The Middle Country

Traverse of Madhesh through War, Colonization
&
Aid Dependent Racist State

The Middle Country

Traverse of Madhesh through War, Colonization & Aid Dependent Racist State

Ram Manohar Sah

ADROIT

Adroit Publishers
New Delhi

ISBN : 978-81-87393-23-8

First Published in 2017

Published by
ADROIT PUBLISHERS
4675/21, Ganpati Bhawan, Ansari Road,
Daryaganj, New Delhi-110 002
Phone : 011-23266030

Exclusively Distributed by:

Vijay Enterprises
4675/21, Ganpati Bhawan,
Ansari Road, Daryaganj
New Delhi, INDIA
Mob.: +91-9899717865

Typesetting—Gaurav Graphices, Delhi-110002
E-mail: gauravsingh1908@gmail.com
Printed at: Radha Press, Sahibabad, Gzd.

Acknowledgements

It happened in Delhi University, while I was doing Masters, a hilly origin friend from Biratnagar yelled at me saying, "hey you Bihari". I was not offended on his content, but the way he expressed the racial hate. I was speechless. The whole night I googled to find reason for this racial acrimony. I was not doubtful about my historical background. After all, my forefathers were the first inhabitants of Jaleshwar, a southern town, having traceable history since Sen Dynasty of Makwanpur, way before Shah King's establishment. Our extended families can trace 12th generations living in Jaleshwar, which could be estimated around 275 years. The time matches with the Sen Kingdom Rule in Jaleshwar. The history goes, our forefather Amar Mehtari was a merchant selling grain in the nearby Bhitta bazar (mart). They were frequent visitor to the mart from Sakhuwa Maran, currently located in Dhanusha District on bank of Kamla River, and often had to stay in ascetics Jagadish Giri (Das) hermitage. Jagadish Giri had found underground Shiv-linga, after divine appearing in dreaming, and built the temple near a Banyan tree. One day, Jagadish Giri suggested Amar Mehtari to build a house saying, his future generation will always have prosperity. There was already another temple of Shakti in the ruin of an old fort, at about 500 meters south west. The Banyan tree is still alive and standing inside the premise of Mahadev temple and Shakti temple is inside the Girls school, popularly called as Garhi School, whose central land is still very high compared to the surrounding and believed to have hidden ruins of old fort. Between those two mounds, there was another mound, which Amar Mehtari choose for building house. Mehtari, which is etymologically close to ancient district name Mahottari, contributed in region's growth through business and land cultivation. Some Mehtari became supplier of saltpeter, an ingredient of gunpowder, to Nepalese Army in late eighteenth century[1].

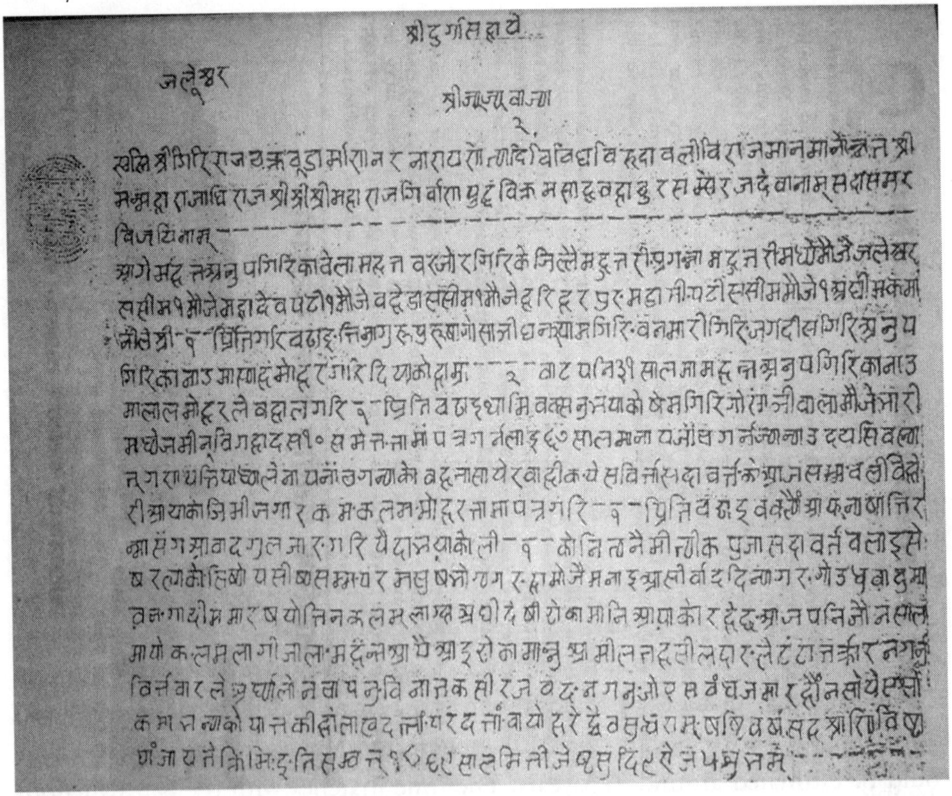

Copy of Royal Order by King Girvan Shah in BS 1869 (1812 AD). The order mention, the successor of Jagadish Giri was reconfirmed land endowment in BS 1831 (1774 BS) for Jaleshwar temple. Source: Journalist Rakesh P Chaudhary.

The night passed in googling and I could find very little resources other than knowing Eighteenth century's Makwanpur Sen Kingdoms was Maithili speaking. I got the connection between Makwanpur's Princess Indra Kumari and Gurkha's King Prithivi Narayan Shah. This finding was encouraging, at the same time, I was still thirsty to find reason for this racial hate in Nepal. Next few weeks, I was desperate to read anything pointing to Makwanpur history. That's when I found the Mahesh Chandra Regmi works achieved on Digital Himalaya website. I want to thank Mahesh Chandra Regmi for his fabulous contribution. Digital Himalaya repository opened door to other research papers. I am not a history student, neither was I organized to read sequentially. The academic pressure left me with little time for my new found interest in History. Since 2007, I had been continuously reading, whenever I get time to find the answer, why racial acrimony? John Welpton's paper 'Being Nepali' was helpful to understand this aspect, and I would like to thank him for also helping understand the different groups in Nepal. 1976's book 'The Silent Cry' helped understand the pain through which plains people passed, while doing so I replaced his 'poor villager' keyword with 'poor Madhesi villager' to make the picture clear. Contemporary writings of Hamilton, Kirkpatrick, and John Wright were invaluable to understand the society as well as history. The collection of Brian Hodgson and papers on Terai by his assistant A Campbell are still exposed like tip of the iceberg, to be explored by future researchers to understand the plains history, culture and economy. Papers respecting Nepaul War is still relevant to understand the strategic complexity of Madhesh lying between China, India and Kathmandu. History book by Ramakant and K.C. Choudhary helped traverse through the political events after 18th century. Grierson, Alexander Cunningham and other writers have helped to recreate cultural history of plain peoples. The unforgettable book of Frederick H. Gaige and PhD thesis of Richard Burghart on History of Janakpurdham are the two gems of Madhesh history. The Panjiar Collection of old historical documents and Prashant Jha's recent notes on political complexities greatly shaped the writing of this book. Leo Rose book was good for knowing the Kathmandu Strategy of survival. Wikileaks and CIA declassified documents has treasure of quality documents on recent politics of Nepal.

I would also like to thank Mr. CK Lal, the great protector of plains people memory through his writing, who helped directly and indirectly, and is always there to help understand the silent complexity of politics and society. Through this writing, I would like to remember all my academic teachers, whose contribution helped me do what I am today; Mr. Sitai Sir (Jaleshwar), Mr. Ram Sewak Sah M.Sc Sir, Mr. Ramesh Thakur (Jaleshwar), Mr. Siya Raghunath (Jaleshwar), Professor Dr. SN Thakur (Janakpur), Professor GL Das (Janakpur), Professor G Dutta (Janakpur), Professor Rajendra Rai (Janakpur), Professor Dr. Subrata Nandi (Durgapur), Professor Dr. ML Singla (Delhi), Dr. Kavita Singh (Delhi), Professor Dr. JK Mitra (Delhi), Dr. Madhu Vij (Delhi), Prof. Dr Simrit Kaur (Delhi), Professor Dr. Vivek Suneja (Delhi), and all others. You all taught beyond books to shape a good human. When it comes to educational contribution, I would like to thank Government of India (and other) for granting 4 years of Columbo Plan Scholarship to many meritorious friends, including me.

I have benefitted greatly from discussion with Professor Dr. Haribansh Jha, Professor Dr. Rammohan Mahato, Professor Dr. Shyam Narayan Labh, Dr. Shreegovind Shah, Dr. Ram Dayal Rakesh, Dr. Jay P Sah, and Dr. Binod Shah.

I thank Former Minister and leader of Sadbhavana Party Anil Jha for always being ready to help understand the challenges of leading from Madhesh. I take this opportunity to thank Dipendra Jha of THRD alliance for always remaining open to share information, Sharad Ghimire for sharing information on 1954's flood and Neel Kamal Chapagain for sharing details on Murtiya Jungle. I would also like to thank friends who helped in collecting resources for writing this book; BP Sah of Hulakinews, Sujit Thakur, Sohan Sha, Puru Shah, Deepak Sah, Niraj Karna, Rameshwar Shah, Subhash Shah, Sunil Sah, Rakesh Mishra, Chandan Singh, Rakeshprasad Chaudhary and Dr. CK Raut. I would also like to thank many other friends who have helped making many occasions memorable that I cherish always.

It also gives great pleasure to thank Mr. Hank Lacy, who shared pictures from his stay in Jaleshwar during 1967-69 as US Peace Corps Volunteer. These pictures speaks invaluable wealth of culture. It also give me pleasure to include two ethnic songs from the region too. Thank you Sasu-Ma (Mother in Law).

This book took almost 10 years to shape. This would not have been possible without the continuous reminding of many friends including Krit Sharma, Dr. Rabindra Yadav, Lalit Jha and etc. Vishal Sirsat, my college friend also deserve the credit, whose questions like a stranger helped to think and structure the book for outsider readers too.

I derived energy from Robert Penner, David Caprara, David Seddon, HRW team, Amnesty team, and Asian Human Rights team to keep bringing truth to the people.

Credit goes to Akhil Sharma and Shanker Nene for making this book publication ready.

It would remain incomplete without mentioning the support of my wife, Sumegha, and kids' and their sacrifice during writing of this book. Rani, Rakhi, Rageeni and Rajni – you all worked and contributed to make a beautiful small world inside me. I want to say "Mommy - you are my first teacher" and "Papa - I love you". Both Barka-Babu (uncle), you have been building blocks. At last, I would like to say to my grandmother, who is among the many starts on the sky, "I miss you-Dai".

Notes

1. Royal Orders of Magh Sudi 14, 1853 (January 1797), Supply of Saltpeter, published in Regmi Research Series, Year 17, No. 6, June 1985

Contents

अलै सुभ के लगनबा, सुभे हो सुभे

अलै सुभ के लगनबा , सुभे हो सुभे
सुभे बोलू दादा , सुभे बोलू दादी
सुभे हो सुभे , आई मंगल के दीनबा , सुभे हो सुभे

सुभे बोलू अम्मा , सुभे बोलू पापा
सुभे हो सुभे , आई मंगल के दीनबा , सुभे हो सुभे

सुभे बोलू चाचा , सुभे बोलू चाची
सुभे हो सुभे , आई मंगल के दीनबा , सुभे हो सुभे

सुभे बोलू दीदी , सुभे बोलू भैया
सुभे हो सुभे , आई मंगल के दीनबा , सुभे हो सुभे

सुभे बोलू बन्ना सुभे बोलू बन्नी
सुभे हो सुभे , आई मंगल के दीनबा , सुभे हो सुभे

सुभे बोलू हजमा सुभे बोलू बभना
सुभे हो सुभे , आई मंगल के दीनबा , सुभे हो सुभे

आज बजे घर घर बजैया
सुभे हो सुभे , आई मंगल के दीनबा , सुभे हो सुभे

आज जनक नगरिया, सुभे हो सुभे
बाबु के दुलरिया सुभे हो सुभे
अलै सुभ के लगनबा , सुभे हो सुभे

- सुनीता पुर्बे

Well Time has Arrived, Well Wishes Everywhere (Ethnic Marriage Song Translated in English)

Well time has arrived, well wishes everywhere
Well Wishes Grandma, Well Wishes Grandpa
Well wishes everywhere, today is auspicious occasion, well wishes everywhere

Well Wishes Mummy, Well Wishes Daddy
Well wishes everywhere, today is auspicious occasion, well wishes everywhere

Well Wishes Uncle, Well Wishes Aunty
Well wishes everywhere, today is auspicious occasion, well wishes everywhere

Well Wishes Grandma, Well Wishes Grandpa
Well wishes everywhere, today is auspicious occasion, well wishes everywhere

Well Wishes Groom, Well Wishes Bride
Well wishes everywhere, today is auspicious occasion, well wishes everywhere

Well Wishes Assister, Well Wishes Minister
Well wishes everywhere, today is auspicious occasion, well wishes everywhere

Today orchestra is everywhere
Well wishes everywhere, today is auspicious occasion, well wishes everywhere

Today feels like Janak Kingdom, well wishes everywhere
Daddy's daughter, well wishes everywhere,
Well time has arrived, well wishes everywhere

- Sunita Purbe

1

Background

The Aitareya Brahmana (Sanskrit: *ऐतरेय ब्राह्मण*) of Rigveda mentions five divisions of ancient world; Pracyadesh (Eastern Country), Dakshinadesh (Southern Country), Praticyadesh (Western Country), Udicyadesh (Northern Country) and Dhruva Madhyamadesh (Middle Country)[1]. Madhyadesh was known as a region where Aryas resided. The term "Aryas" denote people of decent character possessing pure habits[2]. Markandeyapurana[3], one of the ancient Puranas written in Sanskrit, mentions regions belonging to Madhyadesh: Matsyas, Ashvakutas, Kulyas, Kuntalas, Kashi, Koshalas, Arbudas spread over up to Kalingas, Malakas and Vrkas.

Markandeyapurana (32-33)

मत्स्याश्वकूटाः कुल्याश्च कुन्तलाः काशिकोशलाः॥३२॥
अर्बुदाश्चाकलिङ्गाश्च मलकाश्च वृकैः सह।
मध्यदेश्या जनपदा प्रायशोऽमी प्रकीर्तिताः॥३३॥

Manusmrti describes the limit of Madhyadesh between Himavat and Vindhya Mountain, to the west of Prayaga and to the Vinashana, that is, the spot where the river Sarasvati is considered to have disappeared.

Manusmrti (2-21)

हिमवद्विन्ध्ययोर्मध्ये यत्प्राग्विनशनादपि ।
प्रत्यगेव प्रयागाच्च मध्यदेशः प्रकीर्तितः ॥

By the time of Buddha, Madhyadesh expanded towards east to include Bihar till Chota Nagpur, currently located in Jharkhanda state of India.

According to Mahavagga (Vol. V, Chapter 12–13)[4], the Buddhist Vinayapimaka written in Pali language, Majihima-desa, is Pali name for Madhyadesh, extended in the East towards the town of Kajangala (Kankjol in Santhal Parganas), beyond which was Mahasala; on South-East to the river Salilavati (the Salai of Chota Nagpur); on the South-West to the town of Satakannika; on the West to the Brahmin village of Thuna (Malladesh); on the North to the Usiraddhaja Mountain (lower range of Himalaya)[5]. The Majjhimadesa was three hundred yojanas in length, two hundred and fifty in breadth, and nine hundred in circumference[6]. It contained fourteen of the Mahajanapadesas. Gandhara and Kamboja were parts of Uttarapatha. The people of Majjhimadesa were regarded as wise and virtuous. It was the birth place of noblemen, including Lord Buddha, and all kinds of marvelous things happened there.

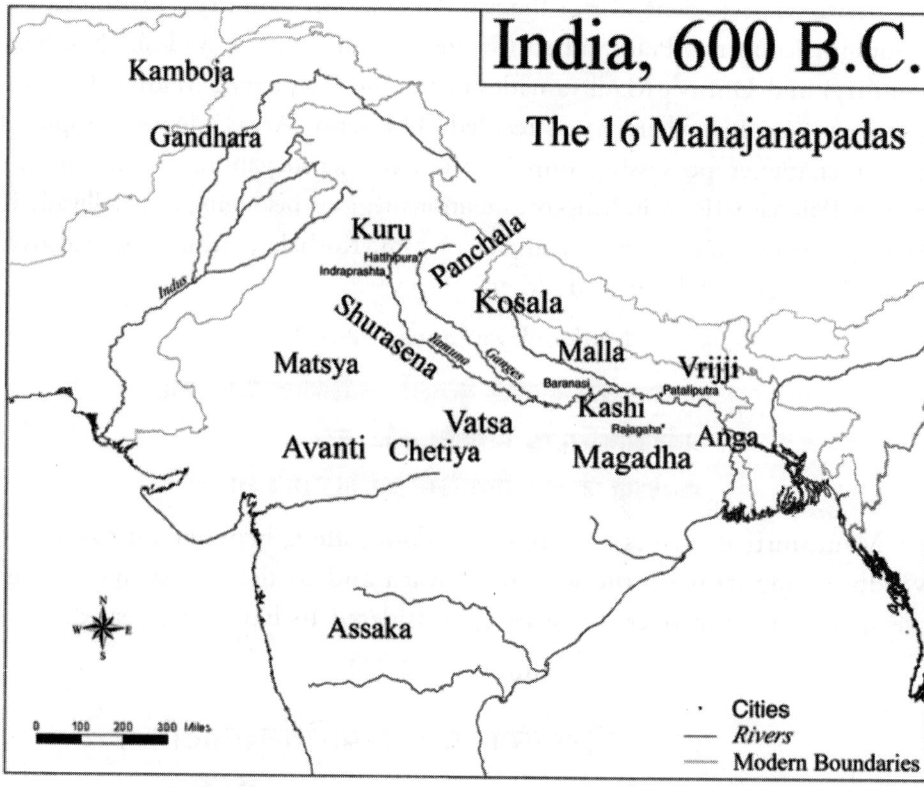

Estimated Sketch Map of India During 600 BC

In the eleventh century, Muslim scholar Al-Biruni, who visited India with Ghazni, wrote "Madhyadesha, i.e. the middle country, the country all around Kanauj, which is also called Aryavarta".[7] Kanauj lies on the southern bank of Ganga in the vicinity of Agra, Kanpur and Lucknow.

The use of term "Madhyadesh" was found till eleventh century A.D., and then it disappreared from common use in native Indian history books, during the Muslim rule in India, when the politics was changing rapidly. However the snail paced changes in isolated Himalaya region have still retained the term Madhyadesh .The use of this term reappeared, when the people in the hill extended their rule in southern plain. The rulers of modern Nepal calls it Madhesh and its inhabitants are known as Madhesi. Madhesh is shorter and easier nickname of Madhyadesh.

Both Gurkha rulers and British researchers in India have mentioned word Madhesh or Madhesi in different contemporary literary sources in last 2 centuries.

- Dr. Grierson's Linguistic Survey of India noticed in 1880 that some part of the Champaran district had the same stock as that of the Bhojpuri spoken in Saran and in East Gorakhpur, and at the same time it carried some linguistic peculiarities borrowed from the Maithili spoken in the neighboring district of Muzaffarpur. The Maithili influence was strongest in the East of the district on the Muzaffarpur border, where, in a strip of land about 2 miles wide and 18 miles long in Dhaka-thana, instead of Bhojpuri, Maithili is spoken. As Dr. Grierson proceeded westward, the Maithili influence appeared diluting on the banks of the river Gandaki. Here, the spoken dialect was the same as that spoken in North East Saran and in Eastern Gorakhpur. This dialect was locally known as **Madhesi**. In 1907, Bengal district Gazetteer[8] further adds that Madhesi was an appropriate and adequate name for the language of the country situated in between the Maithili speaking country of Tirhut and the Bhojpuri speaking country of Gorakhpur.
- Brian Hodgson, in his collection Volume[9] of 'Newar language and comparative vocabulary from 1830s' that was published in 1946, compared Madhesi vocabulary with other spoken languages or dialects, such as, Parvatyâ (Parbati or Nepali), Nevârî (Newar), Limbu, Lâpchyâ (Lepcha), Bhomyâ (Tibetan or Bhote dialect spoken along the high Himalayan border areas of Nepal), Mechyâ (Meche), Murmi (Tamang), Sunuvâr (Sunwar), Sukhimi Bhomyâ (Sikkimi or Sikkim Tibetan), Dharmâ Bhomyâ (Bhutanese Tibetan), Bhomor *Lhasa* Bhomyâ (Lhasa Tibetan), Kirâti (Rai). Interestingly, the collection also has a page

long text in a Dehâti (=of the Tarai) dialect written in Nagari script (folio 220b). Also, Madhesi language is referenced in Hodgson writing 'Limbu folk tales from Yakthungor Yakthungba Munthung with Madhyesiyâ (Hindi) translation 1846-1846.

- Brian Hodgson has again defined Madhes in terms of geography and administration[10] saying "No part of the lowlands Madhes is subject to the Governor of Dhankuta. The **Madhes** is administered by Subashs, of whom there are seven for the whole". The seven zillahs [districts] of then Nepalese lowlands which extend from the Mechi to the Arrah were Morang, Saptari, Mahottari, Rautahat, Bara, Parsa and Chitwan. The Western Tarai extends from the Arrah and it was lately been restored to Nepal which she had lost in the war of 1816.
- The most definitive demarcation of Madhes realm comes from Hodgson collection of a Gurkha official map from 1830-1840 of Western Nepal. *See image.*
- The earliest official mention of Madhesh word by Gurkha officers is found in the Treaty between then Gurkhas King Prithivinarayan Shah and then Kathmandu's King Jay Prakash Malla.
- Kirat History[11] refers to the Madhesh to describe a group within Kirat people called Madhesia Kirat. The story goes: The Kirat king Parbate helped King Chandragupta in driving away the Greek governor Seleucus from Punjab and Sindh. For this military help King Chandragupta gave the North and East part of the Magadha kingdom to the Kirat king. From that time, the Kirat people again began to migrate to North Bihar and North Bengal. But later on by political tactics of Chanakya, the Kirat chief Parbate was murdered; so most of the Kirat people of Kusumpur and North Bihar left the plains and returned to their mountain homes. From that time onwards, they were called the **Madhesia** Kirat or the Kirat of Kashigotra.

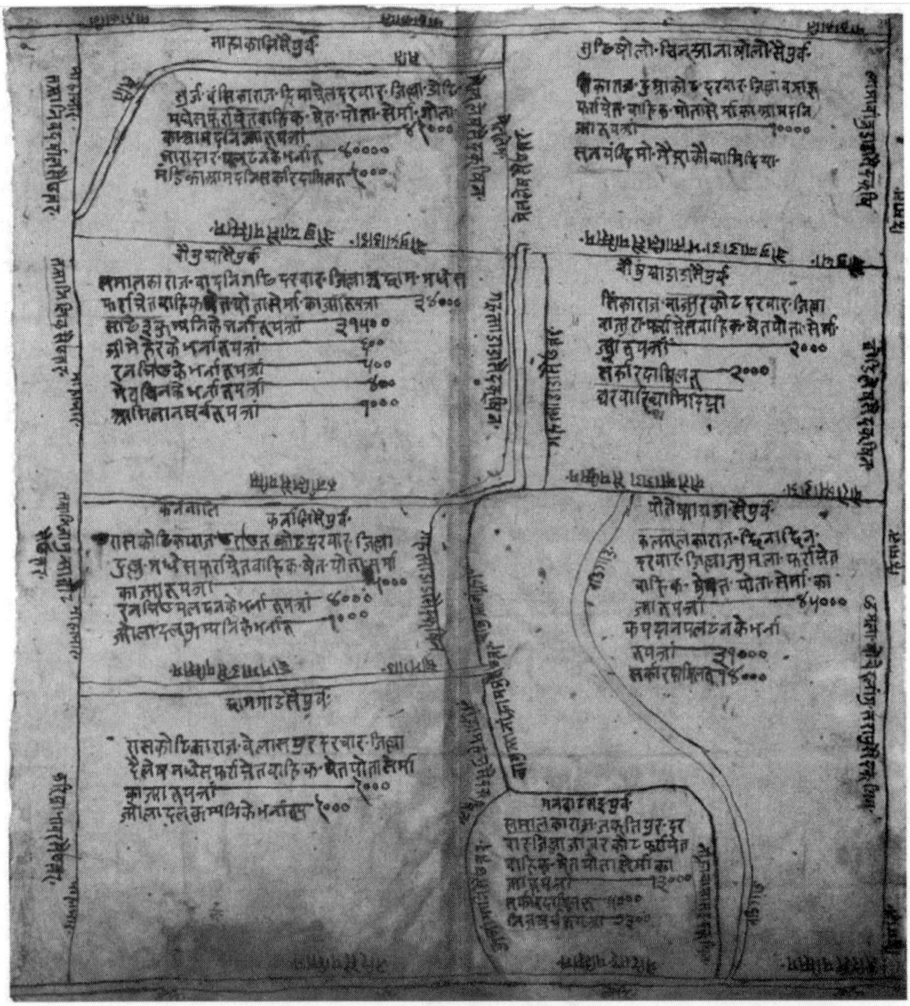

Map of a portion of Western Nepal in the Hodgson Collection (EUR Mss k474 vol 59 folios 26-6), 1830-1840 CE mentioning Madhesh is bordering district of Doti, Achham and Dullu. Implies Eastern lowerland was called Madhesh.

Madhyadesha word and its derivatives Madhes, Madhesis were being used in a limited manner after the 10th century till the beginning of 19th century. The use of these expressions was limited within few geographical pockets. Few scholars used these words in their deliberations. Even if people knew the words, they had no knowledge of the etymological meaning of the words or why these words were being pronounced in that manner. Francis Buchanan Hamilton, who travelled to Nepal in 1802-1803, wrote his paper entitled 'Some Observation on Nepal.' In this deliberation he has mentioned

Madhesh with the same question in mind "Nepal is also named Maddesh or central country, for which appellation I heard no reason assigned"[12]. Hamilton, in his paper, has extensively used the name Terriany for the land situated at lower plain. Hamilton's book 'An Account of the Kingdom of Nepal' is one of the most comprehensive historical works on the country, in which he has also referred to the plain at lower region as Tariyani, Tarai, or Ketoni. In the historical collection 'Paper Respecting Nepaul War', Sikkim King has used the term 'maddies' to denote the lower country[13]. In the paper the King makes a proposal that Sikkim would help British against Gurkha, to conquer lower country. In fact, Sikkim wanted to conquer Hilly part during 1814-1816 war.

पत्र पठाउने—राजा श्री जयप्रकाश
पत्र पाउने—श्री ५ पृथ्वीनारायणशाह
बिषय—भोटमा गोर्षा र काठमाण्डौको वकिल राख्ने वारेको धर्म
मिति—वि०सं० १८१४ पौष वदो ९ रोज ३

स्वस्ति श्रीमन्महाराजाधिराज श्री श्रीमज्जय प्रकाशमल्लदेवले सास्ति श्रीमन्महाराजाधिराज श्री श्रीमन्नृप पृथ्वीनारायणसाहदेवकन धर्मपत्र लिखिदिञ्या. काठमाडौको गोर्षाको टकसार चलाउनु रूपैयामाहा कपट नघाल्नु दुबै टकसारमाहा एकै चाल्नि ··· गोर्षाका रूपैया काठमाडौले चल उनु काठमाडौ ······गोर्षाले चलाउनु भोट रूपैया जिनिस पठाउ······ बरावर पठाउनु भोटमाहा गोर्षा काठमाडौको उकील बसाउनु दुबै उकीलले ठेचि मारि माल चलाउनु दुबैका मत वाहिक ल्यायाको लैगयाको माल षोशनु काठमाण्डौले षोस्या. आढा गोर्षाकन दिनु गोर्षाले षोस्या आढा काठमाडौ कन दिनु काठमाडौका रूपैया ताहां गोर्षाले···सास्ति गर्नु. दण्द गर्नु गोर्षाको रूपैया इहा काठ····नचलाया सास्ति गर्नु दण्डगर्नु पाटन बाटो आयाका··जन लुटि नषानु काठमाडौमाहा गोर्षाको उकील वशाउनु गोर्षामाहा काठमाडौको उकील वशाउनु. उकील ··· मतले भारि फोर्नु माल हेर्नु. भोटवेपार गर्दा नवाकोटको बाटो गर्नु गोर्षाको माल जाहिर गरी ल्यायाको काठमाडौले नषोसनु. लुकाइ ल्यायाका षोशनु. काठमाडौको माल जाहिर गरि ल्यायाको गोर्षाले नषोशनु लुकाई ल्यायाका षोशनु भोट बाटो आयाका सुना रूपा बरोबरि लिनु मधेश बाटो आयाका सिक्का बरोवरि लिनु. पाटन गोर्षाले षानु नालदुम् काठमाडौलाई दिकन काठमाडौको काम गर्नु पाटन गोर्षाका हाथ नहराका दिन काठमाडौले थामनु पशनु काठमाडौको हाथ आयाका दिन. गोर्षाकन सोपि दिनु. अघि गोर्षाको पछिका······काठमाडौको ऐसकरार-माहा······धर्मको वृद्धि होस् करार नराष्या पंचमहा-पातक लाग·····संव्त १८१४ रो ३ मिति पोष बदि ९ लिखितमिति शुभं ——

Treaty between Gurkha King Prithivinarayan Shah and Kathmandu King Jai Prakash Mall having mention of Madhesh as trade center on the south of Kathmandu Valley in 1757 AD

Alternative Nomenclatures

Madhesh was known with different names depending upon the fact that to which area the people belong. Even today, one can hear native rural old people calling their land as 'Desh' and the inhabitants as 'Deshbali'. Hilly people called the land as 'Madhesh', which is different from the word "Muglan" often used for Indian plain.

Cunningham, referring to Chinese traveler Hwen Thsang, writes[14], "According to Hwen Thsang the country of the Vrijis was long from east to west and narrow from north to south. This description corresponds exactly with the tract of country lying between the Gandaki and Mahanadi rivers which is 300 miles in length and 100 miles in breadth". Mahanadi (Mahananda in Hindi) is known by the same name in Nepal Bengal, which flows through Indian states of West Bengal, Bihar, and, indeed, Bangladesh. Its right bank tributary, the Mechi River constitutes part of Nepal's Eastern boundary with West Bengal. The description of boundary of Vrijis confederation, given by Cunningham, matches with the boundary of Karnat dynasty Kingdom before it was plundered by Ghiyas-ud-din Tuglak in 1325 AD[15]. This indicates Madhesh was known as Vriji at the time of Hwen Thsang's visit in 7th century.

Recent native scholars described the place as combination of Mithila, Awadh or Morang (also called Coochh). In Hindi language, lower land is called 'Tal-hutti', and this is used often for Madhesh too. Tharu people were insistent on calling it as Tharuhut whereas the British chose the ecological name 'Terai' or 'Tarai' or 'Terriany' to signify the fact that plain has climate, water, air, flora-fauna, geography and altitude, which are different from the hilly areas dominated by Gurkha rulers. Father Giuseppes, in his account, has used name Teriani. Father, who was expelled by King Prithivinarayan Shah from Kathmandu for being Christian missionary, has nicely put characteristic of plain as fabled in hill 'At the foot of the hills the country is called Teriani; and there the air is very unwholesome from the middle of March to the middle of November; and the people in their passage catch a disorder, called in the language of that country Aul, which is a putrid fever, and of which the generality of people who are attacked with it die in a few days. Hamilton's book notes the geographical and economical dimension of the region in these words 'in general, about twenty miles in width. In this space there are a few scattered small hills, and much poor high land overgrown with trees and bushes of little value ; but there is, also, a very large proportion of rich land, and on the whole the soil is much better than in the adjacent parts of the Company's territory'. He further elaborates on the features of native people 'The inhabitants of this part of the Tariyani, which I had an opportunity of seeing, are quite the same in terms of their circumstances, language, dress, persons, and customs, as the Hindus of the northern part of Behar (Bihar). The peasantry are extremely nasty, and apparently indigent. Their huts are small, dirty, and very ill-calculated to keep out the cold winds of the winter season, for a great many of them have no other walls but a few reeds supported by sticks in a perpendicular direction. Their clothing consists of some cotton rags, neither bleached nor dyed, and which seem never to be washed. They are a small, hard-favoured people, and by no means fairer than the inhabitants of Bengal, who are comparatively in much better circumstances'.

Physiographic regions vis-à-vis major geological formations of the Nepal Himalaya. Source DWIDP (Department of Water Induced Disaster Prevention) as quoted in Khanal, Narendra. R (2007), Preparing for Flood Disaster, pp 5.

Notes

1. Aitareya Brahmana VIII.38.3 op cit in Sharma, Subhra (1985); Life in the Upanishads, Abhinav Publications, 1985, pp 61
2. Chakladar, Haran Chandra (1990); Social Life in Ancient India: Studies in Vâtsyâyana's KâmaSûtra, Asian Educational Services, Jan 1, 1990, pp 42
3. MARKANDEYA-PURANAM, translated into English by F. Eden Pargiter, pp 253-255
4. Vinaya Texts: The Mahâvagga, V-X. The Kullavagga, I-III, Translated from Pali by Rhys Davids and Oldenberg, Clarendon Press, 1882
5. Dr. Radhakrishnan, Sarvapalli (1958); The Cultural Heritage Of India, Vol I, The Early Phases, The Ramakrishna Mission Institute of Culture, Calcutta, India, pp. 46.
6. G.P.Malalasekera, Dictionary of Pali Proper Names: Pali-English, pp .418-419
7. Dr. Sachau, Edward C (1910), ALBERUNI'S INDIA, An Account Of The Religion, Philosophy, Literature, Geography, Chronology, Astronomy, Customs, Laws And Astrology Of India About A.D. 1030. Vol I, 1910, pp 173
8. Bengal District Gazetteers, Volume 10, Part 1, Bengal Secretariat Book Department, 1907, Page 39-40
9. Hodgson Collection Volume 83, Newar language and comparative vocabulary 1830s.
10. Hodgson, Brian Houghton (1880), Miscellaneous Essays Relating to Indian Subjects, Volume 2, Page 202
11. Chemjong, Imanshing (2014); History of The Kirat People, 2014
12. Op Cite Lecomte-Tilouine, Marie (1998), On Francis Buchanan Hamilton's Account of the Kingdom of Nepal, European Bulletin of Himalayan Research, 1998, Number 14, Page 55.
13. PRNW, pp 429 and pp. 392.
14. Sir Cunningham , Alexander (1871); The Ancient Geography of India: I. The Buddhist Period, Including the Campaigns of Alexander, and the Travels of Hwen-Thsang, Trübner and Company, 1871, pp. 445.
15. Hodgson, Brian Houghton (1841), ACCOUNT OF A VISIT TO THE RUINS OF SIMROUN ONCE THE CAPITAL OF THE MITHILA PROVINCE, Illustrations of the Literature and Religion of the Buddhists, 1841.

2

Being Madhesi: Form and Magnitude of Discriminations

After the construction of Tribhuwan Highway connecting Kathmandu with central Madhesh, removal of visa system to enter Nepal Valley, escalation of migration phenomenon and change in political system, access of people from plain to Kathmandu became reality, post 1958. Since then people have gradually been going to Nepal Valley either for (1) official purpose or (2) in search of financial opportunities. The introduction of Madhesi in the Kathmandu valley has not been a smooth phenomenon and witnessed a great deal of pain which was beyond description. At the same time, the attitude and treatment of state administrative machinery towards these people have been equally shocking. Captured below are a few of the narratives from leading Madhesis, who are also icons of Madhesi society, which reveal glances of structural and systemic discriminations.

Personal Stories of Discrimination

Santosh Shah (age 35, the founding President of bi-monthly English magazine "Today's Youth Asia" and an anchor and producer of the television talk show "Power Talks") - incident took place in 2010. In an interview given to the Pakistan's leading newspaper, Santosh Shah stated[1] "The most challenging part of launching his TV program was gathering the finances. Most advertisers found the idea interesting, but they were unwilling to invest in a black man".

Salik Shah (age mid-20s, Journalist, Writer, Editor, Creative Director, Founder of "Mithila Review") – incident took place in 2010. Salik became increasingly aware of bigotry in the capital Kathmandu, where he was born, raised and went to school. In his word[2], "When someone would label me "bhaiya" (big brother) or "marsiya" (a distorted form of Madhesi) I used to feel bad". Salik adds, "They have even degraded the original meaning of Bhaiya and Dhoti as dignified by Mahatma Gandhi, who wore white cotton dhotis all his life."

Ravin Pandey (age mid 50s) - incident of 2000

Ravin Pandey, belongs to a village located in Mahottari districts, in southern plain near Janakpur and was a student leader. He went to attend a 1990 political convention of Nepal Sadbhavana Party in Tudikhel, one of Kathmandu's stadiums, just after democracy was restored by King Birendra after 30 years of partyless panchayat system. The people of hills threw stones on the plain's people and their leader because they delivered their speeches in Hindi, a link language common in Madhesh.

Lumbini (birth place of Lord Buddha) - incident of 2014

Prof. David Seddon, Principal of South London College and professor of Politics and Sociology, wrote in Nepal's top English magazine[3] after his visit to Lumbini. He wrote *"The site at Lumbini is a monument to the Gautam Buddha, but even Buddha himself would avoid staying very long at the site due to its neglect by development agencies. The 2500 years old Ashoka Pillar and Stupa are at the risk of collapse and/or disintegration".*

Dr. C K Raut (age mid-30s, Cambridge PhD, Scientist, Leader) - incident of 2000.

Dr. CK Raut was a topper in Government Engineering College located in Kathmandu. In one of the narratives in his autobiography[4] he alludes "One day he heard his professor saying 'These Dhotis snatch our opportunities, and are now becoming toppers in classes too'-". In another account, he mentions that his father has to bear physical assault in front of him for wearing the ethnic attire Dhoti on the street of Kathmandu". In yet another account, he says a professor made physical assault on another member of collage staff simultaneously yelling at him "Dhoti, bastard Madhesi, I will throw you out, do you want to see my power" and all this happened on the minor issue of cycle parking. Dr. C K Raut is currently leading a political movement advocating for and demanding sovereign state for Madhesh.

Badrinath Jha (age early 40s, Engineer and Senior Manager) - incident of 2015.

He, along with his wife and 12 years son, stayed in Pokhara for more than a year. While in school or on street, his son was constantly being teased with slurs like Dhoti, Madhesi, Indian, black (even though his skin is white). He could never fathom out the reason for teasing. He narrated such incidents to his parents back home. Parents ignored thinking it was an effect of cultural sock. One day, kid came running and crying to the parents from Karate class. He was physically harassed in front of teacher who tried to pacify the aggressive group yelling as Dhoti, Madhesi, Indian, and black. Kid, having Nepali Passport since his birth, asks his parents 'Am I not Nepali'? And kids father, in turn, raised this question on social media, "What more should he do to become Nepali"?

Sitaram Agrahari

A leading Madhesh oriented media, Madhesh Vani, reported[5] in February 2016 that Government owned Gorkhapatra, the oldest national daily newspaper, had dishonored the order of Supreme Court. Supreme Court had ordered Gorkhapatra to reinstate Sitaram Agrahari as Chief Editor of Gorkhapatra Daily. Agrahari was removed from the post and was appointed the editor of Madhupark Monthly. Agrahari filed a petition in Supreme Court. The joint court of Chief justice Ramkumar Prasad Sah and Jagdish Sharma Paudel gave verdict to reinstate Agrahari. Agrahari belonged to Madhesi community so the decision was deliberately delayed.

Dr. Sukhdev Shah (age 80's, former IMF employee, Economics Professor)

Sukhdev Shah belonged to the early generation of Madhesh. He after graduating from India, began his career with Nepal's central bank. This was the time when there were no facilities of higher education available in Nepal and talents educated in India were greatly sought after. Soon, he came to USA for higher education and started his job in International Monitory Fund (IMF) in Washington DC. He has many experiences to share and has written several articles which have been published in the leading newspapers.

On a social forum he wrote "I have observed over a long span of some 40 years that I spent in Washington and New York, where we maintain two diplomatic missions in these places, staffed by dozens of Nepalese citizens, and, over these years, close to a thousand of them have served in high and low positions. However, I do not recall even a single Madhesi serving at these missions, even as a lowly clerk or a cook!"

"Similarly, there has never been a case of any Madhesi being part of Nepalese delegation to the meetings of UN, World Bank, and IMF, which are annual events and dozens of Nepalese delegates come for these meetings each year. Why would even one of these not be a Madhesi who comprise over half the country's population?"

On his return to Nepal from his visit Dr. Shah further adds to his personal experience: "I have never encountered a Madhesi hostess or a pilot on any Nepalese air carrier, although I have flown for many decades. Similarly, landing at the international airport in Kathmandu, even these days with Madhesi politics in buoyancy, I can hardly see a Madhesi helper—even a baggage carrier— serving the passengers."

Rakesh Mishra (age mid 40's, Fulbright Scholar)

After the 2006 constitution included conservative citizenship provision for the female marrying Nepalese citizen as well as their offspring. Rakesh Mishra took to Facebook and gave vent to his feelings. His father was a political activist, who was imprisoned for years for participating in pro-democracy movement pre-1990. Rakesh's wife is medical doctor and Fulbright scholar too, and was Indian citizen before marriage. Mr. Mishra posted on Facebook *"I am not able to look at my 70 years old mother, who is a naturalized citizen of Nepal.....she got citizenship certificate after I got one.....Not able to confront my dear wife Sangeeta who was generous enough to renounce her Indian nationality because I insisted.....Not able to confront photograph of my late father Ramchandra Mishra who spent his life fighting for democracy, human rights and Madhesh dignity.......I am sorry to all of you that I remained a Nepali like my father.....not anymore......I am a proud Madhesi ....I will live and die here but will resist Nepali aggression on my land till I die.. I have lost faith in anybody who is a proud Nepali..."*

Prof Dr. Haribansh Jha (retired Professor of Economics)

I was employed as economic advisor in Nepal Foreign Ministry and was also very close to the Nepal Royal Palace. Leo Rose, a noted historian, wrote a book on Nepal. Regarded as an expert in the Nepalese affairs, Leo Rose made a comment favoring India, in one of Kolkata's conference. This comment shook the foreign ministry. It was decided at the top that Leo Rose be countered in a conference to be held, sooner than later, in Kathmandu. A message came from the top that Mr. Jha should be assigned with a set of question to confront Mr. Rose in the upcoming conference. There were two Jha in the office, and my colleague Mr. Jha's name was sent, later to be pushed from top that they wanted me to question Mr. Rose. Preparation was made that I will ask question after so and so presentation. As planned, at the end of presentation, I raised my hand to ask question. After Mr. Rose's nod, I asked a question. Mr. Rose was not prepared that someone in Kathmandu will ask a foreigner that kind of question in a country which is so much dependent on foreign aid. This incidence exposed and threw me open to heavy criticism in the diplomatic circle. However, I was happy and was convinced that I did something good for my country. My conviction, however, shattered to pieces in no time after another experience. It was again during 1989-1990 Indo-Nepal blockades; there was effort to open communication with Indian authorities to normalize the relationship. A team of five people was constituted and I was one of those as economics expert. And I was only Madhesi among the team. We were a team of five people and heralded great importance as we left Kathmandu and landed in the Indian capital New Delhi. While on the way to hotel, during the offline conversation, I came to know that a government officer had come at the Kathmandu airport just before the take off. All other members of the team were given cash to take care of their personal expenses while visiting Delhi, except me. I was surprised at this blatant partiality, and questioned myself, am I different from other delegates because I am of Madhesi origin? We had different meetings with Indian officials during the Delhi visit. After return from Delhi, I got chance to come face to face with the then PM Marich Man Shrestha and I specifically mentioned this incidence of partiality shown in my case during Delhi visit. He assured of conducting investigation, which never happened. Then, on one occasion, I got chance to be 1 on 1 meeting, with King Birendra. There again, I mentioned the Stipend related discrimination to the King. He listened, but, till date, I haven't received the stipend. In the same conversation, he asked me, 'Dr, what are you doing these days'? I answered 'Your Majesty, I am writing a book on Terai'. King was taken aback for a few seconds, then he counter questioned, 'Dr., suggest me what can I do for Terai'? I mentioned, 'Your Majesty, you can do a great deal of service to Terai without costing a big money and this is within your capacity. You have 5 personal secretaries. You can appoint 1 more person of your trust from Terai to be your 6th secretary'.

Rita Sah (Age Mid-30s, Nurse, Social Activist, Writer)

Rita Sah is one of the vocal Madhesi women, who writes and participates in civil rights movements. She did her schooling from Rajbiraj, then did certification in nursing from a place close to Rajbiraj. She shares her experience[6] "While I was studying in nursing in my native place located at Bhardah, 300 km south of Kathmandu, most of the students and teachers were from Pahari community. It was challenging to mix up with them due to difference in food, language, habits, and clothing. There were few Madhesis from the neighboring villages who were discriminated against and humiliated almost on daily basis by the teachers and fellow students for following native rural lifestyle. One day, I gathered courage to ask teacher "why do you humiliate and verbally assault them"? Teacher had no reason but weak academic record. "We all worked hard, studied day and night. However, we all knew we are getting low marks."

Rita moved to Nepal's capital Kathmandu after marriage. During her 15 year-long stay in Kathmandu, she had suffered from several incidents of discrimination. Sharing experience she posits[7] "I asked vendor for the price of an apple in Nepali. Another buyer appearing to be in 60s and educated questions me, why are you speaking in Nepali with the vendor, he too looks Indian. I replied, I am from Saptari, a district in Nepal and the gentleman came back saying then your maternal home must be in India". Such incidents show as to how Madhesis are being ostracized in their own Capital.

Prof. Dr. Ramawatar Yadav (age 70's, Former Vice Chancellor. Purbanchal University Nepal, Former Joint Secretary, Education Ministry, Senior Fulbright Scholar)

Prof. Yadav is among the first generation of Madhesis who reached Kathmandu in search of employment on the strength of higher education in India. He recollects[8], he had to visit government office infinite times during early 1980s to get government ID card, which could have been so simple process had he been looking like Burmese with high cheekbones and flat noses. Prof. Yadav has three specific instances to share where his upward career mobility was hindered for the reasons linked with being Madhesi.

- In 1965, Prof. Yadav was selected for British Council Scholarship by Mr. Lyndon Clough, the British Council Representative. Ministry of Education simply would not permit him to avail of the scholarship rather number two student got the scholarship. Prof. Yadav had to wait for 3 years when another Englishman, who occupied the English Chair in the University, initiated him to get the scholarship.
- In 1973, Prof. Yadav was selected in first spot for the Fulbright Hays Scholarship to pursue a PhD course in Linguistics. However, his name was demoted to second place in the education ministry. In the meantime, Mr. Gabriel Campbell, Director of the US Education Foundation, announced that two candidates had received "confirmation" from a U.S. University for scholarship. The hurdle was created, questioning, why in real fact two students in linguistic should go for PhD study from Nepal, a small country? The situation persisted until the matter was sent to Manpower Planning Division of the Planning Commission.
- Prof. Yadav was transferred numerous times. He worked under countless Secretaries in the Ministry of Education—one of whom had started his job eleven years after Prof. Yadav.

Lastly, in Prof. Yadav's word "Throughout, I have faced an unseen enemy—my Madhesihood—although I cannot quite calibrate the exact extent to which Madhesihood might have been a robust and an undisputed deterrent to my upward mobility in life".

Prashant Jha (Age Mid-30s, Author, Associate Editor, Hindustan Times)

Grandfather of Prashant Jha was asked by college friend Dr. Tulsi Giri, former PM of Nepal, to come to Kathmandu. In no time Prashant Jha's grandfather made good connections and got established in the power circle, that be, of Kathmandu. He even acted as a go-between the King Mahendra and power handlers in Delhi. Prashant, third generation in Kathmandu, was born to the parents, who were well-off and properly established in the business and professional circle of Kathmandu. Despite all these, there was something unusual, which the young mind of six class student could not understand and fathom out at that point in time. He narrates that as young kid, while he was eating lunch, a friend said, in a mix of seriousness and jest, "You are a Dhoti". I discovered that the term- definitely derogatory- was associated with Madhesis, who, in turn, were equated with Indians. I tried hard to run away and distance from my identity. I hung around with Kathmandu kids, myself got indulged in calling the other Indians in school 'Dhoti', and rationalized studying Hindi by saying it was what my parents wanted. But I could not run away from my identity too far. The differences were too many: we went vegetarian during Dushera as Kathmandu feasted on meat; we didn't do Tikka; Tihar was the one-day Diwali for me. My father, short and on the darker side, made it a point to wear kurta-pajama. It was a dress I took to later and with the accented Nepali and the surname, often invited the remark that "we do not look Nepali."

Gopal Thakur (Age Mid-50s, Writer, Activist)

Thakur has done Masters in Nepali literature, yet he found it difficult to have been accepted as one of the Nepali speaking people[9]. He mentions, "I have worn Nepali dress Daura-Suruwal from time to time, but they do not accept me as a Nepali simply saying Nepali style is missing" and thus usual questions and answers too, "What is Nepali Style? I don't know." Thakur further asks "If my face, dress, language, accent, land, lifestyle do not match with Gorkha people then how do I fall under their established notion of Nepalese identity, if not, why should I be in illusion?"

Dr. Binay Panjiyar (Mid 20s, Medical Doctor, Activist)

During the 2014 SAARC summit, Dr. Binay Panjiyar was arrested from Sundhara[10], Kathmandu, with his friends on 25 and 26 November for attempting to hold a rally in Kathmandu along with Dr. C.K. Raut. The Nepal police and Central Investigation Bureau (CIB), jointly, arrested more than 300 people and detained some 30 individuals for up to 48 hours. Amnesty International was closely monitoring the incident and they published press release on Dec 5, 2014 with details[11]. Dr. Binay Panjiyar, along with others, gathered there to rally on Dr. Raut's call for "independent Madhes". However the salient feature of the event was, racial and feature-based arrest. On the day of the proposed rally, Nepal police entered Sundhara and openly began arresting anyone with the physical appearance matching with a "Madhesi." This discriminatory tactic also led to the arrests of a handful of non-Madhesis whom police officers considered to have "Madhesi" features, and Madhesis in the vicinity who were not Raut supporters. CK Raut himself, along with

25 of his supporters, was surrounded by police and charged with "lathis" (long wooden sticks). Deepak Sah, Roshan Jha and Dharma Lal Rai Yadav, who are close to Raut, were detained for 40 hours without access to a lawyer, and their families were not informed of their whereabouts. Sah's laptop and mobile phone were also confiscated. Other Madhesi members of Raut's movement in southern Nepal, home to the majority of Madhesis, were prevented from travelling to Kathmandu for the rally.

Shekhar Golchha (Age Mid-50s, Businessman, Owner of Golchha Organization)

Shekhar Golchha joined the Golchha Organization, set up by his grandfather Ram Lal Golchha, 27 years ago with a management degree from the UK. Today he is considered as a major entrepreneur. In his enterprise he has 300 employees and volume of business overseas is worth Rs 1 billion, annually. He is Managing Director of Him Electronics, Hansraj Hulaschand and Hulas Investments. Mr. Golchha is also the director of Hester Nepal Pvt. Ltd., Neoteric Nepal Pvt. Ltd., and Eastern Sugar Mills Ltd. He belongs to Marwari community, which is believed to have migrated to throughout the world, including Nepal, in late 19th century. Marwari community has controlling stake in the Nepal's business and industry. Golchha organization, which originated from the small jute business of the Golchha family, started way back in 1931, today provides jobs to more than 18,000 people. On the social sector, Golchha Organization has contributed mainly to the health sector. Ram Lal Golchha Eye Hospital in Biratnagar is a free-service hospital. Parop-kari Shree Hansraj Golchha Chikitsalaya in Lalbandi is another example. Besides, the Organization has been continuously extending its financial assistance to many areas of social services, particularly to the religious institutions. Shekhar's father Hulaschand was interested in Nepali literature and was a Nepali Poet.

Despite all these track records and status in Nepal, Shekhar, who was born and brought up in Kathmandu, has his "piece of cake" that he shared though his Facebook page. He described encounter with another well-known businessman in a restaurant, one evening. The businessman shared with Shekhar that he had complained to the Nepal's Ambassador that there should have been at least a Nepali representative in the business delegation gone to Mumbai sent though Nepal Trade Unions (*Nepal Udhyog Banijya*). Shekhar was surprised and asked, "Dear brother, I was also in that delegation. Aren't we Nepali?" The businessman replied back, "I mean Nepalese Blood". Mr. Golchha ends his paragraph asking "What should I do more to become Nepalese".

Notes on Structural Discrimination

Racist Remark by Shanker Pokhrel (Member of Communist Part of Nepal-UML Standing Committee)

On September 06, 2016, a central leader of Nepal Communist Party twitted, referring to skin color as discussion point. The tone of the comment is "Madhesi, you are Black people, and you cannot "protest" against dissatisfaction". There was widespread protest on this racist comment[12]. After the controversy, in the follow up twitter comment, instead of being apologetic, the leader made specific comment saying "Black color is associated with racial discrimination in European, thus he does not like [Madhesi also using Black as symbol of protest declaring Black Day]". Few months earlier, similar racist remarks came from his party leader and former Prime Minister K.P. Oli, who equated Madhesi protest like 'flies' and killing of Madhesi by police force like 'falling Mangoes' during the six months of 2015 protest[13]. About a year before, during the meeting with plain origin politician, KP Oli had also attacked plain people in the satirical tone suggesting they are blood relatives of Indians in Bihar and UP. Thus their demand in Nepal is irrational. Instead, they should put their demands to India. Politicians of origin in Plain have been demanding state of their own in the proposed state boundary of the federal structure, consisting of all the plains land that had traditionally been dwellings of the people of plains. This land included the plains-land where a great deal of migrations of Hilly people took place in the last 5 decades. On this demand Oli response[14] was "Do you want all of the plain land? In that case, do you also want to have UP and Bihar states of India?"

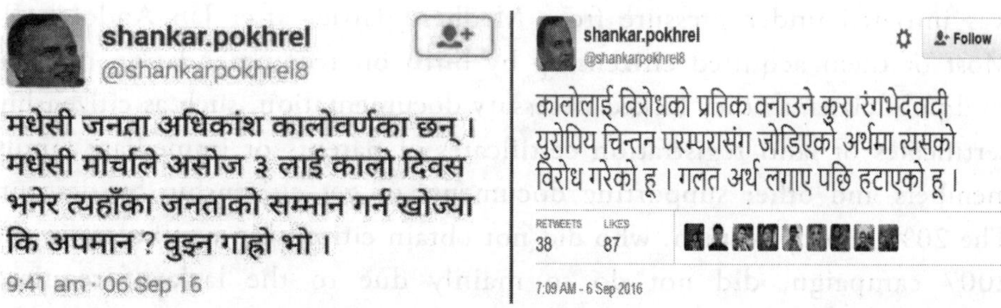

Screenshot of first and follow-up twit from Shankar Pokhrel. Source https://twitter.com/shankarpokhrel8

Santhal Community of Jhapa Facing Combined Threats of Citizenship, Land and Migration

Santhal were the initial inhabitants of Jhapa district. They were not aware of significance of citizenship card when it was first distributed in 1952. So, they did not try and acquire it. They continued to cultivate land as tiller as they were not the registered owners of land. In fact there was no such need of registration at that time. The land reform program of 1967 did not help the situation as at that time most of the Santhal did not possess the citizenship certificates required for landownership. When Santhal migrated from the hills, government officials falsely implicated them in thefts of animals, cow slaughtering and collaboration with armed political groups[15]. This resulted in their displacement from their traditional lands and people close to government officials and local landlords, mostly of hill origin, took over their land and became property owners.

Immediate impact of Santhal not having citizenship certificates was that they were not eligible to purchase land. Shyam Tudu of Jalthal VDC-6 had to register the land that he had bought 20 years ago in the name of his neighbor (a family of hill origin) because he did not have a citizenship certificate[16]. He further explained that later on he had to take a loan from the same neighbor, who eventually acquired the same very land at a very low price, because Shyam Tudu could not pay off the loan. Result of all this was that he was rendered landless.

According to Nepal Santhal Adivasi Utthan Sangha, nearly 80% of the Santhal in Jhapa district acquired citizenship certificates during the large scale campaign of distributing citizenship certificates in 2007. The campaign was initiated under pressure from Madhesi parties after Jan Andolan II. Most of them acquired citizenship by birth on recommendation of local level politicians, as they lacked necessary documentation, such as citizenship certificates or land registration certificates of parents or immediate family members and other supporting documents to get citizenship by descent. The 20%, mostly women, who did not obtain citizenship certificates in the 2007 campaign, did not do so mainly due to the lack of required documentation proving their length of residence in the country. This happened as there was also a lack of awareness of the campaign among them, or because they were absent from the village at the time of distribution of citizenship certificates. Sarita Tudu, a landless woman from Garamani VDC, for example, was working on a distant farm at the time of citizenship certificate distribution campaign in her village and thus failed to obtain her citizenship certificate[17]. Bishwo Nath Murmi, 80, of Lakhanpur VDC said "we have been living here for the past six decades but we are yet to receive citizenship certificates". He lamented that due to the lack of a certificate he was deprived of getting old-age allowances provided by the government[18].

Due to the lack of citizenship certificates, elderly Santhal could not receive social security allowances from the government. They cannot open bank accounts where they can deposit their savings. Citizenship certificates can open doors to better employment prospects, especially when employment related to migration to gulf countries requires citizenship in order to acquire passport for travel.

The Santhal, who are living at Gauradaha, Lakhanpur, Gaurigunj, Juropani, Mahabhara and Korobari VDCs of southern Jhapa are facing various problems due to the lack of citizenship certificates.

Electoral and Budgetary Representation Policy

Prior to the promulgation of constitution, people of lower plains had demanded: (1) lands situated at lower plain be exclusively the part of plain states in federal structure and (2) plain lands should be able to send around 50% of the candidates to be elected in the central election as their representatives in the parliament. The second demand was in line with the 2011 census, which makes provision of plain land accommodating 55 percent of Nepal's population including inner Madhesh, which forms around 10% of population.

The constitution was published in 2015. Even amended twice after Madhesi agitation, that killed around 50 people, the constitution falls short of Madhesis expectation. The plain land was divided zig-zag and tagged with Hilly district to prevent consolidation of political franchise of plain's people under their own federal state government. Secondly, the electoral constituencies that would send representatives to central parliament, are constituted and delineated in such a way that plain people have less chance of winning into First-Past-The-Post (winner takes all) electoral method. As per expert estimates, in this method plain lower land will get only 41% seats, 71 seats out of total 165 First-Past-The-Post seats, despite having around 50% to 55% population[19].

In another parallel and concurrent discussion regarding restructuring of local level bodies, the Kathmandu based decision makers leverage lowland differences with the highland hills. The Local Level Restructuring Commission (LLRC) divided Nepal into three distinct geographical entities - Himalaya, Hill and Madhesh. Madhesh districts consist of Jhapa, Morang, Sunsari, Saptari, Siraha, Udaypur (inner), Dhanusha, Mahottari, Sarlahi, Sindhuli (inner), Bara, Parsa, Rautahat, Chitwan (inner), Makwanpur (inner), Kapilbastu, Nawalparasi (inner), Rupandehi, Dang (inner), Banke, Bardiya, Surkhet (inner), Kailali, and Kanchanpur. LLRC further proposes restructuring village council having the population size in mountain districts to be from 13,000 in hill districts to be 22,000 and in Tarai districts to be 40,000. Similarly, for each municipal council, the population size in mountain districts has to be 17,000, in the hill districts 31,000 and in Tarai districts 60,000[20].

Making sense of the above two different levels of structure and treatment to lowland people, it will further indicate the impact on the local residents. In 1995, the Government started providing village development committees (VDCs) with grants of 300,000 rupees a year to fund local development. In 2008/09 the amount was increased to at least 1.5 million rupees per year to all of Nepal's 3,915 VDCs up to 3 million rupees in certain VDCs[21]. Municipalities were provided minimum grant of 400,000. As of 2011, Rs 1.5 billion was being distributed among the country's 75 DDCs (on average, about Rs 56 per person), whereas almost Rs 9.2 billion was distributed among the country's 3,915 VDCs (in aggregate, approximately Rs 348 per person).

The local level structure receives huge amount of grants from central government, unlike the developed countries, where local bodies arrange local finances. As per a UNDP report, on average 77% of revenue of the High hills VDCs, 70% of the revenue of the Mid hills VDCs and 53% of the Terai VDCs' revenue came from central government grants in the two fiscal years (2006/2007 and 2007/2008)[22]. Thus, having more local bodies in hill means drainage of more central resources[23], a big chunk of cost of which is born by plains. Additionally, the central level parliament makes policies and allocates resources for major projects, and thus asserts its control in central governments through skewed proportion of parliamentary seats.

Comment by Dr. Harka Gurung on Extractive State (1939 – 2006, a Nepalese Geologist, Anthropologist, Author, Politician, and Conservationist)

Dr. Harka Gurung wrote in an article about the socio-economic status of Madhesis: "Based on 1987 data[24], of the total development expenditure of NRs 3,297 million during fiscal year 1985-86, the Hill region claimed 59.8 percent against 33.9 percent for the Tarai and 6.2 percent for the Mountain".

The total estimated GDP of Nepal was valued at NRs 4,174 million at current price of 1984-85. Of that amount, 56.5% was contributed by the Tarai regions. The share of Hill regions was 39.2 percent and that of Mountain regions was only 4.3 percent. Central Tarai ranked first and Central Hill second; Eastern and Western Tarai ranked third and fourth in GDP contribution.

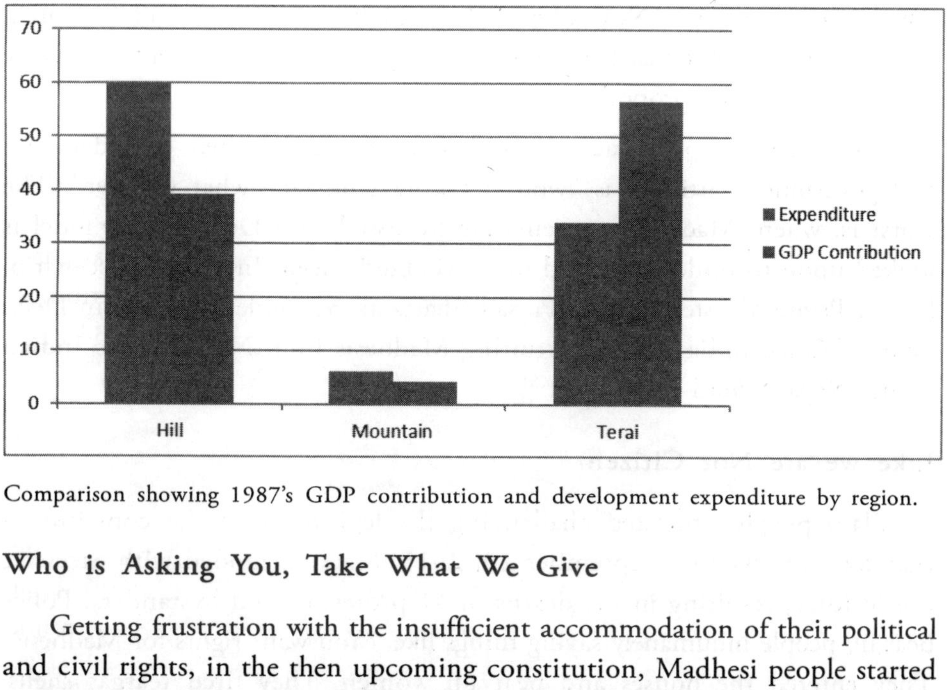

Comparison showing 1987's GDP contribution and development expenditure by region.

Who is Asking You, Take What We Give

Getting frustration with the insufficient accommodation of their political and civil rights, in the then upcoming constitution, Madhesi people started agitation in August 2015. Madhesis are natives of lower land plains, and since Nepal government rules over Madhesh, the issues raised by Madhesis with Nepal government are naturally domestic in nature. However, in December 2015, out of the blue, Foreign Minister of Nepal, Kamal Thapa flew to Delhi, without disclosing to Madhesi leaders, and presented four points formula to address Madhesis' demand[25]. Madhesis came to know about the four point formula through Indian Ambassador in Kathmandu. Thapa hoped that agreement of Delhi will be sufficient to address the Madhesis' demand.

In the follow up events, Prime Minister Sushil Koirala added the amendment to constitution, which was promulgated in September 2015, to address the Madhesis demand, without consulting Madhesis[26]. After constitution amendment bill tabled without the consent from Madhesis, Morcha announced fresh protest[27]. The constitution was amended in January 23, 2016 to address the demand for Constituency Delimitation among other demands. Government passed the amendment, however it didn't pacify the agitating Madhesis[28]. The agitation, which continued for record six months, faded in the following weeks for logistic reason and people's pressure to normalize the supply chain. After change of government on August 4th, 2016, the new PM Prachanda vowed to address the Madhesis' demand. However, again, the repetition of same - missing Madhesi's consent - was observed, when Prachanda tried to file the amendment in November 2016[29]. Mahanta Thakur, leader of plain based TMLP party, refused to comment on proposed amendment, saying he was not shown the proposal[30].

The people of plain lack the rights to consent to their own demand, and government attitude is "who is asking you, take what we give". The worst is, when, Madhesis consents are bypassed, and Delhi's role model is looked upon to understand and meet Madhesis need. In a similar scenario, former Prime Minster Krishna Prasad Bhattarai, responded in 1990 in Delhi saying, "Once India started recruiting Madhesis from Nepal in the Indian Army, Nepal would follow suit"[31].

Like we are Not Citizen

Plain people protested challenging the legitimacy of the constitution that was approved on September 20, 2015. State responded with excessive use of force, resulting in the deaths of 41 protestors and bystanders. Police beat up people inhumanely saying things like, "You want rights for Madhesi?" They entered the houses and beat up women. They fired teargas shells, scared the children. In a field survey by Human Right Watch team, a native stated "We are being treated inhumanely, like second-class citizens. Like we are not Nepalis, like we're criminals or terrorists"[32]. For instance, on Sep 9th, in a berserk response to protest, four people were shot dead in Jaleshwar by the police, not necessarily protester, including Rohan Chaudhari. Rohan Chaudhari, a 17-year-old secondary school student, was shot dead in front of official residence of the district judge building, he was returning from a private tuition class, carrying a bag of school books. Two days later on Sep

11th, two more was killed in Jaleshwar. Co-incidently, one of the killed was Ganesh Chaudhari, grandfather of Rohan Chaudhari. Ganesh Chaudhari, a noted local social worker who had been decorated by the former king, had headed to a rural market, a few kilometers from the outskirts of Jaleshwar, to buy vegetables. Ganesh Chaudhari was riding his bicycle along a footpath away from the road and was about 30 meters from the road when he was shot, when he was shot in head from a police vehicle. For six days, burial was denied to the 6 people killed by police in the Jaleshwar, as curfew was enforced making way for constitution promulgation in Sep 20th.

On the same day, Sep 11th, three people was shot dead in Janakpur, 10 miles north of Jaleshwar. One of the shot was Nitu Yadav, 14 years boy, who had joined protest program against constitution. Nitu was dragged from his hiding place by police officers, thrown to the ground, and, while an officer stood on his legs, shot dead in the face at point-blank range. In another horrific police firing, where 200 police indiscriminately fired in the local market, six people were killed on Sep 15th in Bethari Chowk of Bhairahawa, including 4 years old boy Chandan Patel[33] and 12 years old girl Ranjana Singh. Ranjana was preparing tea in her grandparent's house, and as firing started outside in the market, she tried to watch from the window and a bullet hit her in her neck[34]. Chandan Patel's killing FIR case had not being accepted by local administration even after a year despite multiple efforts by his father[35].

THRD Alliance and AHRC investigated[36] 37 deaths out of total 41 reported; of the 37 protesters killed, 89% were wounded in the head or thorax, contrary to the government rules, which requires police to aim below the waist. In 12 cases (33%), those killed were peaceful protesters and in 18 cases (51%), those killed were not involved in the protests and were mere bystanders or people killed in their houses in the surrounding areas of protests. In addition, in eleven cases, police obstructed the efforts of family members and others to transport the victims to hospital.

Notes

1. Dawn, Young today leaders tomorrow; Published Jan 14, 2010; http://www.dawn.com/news/911310/young-today-leaders-tomorrow
2. Shah, Santosh Salik (2007); Balkanization Threatens Nepal, Discrimination driving separatism in Terai, Ohmy News, Published 2007-01-24

3. Seddon, David (2014); Forget the past - The shocking neglect of Nepal's Tarai heritage in Lumbini and Janakpur; Nepali Times, 12-18 September 2014 #724
4. Dr. Raut, CK (2013); Autobiography, Vairag Dekhi Bachab Samma; March 2013
5. Gorkhapatra dishonored order of Supreme Court; 10 Feb, 2016, http://Madheshvani.com/en/details/3473/news
6. Sah, Rita (2014), ke madhesi haru alien hun , Samta online magazine, published on Dec 26, 2014, downloaded from http://esamata.com/np/2014/के–मधेसीहरू–एलियन–हुन
7. Sah, Rita (2013), Being Madhesi in Kathmandu, The Kathmandu Post, Daily, Kathmandu Published on 2013-10-06 downloaded from http://kathmandupost.ekantipur.com/printedition/news/2013-10-05/being-madhesi-in-kathmandu.html
8. Dr. Yadav, Ramawatar (2010); Himalaya, the Journal of the Association for Nepal and Himalayan Studies, Volume 29, Number 1 The Tarai: History, Society, Environment, 2010; http://digitalcommons.macalester.edu/cgi/viewcontent.cgi?article=1870&context=himalaya
9. Thakur, Gopal (2015); Esamata online Magazine, Ab Malai Nepali na bhana (Now Don't Tell me Nepali), June 2015, http://esamata.com/2015/insight/अब-मलाई -नेपाली -नभन/
10. Panjiyar, Binay (2015); Madhesh: Integrated or Independent, 25 oct 2015, downloaded from http://shahvizay.blogspot.com/2015/10/story-telling-1-Madhesh-integrated-or.html
11. Amnesty (2014); Nepal: Dissenting Voices At Risk, Amnesty International, Index number ASA 31/008/2014, Published on 5 December 2014, downloaded from http://www.amnesty.org/en/documents/ASA31/008/2014/en/
12. Online Khabar (2016); Controversial tweet from UML leader Shankar Pokharel sparks protest in Rautahat HQ Gaur, Onlinekhabar , published September 7th, 2016
13. Manandhar, Narayan (2015); Olitics – Politics, Madhesi Youth Online Website, published on November 10, 2015 downloaded from http://www.madhesiyouth.com/opinion/olitics-politics/
14. Ekantipur (2016), Oli refuses to apologise to Madhesis, The Kathmandu Post, Published January 08, 2015
15. UN (2011); State of stateless citizens: A case study on citizenship and landlessness issues of the Santhal community, United Nations Resident and Humanitarian Coordinator's Office, Issue No.: 5, May 2011
16. UN (2011); State of stateless citizens: A case study on citizenship and landlessness issues of the Santhal community, United Nations Resident and Humanitarian Coordinator's Office, Issue No.: 5, May 2011
17. UN (2011); State of stateless citizens: A case study on citizenship and landlessness issues of the Santhal community, United Nations Resident and Humanitarian Coordinator's Office, Issue No.: 5, May 2011
18. THT (2006); Santhals migrating to India; The Himalayan Times, October 30, 2006

19. Jha, Dipendra (2016); Terai Will Get 71 Seats, Not 80, Even After Amendment, Madhesi Youth, published Feb 16, 2016 downloaded Nov 2016 from http://www.madhesiyouth.com/analysis/constitutional-amendment/

20. Sedhai, Roshan (2016); Madhes-based parties find fault with LLRC's criteria, term it biased, The Kathmandu Post, published Oct 23, 2016

21. Inlogos (2009); Assessment of Village Development Committee Governance and the use of Block Grants. Kathmandu: Ministry of Local Development and United Nations Development Programme (UNDP), 2006, pp 1

22. Inlogos (2009); Assessment of Village Development Committee Governance and the use of Block Grants. Kathmandu: Ministry of Local Development and United Nations Development Programme (UNDP), 2006, pp 5

23. Neupane, Gyan P (2017); Govt to release at least Rs 10 million to each of 744 local units for operation, My Republica, March 8, 2016

24. Gugung, Harka (1990), Making of a Dynamic Region, Tarai: Backwater or New Frontier, Himal, ALTERNATIVE Bl-MONTHEY Magazine Vol. 3, Sep/Oct, 1990

25. In Delhi, Kamal Thapa signed four-point 'commitment' to end Nepal crisis, Online Khabar, published on December 5th, 2015 Downloaded on Nov 24, 2016 from http://www.onlinekhabar.com/2015/12/358807/

26. PTI, Amendment was forcefully tabled, say Madhesis, The Hindu, Published on December 26, 2015

27. After constitution amendment bill tabled without its consent, Morcha announces fresh protest, Reporters Nepal, published 2015/12/18

28. Jha, Dipendra (2016); Problems with first amendment made to Nepal's new Constitution, Madhesi Youth, January 27, 2016

29. Post Report, Govt to table constitution amendment bill without consent of UML, [Madhesi] Gathabandhan, The Kathmandu Post, Published Nov 21, 2016

30. Post Report, PM to split Province 5 to woo Madhesi forces, The Kathmandu Post, Published on Nov 23, 2016

31. Sinha, Shreenivas Kumar (1992), A Soldier Recalls, Autobiographical reminiscences of an Indian Army officer, Lancer Publishers Page 367

32. Human Rights Watch, "Like We Are Not Nepali" - Protest and Police Crackdown in the Terai Region of Nepal, Published October 16, 2015

33. 4-yr-old among four killed in Rupandehi police firing, The Kathmandu Post, Published Sep 16, 2016

34. NEPAL: Protest & Repression - Special Report on State Responsibility for 37 Killings During Protests in Terai, Asian Human Rights Commission (AHRC) and Terai Human Rights Defenders Alliance, Published May 23, 2016

35. Harijan, Raksha Ram (2016); Is four year also killed during protest encounter? चारवॉं केटा पनि मुठभेडमा मारिएको हो र सरकार ?, Published September 25, 2016 Downloaded from http://esamata.com/insight/चारवॉं केटा पनि मुठभेडमा

36. NEPAL: Protest & Repression - Special Report on State Responsibility for 37 Killings During Protests in Terai, Asian Human Rights Commission (AHRC) and Terai Human Rights Defenders Alliance, Published May 23, 2016.

3

Culture, Archaeological Heritage, Local Heroes, and History up to 1814

Culture

Culture is defined as that complex whole which includes knowledge, belief, art, morals, law, custom and any other capabilities and habits acquired by man as a member of society. Some aspects of human behavior, such as language, social practices such as kinship, gender and marriage, expressive forms such as art, music, dance, ritual, religion, and technologies such as cooking, shelter, and clothing are said to be cultural universals, found in all human societies.

Let's start with Art found in the Madhesh region. Madhesh region is naturally divided by river system into 2 broader cultural groups: East of Gandaki having greater impact and influence of Mithila region and West of Gandaki having greater influence of Awadhi culture. This Culture can be divided, even further: East of Koshi, Koshi to Gandaki, Gandaki to Rapti and west of Rapti.

- Art – Madhesh people are rich in art which has been carried forward since Vedic times. It is believed, in the King Janak's time, other people were surprised at the bamboo arts. The Madhesh region, being at the foot of Hilly range after Himalayan range, is having less of Sand, stone and gravels. Earth is formed with different types of mud. A white mud, locally called 'Chikni Mati' dug from deep inside the earth is found extensively in rice fields. Also, people collect mud from river, left over by the floods. This mud is brought by flash flood from high lands in rainy seasons. Women and men bring mud, mix farm residual husk in it and use for (1) building house foundation and wall (2) building grainy storage and (3) paint house and its surroundings using additional colors bought from local market; red from the red mud called Geruwa and white from lime stone. After each rainy season, paintings in the houses are refurbished with new mud and colors before local New Year's Sukrati festival; local name for Diwali, the festival of light. The warehouses to store grains, locally called "Kothis", are made of bamboo and covered with mud plaster. They are painted with the colors. More often, animals like elephants are depicted in these paintings. Similarly, flowers, bamboo trees, figures of deities find place in such wall paintings. It is only from these paintings that the inspiration of modern Mithila paintings on paper was derived during the earthquake of 1934 to leverage the painting as commercial profession for supporting women in the region. Mithila Women Development Center in Janakpur has been established with the same goal. It brings the artists from different villages together and provides channel to sell their works of art. There are other forms of art that are equally popular in Madhesh. Threading and knitting arts are more attractive in the small towns, where women make use of cotton threads, clothes, plastic threads and other reflective materials, and produce beautiful quilts, toys, sweater, table cloths, chair covers, window curtains, door curtains, pillow covers, bed sheets, etc. Some of these arts also end up in glass frame, hanged on wall or hanging from house ceiling. Weaving is available as hobbies as well as commercially. Both men and women can be found weaving mates using the rice husk. Few people commercially produce floor mates that are sold in local markets. Women stranded inside house in the rainy season use their time productively weaving baskets using local big soft grass called Sikki. Sikki baskets are time consuming and expensive. These produces are generally gifted to dear ones at special occasions. Bamboo arts are commercially adopted by Dom caste, lowest in social hierarchy, and their produces have high demand in villages and towns. Bamboo art produces different types of baskets used for house hold activities or as heavy carriage. Bamboo art also forms part of marriage ritual, where a big colorful decorative tree shaped product goes from groom to bride's place. During the marriage, Mithila paintings are drawn in the form of bamboo and flowers in deity room or Kohbar room.

- Performing arts such as dramas, Dances, Music, are indispensable attractions during festivals and special life events. Heroic tale of Alha-Udal, Rajput from Chandel King Court who lived in 1182 CE in Bundelkhand Region of North India and fought with Prithviraj Chauhan. An Alha-Udal ballad has been entirely handed down by oral tradition and presently exists in many recensions; which differ from one another both in language and subject matter throughout North India. The original language of this work has been continuously modernized over the centuries to suit the dialect of the reciter and it has been lost wholly in this process. Alha-Udal is top choice in the drama enacted during Durgapuja or in some local fairs. Other choices are story of Ramayana, Mahabharata, and Vikram Betal. Story of Lorik, mentioned in earliest Maithili book 'Varn Ratnakar' written in 1224 AD, is orally narrated and also enacted through play. King Salhes forms themes of Mithila painting. Maithili women enact the songs of 'Dom-Katchh' with the turn of Dholak music during marriage ceremony in bride's house, while men are away on 'barat'. Tharu women are vibrant with their dances and dressing during occasions like Sankranti festivals. Young girls sing songs for their brothers in 'Sama-Chakewa' festival that continues each night for a month during October-November. Neighbor women gather in groom's or bride's house and sing songs, mostly of Poet Vidyapati, starting few weeks before marriage. They also have songs for different festivals like Chhat, and Daha festivals. During Daha, both Hindus and Muslims come together for processions, where Muslim women sing and men mourners beat their chests and shout 'Ha Hussain, Ho Hussain' to commemorate the martyrdom of Hazrat Imam Hussain, the younger grandson of the Prophet Muhammad, in Karbala over 1,400 years ago. Hindu would take vows in Daha wishing his/her dear one's health to remain good. Hindu festival season starts with "Naag Panchami" locally called "Lag panchee". On this day snake is worshipped. "Naag Panchami" falls on the fifth day of bright half of lunar month of Shravan (July/August), and ends with Holi. Holi is most lively festival of color on which people have full liberty to eat exotic foods, drink liquor and make funs with people of any genus. People apply water color or vermilion to other's face and men also mix with women to apply colors. Music bands come together singing exotic songs and youth can be seen dancing on drummer. Elder generations also come together playing music on devotional songs towards evening. Festival closely similar to Holi is "Joor Sital", which falls on the second day of Hindu New Year, approximately corresponding to April 15th, is only celebrated in Madhesh-Tharu culture, and nowhere else in South Asia including Nepal and India. "Joor Sital" is festival of water on New Year day, and matches exactly with the celebrations that take place in Southeast Asian countries such as Myanmar, Cambodia, Laos, and Thailand as well as Yunnan, China. "Joor" means heart and "Sital" means Cool, thus with the belief that cold water will keep the heart cool through the remaining year, in the early morning, elder sprinkle cold water on the heads of younger while they are still on bed; young pours water on plants, trees and animals. Socially, people sprinkling water on street passersby or friends can be seen playing in muddy puzzles. "Joor Sital" also witnesses a lot of variety of food preparations in kitchen to celebrate New Year and leaves the question open in mind, what is the connection of Madhesh with the Southeast Asian countries those celebrating the water festivals. There are many Folk tales that Grandmother has been telling to kids like; (1) story of seven brothers and sisters (2) King and eggplant (3) Kid, monkey and deity. Grandmother and mother sing songs for kids while doing massage, while playing or while making them sleep. There is also a caste of musicians called "Pamaria" who visit once to the house which has been blessed with new baby, where they dance and sing holding kids in hands. Songs are also on rivers like Koshi and Kamla, which are addressed as mothers.

- Musical instruments popular in Madhesh are big Dholak, Tabla, Dafli, Tasha, Piphi/ Shehnai, Jhael (Indian Chime), Kirtan, Damru, Flute. Religious processions make use of musical instruments too.
- Custom, Habit, Law, Morals, Rituals – Elders are respected, they are never called by names, names of women are not known in public life after marriage, women take care of house chore, people greet each other as "Ram-Ram" or "Pranam", "Namaste", "Salam" or "Khuda Hafiz". Juniors greets the elders by touching feet with hand, if they meet after long intervals. Mostly, they are hostile to new people and would prefer not to greet if they have met on road. Joint families

are common practice with guidance from elders on home affairs, who might be sharing same roof and in the best case of joint family all women would share responsibilities to cook food for whole family. Option is also open for each brother to have different kitchen under same roof. Women take care of household, backyard and sometimes also take up the outdoor responsibilities. Men take care of the intensive manual works and outdoor works that need heavy interactions. In rural places, women might leave behind curtain or at least try to cover faces in front of elders, men members of family or in front of people from outside. Things are lately changing, as women are left at home to take care of both indoor and outdoor responsibilities while most of the men members are immigrating for employments in gulfs or Malaysia and Korea. Relatively, lower caste women have been doing outdoor works for longs time, who are under pressure to make the both ends meet daily, and they can be seen helping landlords in planting paddy and harvesting crops. Low caste women can also be seen along with their men cutting grass, grazing goats, cow and buffalos, which they own for income by selling milk to well-off high caste neighbors. Caste system, which is hereditary, is found among Hindu, and to some extent it is found among Muslims too. A particular caste is well skilled in one form or the other in the fields of trade/service. For example Dhobi specialize in washing clothes, Haluwai specialize in making sweets and confectionary, Chamar specialize in leather works, Brahmin specialize in religious rituals, Baniya specialize in trading and Hajam specialize in manicure, Lohar specialize in iron works, Sonar specialize in gold jewelry, Malee specialize in growing flowers and gardening, Kumhar specialize in earthen pottery, Mallah specialize in fishing, so on and so forth. Caste system is prevalent in the whole of Indian subcontinent. This system in Madhesh is part of the same structure and there is nothing unique so far as Madhesh is concerned. In old setting, inter-caste interactions happened through Jajmani system. Under this system goods/services are exchanged as per barter system in which social contracts were very well pre-defined. Jajmani system also covers Hindu interactions with Muslims. For example, Hindus getting services from Dhobi (cloth washer) or Dhuniya (quilt makers). With immigration being escalated and open trade being evolved Jajmani system is gradually petering down. Beside, people now tend to break caste system to adopt, which was once a taboo, skills of other castes. Indeed, caste system still survives in terms of practice of inter-caste marriages, where marriages are mostly arranged ones. It is also prevalent in the notion of untouchability, which is a dominant part among higher castes, according to which members of higher caste should not accept water/cooked food from lower caste directly or even if they have touched during transportation. Whenever there is conflict between members of two castes, groups of people belonging to the particular castes flock around their corresponding caste, and elder members of two castes sit together to resolve issue, and in those cases higher caste mostly have upper hands. In villages and old cities, it is quite common to have caste based house clusters. Caste has an additional unique character; each caste has its own family deity. Within the caste too, there can be different family deities. The social setting is secular in the sense that each caste is dependent on other in the context of either Jajmani system or open market or local customs or belief. For example, Hindu builds big monumental structure of Daha in Muslim festival of Muharram. All castes and creeds join procession of Dusad's Salhes puja by singing-dancing. Similarly, all castes together celebrate village Barham-puja. In case of Sudhi caste, Muslim saint Mira Sahib is family deity and Muslim priest, locally called Olia, officiates the rituals. Ponds and rivers are worshiped as gods and mother goddesses whereas trees are worshiped as adobe of God. During special lunar calendar dates, ponds and rivers are visited for bathing and fairs are also organized there. Koshi and Kamla Rivers command high regards in the region having many legends attached and songs sung. Ramayana Stories, the prominent Hindu epic conceived at least 5000 BC, revolves around the region of Mithila and Awadh.

- Other recreational activities are in the form of Games, both indoor and outdoor and Gambling. Gambling is too penetrated in young and elderly men. Ethnic gambling is played with Cowries or seashells which were once ancient form of monetary exchange medium. In the newer form of gambling cards are also played. Popular physical games are Kabbadi, wrestling locally called "Kusti", swimming, athletics, football and Cricket.

- Superstition is very mild term and might be out of context vis-a-vis the scenario taking place in the concerned field in Madhesh region. People resort to the old beliefs and customs when in trouble and have claimed to get benefitted from the practice too. Ghost stories are too much alive and people believe there are some places more prone to have their presence, like big tamarinds tree, big Jamun tree; a native Indian tree and black fruit tasting like cherry and also appearing like cherry. Evil ghosts, generally terms "Bhoot", are also supposed to enter someone's body either voluntarily or on the instruction of spiritual guru locally called "Ojha" or "Bhakta", and caste psychological impact on the possessed people to change in such a way that the person begins to impersonate and imitate the style in terms of talks and behavior of other person (supposed to be of dead people whose spirit has become ghost). The impersonation can last for few minutes to few hours; however the duration is painful for the person impacted. Impacted person might get the attacks frequently. Family person visits another "Ojha" or "Bhakta" for permanent recovery, who might ask for animal sacrifice and/or deity's storytelling in the form of poem along with music, locally called "Bhaktaee", if things go well. Such local deity can be inside the house of spiritual leader or it can be one in a village or at some place famous in the region. Animal sacrifice can also be a ritualistic thing depending upon family or region, for example, once in a year Gadhimai temple near Birgunj witnesses thousands of goat sacrifices from people coming from far and wide places. "Ojha" and "Bhakta" are males, and females with similar powers are called "Daayan". The term "Daayan" is mostly considered a term depicting cruelty believed to prey upon new born kids or during pregnancy. Spiritual leaders transfer their knowledge and can also transfer spiritual powers, supposed to have consisted of both Mantras and obedient ghost to their inheritor. The other forms of ghosts are (1) Devi, female young ghost, who tries to make love with young boys, (2) Panduba, a ghost who was drowned in ponds or river and (3) Manush-deva, small shaped rugged ghost who works for its master to accumulate Wealth. There is one more belief that credit should not be extended either in morning or night, similarly new cloth should be worn on specific day of week, and manicure should be done on some specific day of the week too.

- Five major life events, called Sanskaras in Hindu religion, are (1) Birth (2) Education (3) Marriage (4) Renouncing of or retirement from materialistic life (5) Death. Madhesis celebrate each of these Sanskaras in social gathering by inviting people to their houses. After birth, child is hidden from the world for at least a week, and more depending on the caste and family. After six days, child's Chhatiyar is done, when child gets to wear new cloth for first time. Before Chhatiyar, kid wears old cloth of other kids. Chhatiyar is also the first day when people from outside get to see kid for first time, and it is a big feast day where guests come together and provide blessings to new born. Chhatiyar, is followed by naming of kid after few weeks, and then followed by first grain food during six month around. First grain food could be big celebration depending on the caste and is locally known as "Anna Prashana". When kid is ready for education or to acquire formal skills, it is preceded by Mundan i.e. hair offering to the god. Mundan is only for boys. Marriage is a big celebration for the families both of groom and bride. People from Groom's side go in a group of people called "Barati" to the bride's house during evening. Baratis are given very warm welcome and are received with great respect. Barati People are served quality food. Decorations are made rather extravagantly. Religious leader/priest performs rituals and makes bride and groom take marriage oath. Next day, groom brings bride to his family. 2-3 decades before, Barati used to stay at bride's place for 2 nights, and leisure time was spent enjoying stage plays, locally called naach-gaan, organized by the family of bride. In the celebration program, professional artists called natuwa or also called as launda-laundi are brought. Muslims also have almost similar 1-2 days marriage ceremony having some variation in religious rituals. Remarriage in Muslim is allowed as per religious law. In Hindus, remarriage is not uncommon, although this gets tougher and tougher, according to the caste hierarchy. Polygamy is rare, though it was common few generations back. Ritual driven fictitious marriage with mango tree is also common in Hindu caste a day or two before the actual marriage, to remove any celestial bad omen. Renouncing was a big celebration once upon a time and is mentioned in religious book as Sannyas. Sannyas or renouncing is done after "Vanaprastha" or "Ban-prasthan" meaning leaving house and moving to peaceful jungles. Now a days, Sannyas and renouncing are not practiced in core sense of the terms. The last Sanskaras is death. Upon death, Hindus are burnt and Muslims are buried in soil. Hindu unmarried saints or new born kids, if die before certain age, are also buried in soil. Before burning, Hindu symbolically buys land by placing Cowrie or seashells at the four corners of land where dead body is burnt and buys fire from Hindu lower caste "Dom", who is believed to be king of cremation site called "Smashan". Hindu follows around 13 days of rituals, when relatives/friends gather and big feast is organized for them. The eldest son of the diseased, or some close relative in the absence of a son holds the pyre and wears white cloth during the 13 days of mourning rituals. After pyre burning or cremation, the remains like ash are collected and taken to Ganga River for immersion. Post death, eldest son performs funeral rites or Shraddha, then offers libations in the form of water, every subsequent year, on father day also locally called 'Pind Daan'. This continues till such a time that eldest son visits Gaya for final 'Pind Daan' at Falgu River.

- Jewelry and Makeup – Women have many types of ethnic jewelry made of Silver and Gold. Stones and Pearls are not a big choice. Bangles of varied thickness made either of glass, or lac or precious metal is a must for married women to be worn. Married Hindu women also put red small sticker, locally called "Tikli" or "Bindi", in the center of forehead and apply red color vermillion, locally called "Sindoor" in the center front part of head. Women have precious metal jewel for forehead, wrist, ear, nose, neck, shoulder, hand finger, leg finger, leg ankle and waist's metallic belt. Poor, both men and women, wears neck chain containing old coins too. Men wear neck chain and finger ring more often and bracelets occasionally. Earlier, men used to wear small jewelry in ear too. Men of all ages wear small metal coin and/or Cowrie or seashells knotted in thick round thread, locally called "Dnara" between stomach and waist, which is invisible to people. Dnara signifies how people used to carry money from one place to another in old days. Women apply Mehndi or henna very often on hands and on legs too, giving impression of tattoo. Red water color is preferred to Mehndi for legs. Permanent tattoo can be found in old generation. Before marriage ceremony, people use traditional facial paste called "Uptan" made from the mix of turmeric and mustard oil. Mostly women and occasionally men also do eye makeup using black Kajal, locally prepared out of smoke produced from mustard oil and charcoal. Women love their big hair, and use two types of traditional combs (1) Thhakri, which looks like a broom made of midrib of dried coconut leaf and (2) Kakhi or Kanghi made of wood or plastic in modern time. Traditionally, hair were washed using the white soil called "Chikni-mati" or Oil-cake called "Khhari", which is now being produced in the form of soap or detergent shampoo and which is now promoted commercially. After bath, people apply mustard oil or sesame oil in hair. These oils are locally produced. They also use imported coconut oil or perfumed oils.

- Food and Cooking - Day of Labor class people begins with breakfast, whereas all other groups, middle class, businessmen and higher class prefer meal as first food of the day. Rice is main staple diet, as well as status symbol over bread. Bread is associated with poor labors. There are many varieties of rice. Aromatic Basmati Rice is the first choice. Similarly, bread made out of flour is preferred to rice. Pearl millet and barley are also used occasionally. Many people plant rice, twice a year and wheat or maize once a year. And just before rice, people might also plant finger millet, locally called "Maruwa". Other grains produced and consumed are pulse, pigeon pea locally called "Rahhri", split red lentil locally called "Masoori", split green gram locally called "Moong", chicken peas locally called "Chana", and split black gram locally called "Urid". Third category of important food items consumed is cooked vegetables. These include potato, onion, tomato, cauliflower, eggplant, bitter guard, pointed gourd, locally called "Paror", green beans, pumpkin, green jackfruit, capsicum, Chili etc. People use several other side items as taste enhancers which can be broadly categorized as (1) Chutney; grinded semi-liquid Flex seed, sesame seed, green coriander leaf, mint leaf, green mango, onion etc., and (2) Achaar; fermented and preserved green mango piece deep into spicy oil. Use of milk curd during and after lunch is supposed to have good omen, and thus people also take curd before leaving on an important assignment at long distance. Concentrated butter locally called "Ghee" is highly admired and used during lunch and dinner. Ethnic Rice chips fried into deep oil is unique to this region, and is similar to the Sabudana (Tapioca Sago) chips popular in South Asia. Papad, a thin wafer, is either roasted or deep oil fried. To supplement the vegetable curry, deep oil fried vegetables having a layer of chickpeas spicy batter, and locally called "Pakora", are occasionally consumed for lunch/dinner and more often used as snacks. Sliced potato or eggplant having a cover of a light rice flour batter and properly grilled in light oil is very tasty locally called "Taruwa" and is highly desired dish when some guests are invited for lunch or dinner. Fresh Fish, which is available in plenty, is also taken as "Taruwa" in addition to Fish Curry. Fish are either wild, found in river or ponds too. Poor people also catch tiny fish using net, locally called "Chachre", laid in the water channels in the rice fields during August-September. Its taste is awesome. Crab (locally called "Kokra"), shrimps (locally called "Jhinga"), whelk (locally called "Ghongha"), tortoise (locally called "Kachhuwa") - found in rice fields, rivers and ponds – are delightful dishes of poor families. Oysters are found, though not like before. It is not taken as food rather its shell is used for making food quality lime to be used in Betal leaf also called "Pan". Meat, mostly of goat or chicken, is preferred with curry rather than grill. Rice pudding is served occasionally post-dinner. Spices are part of curry ingredients. Among these writ of turmeric powder, chili powder and coriander powder runs large in every kitchen. Dried vegetables are stored for rainy season. Dry fish are preferred to cabbage. Additional food storage is in the form of popcorn shaped lentil batter granules which are dried in the sun. It is locally known as "Ba-ri". In the same league comes grinded and dried popcorn shaped white Chinese winter melon granules locally called "Kumh-rauri". Other eatable unique to Madhesh is "Bageeya" made post-harvest of new rice crop. It is a sort of dumping in a sense. However, triple in size and preparation, it is stuffed with lentil and is boiled rather than steamed. In winter sesame laddu, locally called "Tilwa", is made, which is small ball of sesame seeds glued tightly together after mixing with Jaggery. Similarly prepared is small ball of puffed rice (called Murhi) and flattened rice flakes (called Chuwda) which is locally called as "Lai". Chuwda and Murhi are reserve foods that can last for few weeks, and forms good company during long travels. Similarly, roasted chickpeas batter locally called "Satuwa" is preferred to reserve food during hot summer and believed to be heathy choice, given its protein percentage which only requires water to mix and drink. During family festivals, thick bread mixed with Jaggery and deep fried in oil, are prepared and are locally called as "Thakuwa"; and if little refined flour is used along with sugar instead of Jaggery, it improves the taste considerably, and is locally called "Khajuriya", also to be found in sweet shops. Locally grown fruits are Mango, Litchi, Coconut, Khajur (Dates), Tarkuwa (Baby Palmyra Palm fruits), Bael (Bengal quince or golden apple), Jamun, Ber (Indian plum), Pomegranate, Papaya, custard apple of two varieties, Guava, Banana, Goose berry, Jack fruits, watermelon, canary Melon, etc.

- Clothing – Ethnic men wear are Kurta (similar to shirt) and Dhoti (piece of long plain cloth tied around the waist and extending to cover most of the legs). Gamchha, a cotton scarf, is common around the neck of working men that helps them clean dust or sweat or protect during winter. Shirt-Pant has lately become de-facto wear of professionals and Vest-Jeans are very popular in the new generation. During summer, to beat the heat, working men can be seen in thin vest and sometime naked top half body. Ethnic wear of married women is blouse and Sari (a drape around 5 meters in length and 1.5 meters in breadth that is typically wrapped around the waist, with one end draped over the shoulder, baring the midriff). Young girls wear Kurti (female version of Kurta), leggings and scarf. Western wears such as tops and jeans are slowly and steadily making impression on women too. Fashion accessories for ethnic women are Kajal, Bindi, and ribbon.
- House & Surrounding – Traditional houses are made from bamboo and tree stems forming the base structure; roofs are thatched either with dried grass or terracotta tiles; and walls are thatched either with dried grass or woven bamboo net or mud or mix of all. Kitchen is generally in separate room, which emits a great deal of smoke. Kitchen stoves, locally called "Chulhi" or "Chulha", are made of mud on ground and for fire energy wood or dried glass or dried cow dung cakes, locally called "Goitha-Chipri", are used. Today, modern houses are made of bricks, cement and iron rods; and a few decades back modern houses were made using mix of bricks, lime

stones and wooden pillars. Roads, both rural and urban, are not so good and are always having ongoing work, primarily due to excess water or flood, which is common in the region. Region is well supplied with water sources like ponds and rivers. Thus, fish is a popular staple diet and source for protein in addition to milks from cows and buffalo. Water, which is generally still or slow flowing due to flat terrain, is breeding ground for mosquitos. This state of affairs have escalated recently in urban centers with the decreasing population of frogs and increasing dumping of solid organic waste in the sewage that are mostly open and ill managed. A few other creatures easily spotted in Madhesh are ant, moth, flies, spider, snake, cat, dog, donkey, pig, cow, buffalo, hen, duck, sparrow, pigeon, parrot, mynah, crow, eagle, Asian koel, woodcutter, owl, etc. Easily spotted herbs and shrubs are Mango, Pipal, Banyan, Neem, Dalbergia sissoo, Sal, Mahua, bombax or Simmal, Ashoka, bamboo, jasmine, orchid, rose, marigold, sunflower, lotus, Chinese rose, etc.

- Weather – As everywhere else, in this region also there are winter, spring, summer and rainy seasons. Summer is really tough with common temperature at around 40 degrees Celsius. The temperature increases further. There is also humid environment which ushers flocks of mosquitos. Rainy season is most awaited one. However, it becomes very painful when there is excessive flow of water from Himalayan region, which creates flood havoc. In recent times, winter is not good since pollution from Indian subcontinent creates thick fog below Himalayan range impacting access to sunlight which is required for basic transportations.
- Lifestyle – Morning starts very early, and many elderly people wake up as early as at 4 AM, because they go to bed early. They go to bed early because of lack of sufficient supply of lights on the roads and recently due to increasing security reasons. In rural areas, in general, there are open air toilets, whereas in urban areas there are pit toilets. For cleaning water is used instead of toilet papers. Traditional toothbrush is made from Neem twigs or bamboo stick; that is used one time and thrown, daily. Commercial branded tooth paste and tooth brush have made inroads strongly. Mouth brushing is mostly followed by bath in middle class and upper class, before taking lunch. Labor class people mostly go to work after brushing and take

bath in the afternoon. Traditionally people bath in ponds, and in last few decades hand pump counts have made good progress. Hand pumps supply most of the drinking water in Madhesh. Traditionally drinking water was sourced from wells and before that from ponds or rivers, about a century back. Most of the offices and shops open at 10 AM and people might start working even late. Small mom-pops stores supply the daily commodity, and in most places it also has weekly haat or bazar. Rural people visit urban centers for office works, in addition to shopping. Most of them can be found hanging around in courts during non-agriculture season, because property disputes are very common within families or neighbors, and probably this gives them opportunity to connect with politics of outer world. People return home very early and sleep also early. Theft rather than robbery is very common during the nights. Houses are thatched, locally called houses of "Phus". In such houses thieves enter inside, having made tunnel or "Sendh" very quickly, and they generally do this around midnight when people inside the house are in deep sleep. While doing so, they apply oil in the body so that they can escape easily if someone tries to catch them. Madhesh region has old tradition of burglary. The fact is that such burglaries are not only ignored, but also have state protection for last several centuries, when conflict between British India and Nepal was at peak. Burglary in this region predates King Prithivi Narayan Shah's rule and is even proudly mentioned in the famous story of "Salhes". Old stalwarts of two villages, Jhijha and Akaura, were rehabilitated by grant of lands from both Bihar Government and Nepal Government few decades back, getting their promise that they will leave their notorious robbery profession[1].

- Kinship – Madhesh region is more of a political boundary today than the true representation of cultural boundary. Madhesh is common name to represent part of Mithila, Bhojpuri region, Awadh and Tharuhut currently situated at Nepal boundary. Thus, from cultural perspective, it has reach to and connection with regions all across Mithila, Bhojpuri region, Awadh, and Tharuhut, that spans very deep into northern Indian State. Probably that is the primary driving factor which has made it possible to have open border between India and Nepal. The people across has deep marriage ties. Most of the marriages are within 50 miles of radius. However, given the bad state of road network, relatives appear to be at far away distance. Madhesh has strong sense of relationship. Madhesis gather together during special occasions like marriage or someone's death ritual. Unlike English, kinship is well defined. A family constitutes mother (called "Ma" or "Mai"), father (called "Bau", "Babu" or "Pita"), sister (elder called as "Didi" and younger called as "Bahin"), sister's husband (called "Jija" or "Pahuna"), brother (elder called as "Bhaiya", younger called as "Bhai"), brother's wife (elder called as "Bhauji" or "Bhabhi", younger called as "Bhabho"), grandfather (called as "baba" or "Dada"), grandmother (called as "Dai" or "Dadi"), uncle (called as "Kaka" or "Chacha"), aunty (called "Kaki" or "Chachi"), cousin (called "Bhai", "Bhaiya", "Bhahin", "Didi"). In the extended family, relationship is equally given importance on both mother's side and father's side. Mother side: grandfather (called "Nana"), grandmother (called "Nani"), uncle (called "Mama"), aunty (called "Mami"), and cousin (called "Bhai", "Bhaiya", "Bhahin", "Didi"). Father's sister is called "Phuwa" or "Phuphu" or "Didi", and her husband is called "Phupha". Mother's sister is called "Mausi" and her sister's husband is called "Mausa". Wife's side: father is called "Sasur", mother is called "Saush", brother is called "Sala", sister is called "Sali", brother's wife is called "Sarojhani", and sister's husband is called "Sadhu". Husband Side: Father is called "Sasur", mother is called "Saush", bother is called "Bhhaisur", brother's wife is called "Bhabho", sister is called "Nannd" and sister's husband is called "Nandosi". In Hindus, marriage within blood relationship is prohibited for seven generations across both mother's and father's side. High castes like Brahmin and Kayastha have recorded family trees from centuries. Among them also marriage within same gotra is prohibited. One's son is called "Beta", and daughter is called "Beti", at son's side grandson is called "Pota", at son's side granddaughter is called "Poti", at daughter's side grandson is called "Nati" and at daughter's side granddaughter is called "Natani". Brother's son is called "Bhatija" and Brother's daughter is called "Bhatiji". From male perspective, sister's son is called "Bhanja" and sister's daughter is called "Bhatiji". Sister's son is called "Bahinput" and Sister's daughter is called "Bahinputri". While addressing relatives or friends by name, "Jee" is added after the name. Male name is prefixed with "Shri", and female if married is prefixed with "Shrimati" else "Sushri".

- Wealth and Commerce – Traditionally, first level of wealth is generated from (1) agriculture (2) animal husbandry (3) fishing and (4) Immigration. Other commercial activities generating the secondary level of wealth are goods trading and services. The wealth goes out from the region in the form of (1) financing imports of essential commodities like salt, medicine, cloth and construction material as well as recent trend of luxury goods, import of goods like Motorbike, electronics goods (2) Tax (3) outward investment. There are industrial production activities. However, their impact on locals in terms of native men's employment, raw material sourcing and market is negligible. There are plenty of jungle resources having timbers; however access of local people to such resources has been prohibited. Social lending is accessible method, though interest rates are steep high at 3% per month, for short term financing, unless someone is highly connected with political elites to get from banks. Banks here are mostly for collecting retail deposits, that immigrants are bringing but don't see any other productive outlet for investment except land purchase.
- Physical appearance – Men and women are of average heights around 5 feet 3 inches. Facial structure is divided between Tharu and the rest (Maithili, Bhojpuri and Awadhi). Tharu face looks like Chinese and faces of the rest of the people look like Indians. Body structures look similar. They are lean-thin, except tummies bring a little larger and oversized in men. The main reason for this is that they are rice eaters. Having large tummy is considered to be a sign of prosperity. They are of dark complexion given their exposure to the hot and humid climate, genetic carryover notwithstanding. Generally, the higher castes have more physical height, attractive face with longer nose, more body weight and fair complexion compared to the lower castes.

Archaeological Heritage

Orally descended ancient history of Mithila and Awadh links them back to "Pouranik" age of Ramayana, a Hindu epic considered to have been conceived at least about 5,000 years ago, in which the main woman character Sita belonged to Mithila and main man character Rama belonged to Awadh. Coming down to the recorded and more traceable history, there is mention of Videha -another name of Mithila - in the works written during Buddha's time about 600 BC. Gautam Buddha himself belonged to Awadh region. In other earlier Buddhist canonical literature such as "Vinay Pimaka", the region has been depicted as culturally rich, socially mature, politically active and economically strong. As per Buddhist literature and Jain literature of contemporary period, Videha was federation of republics of eight clans together called Vajji or Vrijji Republic, which was first known republic in the world that existed in 6th BC. Since then, many rulers came into the region. This can be born out very well from the archaeological excavations, though very limited work in this area has been done.

The Tarai has independent history of ancient times, although those kingdoms had connections both with Gangetic plains and Nepali hills. Lumbini, Kapilbastu, and Devadaha are all important sites in the West. Simraungadh and Janakpur are important in the East. Kapilbastu was an important early Buddhist center associated with Gautama. These early kingdoms were decimated by disease and were largely reforested until Simraungadh was founded near the former site of Janakpur. Simraungadh was later destroyed by the Moslems in the fourteenth century and the region was again naturally reforested[2].

From the twelfth century downward, the tide of *Mussulman* conquest and bigotry continued to sweep multitudes of the *Brahmans* of the plains from India or *Bharat* into the proximate hill, which now compose the Western territories of the kingdom of Nepal[3].

In the following sections, we are going into details of some of the important and known archeological sites:

Simraungadh

Simraungadh (or Simraun) represents the magnificent account of History of Tirhut. Simraungadh was established in 1097 AD by a King originally from Karnataka of south India named Nanya (Nanyupa) Deva. A King coming to extreme north from south might look surprising in first thought, however this was not unusual given the fact that Kathmandu's Pashupati temple had been getting main priests from Shankaracharya Peeth located in Sringeri of south Indian state Karnataka. The tradition of having South Indian as main priest in Pashupati is believed to have been started on advice of Adi-Shankaracharya in 8th century.

About 15 miles from the base of the hills and at a nearly equal distance from the Bagmati River, in the South of the former and extreme West of the latter, stand the remains of Simraungadh in the Nepalese district of Bara and opposite to the Champaran district of India.

Simraun has been the integral part of History of Mithila and represents the glorious period of History. Minimal inscriptions have been found about Simraun. However, according to the local narratives, as noted by Brian Hodgson in his account, four kings Rama, Nala, Pururava and Alarka preserved their wealth in a water tank (named Isra) which was guarded by a snake. Nanya Deva destroyed the snake, appropriated the wealth and built Simraungadh with it[4].

Simraungadh was a city built within the fort spanning about 12 miles in circuit. The fort was full of the works of fine architecture, having parallelogram shape, and surrounded by two layers of wall, of which outer wall was made of fine burnt bricks each having a cubit square and weighing about 40 kg. The whole building turned into ruins except only the water tank (Isra) which remained in good shape.

About two dozens of idols found in the ruins, are all mutilated. This supports the common belief that the Muslim aggressor Ghiyas-ud-din Tuglak from Delhi completely destroyed the Hindu kingdom of Simraungadh in 1325 AD, and its last king Harisimha Dev ran away with his family and made abode in Kathmandu valley.

The earliest written account of Simraun is by Italian missionary Father Cassiano (more popularly known as Givanni Beligatti), who travelled from Patna to Nepal Valley several times during 1739 and 1754. Father Cassiano's handwritten account was first published in 1901 by A. Magnaghi under the title "Unpublished relations of a trip to Tibet by p. Cassiano Beligatti". The book was republished by L. Petech in 1952-53 under the title "Italian missionaries in Tibet and Nepal"[5]. In his book Father Cassiano describes Simraungadh in the following words:

> *We saw various ancient ruins indifferent sites and some were obviously remains of important build—I could not understand, how in a wood so vast, whose age-old trees showed its -ancient origins, there could have existed constructions of a certain consideration. During the following years, when I made my abode in Nepal, I inquired about those ruins I was assured by many Nepalese from Batgao [Bhaktapur] that said ruins were small vestiges of the famous and very ancient city of Scimangada [Simraungadh], from whence came their kings, and Which could not*

be approached if not after having circled around and around it for approximately a month, the city being situated in the centre of a labyrinth closed by high walls, a labyrinth with only one entrance, and having found the right path, before arriving to the city one had to pass under four forts, which were distributed equidistant along the way with-in the walls of the labyrinth, each wall distant from the next 2 kose, i.e., 4 miles, and the walls which were extremely high were also proportionately thick. Between one wall and another there were delightful fields and small creeks which watered them.[6]

In the court of Hari Singh Dev, the last Karnat dynasty King of Simraungadh, the Royal Priest was Pt. Jyotishwara Thakur, the author of 'VARNA RATNAKAR', which is considered to be the first prose, an encyclopedia in any north Indian language. Many other books were written during his period in Maithili and Sanskrit languages.

The kingdom of Simraun extended from the Kosi River to Gandaki and from the Ganges to the hills of Nepal; at least these were its boundaries in the days of its greatest splendor[7].

Hamilton also visited the site at the end of eighteenth century and tried to compile several oral historical accounts from local people. Hamilton provides more details on the scenario related with the period when Harisingh Dev was thrown out of throne. Most of the regions, especially the lower area close to Ganga, came under Tuglak regime. The Eastern side of Tirhut was given to a Maithil Brahmin to collect taxes and in due course of time his family established and asserted its inheritance over the throne, having Darbhanga as capital. The Western lower region was given to Sallaria Brahmin named Guzz Singh having his capital in Bettia[8]. The upper north region close to hill was given to Pt. Kamleshwar, who later became founder of Oinwar Dynasty having capital in Mahottari district. Oinwar ruled till they were dethroned by King Lohang Sen.

Today, Simraungadh archeological heritage stands neglected in absence of state priority[9]. Local people very often find historical artifacts, metallic and terracotta, while digging ground in surroundings[10].

Lumbini - Kapilbastu

Lumbini is birth place of Gautam Buddha, who was born as Prince Siddhartha Gautam in 623 BC. As per Pali literature, Queen Maya wanted to give birth to her child at her parent's house in Devadaha, however failed to make full journey on time, and thus gave birth to son Siddhartha in half way at Lumbini. The Buddhist literature mentions that the Sakyas of Kapilbastu and Koliyas of Devadaha jointly maintained the garden of Lumbini.

In early phase of life, Prince left his Kingdom one night in search of answer for the pains that human being suffers during the life. He moved around many places, including Videha (ancient name of Tirhut) which was famous among scholars, and finally found his enlightenment in Gaya, now situated in Bihar. This place is now known as Bodhgaya. Buddha was able to connect to people because he was able to explain the emancipation from suffering in simple terms and still enabled people to get god's blessings, compared to the complex Brahmanical procedure prescribed in Hindu religion. In those times, Brahmanical doctrine instituted the advancement and supremacy of Brahman Caste. Buddha, as a champion of religious liberty and social equality, attacked the Brahmans in their weakest and most vulnerable points, - in their impious assumption of all the mediation between man and his maker, and in their arrogant claims to hereditary priesthood. Buddha, was a great social reformer of that time[11].

The predecessor of Buddha to challenge caste inheritance was King Janak of Videha (later named as Mithila, Tirhut) having capital at Janakpur. "Janak" was a dynasty and Sita's father Janak was 19th among them having name Sirdhwaj Janak[12]. Brahmana scholars of the corresponding period approached Janak kings to acquire knowledge. One such episode is very popular. Ashtavakra, a great scholar and ascetic went to Janak and had philosophical and spiritual debate with him, contents of which are compiled in the famous Ashtavakra Gita. Janak Kings were great patrons of scholars and great philosophers themselves. King Janak used to invite scholars to participate in Shastarthas or scholarly debates. At one occasion, King Janak announced a prize of one thousand cows for the most prominent scholar in which Yajnavalkya was declared winner after he defeated other scholars one by one with his reasoning and excellent logic[13].

Jain religion, which was also popular in those days in the Gangatic plain, had impact on Buddha. However, Jain religion was still harder to follow for the common people due to the requirement of strict self-discipline.

After around three and a half century, in 249 BC, emperor Ashoka visited Lumbini in the 20th year of his coronation and erected a stone pillar with Pali language inscription to pay homage to Lord Buddha's birth place. The Ashoka's inscription on the pillar is in Brahmi script and has been translated as: By King Piyadassi, the beloved of the gods [who] having been consecrated twenty years [having] come himself personally [here] to offer homage, or celebrate, because Shakyamuni Buddha was born here, was caused both a Silavigadabhica to be built and a stone pillar to be set up. [And], because the Lord was born here, the Lumbini village was made free from taxes and liable to pay [only] one-eighth part [of the produce][14]. Emperor Ashoka declared Lumbini village a tax free zone to mark the auspiciousness of the place.

In the years 350-375 AD, a Monk Seng-tsai belonging to the Qin Dynasty made a pilgrimage to Lumbini. He wrote accounts of his visit. Subsequently another Chinese traveler named Hwen-Thsang visited Lumbini in 636 AD and described Lumbini as "a deserted place, and wild animals roamed around enough to warn off travelers".

The last person to visit Lumbini and leave behind the evidence of his visit, before Lumbini went missing for centuries, was, King Ripu Malla in 1312 AD. Lumbini, the most important sacred place of Buddhist pilgrimage, was slowly converted into bush land and faded from memory for a long time. Some Scholars suggest that reason for this going into oblivion was natural disasters, such as drought, famine, flood caused by incessant rains that region attracts during rainy season and major earthquakes that this region witnesses each century. Major earthquakes occurred in 1344, 1408, 1505 AD[15] impacting Lumbini region. Other group of people link the cause of oblivion to the invasion of Muslims and revival of Hinduism. There is little research conducted on this question and it would be worthwhile undertaking further study of history between fourteenth to nineteenth centuries.

During five century-long oblivion, most part of the Asoka pillar was covered by the earth. When Dr. Alois Anton Führer first went to the site at the end of November 1896, only 10 feet of the pillar was visible above the ground and remaining 12.4 feet were buried in earth[16]. The site's surrounding was inhabited, so it's possible that the local people never gave any attention to the archaeological structure and were unaware of its importance. The people who live around Lumbini are Hindus and Muslims, and not a single Buddhist is in sight[17]. After Lumbini came to light, Buddhists around the world visit it and there are many tourist guest houses built by different international government grants. Hindus also pay visit to the Lumbini Buddhist shrines.

Lumbini is located close to India-Nepal border and is about 10 miles away from nearest border point and 15 miles away from the Hill. Lumbini is hot and flat and belongs to sub-tropical climatic zone, having all four seasons. It has long summer starting May-June with high temperature (up to 42.5°C), thunder showers, heat waves originated from land. From July to September summer becomes tougher with humidity. A great deal of mud, winds, and hailstorms are the side results of monsoon rains. October and November is the autumnal season, having dry and warm climate during daytime and cold at night. December to February one experiences winter with dense foggy morning impacting visibility and cold temperature occasionally dropping to 5°C. Due to the global warming, weather pattern has changed a lot. Rainy season has become shorter, average temperature has increased and fog is getting worse and worse day by day.

There are two rivers close to the Lumbini Garden.

- Harhawa River: The catchment area of the Harhawa River is 21 km. The flood discharge at peak is estimated at 160 cum/sec[18]. The river basin gets flooded several times each year and each flooding lasts four to five days. The river develops a typical floodplain of 100/120 meters in width – one to two meters below the surrounding grounds along the river course.
- Telar River: The Telar flows from East to the Sacred Garden. The name derives from the word 'tel', which means oil, since the water is thought to be oily in nature. This river is a landmark, mentioned by the Chinese travelers, as it flows close to the birthplace of Lord Buddha. The type of soil is clayish, permeability is very low, sodium level is high and the available phosphorus is very low. The soil is firm and the alkalinity level is high.

As per Tara Nanda Mishra and Bidari, flood was the reason for Lumbini having been abandoned for 5 centuries. 'It is also possible that some natural disasters, such as drought, famine, floods in the rainy season, or earthquakes caused people to abandon Lumbini'[19]. The swampy ground further deteriorated the land and brought about diseases such as malaria making the area uninhabitable for humans. This took centuries to counter this menace by draining the swamps and eradicating the malaria using large quantities of toxic chemicals and by turning the jungles into farmland.

The chronological sequence[20] of dynasties at the Lumbini site, as per Tara Nanda Mishra who did further excavation of Lumbini, is as follows:

- 4thB.C. Pre-Ashokan
- 3rdB.C. Mauryan
- 1st – 2ndB.C. Sunga/Mitra
- 2nd BC – 1stA.D. Kushana
- 3rd – 8thA.D. Guptal
- 9th – 13thA.D. Khasiya Malla

These dates interestingly match with the foundation of the capital of the Sakya Kingdom in Tilaurakot (28 Km West of Lumbini), which dates back to 7th century B.C.[21].

However, Government of Nepal has neglected all the Buddha sites, except the sites where foreign donations are forthcoming or where India claims its closeness to Buddha heritage. As per British professor and writer David Seddon, who visited Lumbini in 2014, Lumbini is in miserable condition due to cold response from government and its agencies. As per professor Seddon, the famous Ashoka pillar is submerged in an overgrown and rubbish-strewn pond which is surrounded by decrepit and broken railing. Several cracks have appeared in the pillar which can be taken care by "loving care"[22].

Janakpur

Janakpur is mentioned in Hindu epic 'Ramayana' as capital of Mithila, where the king was Janak, the father of Sita, also known as Janaki, Maithili or Vaidehi. Mithila, also known as Videha or Tirhut, has rich history, culture and commands a significant place in Indian subcontinent. However, there is little archeological evidence from the period of Ramayana, which is believed to have happened, as mentioned above, at least 5000 years ago. But in this matter there are different opinions. Overall, period of Ramayana is believed to be 3500 to 5000 years before. Mithila's ancient capital Janakpur is also victim of the lack of archaeological evidences. Its location has been located on the basis of people's belief and very few of the geographical features mentioned in Ramayana. Mithila was known as Tirabhukti or Videha in the past, and is considered to be the present Tirahuti or Tirhut. As per Alexander Cunningham[23], "the modern town of Janakpur in the Mithari district, is acknowledged by the universal consent of the natives of the country, to be the same place as the ancient Janakpur, the capital of Mitihila. It also corresponds exactly with the position assigned by Hwen Thsang to Chen-shu-na, the capital of Vriji. The correct rendering of the name is doubtful but if the bearing and distance recorded by the Chinese pilgrims are correct it is almost certain that the capital of Vriji in the seventh century must have been Janakpur". Cunningham has misspelt Mahottari district as Mithari, otherwise he insists that Janakpur has been there in 7th century when Chinese traveler Hwen Thsang visited Indian subcontinent. Hwen Thsang, also known as Yuan Chwang, Hsuan Tsang and Hiuen Tsang, visited Kathmandu valley from Vaishali and then returned to Vaishali. From that time onward till recent times the route to Kathmandu has been popular through Sindhuli or along the bank of Kamla, and both of them are accessible from today's Janakpur. This could have been the route through which Hwen Thsang travelled between Vaishali and Kathmandu.

However, the ensuing discussion is not to approve or disapprove the people's belief on the basis of which current location of Janakpur had been identified. The discussion below is restricted to the terms of human settlement, history and archaeological evidence about the place, which is currently known as Janakpur.

Coming back to Cunningham, he further spills the details on Janakpur saying, "According to Hwen Thsang the country of the Vrijis was long from east to west and narrow from north to south. This description corresponds exactly with the track of country lying between the Gandaki and Mahanadi rivers, spanning 300 miles in length by 100 miles in breadth. Within these limits there are several ancient cities, some of which may possibly have been the capitals of the eight different clans of the Vrijis. Of these Vaishali, Kesariya and Janakpur have already been noticed; the others are Navandgarh, Simraun, Darbhanga, Puraniga and Motihari. The last three are still inhabited and are well known but Simraun has been deserted for upwards of 550 years while Navandgarh has probably been abandoned for at least fifteen centuries Simraun has been described". Mahanadi (Mahananda in Hindi) is known by the same name in Nepal & Bengal, which flows through Indian states of West Bengal, Bihar and the country of Bangladesh. Its right bank tributary, the Mechi River forms part of Nepal's eastern boundary with

West Bengal. The boundary of Vrijis confederation, as given by Cunningham, matches with the boundary of Karnat dynasty Kingdom before it was plundered by Ghiyas-ud-din Tuglak in 1325 AD[24]. This indicates that land of Vrijis were again powerful and prospering under Karnat dynasty, whose capital was in Simraun about 80 miles West of Janakpur.

Further, we will discuss the archaeological evidences that indicate there was human settlement in Janakpur in ninth-tenth centuries. Before that, I would like to find the answer to what happened to the people who migrated from Janakpur area after 14th century, which matches with time when Lumbini also witnessed absence of human settlement.

As per tales in Awadh of North India[25], Rai Amba and his son went to Janakpur in Tirhut with cavalry of 5,000 army from Rai Bareilly. On his way back, a Brahmin complained to him that a nearby Bhar King of Hastinaghat (now called Hasanpur) had made offer to marry his daughter, but he did not want it. On this, Rai Amba suggested to Brahmin to go to Hastinaghat king and pretend to submit to the desire of Bhar. Brahmin went and told King, he is happy with the proposal and he can come at earliest to take her daughter. Bhar King got excited listening to the Brahmin and immediately came unsuspecting into the trap. The Bhar king fell to easy inglorious pray to the arms of Rai Amba. Rai Amba got the Kingdom, which was ruled by his son Rai Bidad and succeeded by his son Rai Dudhich, who subsequently became Muslim. Ancient Bhar Kingdom ruins exist currently in Basti district of UP, India[26].

This event took place in the fifteenth century. There are two accounts to estimate the timeline. As per one account, father of Rai Amba was famous Tilok Chand, who died half century before Akbar's accession to Mughal throne in 1556 AD[27]. Thus, Rai Amba might have visited Janakpur before the end of the fifteenth century. In another account, Rai Barar, son of Rai Amba, led the cavalry against Bhar King. Great grandson of Rai Barar named Palhan Deo is said to have become a Muslim during Sher Shah Suri's reign (1540 –1545 AD). By this account, attack against Bhar king happened four generations before Sher Shah Suri's reign, which comes to be around middle of the fifteenth century.

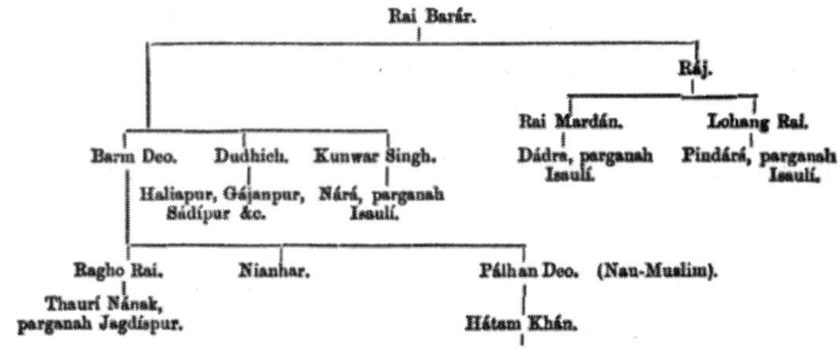

Genealogy of Rai Barar as given by A F. Millett in 'Report on the settlement of the land revenue of the Sultánpur district. [With] Accompaniments, Volume 1, 1873, pp. 182

Another family clan from Uttar Pradesh of India belonging to Kurauna of Sitapur district has also direct linkage to the history of Janakpur. As mentioned in the Gazetteer of Awadh, written in third quarter of nineteenth century based on the survey, the Jamindar Deo Singh and Madho Singh families came to Kurauna four centuries back from Janakpur in Tirhut[28]. The report mentions, the detail about the family history was lost, except the fact that their father Raghunath Singh died in 1850 after enjoying the estate for 72 years and their grandfather enjoyed the estate for 75 years, together one and a half century. By this account, we can estimate the families of Jamindar Deo Singh and Madho Singh migrated from Janakpur around middle of fifteenth century.

Both the above historical mentions of Janakpur elude to the fact that Janakpur had human settlement till middle of fourteenth century. This is corroborated by the history of Maithili Poet Vidyapati's presence in village Banauli[29], three miles Southwest of Janakpur, where he is believed to have died in 1448 AD.

The history of Janakpur for next three centuries, from fifteenth century to eighteenth century, seems to be ruled by long grass and jungle that grew in the absence of human settlement. The reason for migration of people from Janakpur to other region is not known. But it would appear something similar to the trend that is observed from the ruin of Simraungadh and Lumbini. All eluding to the direction that, there was devastating natural calamity (flood, earthquake or drought) that forced people to move to other places like Uttar Pradesh.

Janakpur was rediscovered in early eighteenth century[30] by two Hindu ascetics Caturbhuj Giri and Sur Kisor. Sur Kisor established a foundation for Janaki temple and Caturbhuj Giri constructed a Ram temple, which is very much there in Janakpur prominently visible even today. A good commodity market was in place, when Captain Kinloch passed through Janakpur on his way to help King Jay Prakash Malla in 1767, where he planned to buy plenty of grains[31].

There is little archaeological evidence of significance in central downtown Janakpur. However, in the areas surrounding a radius of few miles, researchers have found remains of archaeological sites of considerable importance. Such areas are: Banauli, Kapileshwar, Bhutahi, Duhabi and Bega Shivapur.

- Kapileshwar is situated half mile to the East of Janakpur. This place is replete with ruins. The first report of light excavation was produced by Janaklal Sharma of Department of Archaeology in 1958.The report[32]indicated detailed research for the place. This place is high compared to surrounding. The old temple of Shiva comprises Shiva Sculpture from Sen Reign. On doing further exercise, Sharma found a beautiful figurine of a Kumar estimated to be of 10th century. Further down the temple, he found Yogmaya statue appearing to have been of 9th century during the period of Pal dynasty. This figurine he noted to be most beautiful statue ever found in Nepal till 1958. A young lady feeding milk to her kid while sleeping on bed and many helpers servicing the lady. This statue was taken to National Archive in Kathmandu in 1958. Sharma also mentions a villager named Jenul Dafali, who found seven ancient plates two feet below ground while digging.
- Banauli: Banauli is located 2 miles in the South-East of Janakpur. This place is linked to the history of famous Maithili poet Vidyapati. Vidyapati is believed to have stayed there for more than a decade as guest of King Puroditya in search of personal safety along with Queen Lakhimi Devi after Oinwar King Shiv Sinha defected and was taken away by Sultan of Delhi. About 1 hundred yards West of the village lies a ruined brick foundation and in the South of the foundation is a pond in which an idol of Lakshmi Narayan was found about 200 years ago. The brick is the foundation believed to be of Poet Vidyapati[33].
- Bhutahi is situated 2 miles to the East of Janakpur. Archaeologist Janaklal Sharma found many archaeological evidences on his tour[34]

in 1958. He was sent to Bhutahi on request of local officer after local villager reported of finding of half a ton of Cowrie/seashells while digging earth. Upon survey, Janaklal reported to have seen following things after digging 3 feet below a ruin foundation:

- Lakshmi Idol
- Sarasvati Idol
- Vishnu Idol, damaged on right hand
- Kamlasan Idol
- Torn Idol

Janaklal also noted some written letter on idol of Vishnu in unknown script. He found ruin spread in about 12 Bigha land that he suggested for further excavation.

- Shivapur Gadhi is located about 1 miles from downtown Janakpur and is ward no 19 of Janakpur municipality. In an excavation done in April 2016 under supervision of Archeologist Bhaskar Gyawali of Department of Archaeology, he found baked brick wall, Mud Oven, Pots made of mud, terracotta ornaments and Cowries/seashells. These were found about two meter below ground level in a barren plot of 52 Bigha (32.5 Acre) and belong to medieval age[35].
- Duhabi: Another place of archeological importance is Duhabi lying about 10 miles from Janakpur in the South-East direction near Mainathpur railway station. In a partial excavation of this place in 1960s villagers found a circular brick foundation, tantric symbols styled like Bhubaneshwar temple in India, an inscription "ma" and statue of Ganesa[36].

Murtiya Jungle in Sarlahi

This place was once in the middle of 4 Kose-Jhadi (2.5 miles long strip of Jungle) in the northern limit of Plain that was separating it from hill. The name "Murtiyan" of this place literally means "a number of murtis (idols)"[37]. This place is 3 miles in the North-West of Malangwa. Janaklal has mentioned three sites in the Murtiya jungle: (1) Murtiya Well lies 4 kose of Malangwa where Gupta period sculpture was found in 1950s, (2) Heritage Well, locally called "Dharohar Inar", lying 2 kose north from Murtiya Well, (3) Murtiya Jungle main site lies 5 kose from Malangwa in the North-West. Three miles West of main site and East of Bagmati River, there are five big ruins appearing to be remains of a castle.

The main site of Murtiya Jungle comprises remains of ancient collapsed temple, with big size bricks scattered all over the site. Some of the stone fragments of the temple are also used by the local population for religious purposes on site, and some stones have even found their place in some domestic uses in the vicinity. Few of the best sculptures were found in this place that are estimated to be of 12th century. The idols of various Hindu and Buddhist gods and goddesses, and animals with divine attributions are found abundantly in this village. This place became victim of rapid jungle destruction and human settlement. Many idols were stolen[38]. The sculpture is comparable to statues of Simraungadh[39].

Picture showing site of a ruined temple complex at Murtiya. Picture taken in 2001. Source Neel K Chapagain.

Kakre Bihar

In Kakre Bihar lies a ruin of an ancient Hindu-Buddhist temple on top of a small hillock in Surkhet Valley. It is 'Shikhar Saili' temple of Kakre Bihar, believed to be built in the 12th century. It is considered to be only second to Lumbini in terms of archaeological and historical significance. The temple is built of solid stone and contains bronze statues of Lord Buddha as well as numerous Hindu deities. During the excavations of remnants at Kakre Bihar in February 22, 2001, some 2,028 artefacts of archaeological and historical significance were dug up[40]. Along with various statues of Lord

Buddha, statues of Sarasvati, Lord Vishnu, Padma, conch shells and chariot wheels were found during these excavations. Reason behind the construction of the temple on a land spread over approximately 180 hectares in the middle of a jungle, is shrouded in mystery and is yet to be ascertained. Although there are various theories regarding the origins of the temple, no concrete evidences to back them up have been found till date. According to some accounts, to halt the spread of Buddhism, Shankaracharya's followers and apprentices had demolished the structure while heading to Tibet. According to another school of thought it could have been victim of Muslim attack during 14th century[41]. Some believe, there was this reason that the person or king building this temple had no more funds to continue building further. According to archaeologists, the 12th century temple turned into ruins towards the end of the 16th century.

The Department of Archaeology started restoring a 12th century temple at Kakre Bihar in Surkhet Valley in March 2016 with the original pieces that were lying scattered in the vicinity[42].

Image showing Kakre Bihar temple being restored. Source: The Kathmandu Post.

Salhes Phulwari (Garden)

Some four kilometers West of Lahan lies Siraha, marvel of a garden of Mother Nature. There is a legend of king Salhes, chronicled to have ruled this region during the latter mid-13th century. In this ancient densely forested garden spread over an area of some six hectares, there grows a unique

Haram tree that bears flowers only once a year that too on the Nepalese New year Day of Baisakh. The buds start appearing on the last day of the previous year and as the hours pass by, the buds blossom into flowers and by the New Year dawn takes full shape of a garland. As the day advances the flowers wither and fall. They will not again bloom until next year's Day[43].

There is also a temple of Salhes, the king of mountain. There is an idol of Salhes sitting on an elephant. On its left and right side there are two attractive idols of Dauna and Kusuma.

There is another place called Salhesgarh, which has a mound. This mound is in the state of remains. There is a Gahwar (small temple) of Salhes[44].

As per Ram Dayal Rakesh[45], Salhes was born and ruled here in about fifth and sixth centuries. His father's name was Bhairav Bhupal Soman and his mother's name was Mandodari. He had two brothers namely Motiram and Budhesar. Salhes was a very handsome and famous warrior who later on became king of that state. He was fond of moving around gardens, mountains, forests, rivers, lakes and ponds. Once he met the daughter of the Hindu king named Maheshwar Bhandari of Taregna province. He fell in love with Dauna.

A Few More Archaeological Sites

Rajbiraj

Chanarbhoga near Rajbiraj, towards the North of the Rupani-Sambhunath section, in the Chure hills there are ruins of an ancient temple lying helter-skelter. Remnants of large pillars, temple columns with carved idols, pedestals, large baked bricks, and blocks of sandstones lie unattended. Select temple parts and idols, however, have been collected and placed on a small cave-like dugout in the hill. The villagers from that area consider it the main temple deity[46].

Sonukhara of Mahottari

Sonukhara is situated at a mile north of Jaleshwar. About 150 years ago, while digging earth for some purpose, a person found a piece of gold which was brought to Jaleshwar temple. Janaklal reported that people have found remnants of walls and building while tilling the field, hence, the name Son-

Ukhara meaning Gold-excavation. He also found a few structures in ruined state[47].

Bhediari of Morung

Bhediari is located nearly ten kilometers south of Biratnagar. Many important brick temples have been excavated and they appear to have been built during the Sunga period. A number of silver punch-marked coins have been found, but no stone or terra-cotta idols have been found[48]. It is believed to be a town of Sunga period (200- 100 BC).

Baraha Kshetra

It is an important temple site located at the confluence of the Koka and Koshi rivers. This site belongs to the later Gupta period.

Narsingha Tappa in Sunsari

Some years ago, while cultivating lands at Narasingha Tappa, close to the present town of Ithari, an idol of Vishnu was discovered. The idol belongs to the fifth or sixth century A.D., and is based on the Gupta art tradition and has been temporarily kept inside a local Shiva temple.

Bhawanipur in Rupandehi

An excavation carried out in 2014 by the Department of Archaeology at Bhawanipur of Kerawani VDC in Rupandehi has discovered items belonging to Licchavi-era. The excavation conducted from January 17 to February 1 has unearthed stone idols, copper currency, earthen vessels and playthings. The items found through excavation rather suggest that the structures date to either Licchavi or Gupta-era[49].

Panditpur in Kapilbastu

A team of archaeologists excavated substantial evidences suggesting that Panditpur of Banjariya VDC was the capital of the ancient state Koliya. In 2015 excavation, the archaeologists found ring wells, topaz, bangles, glasses, stones, and human statues dating back to the Kushan era[50]. The team excavated the foundations of boundary walls erected to protect the city which suggests that the site was the location of the administrative headquarters in Antonagar. The team has also found glasses belonging to the Mughal era suggesting that even the Mughal Kings might have visited the area[51].

Rural Heroes – Epic stories

Lorik

Story 1: Lorik Story (Shahabad Version) as Given by William Crooke[52]

The legend of Lorik is very popular among the Ahir tribe.Multiple versions of the legend are popular throughout north India and plain of Nepal. The story is related at wearisome length, but the main features of it, according to the Shahabad version, are as follows: Siudhar, an Ahir, marries Chandani, and is cursed by Parvati with the loss of all passion [impotence]. Chandani forms an attachment for her neighbour Lorik and elopes with him. The husband tries but fails to persuade her to return, fights with Lorik and is beaten. The pair goes and meets Mahapatiya, a Dusadh, and the chief of the gamblers. He and Lorik play until the latter loses everything, including the girl. She urges that her jewels did not form part of the stake, and induces them to gamble again. She stands opposite Mahapatiya and distracts his attention by giving him a glance of her pretty ankles. Finally Lorik wins back everything. The girl then tells Lorik how she has been insulted, and Lorik with his mighty sword cuts off the gambler's head. Right at that time the head and the body got turned into stone.

Lorik and Chandani, after killing the gambler, went on to Hardoi, near Munger, where Lorik defeated a Raja and conquered his country. Lorik was finally seized and put into a dungeon, from where he was freed by the aid of the goddess Durga.

He again conquered the Raja, recovered Chandani, had a son born to him, and gained considerable wealth. So they determined to return to their native land.

Lorik had already been betrothed to a girl named Satmanain, who was not of age and had not joined her husband. Lorik had an adopted brother named Semru.

In the mean time Semru had been killed by the Kols and all his cattle and property were plundered. Lorik's first wife, Satmanain, had grown into a handsome woman, but still remained in her father's house. Lorik was anxious to test her fidelity; so, when she came to sell milk in his camp, not knowing her husband, he stretched a loin cloth across the entrance. All the other women stepped over it, but the delicacy of Satmanain was so excessive that she would not put her foot across it. Lorik was pleased, and filling her basket with jewels, covered them with rice. When she returned, her sister saw the jewelry and charged her with obtaining them as the price of infidelity. She indignantly denied the accusation, and her nephew, Semru's son, made preparations to fight Lorik to avenge the disgrace brought on his aunt by Lorik. Next day the matter was settled amicably to the satisfaction of all parties.

Lorik then reigned with justice, and incurred the displeasure of Indra, who sought to destroy him. So, the goddess Durga took the form of his mistress Chandani and seduced him. He succumbed to her wiles. She subsequently struck him so that his face turned completely round. Overcome by grief and shame, he went to Benares, and there he and his friends were turned into stone.

Story 2: Lorik Story as Narrated by Sir Alexander Cunningham.

Lorik deserted his wife Majhar and eloped with Chanayin to a place named Hardi, where he was opposed by Raja Malwar, an Ahir, whom he conquered. Then the two chiefs became friends and went to bathe together. When Raja Malwar's sheet dropped from his shoulders, his back was seen to be marked with numerous scars. "What are those scars?" asked Lorik. Malwar answered, whenever Harwa and Barwa come this way they bite us and leave these marks. Lorik declared that he would not eat in that village until he had met Harwa and Barwa. But Malwar told him that he could never reach them on foot, and so he lent him a horse which carried Lorik to Newarpur. By sunrise the next morning Harwa and Barwa were out hunting but Lorik went after them and fought with them. Lorik killed all their followers. The brothers then sought the aid of their sister's son Kumar Angar but Lorik killed all the three after which he returned to Hardi, where he lived happily with his mistress Chanayin and gave away the kingdom of Newarpur to Bari Chakidar Dusad. Such is the story of Harwa and Barwa and their conqueror Lorik.

Barwa is a village in Narkatiganj, West of Champaran district of Bihar. Harwa is a village near Araria district of Bihar. Both of them seem to be at a day's distance away from nearest hill in current Nepal. Newarpur indicates a village of Newar, which is centered in Nepal Valley. The story of Lorik is mentioned in Varna Ratnakar of Jyotisvara. The Lorik story was originally cast around Saharsa district of Bihar[53].

Goraiya – the Robin Hood

Goraiya character is a bandit belonging to a low caste. He steals merchandise, loots the shops of wealthy traders, destroys their account books, redistributes the booty to the poor and oppressed, and hides in pigsties to elude his pursuers[54]. Goraiya holds travelers or rich merchants to ransom[55].

Goraiya is the god of the village boundaries along Bandi and Sokha which form the triad worshipped by most of the lower castes in Northern Gangatic plain and by the women of the dominant caste of the Babhan [Brahmin][56].

The higher castes make offerings of meal, the outcastes sacrifice a hog or several young pigs and pour out libations to spirits, on the ground[57]. The usual representation of Goraiya is a stone or mound of earth under tree outside the village, at which offerings of goats, sweet meats, milk and ghee are made, to be taken away afterwards, by the Dusadh[58].

It is believed, Goraiya has two wives— the goddess Bandi, the forest (bun) goddess of the uninhabited waste land, and Sokha, the witch goddess[59]. However, I doubt if this is believed uniformly across by all the people.

Hirni-Birni

The story is about two sisters, Hirni and Birni[60]. They own ox, raise fighting cocks that they produce at every stage of their journey while going from Bihar to Terai. Both sisters decide to visit akharas or armories in search of able strong boy, who can tame their ox and put a rope to its nostrils; only man capable of this feat will be worthy marrying them. After several search, they could find a Rajput warrior Posan Singh, who could meet the sisters' criteria to subdue the beast. Posan Singh was married but he left his wife and parents to marry both sisters. Then begins a long series of exploits along the Terai roads. After marriage, Posan Singh lost his Rajput caste affiliation. No one was willing to accept him as Rajput and thus at the time of visits to different Akharas on the way, he was not being introduced as Rajput. The two sisters could manage income from their tattooing and thievery. One day, Posan Singh won a tournament, got prize and became rich. He then made his wives' life full of luxuries, raised their social status and enabled the duo sisters to leave their activities. Their union bore children who were educated by their father in battle skills. The children, however, regained the status that Posan Singh had lost. The kids got married to prestigious young Rajput girls of high lineage.

Shobha Nayak Banjara

The story was compiled in details by Grierson[61]. The story is of a merchant family and the difficulties they pass through. Shobha Nayak is son of a major merchant from Belupur in Saran district. His father arranged a girl to marry him. The bride, named Jasumati or Bari, came from a rich Mithila merchant family. The wedding took place without any difficulty. However, on the very next day of the marriage, Shobha was required to leave his conjugal abode and go to Morang to lead his caravan of six hundred heads of cattle and six hundred caravan drivers. His caravan used to visit far-flung regions and sell a variety of goods: turmeric, cloves, betel nuts, pepper etc. They have to go through many hurdles on the way to Morang; customs offices on both side of the border, exorbitant taxes by local officers, custom officers imposing lengthy halts in their chauki, highway robbers and thus requiring them to hire armed soldiers for their protection. These soldiers were from Netaus or ascetic warriors such as Nagas or naths.

In the absence of husband, Bari Jasumati had to go through the cruel treatment meted out to her by in-laws. On sixth month of marriage, Bari disclosed she is pregnant and in-laws called it illegitimate. Her brother-in-law was on her side; however he had little voice to resist his mother. Bari was thrown out of house to live in a place where livestock was kept. She gave birth to a child, Nand Lal, in her husband's absence. However, her mother-in-law didn't accept her, saying the child was illegitimate. She went to live with one of her relatives. She raised her son, taking him to field while she herself worked. She collected dry cow dung and wood for combustion. After 12 years, Shobha returned from Morang. Not finding Bari in house, he asked her mother about Jasumati. His bother told him the whole story. Then, Shobha went to Bari Jasumati and brought her back with him and provided seat on his throne. Then they lived happily forever.

Chuharmal

There are multiple versions of Chuharmal story. Given below are three stories that manifest three different shades of the persona of Chuharmal; as a justice seeker, as a lover and as a thief. Lover story is popular in Magadha and thief character is famous in the story told in Mithila.

Story 1

The hero of the legend is Chuharmal. His father was Beharimal, his uncle Bandimal, his brother Dukhamal. Chuharmal was born when his father was away ploughing in the field; no midwife or assistance was available. He, however, sat up, and when his father came and was followed by the midwife, the child would not allow the midwife. When he became a few years old, he prevailed on his father to remove him to the village of Turki Kainjni, because at Mokdma his house was close to the Kacheri [court], and the females of his home were being annoyed by the officials. Budhwa was the cowherd of his father's flocks; he persuaded him to carry him to the akhada (gymnasium) of Daljit. Daljit was the cowherd of his uncle, and would not allow Budhwa to pasture Chuharmal's cattle near his, and Chuharmal went to fight with him, but on second consideration he sent Budhwa to his uncle to represent matters, and solicit orders on Daljit to let him pasture his nephew's cattle at the place. Budhwa went to Chuharmal's uncle, Bandimal, but he declined to interfere; he was living in Mara Mokdma (old name Mokama).Noticing that his uncle would not interfere, Chuharmal went to Daljit's akhada again, fought with him and slew him and carried off the cattle to their owner, his uncle, telling him what he had done.

The above version of story was compiled from 1872-73 field survey in Mokama by J. D. Beglar.[62]

Story 2

This story is mixed with the Salhes and is being told in Mithila region. The version of story is in Grierson collection[63].

Salhes was married to Dauna Mali and lived in Pakaria, (a parganna in Saptari district) near Morang. He was employed by King Bhim Sen to take care of security and maintain the law and order of Pakaria. Parkaria's expanse is in 9 miles (i.e. 14 Kose). Salhes responsibilities included, maintaining peace all around also to make sure that people and king are happy without any fear of theft. Chuharmal was resident of Mokama, past Ganga River, and he was jealous of Salhes reputation. Chuharmal decided to defame Salhes. Although Chuharmal had never indulged in any theft before, he planned to steal queen's jewels. As mentioned, security of the whole Pakaria region, including that of the palace, was responsibility of Salhes. Chuharmal came to Pakaria and in the midnight dug a mine (*sendh*) of around 2 miles up to Queen's bedroom. Queen was asleep. He thought to take away the golden bed on which Queen was sleeping and the golden necklace of Queen. Chuharmal put the sleeping Queen on another bed and also took out the necklace from Queen's neck. Before morning, he was able to carry the goods through tunnel and cross the Ganga river. Next morning, when sweeper woke up the Queen, they were surprised to see the *Sendh* or tunnel in the room and missing necklace along with golden bed. She wrote to King and King sent police to bring Salhes to Palace. Salhes was present in the judicial court. On hearing all this Dauna Mali was upset; she invoked her spiritual power to know that Chuharmal was the real culprit. In King's Court, Dauna Mali gave a bond and stood guarantee for Salhes and requested the King to let Salhes free, and if she was not able to prove innocence of Salhes in seven days, then she would marry the King.

After getting Salhes released, Dauna asked Salhes to bring costume of dancer. She disguised herself as dancer and went to Monger. Through her spiritual power, she found the Chuharmal house and knocked on his door. She found the necklace in house and asked for it from Chuharmal in return of any of his desire. Chuharmal obliged and gave the necklace telling it was from King Bhimsen's wife. Dauna asked him to come to her tent without telling him about Salhes, who was waiting for fight. After 3 days and 3 nights of fight, Chuharmal was captured by deceit with the help of Dauna again. They brought Chuharmal to King Bhimsen's court within seven days. Chuharmal confessed the crime. Salhes got released and also got praise from King. After that Salhes and Dauna lived happily.

Story 3

This version of story is narrated by the lower caste people of Naubatpur (Patna)[64], who perform the play of Virmal Chuharmal (brave warrior Chuharmal) during a drama sequel called "Reshma". Reshma, the sister of Ajabi Singh, a Jamindar of the city, is the heroine of the story. She is very beautiful and also proud of her beauty. On hearing of the bravery of Chuharmal, she falls in love with him. One day, without telling her mother, she goes to meet Chuharmal who is also a Gurubhai of her brother Ajabi Singh. After a short while Chuharmal comes to the river to drink water. Believing him to be a passer-by, Reshma asks him his name and address. Realizing that he was Chuharmal himself, she requests him to come to her house to drink water. She also expresses her feelings for him. On this, Chuharmal gets angry since she belongs to an upper caste. She also happens to be his

Gurubehen (sister by dint of being a disciple of the same Guru). So, it was not possible for them to have a love relationship. At this, Reshma feels humiliated and reports to her brother that Chuharmal had misbehaved with her. Ajabi Singh gets ready for battle with Chuharmal. Chuharmal prays to Goddess Durga for power. She gives him a sword with which he vanquishes the entire army of Ajabi Singh. Ajabi Singh also dies in the battle. In sorrow for killing his Gurubhai, Chuharmal decides to undertake Jal-Samadhi (killing oneself by immersing in water). When Reshma hears the news of Chuharmal's proposed Jal-Samadhi, she wears the garb of a widow and visits the site of the Jal-Samadhi. She prays to God that if her love is true she should also die along with Chuharmal. She then breathes her last on the Samadhi of Chuharmal.

Salhes

There are many versions of Salhes story. We read one above in Chuharmal's story. Another story on Salhes is given below:

Salhes was of Dusad caste and his full name was Jay Bardhane. He was born in Mahisautha of today's Siraha District. After becoming King, he made this place his capital. Every day he used to take his bath in Manik River. Chandra, Princess of Pakaria, used to go there to pluck flowers. One day, Princess Chandra expressed her love to King Salhes. However, Salhes out rightly rejected her endeavour. Offended Princess decided to defame and bring bad name to Salhes. She went back and complained to her father that King Kulheshwar of Pakaria had killed her deer. King invited Salhes to dice with precondition that whoever loses will become slave of other. Salhes was defeated, thus he was made security guard (Chokidar) of Pakaria. The remaining story is linked to Chuharmal of Monger and is given in Chuharmal section.

Salhes story has been in vogue since centuries. Connecting the dots of History, we find following narrative linked to King Salhes:

Harshavardhana of Kanauj and Chinese were having diplomatic relation through their common interest in Buddism. However, when a Chinese diplomatic mission reached Kanauj in 648, Harsha was dead and Kingdom was in distress[65]. The Chinese mission was attacked on the way, and most of the members of the Chinese embassy were either killed or captured and all of their goods were robbed[66]. Only Wang Xuance and his second in command Jiang Shiren escaped. After they reached Tibet, they assembled a regiment of 12,000 mercenaries and more than seven hundred Nepali soldiers. Then Nepal and China were linked with marriage, with exchange of princess[67]. Tibetan force attacked Indian plain in 649 and war had lasted for 3 days[68]. Tibetan Army entered Indian plain through Chumbi pass between Sikkim and Nepal[69]. An exaggerated account says Wang Xuance took captive 13,000 people, male and female, together with 30,000 heads of cattle and horses[70].

Some historians have linked the attack on Chinese mission to King Arunasa of Tirabhukti[71] – the modern Mithila. The ancient route from Tibet to Kanauj via Sikkim passed through Tirhut the flat land, rather than the hilly range. The account indicates the conflict between Tibet (hill) and Tirhut (plain), where Nepal (hill) allied with Tibet against Tirhut. Arunasa is not identified in the history of Mithila.However the name King Salhes is linked to Tibetan-Tirhut conflict of that time. As per Maithili historian, King Salhes defended the region[72]during those time from Hilly people's attack, and thus his name was changed to Salhes, King of Mountain, from King Jayvardhan. His Kingdom was in Mahisauth, a place near Lahan, 250 miles South-East of Kathmandu, which is geographically located in the path between Sikkim and Kanauj, if one traves though Tirhut plains.

Dina Bhadri

This Epic is of Mushar caste and is linked with Saptari district. There are seven parts of the story, as given in Grierson paper of 1885[73]. In the last part, story of Jorawar Singh is gven. Dina-Bhadri had an associate Gulami Jat. Gulami Jat said to Dina-Bhadri that there was a Jorawar Singh in Kanauli who owned seven hundred wrestlers. Gulami Jat also said that Jorawar singh was such a tyrant, he would not allow brides to go either from East to West or from West to East, from North to South or from South to North.Instead he seized them all and took them captive.

Gulami Jat, along with Dina-Bhadri, made a plan. Gulami Jat went to Jorawar Singh and challenged him for wresting. In the first round Jorawar singh defeated Gulami. Gulami asked for second round, and he defeted Jorawar. As Jorawar fell down, Dina and Bhadri tied him in rope and killed him.

Family Deities

A family is most likely to have more than one deities in their worship. The family deities are offered yearly or bi-yearly worship, and the offerings are of homemade foods, bread, rice pudding, sometimes meats along with flowers and oil lamp. Family deities are worshipped in families and continued being worshipped as inherited deities within the lineage with specific pattern across the same caste. Different families of the same caste can have different set of deities for worship.

Further detailed research is what is needed in this area. Based on the limited survey, caste and their deities were explored, and it came out that there is no singular pattern of worship among castes for deity. On the other side, there are few deities which are worshiped across multiple castes showing secular behavior among different caste groups.

Female deities Kali and Bandi are widely worshipped. People rarely have both together though not as a rule. Kali is found across all classes: high or low, trader or farmer, touchable or untouchable. Castes worshipping Kali are Brahmin, Rajput, Dev, Dom, Halkhor, Dusad, Kayastha, Hajam, Sonar, Teli, Kalwar, Rauniyar, Yadav and Tharu. Similarly, Bandi is also worshipped across all castes and classes and can be found in the houses of Chamar, Dusad, Dev, Rajput, Rauniyar, Sudhi, Teli, Yadav, Hajam and Mallah.

Among the male deities, Goraiya, Sokha and Hanuman are widely found in the list of family deities. Goraiya is found to be worshipped by Kayastha, Kalwar, Sudhi, Teli, Rauniyar, Yadav, Dusad, Mallah, Dom and Halkhor. Goraiya, who also has heroic character like Robinhood, is believed to be savior of ordinary people, and its cult seems to have expanded after introduction of Muslim rule in India. Goraiya's traditional sacrifice is pig, a taboo for Muslims, thus the follower of Goraiya felt themselves protected from Muslim rulers, who forcefully married Hindu girls snatched from their parents. Muslim rulers kept away from families, where Goraiya was worshipped[74]. The vestigial tradition can still be noticed in some families, where brides are gifted Pig's nails in Sari pallu called "*Khhoicha*", while they prepare to leave for groom's house. The pork is not widely consumed among Hindus. Thus, after sacrifice, the pig is taken away by Dom, Halkhor, or Dusad. The animal sacrifice is slowly discarded in favor of the offerings in the form of sweets.

Sokha is family deity of upper caste Hindu and is worshipped by Brahmin, Rajput, Kayastha and Bhumihar[75]. Sokha is also found to be worshipped among few Koiri, Kushwaha and Sudhi families.

Hanuman is worshipped by most of the people and is represented by flagpost in big bamboo, outside house having triangular shaped red flag. The flagpost is changed each year on festive occasion.

Mira Sahib, a Muslim saint, is found to be worshipped by Dusad, Chamar, Dev, Sudhi, Teli and Yadav. Mira Sahib is also worshipped along with Karikh. Karikh is worshipped by Haluwai, Kanu, Yadav, and Sudhi. Ganinath Gobindji is the family god of Teli and Kanu, a grocer by caste, who doesn't take wine and toddy. Few other Telis or Oilman castes worship Brahman and Narasimha as their family gods. Dharmaraj is also found among Telis house and Narasimha is also found as god among few Brahman and Raute families.

Bhairo Baba is found to be worshipped by Dev, Sudhi, Kalwar and Rajdhov. Bishara, a snake deity, is common among Chamar, Dev, Rajdhob, and Rajput. Salhes is primarily worshipped as community deity, outside temple, whose primary devotees are Dusad followed by other castes. However, Salhes is also worshipped as family deity in a few Dusad and Sudhi households.

There are a few deities which are worshipped, in a limited way, in specific castes; Chitragupt is worshipped by Kayastha, Dharmaraj by Teli, Amil by Sudhi, Raktagala by Chamar, Mohmaya by Teli, Bageshwari by Dev, Torar by Chamar, Surya Narayan (Dina Nath) by Kalwar, Gahil by Yadav. There are many common deities being worshipped by Dusad and Mushar. Similarly, Dom and Halkhor have common deities like Bamait, Khandma and Trifhul. The deity Luk Devi believed to be found at riversides at the dead of night with Masal or torch in her hand, is worshipped by Dom, Halkhor and Chamar.

Kabir, a reformist sect, who doesn't accept other deity, is also found in the region and can be found among Yadav, Teli and few other castes.

A Few of the deities are discussed in detail below, whose stories are connected to Madhesh region and have wider follower base.

Karikh

Karikh, also called Karikh Maharaj, is worshipped as family deity generally by lower castes and his follower would not consume alcohol or palm juice (*Tadi*). There is a dedicated temple of Karikh in Paraul, a place 10km North of Jaleshwar. Even high caste people go there and sacrifice animal outside the temple premise. It is believed, Mira Sahib, a Muslim saint, lives outside Karikh's temple premise and the sacrifice is offered to Muslim saint. Karikh is worshipped as family deity and his followers organize grand puja on special family events. Grand Puja continues for about 3 days, during which time priests, who are lower caste origin, sing songs depicting Karikh's life story. At the end of the third day, animal sacrifice is made, and prepared meat along with bread is offered. Offer is also made to Mira Sahib, who is verily placed outside Karikh's sanctum and is considered to giving company to him.

One of the stories of Karikh was compiled during field research recently, which gives the following account: Once Karikh reached an ancient kingdom named Raj Sariasa during his world tour. The kingdom was full of Mughal Pathan. There was habitat of fourteen hundred Mughal Pathan families in the Kingdom. The Kingdom had only one Hindu family. Chief of the Hindu family was Beni Raut. Since the family of Beni Raut was only one Hindu family in the whole kingdom, Karikh Maharaj started to live at his house. He was employed by Mughal Pathan. His job was to look after their cow and livestock. His fortune changed when he began to live at his own house. His family had been making rapid progress and in a little while became one of the prosperous families of the kingdom. He left the job, when he became prosperous. His leaving the job was not acceptable to the Mughal Pathan. They turned hostile to Beni Raut and began plotting against him. One day all the fourteen thousand Mughal Pathan organized a meeting and also called Beni Raut to attend the meeting. In the meeting, the Pathan challenged him to prove the power of his god Karikh Maharaj. They dared him that if his god is really powerful, he should bring back to life the dead cow murdered by them. Beni Raut returned to his home and started crying in fear of Mughal Pathan. Karikh Maharaj appeared and asked him the reason of crying. He told him about his meeting with Pathan and also of all what had transpired. Karikh Maharaj asked him not to worry and accepted the challenge. After four months Mughal Pathan slew a milk producing cow and cut her into many small pieces. They threw the pieces here and there randomly in the large area. Since Karikh Maharaj had accepted the challenge, he now had to bring the cow back to life. He needed to collect the scattered bones and muscles in order to revive the cow. Since, he was a Hindu god; he was not allowed to touch the bones and muscles of cow. Cow is worshipped as mother in Hinduism. So, he required a Muslim person, who could collect the bones and muscles of the cow and put together the cut up pieces and join them in the shape of cow. Then he remembered Mira Sahib.

Mira Sahib was already very much impressed by Karikh Maharaj due to his divine power. Previously Mira Sahib had requested Karikh Maharaj to make himself his associate. There is another story making round behind the relationship of Mira Sahib and Karikh Maharaj. While Mira Sahib was said to be of the renowned 'Raj Dilriya' Karikh Maharaj was considered to be of renowned 'Raj Paraul', currently located 10km North of Jaleshwar. He had been hearing of the fame of Karikh Maharaj. Once he decided to test the divine power of Karikh Maharaj. To test his power, he sent some beef to Paraul and said to his mother that if he really had power, he would not let the beef enter inside the border of his kingdom. Despite the disagreement and disapproval of his mother he sent the beef to Parual. Karikh Maharaj got the information about the plot of Mira Sahib from spies of his kingdom. He stopped the people carrying beef before they were about to enter the border. He converted the beef into flowers using his divine power and returned it to Dilriya. Since that day Mira Sahib acknowledged the divine power of Karikh Maharaj and himself became his devotee. After that incident, Mira Sahib requested Karikh Maharaj to make him his associate.

Karikh Maharaj recalled the incident. He reached Dilriya and asked Mira Sahib for help to collect the bones and muscles of murdered cow. Mira Sahib agreed to help but on one condition. He said to Karikh Maharaj, 'you should keep me with you as an associate, for ever'. Karikh Maharaj accepted the condition. Karikh Maharaj, along with Mira Sahib, returned to Raj Saraisa. Mira Sahib collected the bones and muscles and fastened them together so as to give them shape of a cow. It is said that Karikh Maharaj had 'Amrit' or divine nectar in his index finger. He made the cow drink the 'Amrit' and finally the cow became alive. Since that day Karikh Maharaj and Mira Sahib started to live as an adjunct to each other. Karikh Maharaj also ordered his followers and devotees to worship Mira Sahib.

Mira Sahib

Mira Sahib is worshipped in many lower castes as family deity, sometime independent of Karikh too. On special occasion of marriage, some families offer animals (he and she goat) in sacrifices and its prepared meat is consumed. The special worship is conducted by Muslim priest called Dafali or Aulia. Dafali cut the throat of goat in Muslim style, that is, Halal style. Muslim Dafali took head with them and families prepared the meat from the rest of the body. Then, Dafali came again and took prepared food with him to offer Mira Sahib in his own place. After worship, Dafali brought back food, now called Prasad, for families to distribute among family members. On other days, Mira Sahib is worshipped twice a years along with other deity and Dafali is not present at that time. Prepared food like bread and rice pudding are offered to him. Mira Sahib is placed inside house along with other deity like Bandi or other.

Mira Sahib is believed to possess magical power. With the help of that he is believed to enslave Jinn, supernatural creature. Witch doctors invoke Mira Sahib in their mantra, to get rid of the evil spirit that might have attacked someone. One of the witchcraft verse reads:

बगताई करे बैठे, देऊता बदमान गंगा राम अघोरी (सरभंग), अघोरी सेनाम मिरा	I am sitting here to test out black magic. I will call the defamed gods to fight with evil spirit. Gangaram Aughar is the dirtiest god who could fight with evil spirits. He is most powerful. Mira is even more powerful than Gangaram Aughar.

The practice of worshipping Muslim inside Hindu house as family deity is unique in this region and there are a few stories to establish the connection. In one of the song of Karikh, Mira Sahib is mentioned to be living in West side of Tirhut region. The song of Karikh contains following lines:

पूरबमेदीनानाथओक्राजोरेढुकेघर, उत्तरमेसुग्रिबपाँचोपांडव, पाँचोपकवान पश्चिममेमिरासाहिबआउनकाचड़ेमुर्गाबलिदान, दक्षिणमेशुभगंगा, हनुमान, पाठकेजनौ	Dinanath in East offered milk to Sugrhiv and five pandavs in North offered five dishes Mira in West offered Chicken in sacrifice to Ganga hanuman in South, wear Janeu (sacred thread)

As the above two songs indicate, there seems to be a connection between Karnal located in Haryana of India, which lies West of the West of Mithila region. The ballad in Karnal says, Mira Sahib continues to fight headless to save a Brahmin girl, despite his head was blown by cannon. There are shrines dedicated to Mira Sahib in Karnal district. Lamps are commonly lit at the shrines on Thursdays, but offerings are seldom made except in illness or in fulfilment of a vow; offerings are often made in the form of a fowl or a goat. Goat's head is taken by Muslim faqir[76].

Mira Sahib was believed to have come from Baghdad[77] and he is believed to have been killed by his Jinn. However despite getting killed, Mira was able to subdue his Jinn. He is believed to have been buried at Ajmer as per William Crooke. After Akbar started visiting Ajmer for Dargah of Khwaja Moinuddin Chishti, another Muslim shrine, Mira's shrine in Ajmer also came into limelite. William Crooke writes, Mira Sahib is worshipped all over North India and his Dargahs are at Amroha in the Moradabad District, at Benares and at Bundi[78]. Mira sahib is also found to be associated with magical power in Srilanka[79] and migrants have taken the Tamil version of Mira cult to Caribbean countries[80] too.

As per the Story told in Karnal of Haryana, Mira is said to have led the Sayyad army against the Raja of Tharwa, and had his head cut off by a cannon ball during the battle. He did not mind this and went on fighting. Then a woman in one of the Raja's villages said –"Who is fighting without his head?" upon which the body said – "Haq! Haq!""The Lord the Lord" and fell down dead, calling out "What? Are not these villages upside down yet?" upon which every village in the Raja's territory was turned upside down, and everyone got killed except a Brahman girl, the paramour of the Raja. Their ruins remain to authenticate the story. Now the saint and his sister's son Saiyid Kabir are jointly worshipped.

Additional story as told in Karnal is as follows: There was a country comprising a small shrines of Musalman martyrs or Shahids. It was called Sayyad by the villagers. There was a Raja Tharu in the Nardak, after whom several villages are still called Tharwa, and who dwelt in Habri. He used to levy seigniorial rights from virgin brides. One night the daughter of a Brahman became victim of King's lust. Her father appealed for help to Miran Sahib, a Sayyad. He mobilized a big army of Sayyads, Mughals, and Pathans, and attacked the Raja[81]. The battle extended over the whole country up to Delhi. The girl was recovered but some 500 warriors lost their lives while Miran Sahib escaped with the loss of one hand[1]. He died in 286 Hijri (A.D.899) and his head was entombed at Karnal[82].

According to Tamil version[83] of an Arabic biography this saint Mira Sahib was born at Manikkapuri on the 9th Jamad-ul-akhir AH 910 (AD 1504) and died on the 10th of the same month AH 978 (AD 1570). He was known to his devotees by several names, e.g. Hazrat Mira Sahib, Shaikh' Abd-ul-Kadir, Saul Hamid &c. Among the miraculous adventures attributed to the Shaikh is included a visit to the Maldives, where after thwarting the treachery of the King and his subjects he was empowered to win them over to Islam. He was empowered as he was able in freeing the islands from the dreaded acts of Jinni. Mira Kantiri feast is annually held in Colombo at the Maraddna Mosque during Jamdd-ul-dkkir the sixth month of the Muhammadan year in memory of the saint Mira Sahib. In a similar miracle story from Nagapattinam, Nagore, it is believed that when a Dutch ship was about to get sunk in the sea due to a hole developed in the hulk, some of the passengers in the ship prayed to the Mira Sahib. Mira Sahib was busy shaving his face before his morning bath when the hapless passenger's prayers reached Him. He just swung the shaving mirror to the sea and the hole in the boat automatically disappeared and passengers were saved[84].

Bandi

Bandi (Banni or Bundi) is a female deity and her worship is universal across Gangetic plains irrespective of caste. High caste mostly worship Sokha as major deity and Bandi as auxiliary deity, and lower caste worship Bandi as principal deity[85]. Banni is derivation of Ban (forest) and means forest deity.

There is very little written material on this subject. People who have been having this deity as family deity, continue to do so because their forefathers did that with little knowledge of history.

There are a few links found to Bandi that would indicate the history and significance.

There is a Banni Mata Temple, also known as the Mahakali Banni Mata Temple, which is located in Chamba District, a hill station in the State of Himachal Pradesh in North India. It is an ancient temple dedicated to Devi Kali, a goddess figure in Hinduism, and regarded as forest god. Gaddi families of the region also worship Banni as family deity[86].

As per one school of thought, Bandi is believed to be wife of Lord Siva[87]. Ban-Durga, goddess of forest, is one of the name of Durga, out of known 108 names, including Parvati, Kali, and Sati. Bandi is formed with two words Ban and di, and it appears to be short form of Ban-Durga.

Bandi could also be derivation of Ban-Devi, where Devi is general name for any female goddess[88].

In the northern Gangatic plain, Siva is omnipresent god. So, it looks very probable that people started worshipping something linked to Siva and that could have been also linked to their village life.

Forest is also associated with crude or primitive form of society, so it could be possible, it became favourite with lower caste, who are close to trees and farming.

Each man worships this deity in his own house. People of some standing place a small piece of gold or silver in a plate and call it Bandi. The poor place a lump of clay on the floor[89].Offerings made to her consist of bread and Khir (rice pudding). Sacrifice of a she-goat is also made if the devotee can afford it.[90].

Kali

Kali is a Hindu goddess having appearance of a destroyer, principally of evil forces. She is accepted as absolute divine power. As the Universal Mother she is capable of protecting against evil forces. She also represents Tantric sect. Kali is often portrayed standing or dancing on her consort, the Hindu god Shiva, who lies calmly under her dancing feet.

Historical Account of Tauter Pergunnahs from the Year A.D. 1556 (or 953 Fusilly) till A.D.1771 as Told by Rajah Sitab Ray[91]

Situation

Bounded on the West by Pergunnah Maisey, a district of Sarkar Champaran, on the East by Sarkar Purnia in the Bengal Province, on the South by the River Gandaki and on the North by the skirts of the Nepal Hills called Teriana [Terai].

Revolutions

After the death of Raja Sher Sing and his heirs in the beginning of the reign of Akbar Shah in the year 953 Fusilly Rajah Nersing Ram took possession of the Jamindari of Sarkar Tirhut and after his death his heirs possessed it for some time. During their imprudent and mismanaged Government Beernagur and Purgunnahs adjoining to Purnia were annexed to the Bengal Province and the Mucwanpore [Makwanpur] people, on their own, took possession of Tahter and twenty-three Mahals or small districts together with Januckpore[Janakpur] situated below the hills. There the Jamindars of Sarkar Tirhut were unable to call them to account.

After them, Mahesh Thakur, Loobalker Thakur, Mynaut Thakur and Sindu Thakur and Nerput Thakur, in succession from Father to Son, inherited

Jamindari of Sarkar Tirhut. The above mentioned Mynaut Thakur, together with Isfand Yar Khan, who was Foujedar of Sarkar Tirhut on the part of the king, represented these circumstances to Nawab Fidaey Khan, Subedar of Patna, in the reign of Shah Alumgeer. After obtaining a force and armed, under pretense of a hunting party, surprised the Rajah of Makwanpur unawares in the Tahter Pergunnah, surrounded and took him prisoner. He carried him to Darbhanga the residence of the Foujedar. Foujedar was not willing to put him to death. He, instead, made him a Mussulman and obliged him (as it is said) to give a written affidavit that he would pay 1200 rupees as an yearly Nuzzeruna (or present) which would be paid in the form of elephants. He, then, set him at liberty and having reconciled him to Rajah Mynaut Thakur dismissed him. He paid the Nuzzeruna for some time, till the year 1085 fussily, when Raja Mahomed Syed Khan, Dewan or deputy of the king, discontinued.

This happened ninety-three years ago. Afterwards the Nawab Fidaey Khan, Myr Joomly Seubalou Khan, Khan Summa, Akidut Khan and Muramut Khan Nazims of the Province increased it by force to an amount of 10000 Rs. to be paid in the form of elephants. At that time, Fughur-ul-dowla was Subedar (or Governor of the Province). In the year 1133 Fussilly, Raja Ragoo Sing, Son of Nerput Thakur, Jamindari of Sircar Tirhut, went against Balamund Puddea Naib (who was Deputy at that time) of Mannick Sen Raja of Teriana with a great Force and fought him. Balamund fled and Delput Sen, brother of Mannick Sen, came forward and met Raja Rago Sing and settled the terms with him agreeing to pay two thousand five hundred Rupees, an increase upon the Nuzzerana [tax] to be paid also in the form of elephants. From that time till the year 1160 Fussily, the amount of 12500 rupees was paid at the rate of 1000 rupees Cubit for males and 700 rupees for females. In 1169 Fussily the Gurkhali Inhabitants of the Mountains of Gurka descended with a strong army. Digbandhan Sen the Grandson of Manick Sen was taken prisoner, and seized upon the Pergunnah Makwanpur of which Kunnuck [Kanak] Singh complained to the Nawab Meer Mahomed Kasim Khan in the year 1170 Fussily. In consequence of this Complaint, the Nawab himself crossed over, sending Gourgeen Khan before him, who arrived near Makwanpur where his whole army was destroyed. The Nawab returned to Patna from this time to the year 1174 Fussily. In 1175 Fussily, Prithivi Narayan, the Gurkha Rajah, sent his people and took possession of Makwanpur Kingdom, but did not pay the tribute. Captain

Kinlock was sent there with a detachment of seapoys and drove out the Gurkhas, and Collectors were placed there on behalf of Mr. Golding. On Captain Kinlock's return, the Pergunnahs were again taken possession by the Gurkha Rajah Partap Singh, who agreed to pay the tribute of 12,500 Rupees in the form of Elephants at the customary rate.

List of Mahals in Pergunnah Tauter

- Tauter
- Nundrakajoutly
- Assiboo
- Abijout
- Beya
- Makwanpur Navabad
- Bickerma
- Beera
- Mandu
- Jumna
- Rassary
- Shapore
- Carady
- Bunnrin Mulky
- Sery

Total Mahals or small Districts were 23

Historical Account from 1770 to 1814

A Few Events of the Time that Influenced History in the Making

British East India Company Upgraded Political Role

After the Battle of Plassey, British EIC started gaining political foothold on Indian soil. Nawab of Bengal was getting weaker and British had not yet completed the hold in new setup. There was political vacuum in between the time of Battle of Plassey and the signing of Allahabad Treaty (Transfer of Diwani rights, or the right to collect taxes on behalf of the Emperor in Bihar, Orissa and Bengal) in 1765.

Economy Blockade

Taking advantage of political vacuum on Indian side, Prithivi Narayan Shah attacked Makwanpur. After that, King Prithivi Narayan Shah started economic blockade of passes between Kathmandu Valley and southern Plain. The five years of blockade ruined the health of Nepal Valley.

Earthquake of 1767

In the months of June and July another significant earthquake hit Nepal. Twenty one shocks and aftershocks of this particular earthquake is said to have occurred in a span of twenty four hours. No written or verbal records survive to indicate any human loss or the magnitude of sufferings and damages caused.

King Prithivi Narayan Shah was waiting for this moment. The Kingdom of Nepal was founded on 25 September 1768 by Prithivi Narayan Shah, a Gorkha king who succeeded in unifying the kingdoms of Kathmandu, Patan, and Bhaktapur into a single state under his Shah dynasty.

Great Famine of 1770

The famine of 1770 was the biggest shock that impacted places in Tirhut and Purnia. It is estimated that around 10 million people died in the region, which was one third of the population of the region. The natural tragedy completely eroded the people's confidence to resist any external force for many years to come.

Sanyasi and Fakir Rebellion of 1770

Sanyasi rebellion of 1770 was like a prelude to India's struggle of independence from foreign rule. The holy men both Hindus and Muslims wanted to pursue their way of living which they had been practicing for centuries, and wanted to be left alone. The Hindu sanyasis or monks and the Muslim fakirs protested against the tax collection by the British company soon after Bengal famine of 1770. Both Hindu and Muslim holy men in those days used to go on a pilgrimage to various places of worship in Bengal and en route they would accept sizable money from rich landlords and Jamindars and this tradition had continued for many centuries. After British came to power, Jamindars and landlords were under tremendous pressure to meet the tax demands from the British and as a result, were not being able to give donations to Sanyasis or Fakirs. Further, the British considered them as looters. The result was that these Sanyasis started raiding the government treasuries and Company's factories. Warren Hastings tried to contain and control the raids by the Sanyasis and his direct action resulted in the massacre of 150 Sanyasis in 1771.

Sanyasis and Fakirs felt safe in Jungle of Terai and they also used this route to travel between Bengal and Banaras. Mohan Giri and Musa Shah were famous leaders of Sanyasis and fakirs respectively. Subhan Ali Shah, disciple of Musa Shah was also famous[92].

Annexation of Madhesh by Shah Kings

Makwanpur Takeover

King Prithivi Narayan first married to Makwanpur Princess Indira Kumari with the selfish desire to get dowry and ammunition from Makwanpur King. Next day of the marriage the cultural difference surfaced between Prithivi Narayan Shah and his in-laws. As per the plains' high class tradition, the bride stays in father's house till first child is born (the custom still prevails, loosely though, in Maithil Brahmin), however, Prithivi Narayan wanted to take Indira Kumari to Gurkha kingdom ignoring the tradition and rituals. Then Gurkha was small Kingdom compared to Makwanpur.

After the death of Hem Karna, the father of Indira Kumari, his son Digbandhan Sen became king. He was not at good terms with Prithivi Narayan and the situation even became worse, when on his second visit Prithivi Narayan Shah slaughtered few policemen in Makwanpur on the pretext that they saluted him wearing shoes. Further relationship deteriorated because Prithivi Narayan wanted an elephant and a necklace in dowry.

In 1762, King Prithivi Narayan Shah attacked Makwanpur without any prior warning and after ten hours of battle, Makwanpur was captured on 21st August 1762. During the war, an estimated one-hundred Gurkha and four-hundred Makwanpur soldiers were killed. Digbandhan Sen escaped from Makwanpur. However, his female members got caught. Then the Gorkhas attacked and occupied Hariharpur, Timalkot and Sindhuli. The Gorkhali troops arrested Digbandhan Sen, the king of Makwanpur, on February 13, 1763. The prominent people who had resisted his attack were put to death by him -some were killed with swords, some hung by rope and some were flayed unto death. Surviving Children of these people were degraded to the most vile and abominable condition of a tribe (Sarki) in order to being educated in their odious profession as outcasts.

King Digbandhan Sen tried to get help from the former Murshidabad Nawab, Mir Kasim, who was engaged in assembling a new armed force to take revenge from East India Company. At that time, Mir Kasim was in need of friends. He also wanted desperately to test his newly organized army. So, he accepted the request of Digbandhan Sen and sent his 2000 strong soldiers under the command of Gurgin Khan in 1763. However, they were defeated in the surprise ambush in night, in the narrow hilly pass.[93].

King Digbandhan Sen and his female family members were taken prisoners. Digbandhan, his wife and seven sons were kept in close confinement and were only prevented from starving by a pittance sent to them by their kinsman the Palpa Raja. King Digbandhan's whereabouts remained unknown after that. In the year 1780, Bhubar, one of the sons of Digbandhan, managed to escape to Betiya, a Company's territory, where he was received with kindness and two villages free from the obligation of paying any revenue were granted to him[94].

After the occupation of Bengal by East India Company, the tax rights to Makwanpur were also transferred to East India Company, since Makwanpur was tributary of Bengal. After capturing Digbandhan, King Prithivi Narayan sent agent to the British and settled the occupancy by agreeing to pay the same amount of tax that former King Digbandhan was paying.

Bara, Parsa, Rautahat, Mahottari Leasing

In the year 1895 Vikram Samvat (1769 AD), Major Kinlock advanced towards Kathmandu Valley[95]. However, his army mission failed due to insufficient ration, harsh rainy weather and unknown hilly territory. Thus, Major Kinlock had to settle in Plains lowland along with his military force. He camped at Baragachee in Makwanpur, and established revenue offices throughout Terai, between Gandaki River and Kamla River; currently represented by districts of Bara, Parsa, Rautahat, Dhanusha, Mahottari, and Siraha. However the climate of the Terai was found to be very unhealthy and proved fatal. After three years, in 1827 Samvat (1771 AD), Gurkha Attorney Dinanath Upadhyay was ordered to go to Durbunga [Darbhanga] in order to make a compromise with the English[96]. He accordingly proceeded and met Major Kelly, the officer commanding in the district. On behalf of his government he made his submission to Major Kelly. He submitted that since the whole of the Terai region was dependent on Makwanpur as the hill country of Makwanpur had come into the possession of this State. Besides, the cultivated low lands also belonged to it by dint of same title; Gurkha Government was willing to pay whatever rent (mal wajeb) had been paid by the Rajah of Makwanpur. Major Kelly referred him to the Chief of the Council of Patna by whom he was informed that the Rajah of Makwanpur used to give annually as tribute an elephant fourteen hauts [hands as measure] in height, each haut consisting of fourteen tunussooks [bond paper]. This Government accordingly consented to give the elephant and gave tunussooks which was due on account of the county. In the latter part of the Samvat year 1827, Major Kinloch and his force were recalled. The amount of the tunussooks given by this Government having been collected from the county was paid through Mr. Hardy and the tunussooks returned. During three years an elephant, fourteen hauts high, was regularly presented as tribute.

In the year 1829 Samvat, there was a default in sending the tribute. The State was desirous to maintain amicable relations with the English. So, it was resolved to enter into a negotiation with the Council of Patna on the same terms as had been usual with the Rajah of Makwanpur. Dinanath Upadhyay was accordingly sent to Patna for that purpose and was required there after getting the tribute fixed to take out a regular pottah. The Nawab Hosheear Jung (Mr George Vansittart) was at that time chief of Patna.

Dinanath Upadhyay showed his documents to Nawab Mohabut Jung and Rajah Ram Narain. According to these documents the fixed height of the elephant to be presented as tribute was at twelve hauts and a half and he desired that a reference might be made to records. He, accordingly, reduced the standard height of the elephant one haut and a half and got it fixed at twelve hauts and a half of twelve tunussooks each[97].

Bijaypur Kingdom

The worst famine of the region extended from 1769 to 1773. The worst affected districts were Purnia, which is situated below Bijaypur and Morang. The condition of that region was more worsened than other famine affected regions. It looks, King Prithivi Narayan took advantage of the famine time and attacked Bijaypur and Morang in July 1774. The former was the capital of later. The Kingdom was situated between Koshi River and Tista River.

Bijaypur Kingdom possessed territories in the hill regions (the modern districts of Dhankuta, Panchthar, Taplejung, Tehrathum and Sankhuwa-Sabha) and the Tarai (the modern districts of Morang, Sunsari and Jhapa)[98].

Saptari and Morang Negotiation

After being attacked by Gurkha army, the Rajah Karen Sen of Bijaypur fled into the English dominion[99]. He requested Mr. Peacock for assistance, offering in return to establish a factory for the English in Beejapore [Bijaypur] and to give the Company ten anas (parts) of the revenue of his country reserving only six anas (parts) for himself and proposing that the English should undertake the management of the country[100]. Mr. Peacock declared his assent to these proposals and told the Rajah that he would refer them to Government and obtain the concurrence of the Council. Having given the Rajah these assurances he wrote to Calcutta accordingly but before he received an answer the Rajah Karen Sen died. On this Mr. Peacock proposed that the Rajah's son who was only a boy and the Dewan should go along with him to Calcutta to meet the Governor where he would procure assistance to enable the young Rajah to establish his authority in his country. Gurkha King was worried with Karen Sen diplomatic mission to Calcutta, accordingly, in the beginning of 1831 Vikram Samvat Dinanath Upadhyay was sent to the Presidency in Calcutta. He went by the way of Rampore and after paying his respects to the gentlemen at that place proceeded to accompany Mr. Peacock to Calcutta. Mr. Peacock, also accompanied by Bhooanesen Upadhyay, the Dewan of Muckwanee King, took him to Calcutta. Soon after their arrival at Calcutta the son of Muckwanee died[101]. Mr. Peacock, after introducing Dinanath Upadhyay to Mr. Hastings and getting for him an opportunity to delivering his letters, returned to Rasepore.

Dinanath Upadhyay remained in Calcutta for five months. This was the time when a number of armed Naga Sanyasis used to come, in groups, from Hurdwar [Haridwar] through the Terai up to as far East as Dinapore. These Nagas used to ravage the Company's territories. When the troops advanced to drive them back they verily retreated and concealed themselves in the Terai where the troops were unable to reach.

The message brought by Dinanath Upadhyay was presented before the Governor-General's Council. At the meeting, the Company government decided that it would give up its claim to the Tarai regions of Ambarpur and Bijaypur, i.e. Saptari and Morang districts, in case the Nepal government undertook to ban the entry into its territory of armed Nagas who plundered people in the area from Haridwar to Dinajpur. An agreement along these lines was actually concluded between the Nepal government and the East India Company[102]. The Company government felt satisfied when the areas ravaged by the Naga bandits inside its territories were resettled.

Palpa Treachery

King Prithvipal was deceived by King Ran bahadur on the pretext of marrying Pritivipal's sister. No sooner had Prithvipal reached Kathmandu with about 400 attendants, than all of them were disarmed and he and his principal officers were put in close confinement and no more mention was made of the marriage. The Raja of Gorkha was however afraid of driving the Palpa family to extremes and compelling it to seek refuge in the territories of the Company which it had received from the Nawab Vazir, he sovereign of the lowland countries. However, in 1804, Prithvipal was killed by Bhimsen Thapa, while he was on killing spree to take revenge of the death of King Ran Bahadur.

Bhimsen acted with utmost promptitude in achieving his object. His father Amar Singh, raised to the English rank of general, was sent with a considerable force. In less than a month's time from his son's elevation, Amar Singh took possession of Palpa unresisted, nor did he hesitate to make advance into the low country which belonged to the Raja of Palpa as a subject of the company. On the approach of General Amar Singh to Palpa in July or August 1804, the widow of Prithvipal, with her son Ratna Sen, his uncle Samar Bahadur, called the Lal Dewan or Nader Shah and his grand uncle Suravir, who held the office of Chautariya, fled to a house which the family had at Madhuvani in Tilpur. The unfortunate lady died there and the Raja was removed to Gorakhpur where he lived constantly under fear of being assassinated. In such a situation it was thought necessary to have his house secured by deploying guard of regular seapoys. The Company granted him a pension[103].

Notes

1. The Dusadhs of Jhinjha, Regmi Research Series, Year-9, No. 4
2. Bista, Dor Bahadur (1999), Fatalism and Development: Nepal's Struggle for Modernization, Orient Longman, Calcultta, 1999

3. B.H. Hodgson, *Essays on the Languages, Literature and Religion of Nepal and Tibet* (Varanasi:Bharat- Bharati, 1971), Part II, p. 37
4. Hodgson, Brian Houghton (1841), ACCOUNT OF A VISIT TO THE RUINS OF SIMROUN ONCE THE CAPITAL OF THE MITHILA PROVINCE, Illustrations of the Literature and Religion of the Buddhists.
5. Cimino , Rosa Maria (1986), SIMRAONGARH: The Forgotten City and Its Art, CNAS, TU, Kathmandu, Volume 13, Number 3, April 1986 (Baishakh 2043) www.digitalhimalaya.com/collections/journals/contributions/index.php?selection=13_3
6. *Petech, 1952-53: 12-13*
7. Hodgson, Brian Houghton (1841), ACCOUNT OF A VISIT TO THE RUINS OF SIMROUN ONCE THE CAPITAL OF THE MITHILA PROVINCE, Illustrations of the Literature and Religion of the Buddhists, 1841
8. Op Cite Lecomte-Tilouine, Marie (1998), On Francis Buchanan Hamilton's Account of the Kingdom of Nepal, European Bulletin of Himalayan Research, 1998, Number 14, Page 60-61
9. Rakesh, Ram Dayal (2016); Landscape archaeology: Neglected gardens; Published: April 14, 2016
10. Based on author's interview with Vijay Kumar, native of Simraungarh.
11. Verlagsanstalt, Akademische Druck-u (1885), The Cyclopaedia of India and of Eastern and Southern Asia, Volume 2, 1885, pp 58
12. Swami Parmeshwaranand (2000), Encyclopaedic Dictionary of Upanisads, Volume 3, 2000, pp 392
13. Swami Parmeshwaranand (2000), Encyclopaedic Dictionary of Upanisads, Volume 3, 2000, pp 392.
14. Japan Buddhist Federation (2001), Archaeological Research at Mayadevi Temple, Lumbini. Tokyo, Japan Buddhist Federation, 2001, p. 75
15. Bollinger. L (2016); Slip deficit in central Nepal: omen for a repeat of the 1344 AD earthquake?, Springer Link, December 2016
16. Dr. Fuhrer. A (1972); Antiquities The Buddha's Birth-Place, Archeological Survey of Northern India, Volumn VI, Published by lndologlcal Book House, 1972, pp 27
17. Crossette, Barbara (1994); A Nepalese Garden Of Buddhist Legend, NY Times, published on October 16, 1994
18. Weise, Kai (2013); The Sacred Garden of Lumbini: Perceptions of Buddha's birthplace, UNESCO, pp 149
19. Bidari, B (2009); Lumbini Beckons. A Glimpse of the Holy Birthplace of the Buddha and its Master Plan and the Ashoka Pillar Inscription and the Marker Stone 'The exact birth spot of the Buddha'. Lumbini. pp 30
20. Lumbini, Present Status and Future Challenges, UNESCO, 2006, pp 76. Also see Mishra, T. N. 1996. The archaeological activities in Lumbini during 1984-1985, in "Ancient Nepal", 139
21. Bidari, B (2004); Lumbini: A Haven of Sacred Refuge. Kathmandu, Third Impression
22. Seddon, David (2014), "Forget the past", Nepali Times Weekly Magazine, Issue 724, 12-18 September 2014. Also available on http://nepalitimes.com/article/nation/neglect-of-nepali-heritage-sites-in-lumbini-janakpur,1653 (downloaded on March 2015)

23. Sir Cunningham, Alexander (1871); The Ancient Geography of India: I. The Buddhist Period, Including the Campaigns of Alexander, and the Travels of Hwen-Thsang, Trübner and Company, 1871, pp 445

24. Hodgson, Brian Houghton (1841), Account Of A Visit To The Ruins Of Simroun Once The Capital Of The Mithila Province, Illustrations of the Literature and Religion of the Buddhists, 1841

25. Benett, William Charles (1870), A Report on the Family History of the Chief Clans of the Roy Bareilly District, Oudh Government Press, 1870, PP 22-23

26. History of Basti, District office website, Basti, UP, India http://basti.nic.in/general%20profile/history%20of%20basti.htm

27. Benett, William Charles (1870), A Report on the Family History of the Chief Clans of the Roy Bareilly District, Oudh Government Press, 1870, PP 22-23

28. Gazetteer of the Province of Oudh: N-Z, Printed at the Oudh government Press, 1877, pp 288-289

29. Burghart, Richard (1978);The Disappearance and Reappearance of Janakpur, Kailash, Volume 6, Number 4, 1978 http://himalaya.socanth.cam.ac.uk/collections/journals/kailash/pdf/kailash_06_04_03.pdf

30. Burghart, Richard (1978);The Disappearance and Reappearance of Janakpur, Kailash, Volume 6, Number 4, 1978 http://himalaya.socanth.cam.ac.uk/collections/journals/kailash/pdf/kailash_06_04_03.pdf

31. Raj, Yogesh (2012); The Journal of Captain Kinloch, Aug 26-October 17, 1767, pp 45

32. Sharma, Janaklal (1958), Archeological places between Chitwan and Janakpur (*Chitwan dekhi Janakpur Saamaka kehi puratawik sthal*), Ancient Nepal, Number 2, January 1968

33. Burghart, Richard (1978), History of Janakpurdham, Phd Thesis, 1978, pp 147

34. Sharma, Janaklal (1958), Archeological places between Chitwan and Janakpur (*Chitwan dekhi Janakpur Saamaka kehi puratawik sthal*), Ancient Nepal, Number 2, January 1968

35. Shashi, Shyam Sundar (2016); Ancient artefacts found in Janakpur, The Kathmandu Post, Published on 27-04-2016

36. Burghart, Richard (1978), History of Janakpurdham, Phd Thesis, 1978, pp 148

37. Chapagain, Neel Kamal (2013); Traditions, Materiality and Community Engagements with Heritage: Re-thinking 'Authenticity' in Living Heritage Sites in Nepal, Paper presented in Revisiting Kathmandu: International Symposium Organized by ICOMOS Nepal, UNESCO Kathmandu, ICORP and Department of Archaeology (Govt of Nepal): November 25-29, 2013, pp 12-15

38. Historical idols at Murtiya await preservation, The Himalayan Times Daily Newspaper, Kathmandu, Published 2014-11-03, downloaded from http://arkonetwork.com/news/nepal/historical-idols-at-murtiya-await-preservation/

39. Bisht, Kapil (2011); Stone Sculpting In Nepal: The Art of Making Gods, ECN media, published on Jan 03, 2011

40. Poudel, Motilal (2015); Kakre Bihar to be renovated at Rs 110 million, The Kathmandu Post, Published on Jan 27, 2015

41. Dr. Shrestha, Ram Kumar (2013); Kakre Bihar in search of its real name (काँक्रेविहारआफ्नोसहीनामकोखोजीमा छ)

42. Paudel, Motilal (2016); Kakre Bihar temple being restored, The Kathmandu Post, Published on March 16, 2016

43. Shrestha, Suniva as quoted by Rakesh, Ram Dayal (2016); Landscape archaeology: Neglected gardens, The Himalayan Times, Published: April 14, 2016

44. Rakesh, Ram Dayal (2016); Landscape archaeology: Neglected gardens, The Himalayan Times, Published: April 14, 2016

45. Rakesh, Ram Dayal (2016); Landscape archaeology: Neglected gardens, The Himalayan Times, Published: April 14, 2016

46. Chaudhary, Sanjib Kumar (2014), Dig to preserve, The Kathmandu Post, Published Oct 06, 2014

47. Sharma, Janaklal (1958), Archaeological places between Chitwan and Janakpur (*Chitwan dekhi Janakpur Saamaka kehi puratawik sthal*), Ancient Nepal, Number 2, January 1968

48. SAARC cultural Center, http://saarcculture.org/2016/01/27/archaeology-6/

49. Licchavi-era relics unearthed in Rupandehi , The Himalayan Times Newspaper, Published Feb 02, 2014

50. KC, Sher Bahadur (2012), Artefacts from Mauryan era discovered, My republica Daily News Paper, 2012

51. Gaud, Bechu (2014); Evidence of Koliya state found in Banjariya excavation site, The Kathmandu Post, Published: 02-03-2014

52. Crooke, William (1894); An Introduction to the Popular Religion and Folklore of Northern India, Printed at the government Press, North-Western Provinces and Oudh, 1894, pp 290

53. Choudhary, Radhakrishna (1976); A Survey of Maithili Literature, 1976, pp 123

54. Servan-Schreiber, Catherine (1998); Indian Epics of the Terai Conquest: The Story of a Migration, Sage Publications on behalf of International Council for Philosophy and Humanistic Studies, 1998, pp 87

55. Markovits, Claude; Pouchepadass, Jacques; Subrahmanyam, Sanjay (2006) ; Society and Circulation: Mobile People and Itinerant Cultures in South Asia, 1750-1950, Anthem Press, 2006, pp 299

56. Hewitt, J.F (1894); The Ruling Races of Prehistoric Times in India, pp 202

57. Crooke, William (1896); The Popular Religion and Folk-lore of Northern India, Volume 1, A. Constable & Company, 1896, pp 197

58. O'malley, L.S.S. (1924); Bihar And Orissa District Gazetteers, Concept Publishing Company, 1924, pp 63

59. Hewitt, J.F (1894); The Ruling Races of Prehistoric Times in India, pp 202

60. Catherine Servan-Schreiber, 'Tellers of Tales, Sellers of Tales: Bhojpuri Peddlers in Northern India', in Markovits et al., Society and Circulation: Mobile People and Itinerant Cultures in South Asia, 1750-1950, Published 2006, pp 291-292

61. Grierson, G. (1889); Selected Specimens of the Bihârî Language. Zeitschrift Der Deutschen Morgenländischen Gesellschaft, 43(3), 468-524. Retrieved from http://www.jstor.org/stable/43362026

62. Begler, J.D (1878); Report of a Tour Through the Bengal Provinces of Patna, Gaya, Mongir, and Bhagalpur: The Santal Parganas, Manbhum, Singhbhum, and Birbhum ; Bankura, Raniganj, Bardwan, and Hughli : in 1872-73, Office of the Superintendent of Government Printing, 1878, pp 101

63. Grierson, G. (1881); Git Raja Salhes, Journal of the Asiatic Society of Bengal, Volume 51, Part 1, pp 3-20 https://books.google.com/books?id=kG47AQAAMAAJ

64. Narayan, Badri (2003); Honour, Violence And Conflicting Narratives: A Study Of Myth And Reality, New Zealand Journal of Asian Sludies 5,1 (June,2003): 5-23

65. Proceedings of the Tenth Seminar of the IATS, 2003. Volume 14: Old Tibetan Studies: Dedicated to the Memory of R.E. Emmerick, BRILL, Aug 17, 2012, pp 227

66. Chen, Qingying (2003); Tibetan History, 2003, pp 17

67. Sen, Tansen (2003); Buddhism, Diplomacy, and Trade: The Realignment of Sino-Indian Relations, 600-1400, University of Hawaii Press, 2003, pp 24

68. Sen, Tansen (2003); Buddhism, Diplomacy, and Trade: The Realignment of Sino-Indian Relations, 600-1400, University of Hawaii Press, 2003, pp 23

69. Keay, John (2009); China: A History, Basic Books, Oct 6, 2009, pp 243

70. Bakker, Hans (2014); The World of the SkandapurâGa, BRILL, Jul 16, 2014, pp 129

71. Sen, Tansen (2003); Buddhism, Diplomacy, and Trade: The Realignment of Sino-Indian Relations, 600-1400, University of Hawaii Press, 2003, pp 23 also see Proceedings of the Tenth Seminar of the IATS, 2003. Volume 14: Old Tibetan Studies: Dedicated to the Memory of R.E. Emmerick , pp 227

72. Dr. Thakur, Prem Chandra (2012); Mithila State, The International Journal's, Research Journal of Social Science and Management, Volume 01, Number 10, 2012

73. Grierson, G. (1885); Selected Specimens of the Bihârî Language. Zeitschrift Der Deutschen Morgenländischen Gesellschaft, 39(4), 617-673. Retrieved from http://www.jstor.org/stable/43361768

74. Vidyarthi, L.P and Chaubey, Ganesh (1971); Bihar in Folklore Study, Indian Publications, 1971, pp 123

75. Vidyarthi, L.P and Chaubey, Ganesh (1971); Bihar in Folklore Study, Indian Publications, 1971, pp 122

76. Gazetteer of the Karnal District, Arya Press, 1883, pp 102

77. Gazetteer of the Karnal District, Arya Press, 1883, pp 104

78. Crooke, William (1896), The Popular Religion and Folk-lore of Northern India, Volume 1, A. Constable & Company, 1896, pp 216-217

79. The Journal of the Ceylon Branch of the Royal Asiatic Society of Great Britain & Ireland, Volume 7, The Branch, 1881, pp 125-127

80. Pillai, Suresh (2013) , Nagore Mira , Muslim God Of Caribbean, 2013

81. Karnal District Gazetteer-1918, Revenue Department, Haryana, 1918, pp 73-74

82. Haryana State Gazetteers, Revenue Department, Haryana, 2001 http://revenueharyana.gov.in/html/gazeteers/hrygazI/Hr-Gaz-Ch-5.htm

83. The Journal of the Ceylon Branch of the Royal Asiatic Society of Great Britain & Ireland, Volume 7, The Branch, 1881, pp 125-127

84. Pillai, Suresh (2013) , Nagore Mira , Muslim God Of Caribbean, 2013

85. Vidyarthi, L.P and Chaubey, Ganesh (1971); Bihar in Folklore Study, Indian Publications, 1971, pp 123
86. Wagner, Anja (2016); The Gaddi Beyond Pastoralism: Making Place in the Indian Himalayas, Berghahn Books, Jun 30, 2013, pp 116
87. Martin, Robert Montgomery (1838); The History, Antiquities, Topography, and Statistics of Eastern India, W. H. Allen and Company, 1838, pp 191
88. Sinha, Vivek R (1999); The Tiger is a Gentleman: Leaves from a Wildlife Photographer's Diary, Wildlife, Jan 1, 1999, pp 112
89. Martin, Robert Montgomery (1838); The History, Antiquities, Topography, and Statistics of Eastern India, W. H. Allen and Company, 1838, pp 191
90. Vidyarthi, L.P and Chaubey, Ganesh (1971); Bihar in Folklore Study, Indian Publications, 1971, pp 123
91. History of Tatar, Akbar time to 1800, Bengal: Past and Present, Volume 44, Part 1, Calcutta Historical Society., 1932
92. Bhattacharya, Ananda (2013); Sannyasi and Fakir Rebellion in Bihar (1767-1800), Islam and Muslim Societies : A Social Science Journal Vol. 6, No. 2 (2013)
93. Unification Campaign of Prithvi Narayan Shah, downloaded on Sep 28 from http://www.historynepal.com/2010/03/unification-campaign-of-prithvi-narayan.html .
94. Buchanan, Francis Hamilton (1819), An Account of the Kingdom of Nepal: And of the Territories Annexed to this Dominion by the House of Gorkha, 1819, pp. 145.
95. PRNW, pp. 378.
96. PRNW, pp. 378.
97. PRNW, pp. 379.
98. Notes On The History Of Morang District-I, Regmi Research Series,Year 3, No. 10, October 1, 1971.
99. PRNW, pp. 379.
100. PRNW, pp. 379.
101. PRNW, pp. 379.
102. PRNW, pp. 380.
103. Buchanan, Francis Hamilton (1819), An Account of the Kingdom of Nepal: And of the Territories Annexed to this Dominion by the House of Gorkha, 1819, pp. 177.

4

War of 1814-1816

The discussion on Madhesi will remain incomplete without the analysis of Treaty of Sugaolee and the Anglo-Gurkha war of 1814-1816. The Sugaolee Treaty memorandum[1] dated 8th December 1816, includes point 7 relevant to Madhesi people, which says:

> *"Moreover, the Rajah of Nipal agrees to refrain from prosecuting any inhabitants of the Terai, after its revertance to his rule, on account of having favoured the cause of the British Government during the war, and should any of those persons, excepting the cultivators of the soil, be desirous of quitting their estates, and of retiring within the Company's territories, he shall not be liable to hindrance."*

In the text that follows in this chapter, efforts are to understand the war, politics, and effect of final treaty on Madhesh and its people.

This chapter and beginning of the next chapter will contain discussion on the following topics:

1. Cause of British-Gurkha War and Parties involved
2. Brief British Rule in Madhesh
3. People of Terai or Madhesh, and its role in the war. Also the politics that created context to include Madhesh related provisions in the Treaty.
4. Demarcation of Border and after-effects of war on the people of Madhesh

Cause of Being Face to Face

There were changes of guard in the region, primarily initiated by Gurkha and British East India Company (EIC). Gurkhas, which had their original capital in Gorkha under King Prithivi Narayan Shah, moved the capital to Kathmandu-Patan-Bhaktapur valley, then collectively known as Nepal valley, continue to expand the border to the East and West of hills. Their priority of expansion - that started under King Prithivi Narayan Shah in 1744 BC - was hill, however in those days, there were little unallocated productive resource left in hill to be prized as compensation to army generals, whose motive was driven by wealth, rather than by the sense of welfare of occupied territory. Gurkha had compulsion to look towards Madhesh as possible wealth pool. After battle of Makwanpur in 1762, against his own brother-in-law King Digbandhan Sen, King Prithivi Narayan Shah occupied Simraungadh, the winter capital of Sen King[2], which has been center of Tirhut/Mithila civilization for the past many centuries. By occupying Simraungadh and surrounding plain lands, Gurkha found the resource they were aspiring for long time[3]. Army elites were allocated lands in Madhesh as salary compensation, in absence of other form of compensation including cash money. Army elite would rent those lands out to the common people for cultivation and upon collection of wealth from Madhesh, seniors would distribute the wealth to junior army personnel.

In the same timeframe, British EIC having concentration in Kolkata, was expanding into Gangetic plains. It will not be out of place to give a brief account of EIC. When they first came in India around 1600s, their primary and obvious motive in India was business. In 1634, the Mughal emperor extended his hospitality to the English traders to the region of Bengal, and in 1717 completely waived customs duties for the trade. At that time company's main businesses were cotton, silk, Indigo dye, saltpeter, and tea. However, to do business at that time, they had to own private armies for safe passage of goods across the sea route. In its first century and half, the EIC used a few hundred soldiers as guards. The great expansion came after 1750, when it had 3000 regular troops. By 1763, it had 26,000; by 1778, it had 67,000. It recruited largely Indians in the troops, and trained them along European lines[4]. Company's political rule in India effectively began in 1757 after the Battle of Plassey. In the Battle of Plassey EIC military force was led by Robert Clive and was supported by hopeful next Nawab of Bengal Mir Jafar. Mir Jafar was commander in chief of the Nawab's army and had rebelled against Nawab Siraj-ud-daulah, the last independent Nawab of Bengal and eventually defeated him[5]. British EIC brought under their rule North Indian principalities like Darbhanga Maharaj,

Rajah of Bettia, Awadh Nawab, Hindur and Sirmur whose rule expanded from East to West and paralleled with hilly state of Gurkha.

In the 30-year, since Prithivi Narayan Shah attacked Simraungadh in 1962, Gurkha's growth as a military and political power was phenomenal till it encountered defeat in War with China in 1792, that arrested its westward expansion. While the aggression on border area remained cold for next decade, sort of cold war situation, during this time, however, internal political situation around King Ran Bahadur were rather volatile. But within a few weeks of Bhimsen Thapa seizing power in Kathmandu in 1804, Gurkha resumed imperial expansion towards Westward Garhwal[6]. The Westward conquest was in hilly territory, which drained more resource than produced, thus compelling Gurkha to keep continuing aggression on fertile and productive lands in south of plains.

Thus gradually Gurkha and British EIC were coming closer day by day and disputes were escalating gradually.

The condition in the northern part of the Bihar district was far from satisfactory[7]. The Jamindars on the borders of Nepal mocked at the British authorities. The Company's Government wrote to the Raja of Nepal on February 3, 1787, complaining that his men were encroaching on the borders of Tirhut with headquarters at Darbhanga. A letter from the Collector of Tirhut to the Board of Revenue in 1788 shows the difficulty in the settlement of disputes regarding some frontier village. The difficulties were further increased by the eternal trouble owing to the incursions of the Nepalese. Attempt to persuade the Gurkhas to aid the British officers in the suppression of frontier dacoits proved fruitless and all remonstrations against their aggression were of no avail. The Collector of Tirhut reported that between 1787 and 1813 more than 200 villages had been seized by them on one or the other unjustifiable pretext. In 1815, again, the collector was obliged to report that the Jamindars complained that in consequence of the incursion of the Nepalese, who had come down and burnt their villages and plundered their property, their Ryots had in many instances deserted and they were unable to pay their revenue. In the war (1813-15) which ensued near Jaynagar close to the Nepal frontier, villages had to be occupied by the British troops but no fighting took place in the district. It was only after the treaty of Sugaolee that Darbhanga enjoyed peace and tranquility.

Lately, both sides realized it was becoming too much. Thus, British authority proposed 'Principle of Limitation' to the Gurkha rulers. The 'Principle of Limitation' was another way of endorsing the idea that had already been mentioned by King Prithivi Narayan Shah in his Divya Upadesh[8], known in English as Divine Counsel, saying "Nepal lies between two rocks" and only thing that was missing was the well-defined line to separate two country sites. King Prithivi Narayan suggested to have amicable relations with both emperors of China and ruler of Indian plain. In a way, King Prithivi Narayan Shah accepted the boundary for Gurkha rulers to the point where it touches the British occupation. On the other hand, the British were like protectors of the plain rules in exchange for some tax, so whoever requested protection, they obliged. Most of the plain rulers were victims of Gurkha military might, and thus started complaining to Company Government. Border incidents along the southern border of Nepalese territory had occurred sporadically since 1806 and had led to a general state of tension by 1810. This made the Governor-General to introduce in the Council a 'principle of limitation' of which Ochterlony informed Kaji Amar Singh Thapa in April 1810. Under this principle, the British would not interfere in 'the proceedings of Nipaul in the hills' and 'the Nepalese authority should on no account be extended below the hills'[9].

This British concept of claiming the lowlands, while recognizing Nepalese claims to the hills and mountains, paid no heed to the fact that a certain border hill states, such as Hindur and Sirmur, annexed by Nepal, owned, or claimed to own, lowland territory. For the Nepalese the control of villages was through military might. Borders were 'rivers, ridges, mountain ranges, and the extent of one's military control'[10]. In response to Governor-General's letter sent in May 1813 through Colonel Ochterlony, in which it was requested that the "Principle of Limitation"[11] be respected, the king of Nepal replied 'As the Honourable Company have, by the grace of God, established their dominion in Hindoostan by the power of the sword, so have I by the same means acquired the possession of the hills together with the lowlands dependent on the territories of former Rajahs, some of whom tamely submitted to my authority, while others were expelled for their conduct'[12].

Why British Wanted to go to War?

The story of Gurkha interaction with British started very early, even before Kinlock expedition. British did not want to interfere in the fights between hill kings, rather had policy to deal with the winner. This is why, many hill kings, when anywhere in their kingdom, asked for help from British, they did not get help. Similarly, British concerns were also driven by expense and benefit components. In the early days of 1771, British had some dispute with respect to Parganna Tautar[13] (central Madhesh). The dispute was about a rented land of Darbhanga Maharaj to Makwanpur king. This was not being initially acknowledged by King Prithivi Narayan Shah. However, British let it go, as it was supposed to be small tribute of just 12,000 per year when Captain Kinloch occupied the district of Rautahat and Parsa. British also let go the 'ancient rights of Tirhut' about Pergunnah Tautar (central Madhesh), even though Gurkha was sending tribute irregularly. According to British assessment 'Inconveniences & Expense' was much more than the advantages. Cost of recovery of these tributes Pergunnah was excessive[14]. The 12,000 tribute, however, continued till 1800 when it was removed in exchange of trade treaty.

Between the time-span of Gurkha-China war of 1789 and emergence of Bhimsen Thapa in Nepal politics in 1804, there was negligible military expedition in any direction. Return of King Rana Bahadur Shah to Kathmandu from Varanasi after 4 years in 1804, during which time Bhimsen helped him a lot and as a result dispute with the British got warmed up. King Rana Bhadur Shah's first target was Sen Kingdom of Palpa, which was holding rented land from Awadh Nawab. King Rana Bahadur called King Prithvipal Sen to Kathmandu offering him his sister in marriage. No sooner King Prithivipal entered Kathmandu he was put into arrest. Talk of marriage was just a tempting lolipop and was never intended. Prithvipal was killed in prison after Rana Bahadur's assassination by his step brother in 1806. Bhimsen massacred ninety-three people, after which he was able to claim the title of the mukhtiyar (equivalent to prime minister). Bhimsen sent army under command of his father Amar Singh Thapa to capture Palpa and hearing the news the families of late King Prithivi Pal sought refugee with British Government. The plain land – that was rented to Palpa Kingdom – was offered to the British as tribute on the similar terms and conditions as Pergunnah Tautar. However British refused the offer this time, which led to the dispute of Butwal and Seoraj region.

There were many other places along the border, where dispute between Gurkha and British got murkier. The Collector of Tirhut reported that between 1787 and 1813 more than 200 villages had been seized by them on one or the other unjustifiable pretext and in 1815 he was again obliged to report that the Jamindars had complained that as a consequence of the incursions of the Nepalese, who had come down and burnt their villages and plundered their property, their ryots had, in many instances, deserted their homes and they were unable to pay their revenue[15].

However, the trigger point was the killing of British Thanedar in an inhuman way. On the morning of the 29th of May 1814, the principal police station in Butwal was attacked by a largegroup of the Gurkha troops, header by Munraj Foujdar a high ranking Gurka officer surprised Company police and revenue stations, murdering eighteen men[16]. The chief Thanedar escaped the massacre but was eventually made prisoner and murdered in cold blood, with peculiar barbarity. Munraj Foujdar deliberately caused him to be tied to a tree and to be shot to death with arrows as an example to deter others from taking office under British against the will of the Gurkhas. British Government's effort to get explanation of this event and punish perpetrators received wholly evasive response with inherent threat and menace. Following the murder, the barbarity of Gurkha continued in effort to destroy the British troops and the subjects of the company and drive them out of the frontier of Sarun, by poisoning the water of the wells and ponds in a tract of considerable extent[17]. British waited for the season to turn favorable and around the beginning of October 1814, the British troops began to move towards their posts. Soon after, army was also constituted and deployed into four divisions: one at Benares, one at Meerut, one at Dinapur, and one at Ludhiana[18]. Britain formally declared war with Nepal on 1 November, 1814[19].

British objective before going to war was to punish the insolent aggression of the Nepalese[20]. Also, in case Chinese raise any issue, as Nepal was under Emperor's protection since Nepal's defeat in Nepal-China war of 1788-1792, convey to China in clearer terms that British had no design of appropriating territory.

War Objective from English Perspective

British objective of going to war is discussed in details in the letter of Lord Moira written to the court and people in London. Though it was awaited and anticipated in 'Rajah Sitabroy's letter' in 1771, it was the new Governor-General of India Marquess of Hastings, with his military background, who put a plan to wage a war on Gurkha. British had almost defined objective while going to war.

The British had image of protector, and thus were obliged to provide protection to its subjects and Jamindars. Additionally, the Gurkha violence on Indian subject was making them abandon the land and field that was source of tax for Britishers. Thus the immediate concern of British was to reinstall the sense in the frontier, and rebuild the image of being protector that meant putting army plan together and marching ahead to the frontier, which was an expensive affair. To meet the expenses, British took loan from Awadh Nawab, and to pay back the loan, British planned to give to Awadh the land occupied in the war. In the scenario emerging as aftermath of war, British wanted to have boundary agreed upon by Gurkha to be demarcated using pillars. In the long term interest, anticipating if any war happens in future, British wanted to gather enough knowledge about the politics of Gurkha, thus wanted to have a residency in Kathmandu. To remove the source of funding war, British wanted to strip away the productive lands and newly occupied lands, from Gurkha clutch, that can be given back to the previous owners of the land in such a way that British can reinstall the image of being savior. There were minor interests too on the table, such as nice to have not been pushed, like reactivating treaty of 1800.

War Objective from Gurkha Perspective

Before commencement of war, there was a discussion among the Principal Chiefs of Gorkha Government with a view to know their opinion about the war hovering over the door. The details of discussion have been covered in the "Translation of a copy of the written Opinions of the Principal Gorkha Chiefs on the Question of Peace or War with the British Government"[21]. Gurkha chiefs were divided into two groups; a group favoring immediate aggression and another advocating peace, who favored postponing of aggression for future occasion. War supporting group was led by General Bhimsen Thapa, Kajee Dilbunjun Pande and Peace supporting group was led by Kajee Amar Singh Thapa, Kajee Rundoj Singh Thapa, Raj Guru Rungnath Pundit, Chautaria Bum Sah and Hustodeel. A close look at groups alludes to the fact that war part was pushed by Kathmandu based elite having proximity to the King, and peace was pursued by those fighting on the frontier. This fact is emphasized in combined letter of Amar Singh Thapa, Bum Sah and Hustodeel saying "The advocate of war [Bhimsen Thapa], who proposes to fight and conquer the English, has been bred up at court, and is a stranger to the toil and hardships of a military life[22]". Two confessions emerge from the letter; (1) Gurkha did injustice to the former kings of the hills and who were forced to flee to English territory and (2) Gurkhas have realized that their occupancy of plain land was inappropriate. In another follow-up letter written to king by Amar Singh Thapa, while war was ongoing on March 1815, says "To restore the relations of amity by concession is good and proper for this purpose it is fit in the first place to cede to the enemy the departments of Butwal, Palpa and Sheeoraj and the disputed tracts (of 22 villages on Sarun frontier) already settled by the (joint Anglo-Gurkha) commissioners towards Barah. If this is found insufficient to re-establish harmony, we should to abandon the whole of the Turaee [Terai] the Doon and the low lands[23]".

Four generations of Gurkhas kept themselves engage in the task of usurpation of domination beyond the original boundary of Gurkha kingdom. King Prithivi Narayan plundered Nepal valley, central Madhesh and area surrounding Nepal Valley. The next generation stretched the Gurkha border to the East of Kosi River. Third generation under King Ran Bahadur subjugated Kumaon-Garhwal and Fourth generation King Girvan saw conquest pushed till Sutlej led by Kajee Amar Singh Thapa. Gurkha general knew they were entangled in the vicious circle of land-war-army-land. They were driven by the temptation of getting revenue generating land. War was the only method through which Gurkhas could snatch lands from other kingdoms. Thus, they needed continuous army recruit to rule and usurpation of new kingdoms. Increasing army size needed new revenue sources that only land was able to provide, because other revenue sources like commerce was dying down after Gurkha's occupation of traditional India-China trade routes. The second reason was that Gurkhas needed Madhesh for Saltpeter, the raw material for ammunition that was harvested from the Madhesh having favorable hot-humid condition for the natural deposit of Saltpeter[24]. Land has man made boundary and thus it brought them in conflict with southern neighbor, British rulers. Initially, the British were new in ruling in India and also in Indian politics. This is why they wanted to have priorities on bigger states of Indian dominations rather than Himalayan Hilly Kingdoms. Also, earlier British expedition to Kathmandu under Major Kinloch saw more causalities than benefit due to unknown hilly terrain and hot-humid summer-rainy weather condition in Terai. Gurkhas were able to create a state of illusion that British will not be able to defeat Gurkha in Hilly warfare and even if English occupy contiguous Terai land, they can not retain Terai due to the unfriendly weather and huge cost of maintaining it. Earlier success of Gurkha against China in 1795 war and against Major Kinloch gave them confidence. In addition Gurkha had overconfidence on natural hill hindrance created by God that was believed to be impregnable. Lastly, Gurkha was hoping to get help from China Emperor and Tibetan Lama to fight against English.

War, Negotiations and Treaty - The Strategy

The first division of army was constituted and was deployed at Patna and Moorshedabad. Its strength was of near eight thousand men including his Majesty's 24th infantry comprising nine hundred and seven soldiers. This division was constituted for the main attack which was intended to be made direct upon the capital of Katmandu through the passes between the Gandaki and Bagmati. Major general Marley was entrusted to command this division. The Ganges was to be crossed by the troops from Patna on the 15th of November. Another brigade was formed from the troops at more distant stations to follow the army and protect its pots and rear as it kept advancing further into the hills.

The second division was deployed at Benares and Gorakhpur, under the command of Major general John Sullivan Wood and his instructions were to penetrate by Butwal into Palpa. This division consisted of his Majesty's 17th infantry of nine hundred and fifty soldiers and about three thousand natives. The 15th of November was fixed as the day on which this force was to take the field at Gorakhpur.

The third division was deployed at Meeruth, under general Gillespie, was to proceed first against the Dehra Doon valley, stretching between the Ganges and Jumna, which was within the first range of hills. After Dehra Doon, the force was to divide; a detachment was to attack snowy range of Gurhwal and Srinagur, and the main body was to proceed to the west of the Jumna, in aid of the operations of Major general Ochterlony against Amar Singh Thapa. General Gillespie's force was made up about one thousand Europeans and two thousand five hundred native infantry. This division and the division under General Ochterlony were ordered to take the field towards the end of October, the unhealthy season when the rains have generally proceeded over to the North West. This happens generally by the beginning or middle of this month. Kumaon and Almora, its capital were to be attacked from Rohilkhund, but according to the original plan this movement was to follow the occupation of Gurhwal to the north of the province and the operations undertaken here in December and January were an afterthought prompted by the peculiar circumstances that prevailed at the commencement of the war.

The fourth division was deployed at Ludhiana under Colonel Ochterlony which was to operate in the hilly country, lying near the Sutlej. The force under this officer's command was exclusively native infantry and artillery and amounted to about six thousand men. It was fixed to advance against the strong and extensive cluster of posts held by Amar Singh and the troops under his immediate orders in western front.

The fifth division was deployed beyond the Kosi eastward under Major Latter and was laced with two thousand men including his district battalion for the defense of the Purnia frontier. This officer was desired to open a communication with the Raja of Sikkim and to give him every assistance and encouragement to expel the Gurkha from the eastern hills was still actively going on when the declaration of war issued. After the war was declared, there was no sign of dilution in the acts of severe subjugation being perpetrated by Gurkha army of the Sikkim country and in the ongoing struggle of the adherents of Sikkim Raja with Gurkha army.

Following is a list of Nepalese Sardars appointed[25] on the 11th October in the command of troops designated for the Terai:

1. Shumsher Rana, the son of Bhasker Rana, was appointed to lead the march on the Dusehrek with seven companies of sepoys and one thousand six hundred archers towards Makwanpur and to remain there until the British troops should advance to that quarter. Rumbur Thapa the brother of Rundhuj Thapa, son of the elder Amar Sing, and Kurbeer Khutteree, the son of the late Dusneth Khutteree, were along with the Anone Sirdar.
2. Bahauder Bhandaree, Soobah Bungsoo Khutteree and Subedar, Banka Khutteree were ordered with four companies of sepoys to march from Nepal on the Dusekreh towards the morning. They were to be joined by all the troops already stationed in the Eastward.
3. Amar Singh Thapa, the father of Bhim Singh Thapa, Runguj Sirdar, Bag Banua, Sutten Sul Thakur Rajput and other officers remained at

Sauseen and Butwal with the ten thousand men already stationed in that quarter.

4. Bum Sah, Jugdeo Bhundaree and Agunt Sirdar had taken post with an army of four thousand men around Haridwar.
5. Kaji Amar Singh Thapa, with a numerous force continued in western hill front
6. Rooder Beer, with one thousand sepoys, remained posted at Peeothameh.

The Attacks – First Campaign

Major general Gillespie was the first to penetrate into the enemy's frontier. On the 22nd of October he seized the Keree pass leading to Doon and from there proceeded to Dehra, the principal town in the valley, without meeting any opposition. The whole of the hill country in the west of the Ganges was still under Amar Singh Thapa, who had deployed a force of about six hundred men under the command of Captain Balbhadra Singh. The first face to face fight was at Nalapani. British failed and lost considerable number of people, and backtracked to Dehra Doon. Their second attempt on 25th November also failed and they lost additional people. On November 30th, after heavy bombardment, the fort wall was destroyed to a great extent, Balbhadra escaped with his men.

Major General Martindale joined the force and took over the command. On Dec 27th December, occupied Nahan, and attacked Jaithak. Major Martindale had to face casualties and retreated. Eventually, Jaithak was captured under the command of Ochterlony.

Ochterlony and his boy were second to come in contact with Gurkha force. He attacked Nahagarh and Malaun under Amar Singh Thapa. After initial hiccups, Ochterlony was able to subdue Amar Singh, and cut off communication lines with Kathmandu. On 11 May 1815, Amar Singh surrendered all the territory in the west of Kumaon and he was allowed to go to Kathmandu with his men. British also got agreement to recruit Gurkha whoever wished to join.

The division at Gorakhpur, under General Wood, assembled on 15th of November. They took time in working out logistics and arranging elephants in Gorakhpur and the operation was delayed. They started late in January. They soon occupied Sheoraj and proceeded to Butwal. General Wood faced water problem on 2nd January, and soldiers were deputed to collect water in leather bags for British and native Muslim soldiers, and for Hindu soldiers on posts[26]. On January 3rd, he was in Jeetgurh near Butwal, at the start of Hill. He faced the Gurkha armies there, with some causalities. Gurkha army Chief Sooraj Thapa was killed too. General Wood was informed by a Brahmin spy named, Kauckunnnddee Sewaree, whose integrity was doubted later, that there were large groups of Gurkhas in ready position to assault. The same day, spies of Rajah Ratan Singh also brought the similar news, upon which General Wood decided to retract from Jeetgurh to Gorakhpur on 4th of January 1815. After that, General Wood's action was limited to become defensive rather than offensive. The strategy to deprive Gurkhas of resources and supplies was adopted with the help of native Tharus of Butwal area. All the crops were destroyed and Tharus were persuaded to migrate to southern area, where they were allocated lands[27]. The Eighth regiment of Cavalry was employed in the task of destroying the crops and villages in the Terai from which the Tharus had agreed to migrate. At the start of rainy season, which was unhealthy for the British, size of troops was reduced, with the objective to minimize cost, and some sections of troops were also redirected to Sarun-Champarun frontier. At one time, twelve hundred sick men of General Wood were in hospital.

The division at Danapur-Patna under Major General Marley was scheduled to have crossed Ganga River on November 15th. However, the division could do this at the end of November. In the meantime, General Marley gave orders to Major Roughsedge, to proceed ahead with Lieutenant-Colonel Bradshaw to attack frontier of Sarun and Tirhut. Bradshaw had dual responsibilities — political and military. Bradshaw's first attack was on Barhawa, a place on the bank of Bagmati River near Gaur in Rautahat. Here, close on the frontier, a Gurkha outpost had been established under Parsuram Thapa and Major Bradshaw, who was in command of the English forces, was determined to attack it. Early in the morning of the 25th November 1814, he attacked with the help of newly constituted Champaran Light infantry consisting native soldiers. This was the first time that this infantry got involved in any battle.[28]. In the attack Gurkha had big loss; fifty-one sepoys were killed, twenty-three were taken prisoners and about fifty drowned in Bagmati River[29]. Among the killed were Parsuram Thapa (Army commander and subah of Bara-Parsa) and Musun Raut (a noted leader of Dacoits who was working under the influence of Gurkha officials and also commanded extensive influence on the lower orders in the Terai). Chandra Shekhar Upadhyay was taken into prison[30] and from him many letters and documents were confiscated. This measure was given effect to by a combined action of the three posts on the boundary. The force at Adapoor advanced to Parsa. Captain Hay's division moved forward and occupied Baragurhee. Immediately after being occupied by the British the Tarai was vacated by the Gurkhas. Bradshaw issued orders to Captain Roughsedge under whose leadership Janakpur[31] was captured on 8th of December 1814. Bradshaw completely handed over Military charge to Major General Marley on December 11th for Champaran and Tirhut frontier. The Commander in chief, Lord Moira believed, had the momentum created by Bradshaw been carried forward and maintained also by Marley at that point, they would have occupied Makwanpur without opposition[32]. Marley insisted, to move forward, battering train should accompany him, which was believed to have reached Bettia towards end of December. Marley, instead of moving forward, engaged himself with shifting armies between posts and took a position near a place called Lowtun, 25 miles away from Parsa and Samanpur. Gurkha armies was watching the activities of the British armies from the fastness and immediate jungle. Inhabitants of this region, probably afraid of army, and British in particular, entirely abandoned their villages and carried vast supplies of new rice produce to the forests. British believed, Gurkhas were also gathering information of whereabouts of their positions from those villagers. British Captain Blackney was posted at Samanpur near Gaur to the north of the district on the extreme right of the line where he was left with a small force without any support. Here he was taken completely by surprise at daybreak on the 1st January 1815, his camp was attacked, the tents were put to fire, the sepoys broke and ran in the utmost confusion and Captain Blackney was killed. His grave is in Majorganj near Gaur. Gurkhas attacked Baragurhee, although their attempts were foiled multiple times. But Major General Marlay became further confused and demotivated. First he tried to go to Parsa, however suddenly changed direction to Betteeah in hope of getting battering-train. The confusion on British side proved advantageous for Gurkhas, and they soon expanded to occupy the whole terai again. The effect was more on Tirhoot frontier and somewhat less on Champarun-Sarun frontier, which was lightly covered by General Marley's army. On January 15th, about six thousand Gurkha armies from Janakpur proceeded towards Rupaitha Garhi, four miles south of Janakpur. Gurkha built a stockade in Rupaitha. Fraser provides insight of Gurkha in Rupaitha: "Close to the village containing these temples, the Gurkhas had erected a small fort, provided with a dry ditch, but of little strength. They had, however, commenced a stockade that would have been highly formidable, had it been completed: it was a square of 11.5 yards each way; the height on the cutside was twenty feet. Bastions were erected at the corners, and at each of the entrances in the center of the sides; in the center of the stockade was a tank, which occupied a large portion of its area. It had every appearance of having been constructed in a hurry, as green and insufficient wood was used, instead of the bamboo, which usually is preferred; and no attempt had been yet made to excavate a ditch."

Watching the activities of Gurkha army being geared up, the terrified inhabitants of Mahottari, then consisting of district between Bagmati and Kamla River, started fleeing towards south into India[33]. The inhabitants told one of the British spy that Gurkhas had plan to occupy Thana Humeer Kurdary in Darbhanga district, Bhita located 3 miles south of Jaleshwar, and Saharghat located around 15 miles south of Janakpur[34]. Upon getting the news of Gurkha occupation of Terai, commander in chief Lord Moira directed more armies towards Tirhut and Sarun frontier from all the possible depots. The strength of the army, after reinforcement, became thirteen thousand from initial eight thousand. Commander in chief wanted to restore the confidence back into army, thus he made all the possible arrangements to add and equip army in Tirhut-Champaran frontier. The challenge to British was increased because the rumors were making rounds about exaggerated number of Gurkha armies in the region, more than the estimated population of the country[35]. At the start of the war, the number of Gurkha army was estimated to be twelve thousand. In the confusion, Marley left the frontier without informing anyone and went to Calcutta. The interim command was handled by Colonel Dick who handed over command to Major General Wood[36] on February 21st. On the preceding day a move was made, in which British occupied village of Pirari. In the early March Major general Wood moved from Baragurhee to Janakpur in the East, and destroyed all the stockades on his route. On the March 10th, Major General Wood wrote letter to higher officer mentioning the whole of Terai was in British possession and the management of Terai should be placed under immediate civil officers of the contiguous districts. The command was again transferred back to

Lieutenant Colonel Bradshaw, Political Agent to the Governor General, who has accordingly assumed the civil administration of those lands[37].

To the Eastward of the river Kosi the military charge of the northern frontier was conferred to Captain Latter, whereas a considerable portion of the Terai of Morang was put in the authority of the British Government. Although the force under Captain Latter was intended to be used for defensive operations rather than offensive ones, on several occasions' advantage was taken to attack the Gurkha positions with great success[38].

On the Western front, Almora was besieged and after a stiff fight the Gurkha commander surrendered in April 1815. Amar Singh Thapa also surrendered in May 1814. These two setbacks prompted Gurkha to seek truce.

Truce, Terms and Negotiations

Successes of the British army at Almora and Malown combined with the general pressure of the war upon the resources of Nepal a desire for peace among chiefs and people, compelled Gurkha ruler to make attempt for seeking the restoration of peace. However Gurkha chiefs knew their strategy to engage the British and buy the time till they are again prepared for retaliation. In a letter written on 2nd March 1815, Amar Singh Thapa, the army commander of western conquest emphasized that British were not successful in previous endeavor to retain Terai, thus he saw no reason to believe, British will again be able to hold Terai. In his words, "Formerly when the English endeavored to penetrate into Sindoolee [Sindhuli] they continued for two years in possession of Barra-Pursa [Bara-Parsa] and Mahatree [Mahottari][39] but when you [Rajah] conquered Nepaul they were either destroyed by your force or fell victims to the climate with the exception of a few only who abandoned the place". Amar Singh Thapa proposed, let the British occupy the Plain land, however, there was no proposal to agree on the written agreement about the cessation, thus in future they could again restart the military enterprise[40]. Thapa further advised the King to send petition to the Emperor of China or to the Lama of Lassa seeking their intervention or support. In the draft letter to Emperor of China, where he wanted China to accept Gurkha as tributary, and as first priority asked for the money and then army support. It should be emphasized here that Gurkhas had not garnered Emperor of China consent before deciding on go ahead on the war with British. Amar Singh went ahead to frighten Emperor of China about the British success saying, next target of British would be Tibetan town Lassa. He further lured Emperor of China with invitation to become savior of Jumboodweep, ancient name of Indian subcontinent, after expelling British from the region[41].

British, on the other side, were preparing the draft treaty that they wanted to be signed, while war was still ongoing. In the letter of 1st June 1814, Lord Moira had listed the terms, the British were contemplating to extract through the treaty[42].

- 1st, The perpetual exclusion of the Gurkha influence, power and authority from the countries west of the Kali river
- 2nd, the secession of all the low lands [Terai], from the Kali Eastward to the Tista, rendering either the foot or the ridge of the lowest range of hills the common boundary throughout that line
- 3rd, the formal renunciation of all the claims of the Gurkhas which led to the war
- 4th, the permanent residence of accredited Ministers from each Government at the Court of the other
- 5th, the exclusion from the Nepalese territory of Foreign Europeans and Americans, and of British subjects, without special permission from the British Government
- 6th, security for the Rajah of Sikkim, and any other Hill Chiefs who may have risen against the Gurkhas, to the eastward, and a good frontier in that direction

Simultaneously in June, Lord Moira was also engaged in collecting information about the revenue of the Plain lands. Based on the limited information, he estimated the gross produce of lands lying between the Gandaki and the Kosi to be eight lacs of rupees per annum, including the produce of Morang and Butwal Terai[43].

Gurkha channel of communication was opened in three different fronts; first via Chandra Shekhar Upadhyay, second through Bum Sah and third through Guru Gajraj Mishra. Chandra Shekhar was the designated Gurkha King's attorney in Calcutta handle any dispute related to British. However, he was captured in surprise attack by Bradshaw in November 1814, and he was encouraged to open channel of communication with Rajah. Bum Sah was Governor of Almorah under Gurkha occupation and he was also linked to rajah by blood relation, so he was designated as Chautaria. During his surrender of Almorah to British, Bum Sah showed interest to reestablish peace by making friendship between Rajah and British. Gajraj Mishra was religious teacher of Rajah's father Ran Bahadur Shah. Gajraj Mishra was grandson of Sriharsha Mishra[44], the religious teacher of Prithivi Narayan Shah. Since the killing of Ran Bahadur and during the rise of Thapa clan, he was staying in Banaras and making living through lands given by British. He was known to British too because of his mediation during 1793s and 1801s treaty negations with British. After war was initiated in 1814, he was called by Rajah and Bhimsen Thapa to Kathmandu.

After having consultation in Kathmandu, Guru Gajraj Mishra returned to Lieutenant Colonel Bradshaw's camp on the 28th May accompanied by Chandra Shekhar Upadhyay. There he produced before Lieutenant Colonel Bradshaw the paper with the Rajah's red seal empowering him to bring to an adjustment through compromise all corresponding matters between the two States. Guru listened to the treaty terms and at the same time cautioned British that the terms will not be acceptable to the Gurkha Chiefs and the most stringent of them was cessation of plain lands between Kosi and Gandaki River. Majority of the Gurkha chief, and primarily Amar Singh Thapa family derived their personal income from the rent free Terai land given to them for their services.

On the separate and concurrent discussions with Gardner, Bum Shah and his brother Rudra Beer Shah asserted that to cede the Terai, would amount to destroying the resources of the Gurkha empire, and a great part of the soldiery drew their subsistence from jagirdari situated in that tract and even the Rajah's household expenses were defrayed from the resources of the Terai[45]. As per their estimate, Terai gave ten lacs of revenue and another ten lacs were coming from the hills. They further nudged Gardner saying, they relied on the generosity of the British Government that they were aware, they could not resist, but that it was better to incur the hazard of the worst consequences than to submit at once to a sacrifice which would destroy their State.

Bum Sah was relative of Rajah, and also closer close British's thought of English-Gurkha treaty. Leveraging the close relationship, British proposed him to cede Doti as buffer state between British and Gurkha state. However Bum Sah preferred to remain with Rajah at tough time and was eyeing bigger role in the central power structure. Probably, Amar Singh might have got the indication of British plan to push Bam Sah directly to Rajah bypassing Thapa group. Bum Sah was of the opinion that Rajah should cede few more plain land, but not close to English demand, to restore peace between states. Similarly Chandra Shekhar Upadhyay was having rent free land in Plain, and like Bhimsen, he was also getting impacted with the plain cessation.

Bum Sah's terms were not different from the Guru Gajraj Mishra and British priorities over negotiation channel with Guru.

In the August, Guru again came and stated the apprehension about the personal loss of few powerful chief who had jagirdari in low land, and so they are opposing the terms of treaty.

The officers in charge of the Terai just before commencement of War, have been mentioned in the letter of June 1805:

Kaji Randhoj Thapa and Kaji Amrit Thapa were granted overall authority to supervise revenue, judicial, and other affairs in the districts of the eastern Tarai region. Local administrators in the region were instructed to obey only those orders that were issued to them through these two kajis. Amrit (Simha) Thapa (A.D. 1785-1805) was brother of Bhimsen Thapa, and Randhoj Thapa, a half-brother.

(1) Subba Sarup Pur, Ijaradar of Morang.

(2) Umanidhi Pantha and Jayanta Khatri of the Morang Adalat.

(3) Dasharath Khatri and Bhotu Khawas, sent to Morang for collecting the Salami levy.

(4) Nain Simha (Khawas), Ijaradar of Saptari and Mahottari.

(5) Laxmi Narayan Pandit of the Saptari-Mahottari Adalat.

(6) Shaktiballabh Padhya, Ijaradar of Bara and Parsa.

(7) Mana Ojha and Tularam Bista of the Bara – Parsa Adalat.

(8) Jalim Simha Khawas, Ijaradar of Rautahat.

Table: Showing officers- in-charge of terai land in 1805 at the hands of Thapas, ten years before commencement of British-Gurkha war.

Noticing such a reservation about Terai among the Chiefs and its impact in their payroll, in September, British proposed the idea of providing two lacs in pension. Guru had no power to agree on cessation of Terai, except on the disputed lands. Thus he went back again to Kathmandu.

Third visit of Guru Gajraj Mishra to Bradshaw took place on September 18th, 1815 Guru offered to sign the treaty if the portion of Terai in the British occupation (lying between the Gandaki and Kosi) were substituted for the offered stipends. This was refused and the negotiators took leave on the 29th of October promising to return in twelve days with the treaty signed.

The British were occupying a part of plain land at that point, however as a punishment and to cover the cost of war, they had demanded the whole of plain land, including the *char-kose* (2.5 miles) strip of Jungle. British again discussed the treaty proposal among themselves and came up with the idea that, they should punish the Gurkhas and also take away their source of income, so that Gurkhas do not get sufficient resource in future to create any trouble. At the same time, Gurkha should be able to respect the terms of treaty after signing the agreement. Thus, they relaxed terms in land between Gandaki and Kosi, and came up with two proposals[46] for plain land; (i) The whole land between Kali and Gandaki to be ceded and (ii) The area occupied by British between Gandaki and Kosi should be ceded and be given to Gurkhas. However, this term was not disclosed to Gurkha in 1815 and was not part of first treaty.

Finally, on 28th November 1815, Guru Gajraj Mishra again came from Kathmandu accompanied by Chandra Shekhar Upadhyay, with full power to sign the treaty agreement[47]. The treaty was signed on 2nd December 1815 with the terms British wanted: cessation of Terai and in return British to Provide 2 lacs in pension. The treaty needed rectification, within 15 days from the Rajah Girvan Yuddha Shah, to become effective.

Second Campaign

The terms of the Treaty signed in December was debated in Gurkha court. War faction, led by Amar Singh Thapa, overpowered the faction advocating peace. Consequently, war hostilities were revived. The treaty was not rectified by Rajah and no response was sent to British after expiry of 15 days of term mentioned in treaty itself.

British army started movement towards the Terai again with the preparation for war. In February, Guru Gajraj Mishra formally announced the decision

Gurkha court to recommend the war. British did not want to start the expedition in rainy season. So they were under pressure to begin the war before that... This time, the command of the 17,000 army was handed over to Ochterlony, with promoted designation, as a prize for his victory in western front over Amar Singh Thapa. He planned his attack on Kathmandu, and divided the army in three groups; first under Colonel Kelly to move from right direction, central under Miller to move straight through Chiriya Ghati and third under Colonel Nicol to move from left. The central force made use of the least known pass to penetrate the hill at night. The path was through the bed of river having steep ascendency. The calculated risk paid to Ochterlony, when he was able to surprise the Gurkha army in Makwanpur on 27th February. Gruesome fight ensued causing heavy loss to Gurkha army (about 800 men killed) and miner loss to British (2 officers and 45 men killed). The Gurkha army was led by Shumsheer Rana[48]. In the meantime, another group of British army had also occupied Hariharpur fort on the right side of Makwanpur. British were only 50 miles away from Kathmandu. As they were approaching Gurkha court, Gurkhas became restless imagining British occupying Kathmandu. In a hurry, Rajah rectified the treaty and Chandra Shekhar Upadhyay handed over rectified Treaty to the British in Makwanpur on 3rd of March. At that point, British mentioned to Chandra Shekhar Upadhyay that they should not expect the previous terms in Makwanpur. British had occupied Rapti Valley (currently spread over Chitwan district and Nawalparasi District), Hetauda and Hariharpur. Ochterlony now added these parts also in the treaty, Gurkhas had to cede these places too on which Chandra Shekhar Upadhyay agreed. Further he agreed to kneel down and present the rectified treaty to General in the presence of all the Vakeels in camp.

General concluded the treaty and dispatched Lieutenant Boileau of his staff to act as Resident at Kathmandu until next person was appointed.

The terms of the Sugaolee treaty were as follows:

1. There shall be perpetual peace and friendship between the East India Company and Nepal.
2. The king of Nepal will renounce all claims to the lands which were the subject of discussion between the two States before the war; and will acknowledge the right of the company to the sovereignty of those lands.

3. The king of Nepal will cede to the East India company, in perpetuity, all the under mentioned territories: i) The whole of low lands between the rivers Kali and Rapti. ii) The whole of low lands between Rapti and Gandaki, except Butwal. iii) The whole of low lands between Gandaki and Koshi in which the authority of the East India Company has been introduced, or is in actual course of introduction. iv) The whole of low lands between the rivers Mechi and Teesta. v) All the territories within the hills eastward of the Mechi river, including the fort and lands of Nagree and the Pass of Nagarcote, leading from Morang into the hills, together with the territory lying between the Pass and Nagree. The aforesaid territory shall be vacated by the Gorkha troops within forty days from this date.
4. With a view to indemnify the chiefs and Bhardars of Nepal, whose interest will suffer by the alienation of the lands ceded by the foregoing Article, the East India company agrees to settle pensions to the aggregate amount of two lakhs of rupees per annum on such chiefs as may be selected by the king of Nepal, and in the proportions which the Raja may fix. As soon as the selection is made, sunnuds shall be granted under the seal and signature of the Governor-General for the pensions respectively.
5. The king of Nepal renounces for himself, his heirs, and successors, all claim to the territories lying to the West of the River Kali, and engaged never to have any concern with those countries or the inhabitants thereof.
6. The king of Nepal engages never to molest or disturb the king of Sikkim in the possession of his territories. If any difference shall arise between Nepal and Sikkim, it shall be referred to the arbitration of the East India Company.
7. The king of Nepal hereby engages never to take or retain in his service any British subject, nor the subject of any European or American State, without the consent of the British Government.
8. In order to secure and improve the relations of amity and peace hereby established between two states, it is agreed that accredited Ministers from each side shall reside at the Court of the other.
9. This treaty, consisting of nine Articles, shall be ratified by the King of Nepal within 15 days from this date, and the ratification shall be

delivered to Lt. Col. Bradshaw, who engages to obtain and deliver to the king the ratification of the Governor-General within 20 days, or sooner, if practicable.

DONE at Sugaolee, on the 2nd day of December 1815. Paris Bradshaw, LT.-COL., P.A.

Received this treaty from Chandra Shekhar Upadhyay, Agent on the part of the Rajah of Nepal, in the valley of Makwanpur, at half-past two o'clock p.m. on 4 March 1816, and delivered to them the Counterpart Treaty on behalf of the British Government.

People of Madhesh, and its Role in the War

People living in Madhesh or their sympathizers can be divided into following categories:

1. **Gosain or Mahant or Abbot:** Gosain, also called Mahant or Abbot, were religious leaders of Hindu hermitage or temples. During the preparation of war, British were interested to get secret intelligence from those religious leaders, because they were believed to have been frequent travelers to Nepal Valley and had sufficient knowledge about paths to Kathmandu, which British were interested to know for military planning. J. Adams, Secretary of British East India Company wrote letter on September 30, 1814 with the same objective to Major Bradshaw[49]. At the same time, W. Moorcroft was preparing a report, in which it is said that the Matihani, a place 7 km East of Jaleshwar, temple Mahant had partial land in Tirhut of India, given by Darbhanga Maharaj and Partial land given by Nepal King. In the same report, these Mahants have been mentioned to have expressed their neutrality. However, the British anticipated them to be close to Nepal King, as both being Hindu had a common bond and believed those Mahants to pass the intelligence to Gurkha kings about the movement of British Army[50]. Thus, the British took conscious decision to hide the activities as much as possible from Matihani Mahant, simultaneously these Mahants were also frustrated by anyone asking for any information from them. At that time, Matihani Mahant had income from the vicinity of Kathmandu. Additionally they drew nine thousand rupees per annum from the village in Charaut, in Tirhut of India, about 5 km south of Matihani[51]. In the early phase

of war, Terai between Gandaki and Kosi was occupied by the British. Six villages were granted to Matihani Mahant under maffee sunned (rent free) by Gurkha Raja. Three of these villages were held as far back as by grant from Makwanpur Rajas and were sequestrated by Colonel Bradshaw. As per the letter written in February 7th, 1816, Ummee Das and Rundhale Das, Mahant of Matihani were kept under gentle detention since 18 months at Sugaolee camp suspecting that they had assisted enemy (Gurkha) during war[52]. Post war, the renegotiation of border boundary shows C curve near Matihani border and indicates, they might have preferred to remain with Nepal. Boundary demarcation is discussed in detail in last section of this Chapter. Even post war, Gurkha Kings maintained relationship with Hindu Mahant across border and good example of this is Mahant of Barahi, near Sursand in Sitamarhi district. Barahi is just on the border. Barahi Mahants, about three generations before, used to visit Kathmandu palace with Mangoes to impress King. Barahi Monastery was granted rent free land grants at Janakpur, Mujelia, Ramgopalpur (Chikna), Ramnagar, and few other places in interior hills[53].

2. **Jamindar:** British people ruling India were Christians and they had replaced Muslim rulers on Indian side. Both of them were looked upon with contempt by King Prithivi Narayan Shah, who claimed to make Gurkha domination as pure Hindu state '*ashal Hindustan*'. Thus, many landlords of the frontier, who were Hindus and lived for honor rather than worrying for daily livings, aligned with Shah Kings, because they did not want to be part of Mleccha state, a derogatory word used for British state, a notion of pure Hindu cult. After the war during border demarcation, there was agitation by a group of nine Jamindars[54] who did not want to be on Indian side of border. Most likely they sided with Gurkha Kings during 1814-1816 war. There is mention of village head Bassun Raut of Rautahat Tappa, who sided with British claim over 22 disputed villages along Champaran-Rautahat frontier.

3. **Common People:** Common people, who were poor cultivators, were busy in somehow managing their daily living. The British had plans to train and arm them. However, the idea, which had originated from Major Bradshaw, was dropped[55] after feedback from Magistrates

of Gorakhpur[56], Sarun[57] and Tirhut[58] reached the central decision makers. The feedback from the letter was as follows

a. Terai people are primarily farmers and their main occupation is agriculture.

b. Terai people are not fighter class, and are too scared, they even do not raise to face dacoits, even if their villages are attacked in night.

c. British giving arms to them might have raised unnecessary panic among people. Also, if Gorkha had even a slightest doubt, these people would have suffered. Gorkha people killed even on the slightest doubt and provocation. Also, Terai people would prefer traditional sticks rather than gun.

d. In case of arms, there was possibility of misuse. The head of village had little control over the people. The Jamindars, who mostly control the villages, were already been provided with arms. The Terai people were more migratory, because the land tenancy was fluid, and was given to highest bidders.

e. Terai people preferred to plunder other people rather than protecting themselves, implying they kept fighting their neighbors rather than invaders.

f. In such an event, where Gurkhas have raided the villages, they were told to approach British police station.

Within few days of war commencement in 1814, British occupied the whole of plains land, engaged local people and collected tax too. During that period of about two years, the common people seemed to be happy about British rule in Terai. In second week of November 1814, Bradshaw wrote[59] to J Adams "The inhabitants in general of the Terraie [Terai] have manifested satisfaction at being taken under the protection of the British Government and security has been received from almost all the civil officers and responsible persons in the Tuppah of Routehut [Rautahat] for the remaining balance of the year's revenue of which one third only has been collected by the Nepalese". He further added "Dia Dhauree the Nepalese Choudheree of the four Tuppahs of Bara lying East of the Bagmati namely Serleheea [Sarlahi], Kooderha, Burumpooree and Aseebhoo has also come in and given security for the remaining balance or one fourth of the annual revenue".

There is mention of Meer Jaffeer Shah, who was well known to Gurkhas[60] and helped British. He advised British to collect large number of elephants, and using elephants go into Jungle, which will make ways for following sepoys[61]. British acted upon the advice too. Similarly, Sheik Bad Ullah, who was formerly in the service of the Rajah of Nepal and then residing at Lowtun, knew the roads in the regions. He was employed by British to gather the intelligence. There are few more names likes Shem Bux, Kerit Nidhi Tiwari, Prem Chaowderee, Lattah Babu, Baddul Pathak, Seyfoo and Gangaram Butt who were employed by British in the plain to gather intelligence[62]. Hera Pathak Tharus and Mushars were also looked upon for help during war for making path through the jungle[63].

4. **Former Employees of Gurkha from plain origin:** Few people of plain origin were employed by Gurkha Raja in Nepal Valley during the initial days. Many of them ran away to plain, when they found themselves under awkward scenarios. Sunhaee Dss, a native of Tirhut, was one of them, who escaped from Kathmandu following Bagmati river route around 1812[64]. British followed him to extract information from him regarding the route to Kathmandu via Bagmati River. Similarly, there was Bahadur Sing who was employed in the office of Dewan at Kathmandu during King Ran Bahadur Shah's time, whose help British were looking forward to.

5. **Kins of Former King of plains:** Kins of former king ruling the lower lands in frontier became victims of attack from Gurkha Kings and fled to India. There they got the news that British were planning to attack Gurkha Kingdom. Among them, Makwanpur's heir, Palpa's heir and Tanahu's heir approached British to help in war, and British assured them that they will receive their kingdom back after completion of war.

   The heirs of Makwanpur family, Rajah Oodee Partap Sen, his brother Dherm Taj Sen and Dewan Soobhan Sen, who were living in Bettia on the grant of two village from Bettia King, reached British camp with few Kirati people, the loyalists of former Makwanpur Kingdom, and made agreement to help them[65]. However, that agreement did not go long way, because British found the influence of Makwanpur Rajah Families had diminished during the gap of around 50 years. Similarly, the agreement with Tanahu's heir Rajah Tej Partap Sen, who was living in Ramnagar (in Champaran) after expulsion, couldn't go beyond some initial discussions because British found them to be linked with Gurkha King through some means, and their loyalty couldn't be ascertained[66]. Rajah Ratan Sen, the son of Palpa's King Prithvipal Sen, and his uncle Samar Bahadur (also called Nadir Shah) helped British with useful information[67].

6. **Raja of bordering states (Bettia, Darbhanga, Awadh, etc.):** The Rajah of Bettia, Rajah Bir Kishore Singh, showed a laudable zeal in the service of British India Government. He was invited to bring forward a body of one thousand Burkundauzes or in such additional number. Also he was requested to form a corps of Rajputs in Tirhut[68]. Rajah of Tirhut, was also asked to raise a corps of Pathans and Rajputs living in the district of Tirhut[69]. Nawab of Awadh and Rajah of Tirhut, living in Darbhanga, provided Elephants during the war. The total number of Elephants employed was estimated in the aggregate at 1,115, excluding those 473 which were furnished by the Nawab Vizier and Rajah of Tirhut[70]. Nawab of Awadh also helped the British with loan of two crore to fund the war expenditure, out of which fifty-four lacs were the estimated expenditure of Gurkha-British war. Amrut Rao of Banaras provided 250 horses to British for the war.

British Rule in Madhesh

British force led by Bradshaw occupied Terai in November 1814. Gurkhas again occupied Terai on Jan 1st 1815. Lord Moira, the British Commander in Chief, made every effort to restore the British supremacy, and they again occupied Terai in March 1815. Since then Terai was under British rule till British handed over the Terai to Gurkha after the survey[71], which was completed in 1817. The understanding to give Terai to Gurkha was mentioned in Memorandum signed on 8th December 1816.

The interest and engagement of British in Terai was extensive. They collected tax during the rule, made arrangement for the security, engaged with different groups of people, surveyed different places.

In the letter written by Bradshaw on 12th December 1814 to J Adam, Secretary to Government, he appraised occupancy of Terai. He also mentioned "The inhabitants in general of the Terai have manifested satisfaction at being taken under the protection of the British Government". During the British rule in Terai, while collecting tax, they faced issues in collecting tax. First, there were many rent free land occupied for religious purpose[72]. And secondly collecting tax while war was still on, had its own challenge. Thus London office suggested Bradshaw not to apply "any compulsory measures for the realization of the revenue of the lands" and press "as lightly as possible" in order to facilitate reconciliation between the inhabitants and the British government[73].

Letter to J Adam, Secretary to Government from Bradshaw

Sir, I have the honour to announce to you, for the information of the Right Honourable the Governor General, that pursuant to instructions received from the Military Department, the Nepaulese Terraie was taken possession of by the force under my command on the morning of the 25th ultimo. This measure was effected by a combined movement of the three posts on the boundary. That at Adapoor advanced to Persah; Captain Hay's division moved forward and occupied Baragurhee; and the detachment at Ghorasehun, under my immediate direction, surprised with effect the Nepaulese force encamped at Burhurwa, and on the following day assumed its relative position six coss in advance at Hebeanpoor. The military details connected with the reduction of the enemy's Terraie on the frontier of Chumparun have been transmitted to the Head-Quarters of the Right Honourable the Commander in Chief. I do myself the honour to forward to you copies, in Persian and English, of the proclamation issued on the accomplishment of that measure, and to apprise you, for the information of the Right Honourable the Governor-General, that having visited the advanced posts of Keleeanpoor in the east, Baragurhee in the centre, and Persah on the west, and thus secured the newly acquired territory, I resigned, on the 11th instant, to Major General Marley the military authority with which I was invested, for the defence of the boundary and reduction of the enemy's Terraie on the frontier of Chumparun and Tirhoot. The occupation of the latter having been entrusted by me to Captain Roughsedge, I have to add that the latest accounts from that officer dated the 8th instant report the execution of that duty as far east as Janikpoor.

2. The inhabitants in general of the Terraie have manifested satisfaction at being taken under the protection of the British Government, and security has been received from almost all the civil officers and responsible persons in the Tuppah of Routehut, for the remaining balance of the year's revenue of which one third only has been collected by the Nepaulese.

3. Dia Dhauree, the Nepaulese Choudheree of the four Tuppahs of Bara lying east of the Baugmuttee namely Serleheea, Kooderha, Burumpooree and Aseebhoo has also come in and given security for the remaining balance, or one fourth of the annual revenue. The other eleven tuppahs of the Terraie are yet to be conciliated, and drawn to a willing submission to the regulations of Government. Those persons who have early come forward to acknowledge the British authority will possess a claim to consideration on the final settlement of the Terraie.

4. I have to inform you that the only prisoner taken in the surprise of the 25th ultimo, besides those who called for quarter, is Chunder Seekher Opadeea, the late Agent from the Rajah of Nepaul, charged with presents to the British Government. He surrendered himself in the evening of the above day on unconditional terms and his property has been shared as prize by the troops of the detachment. Among this person's effects were found three Persian letters under the red seal of the Rajah of Nepaul. One of them is addressed to the Right Honourable the Governor General, one to Mr Well and and one to Meer Jaffier Shah, the same of whom Mr Moorcroft had entertained so favourable an opinion. Previously to the transmission of those letters for the information of the Right Honourable the Governor General, I have deemed it to be proper to open peruse and take copies of them.

Camp Mahadara, 12th December 1814

Signed by

P BRADSHAW

Political Agent

Letter from Bradshaw declaring Terai to be under British Occupation in 1814. Source: PRNW, PP 371

British, during their rule, also contemplated to derive essential assistance from local inhabitants in the further execution of military operations[74].

Local inhabitants were employed in the revenue collection and guide department too[75].

After second time occupation of Terai, British surveyed the Janakpur area and gave detailed account of the region. In James Baillie Fraser word "Janickpore[Janakpur] is a place of much sanctity, where are temples of Janick[Janki] and Ram, described as very curious; their base is a regular square which decreases as the walls rise, and is at top covered with a dome, from which a spire arises. One of the great temples is covered with a plate of metal resembling gold, of great value; it is a building of four stories, from the corner of each of which are suspended seventy-two bells, it is a very great resort of pilgrims."[76]

Re-Negotiation

Boileau was the first Resident to Gurkha court and was replaced by Gardner in 3 months. Starting from the first day, the Resident was facing resistance from Gurkha and which indirectly indicated that there was challenge in the implementation of Treaty. Articles 3, 4 and 8 were the crux of the treaty, other points were more or less automatically taken care of by the implementation of these three articles. The British had, in the beginning itself, told the Gurkha that "either they take Resident or War", so point 8 of the article was also taken care of. Gurkha party was divided on the pension arguing that acceptance would make them subordinate to the British rule. Thus, they let expire the due date of informing British about the list of Chiefs who would get pension. At the same time, Gurkhas, in all the possible meetings, asked them to show generosity and give them Terai. Initially, they defined Terai to exclude jungle, however, soon British clarified, Terai do comprise Jungles up to the foot of hills.

The British understood the reluctance on the part of Gurkhas and were contemplating concession that can make treaty palatable to them. British wanted to have good terms with Gurkhas post-war scenario as good neighbor in the hope that they would allow passage of British commerce through the best route passing through Nepal Valley, compared to the route available in the newly acquired western hills. British also wanted to have good terms, so that the expenses to be incurred on army could be minimized through elimination of possible Gurkha incursion on the border in future. British were in hurry to get the terms of the treaty implemented, especially one related to the cessation of western Terai up to the hill, so that it can be handed over to Awadh Nawab, as promised earlier. The prolonged implementation of treaty implied extended hostility, thus, more expense on the Army as well as slowing down the procedure related with other British affairs in the rest parts of India. Additionally, Lord Moira was being questioned about the inflated balance sheet, where he had to add pension item of 2 lacs each year.

British had gained leverage in terms of acquiring Terai, however, they were not able to show the leverage is substantially beneficial to the British cause. British occupied Terai very early in the War, and since their occupation in November 1814 they collected taxes. During the tax collection, they found many lands were religious endowments[77] (rent free land, also called Guthi) to different monasteries and the total estimated rent was only 1,65,800 rupees which was less than required pension amount of two lacs[78]. Lord Moira was doubtful of the estimates; however, he had to rely on the data coming from the concerned officers. Lord Moira estimated Terai revenue to be eight lacs including Morang and Butwal[79]. Even Bum Sah estimated the revenue to be 10 lacs[80]. Further information was even more worrying for the British establishment. The health of the officers were degrading in the Terai while on posting, and about 1200 officers were sick in Western front alone, at a particulate point in time. The humidity, water current and unhealthy climate of Terai as well as the hot weather was not suiting them. All this together was making it harder to maintain the post[81], especially during the rainy season. Above all, the objective of the war was not territorial expansion. Rather it was to define and secure the northern boundary of the East India Company's possessions and to reinforce the people's faith in Company's government by defending the subjects under its protection[82]. Magistrate of Gorakhpur noted, "I am not aware of any objection to the whole or any part of Terai bordering on the Gorakhpur district being ceded to the Gorkha Government"[83].

Evaluating all the pros-cons, British was all prepared to pass anything, including low land between Kosi-Gandaki, except demand for Residency, to establish peace with Gurkha.

To make the matter worse, Chinese arrived in the northern frontier in the August 1816, while British were working on implementation of Treaty. Bhimsen was in awkward position vis-a-vis Chinese, because the Treaty was signed and they had not paid tax for last few years, a custom enforced upon them by Chinese after 1792 war defeat. However, Bhimsen wanted to make maximum out of this situation. Gurkha tried their best to put Chinese and British against each other, so that dispute erupts between them, and in the ensuing collusion Gurkhas emerge winner. Gurkhas told the British that Chinese were upset because of opening of a Residency and they have not sent present to the emperor. Further, Gurkha proposed that they want to stay aligned with British power and requested British to help push China away from the Nepal. However, British handled the scenario smartly, and said they have no issue if Gurkha continue relationship with China too. Taking this opportunity, Gurkha also asked for recovery of Terai region. On other hand, they approached Chinese officer asking their favor to remove residency from Kathmandu. The minutes of their meeting[84] give details of the communication between Chinese and Gurkha Vakeels, Dilbunjun Pande and Colonel Runbeer Singh Thapa.

Chinese officer Cheeoon Chang said "You Goorkhas are a mischievous race, and have caused the ruin of many Rajas. Digurchee, too, you plundered without any provocation; and now you have thought to enact the Digurchee scene in connection with English, and so murdered their police-officer, after settling the question by negotiation. You have been punished justly; — you wrote to us of war, and have since written off peace; yet still ask for our aid. — What kind of peace is this?" The Nepalese urged that if not inclined to give assistance to recover what had been lost, the Chinese authorities would, at least, lend their good offices to facilitate the removal of the Residency from Katmandoo. Cheeoon Chang replied, "You wrote that it was to establish a factory that the English had come; why should I remove merchants?" Dilbunjun, one of the Vakeels, on this said, "They were not merchants, but soldiers and officers that they desired to be rid of." Cheeoon Chang replied, "The English have written that their object is to cement peace; and it appears you have agreed to receive the Resident. You wrote to us that the English had demanded the passes into Koten China; but we know this is false; — if they desired to come to China, it would not be by that route."

In Lord Moira's letter written on Aug 6, 1816, there is mention of question from British people that "The advantage acquired in the field were not duly insisted on in the condition of peace", on which Lord Moira provides his clarification as:

"The principal of the negotiation on my part was that our future tranquility made it necessary to debilitate the Goorka State as far as might be done without entirely overthrowing the old Government. We should have had infinite trouble in the formation and maintenance of any other Government and we might also have dissatisfied the Chinese by setting up a dependent of our own. But the old Government could not exist without a certain extent of resources. These considerations dictated the instructions to Sir David Ochterlony at the outset of the second campaign that success was not to occasion any demand additional to the terms of the original treaty"

After British agreed on giving Terai between Kosi and Gandaki to Gurkha, Bhimsen Thapa proposed to replace old treaty with new Treaty. British rejected the replacement of treaty, as it could have opened a new cycle of negotiations, and insisted, the concessions were gift, and no negotiation will be done. On paper, it would be in the form of memorandum in addition to the original treaty. However, the issue aroused about the people of lowland plain, who were under British rule since November 1814. British took initiative to communicate with the people of plains, who were not happy with the decision to handover the Terai to Gurkha[85]. Thus, in the memorandum, which was presented on 8th December 1816 and signed on 11th December 1816, there is mention of the provision regarding plain's people to protect them from Gurkha's punishment: "Moreover, the Rajah of Nipal agrees to refrain from prosecuting any inhabitants of the Terai, after its revertance to his rule, on account of having favoured the cause of the British Government during the war, and should any of those persons, excepting the cultivators of the soil, be desirous of quitting their estates, and of retiring within the Company's territories, he shall not be liable to hindrance." This provision was beneficial to the people other than cultivators of the soil. But, this would not have mattered in case of cultivators mostly because, land belonged to the state, and cultivator was nothing more than the renter of small piece of land sufficient to take care of his family and who would keep changing his location, where the favorable terms of the rent was available.

The Eastern and Western border were separated by Mechi and Kali Rivers respectively, thus there was no question on the limit of border. However, Terai was a big plain land with no physical separation line to draw border. Thus, the last point on the memorandum mentions about survey and clear demarcation of border. We will discuss the border demarcation process and other issues.

Border Demarcation

Border concept was new to the different rulers in Indian subcontinent and for them state boundary was boundary of nature like river, jungle, mountain ridge. Village boundary formed the final boundary of state or country. The extension of boundary came with the power of sword and flexing of muscle. Fixed pillar based linear boundary was European concept and Company officials were obsessed with it[86]. During the treaty, Eastern boundary was fixed as Mechi River and Western boundary was fixed as Mahakali River that Gurkhali accepted readily. As per the initial Treaty done on December 2nd 1815, and signed and returned by Gurkha agents on March 4th 1816, "low lands" lying between river Mahakali and Mechi needed to be ceded and attached to Company. However, dispute arose in case of "low lands" lying between river Mahakali and Mechi because "low land" had multiple ramifications to the Gurkha state; (1) Terai provided the financial support for army maintenance and expansion (2) Terai provided the saltpeter required for manufacturing of ammunition and (3) Many army veterans had stake in Terai in the form of land grants. Major Bradshaw first received overtures from Kathmandu regarding Terai cessation, through Raj Guru Gajraj Mishra. He then went to Kathmandu for consultation. In the month of June 1815, to restart the negotiation, Chautaria Bum Shah crossed Kali river and opened communication with Mr. Gardner with the objective of obtaining permanent peace. In the communication he wrote to Mr. Gardner

"Never will we consent to give up to you the Terai; take the Terai, and you will leave us without the means of subsistence, for the hills, without it, are worth nothing. The Terai, is of no use to you, because your people cannot live in it, or keep it, and in wresting it from your hands we will devastate your provinces down to the Ganges"[87]

In the follow up memorandum signed on December 8th 1816, Company agreed to give "low land" to Gurkha king and in return company removed the condition of paying two lakhs of rupee per annum to Gurkha court. Another issue was attached with the new provision; how to draw border in "low land" between Company and Gurkha? Thus through the same memorandum, provision of Commissioner was included with the objective of "arranging in concert a well-defined boundary... establishing a straight line of frontier". There were visible challenge of having straight line frontier (1) establishing the base line on which further refinement of straight line would be done (2) to make the frontier straight, there was need for exchange of lands between state (3) in course of drawing straight line, few individual property was about to be falling in both countries, thus adjustment had to be made such that individual property falls within one country only.

The base line for demarcation started with the former frontier which was agreed in year 1812 between commissioners of two governments. In exchange for annulling the two lakh pension proposal, British was ready to restore Terai situated between Kosi and Rapti, with the exception of two Koses (about 4 miles) of territory in depth from the most Northern projecting point of the former frontier. The disputed portions of territory on Tirhut and Sarun frontier and certain other places of commercial importance (Simraungadh, Janakpur, Jaleshwar, Roopelaugarh) were not to be restored in the deal[88]. Resident Gardner, who was in Kathmandu, reported that Gorkha court showed satisfaction and not a single objection was raised on annulment of pension. However, in the hope of securing as much as possible, Gurkha proposed to consider Southern most point of former frontier and two Koses of territory in depth from that line. Taksari (chief minting officer) Chandra Shekhar Upadhyay, who had land holding in Mahottari frontier and was about to lose, even argued that the reverted Terai would not be equal to two lakhs of rupees. British primary objective of insisting two Koses was to remove all future troubles, therefore resident was advised not to follow two koses rigidly and come to an understanding with Darbar on Principles and insist on lands which were essential for the British subjects. Eventually, Bhimsen and Gardner decided to relax two koses to half kose from Southern most point. The regular compliance of British on their request, convinced Gurkha to request restoration of even the remaining half kose, assuring British that no future dispute would arise after proper demarcation is complete[89]. British agreed to remaining half kose request, given its insignificance to British and fast approaching good season. Accordingly, Resident Gardner prepared a memorandum of restoration of low land (now mentioned as Terai in memorandum) from Kosi to Rapti, and presented to young King Rajendra Vikram Shah on December 8th, 1816, the day of his accession.

After both sides agreed to demarcate the boundary on the basis of actual occupation, another challenge came to the survey officers while going on

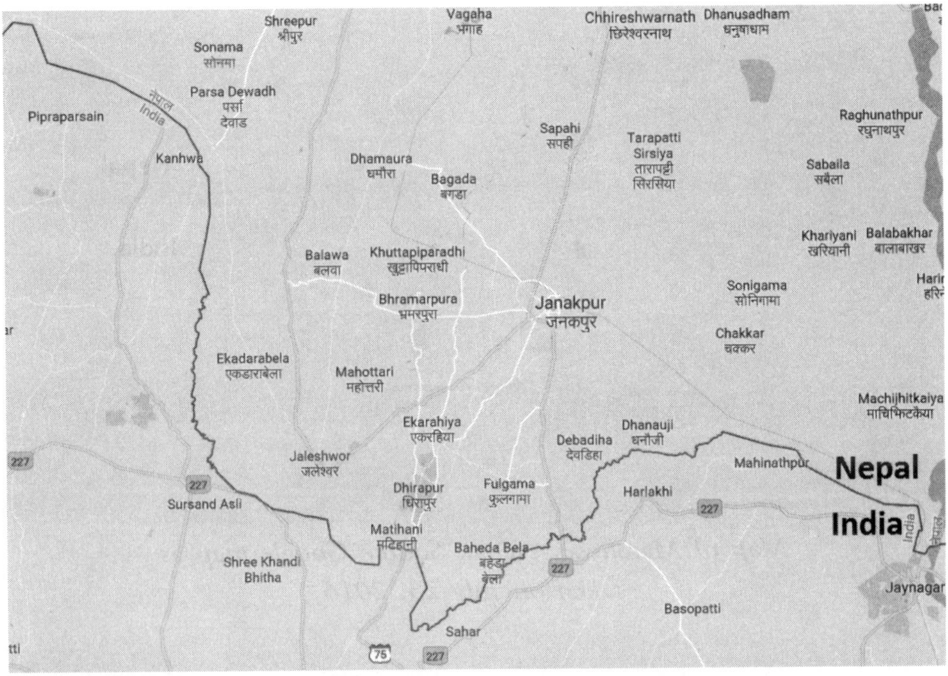

Map of Janakpur showing bulge towards India till Matihani. Source Google Map as taken on July 23, 2016

ground. The inhabitants of villages, which were under the actual occupation of Nepal, suppressed the receipts issued to them by the Nepal government, and defected to the British, because the Nepali administration at the time followed a strict policy against them. This reduced the territories of Nepal, with the result that in Sarlahi the boundary came to be located near the Chure range. But Janakpur was held to be within Nepal's line of control, because the temple had a roof with Jhingati tiles. Thanks to the use of Jhingatis in that temple, the plain areas far to the south of the Chure range within Mahottari district were held to be under Nepal's control. Amar Singh had the temple of Rama in Janakpur roofed with Jhingatis[90].

There were few local landlords (Jamindars) who wanted to stay within Gurkha kingdom. A group of nine Jamindars started movement

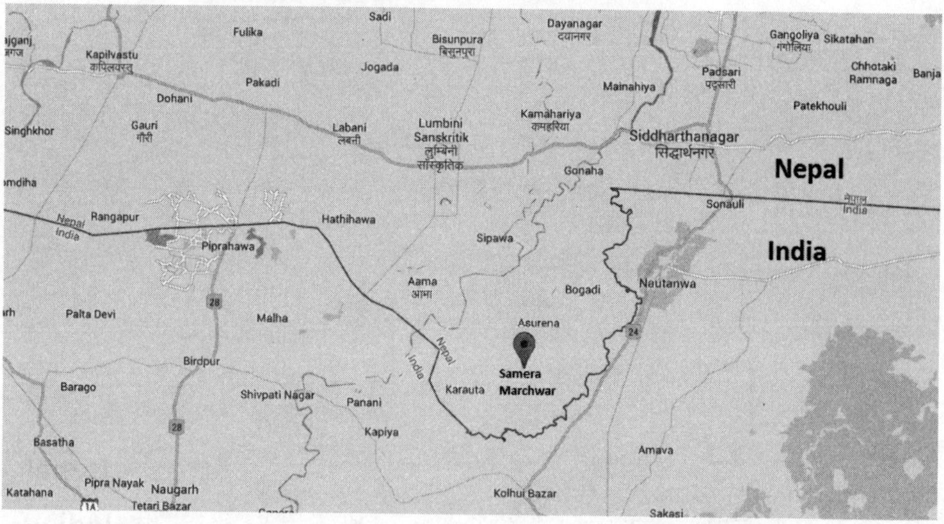

Map of Marchwar, Nepal. Source Google map as taken on July 23, 2016

and went till Kosi River saying they don't want to go with Mlechha (British) occupation, considering religion line. On their way, they had tent in Matihani, a place close to Janakpur and which had very powerful Hindu Abbot of that time having direct reach to Kings, where they were taken in British custody, however released soon as per the pre-agreed terms between governments[91]. Matihani monastery is still present and lies in Nepal barely few yards away from actual border point and most of the nearby people's settlement lies within India. Another point of reference is of Marchwar, close to Lumbini's Buddha Pillar in the western Nepal, map of which looks almost like half-moon attached to the almost straight lines (see google map), who's landlord decided to stay with Gurkha administration[92].

In another instance, Pachrauta (Tappa of Rautahat) was divided in two, with the northern half going to Gorkha and the southern half going to one Ram Bux Singh[93].

The frontier lines along Gorakhpur-Butwal, Saran-Rautahat, Tirhut-Saptari-Mahottari, Purnia-Morang were defined and marked with pillar in 1817[94].

Notes

1. Aitchison, C.U (1863), A Collection of Treaties, Engagements, and Sunnuds, Relating to India and Neighbouring Countries, Volume 2, India Foreign and Political Dept, 1863, PP 208-209
2. Hamilton p. 167
3. Fraser, James Baillie (1820), Publisher London, 1820
4. Gerald Bryant, "Officers of the East India Company's army in the days of Clive and Hastings", The Journal of Imperial and Commonwealth History (1978) pp 203-27
5. Robins, Nick. "This Imperious Company - The East India Company and the Modern Multinational - Nick Robins - Gresham College Lectures". Gresham Colelge Lectures. Gresham College. Retrieved 24 June 2016
6. Cowan, Sam (2009); Ochterlony's men, Himal Magazine, Published May 2009
7. Chaudhury, P.C. Roy (1964); Darbhanga, Bihar District Gazetteers, Secretariat Press, Bihar, Patna, pp 31
8. Stiller, L.F (1989) Prithvi Narayan Shah in The Light of Dibya Upadesh, Kathmandu, 1989
9. PRNW page 680
10. Pradhan, K.l (2012); Thapa Politics in Nepal: With Special Reference to Bhim Sen Thapa, 1806-1839, pp 68
11. Political Consultation, 15 May 1813, No 39, Letter of the governor general to the raja of Nepal, dated 7 May 1813
12. Political Consultation, 2 October 1813, No 39. Letter of the raja of Nepal to the governor general, received 5 August 1813
13. 'Rajah Sitabroy's Account of the Pergunnah Tauter belonging to Sircar Tirhut in the Bahar Province, letter published in Bengal: Past and Present, Volume 44, Part 1, Calcutta Historical Society., 1932 pp 43-52
14. Letter sent to Joseph Jekyll Esqre from Fort William, letter published in Bengal: Past and Present, Volume 44, Part 1, Calcutta Historical Society., 1932 pp 43-52
15. Bengal District Gazetteers, Volume 34, Part 1, Bengal Secretariat Book Department, 1907 pp 23
16. Adam. J, Sec to Govt, The Gentleman's Magazine (London, England), Volume 118, 1815, page 361
17. The Gentleman's Magazine (London, England), Volume 118, 1815, page 361
18. Prinsep, Henry Thoby (1825). History of the Political and Military Transactions in India During the Administration of the Marquess of Hastings, 1813–1823 1. London: Kingsbury, Parbury & Allen, pp 83-85
19. Smith, Thomas (1852). Narrative of a five-year's residence at Nepaul. Vol 1. London: Colburn and Co, pp 187-212
20. PRNW page 722
21. 159. Prinsep, Henry Thoby (1925), History of the Political and Military Transactions in India during the Administration of the Marques of Hastings 1813-1823, Kingsbury, Parbury & Allen, 1825 , pp 457 http://books.google.com/books?id=Tq1jAAAAMAAJ

22. Ibid pp 460
23. Ibid pp 463
24. Supply of Saltpeter, Regmi Research Collection, vol. 39, pp. 305-7
25. PRNW, pp 363
26. PRNW, pp 524
27. PRNW, pp 743
28. PRNW, pp 310
29. PRNW, pp 309
30. PRNW, pp 482
31. PRNW, pp 370-371
32. PRNW, pp 745
33. PRNW, pp 547
34. PRNW, pp 547
35. PRNW, pp 747
36. PRNW, pp 626
37. PRNW, pp 627
38. PRNW, pp 627
39. Bara-Parsa and Mahottari
40. Letter from Amar Singh Thapa to Rajah, PRNW, pp 553
41. Letter from Amar Singh Thapa to Rajah, PRNW, pp 557
42. PRNW, pp 565
43. Lord Moira, PRNW, 565
44. Welpton, John (1991); Kings, Soldiers and Priest, Appendix VI, The Guru Families
45. PRNW, pp 803
46. Letter from J Adams (Secretary to Government) to Lieutenant Colonel Bradshaw, written Dec 9th, 1815, PRNW, pp 852-856
47. Letter from Lieutenant Colonel Bradshaw to J Adam, Dec 2nd, 1815, PRNW, pp 851
48. Prinsep, Henry Thoby (1825), History of the political and military transactions in India during the administration of the Marquess of Hastings, 1813-1823, Vol 1. London: Kingsbury, Parbury & Allen., pp 200
49. PRNW 61
50. PRNW 82.
51. PRNW 83
52. PRNW 918
53. Based on local interview from native of Barahi
54. Lal, CK (2011), Nepaliya hunulai (To become Nepalese), Martin Chautari, 2011, PP 105
55. Letter to Major Bradshaw from J. Adams, PRNW 352

56. Letter from Magistrate of Goruckpore to John Monckton, PRNW pp 415
57. Letter from Magistrate of Sarun to John Monckton, PRNW pp 416
58. Letter from Magistrate of Tirhoot to John Monckton, PRNW, pp 418
59. Letter from Bradshaw To J Adam Esq Secretary to Government, PRNW 370-371
60. PRNW, pp 342
61. PRNW, pp 280
62. PRNW, pp 174
63. PRNW, pp 366
64. PRNW 91, 92, 251 and 252
65. PRNW, pp 375
66. PRNW, pp 374
67. PRNW, pp 316-317
68. PRNW, pp 352
69. PRNW, pp 353
70. PRNW, pp 974
71. Political Consultation, A Campbell's Report on Political Transactions with Nepal, A Sketch of Political Relations with Nepal, 18 September 1837, as mentioned in Bikrama Jit Hasrat's History of Nepal (1871) PP 191-192
72. PRNW, pp 919
73. PRNW, pp 920
74. PRNW, pp 920
75. PRNW, pp 912
76. Fraser, James Baillie (1820); Journal of a tour through part of the snowy range of the Himala mountain and to the sources of the rivers Jumna and Ganges, Rodwell, 1820, pp 23
77. PRNW, 919
78. PRNW, pp 748
79. PRNW, pp 565
80. PRNW, pp 776
81. PRNW, pp 854
82. Cowan, Sam (2009); Ochterlony's men; book review of Britain's Gurkha War: The invasion of Nepal, 1814-16 by John Pemble, The Himal, Published May 2009
83. Ramakant (47), Indo-Nepalese Relations, 1968, pp 47
84. Prinsep, Henry Thoby (1825). History of the Political and Military Transactions in India During the Administration of the Marquess of Hastings, 1813–1823 1. London: Kingsbury, Parbury & Allen, pp 210-212
85. PRNW, pp 849
86. Michael, Bernandro A. (2013), State Making and Territory in South Asia, Lesson from the Anglo-Gorkha War (1814-1816), 2013 PP 95

87. Political Consultation, A Campbell's Report on Political Transactions with Nepal, A Sketch of Political Relations with Nepal, 18 September 1837, as mentioned in Bikrama Jit Hasrat's History of Nepal (1871) PP 186

88. Foreign Secret Consultation, August 24, 1816 –No 7, as quoted in Indo-Nepalese Relations by Ramakant 1968.

89. Foreign Political Consultation, November 2nd, 1816 –No 33, as quoted in Indo-Nepalese Relations by Ramakant 1968.

90. Acharya, Baburam (1975), Social Changes During the Early Shah period, Regmi Research Series, Year 7, No. 9, 1975, PP 166

91. Lal, CK (2011), *Nepaliya hunulai* (To become Nepalese), Martin Chautari, 2011, PP 105

92. Lal, CK (2011), *Nepaliya hunulai* (To become Nepalese), Martin Chautari, 2011, PP 105

93. Napal Correspondence, , Saran Collectorate Records, BSA, as mentioned in PP 183 of Bernandro A Michael State, Making and Territory in South Asia

94. Political Consultation, A Campbell's Report on Political Transactions with Nepal, A Sketch of Political Relations with Nepal, 18 September 1837, as mentioned in Bikrama Jit Hasrat's History of Nepal (1871) PP 191-192.

5

Rent and Silent Cry - Post-war Effect on the People of Madhesh

Rise of Border – Division of Civilization

The 'Low Land' people were all same, their civilization, and culture were same and they are same even today. However, the border lines that were drawn through Sugaolee treaty, are mostly imaginary line on the ground, occasionally get reincarnated into real wall of separation[1]. Since the time immemorial, low lands below Himalayan range were under Awadh and Tirhut/Mithila/Videha cultures, both separated by Gandaki River and connected by numerous links. Tharu culture shares the attributes of either of these cultures though Tharu are unique in their practice too. The Hindu epic Ramayana has hero Ram from Awadh and Heroin Sita from Mithila. Buddha was born in Awadh and travelled to Mithila, the center of education, to make way towards enlightenment. The ballad of Allah-Udal connects Awadh and Mithila. However, the Anglo-Gorkha treaty of 1816 split both the cultures horizontally from East to West. The notion that individuals along the boundary could owe allegiance, taxes and obedience to one government only was gradually enforced. This impacted the blood relationship, families, culture and civilization that keep hurting today too. In many places, a room of house can be seen at one side and other room at another side. Roads along frontier are commonly used by villagers of both sides. The local marts attract people across the frontier. Marriage is common across the border. However in all these, people have to go through the procedural government hurdles which are increasing day by day. Local vehicle cannot cross frontier without registration and paying tolls. Agricultural resources across frontier cannot be shared among families without bribing the custom officials. In case of natural calamities like flood or earthquake that are common in the region and need large scale cooperation to get overcome, people across border cannot come together to strengthen each other's hand.

No Man's Land in Parsa District. Photo Credit The Kathmandu Post

Breaking of Human Ties Between Different Ethnic Groups

Long before rise of Gurkha king Prithivi Narayan, Kathmandu, Lalitpur, and Bhaktapur were collectively being called as Nepal valley, which was, at that point in time, cosmopolitan in true sense. The Nepal valley, which was primarily occupied by native Newar people, was open to all without any barrier. Christian missionary Father Giuseppe lived at Kathmandu during King Jay Prakash Malla rule. Kashmiri Muslim traders were welcomed in the valley. Muslim had built architectural buildings, including Rani Pokhari[2]. Tirhutia Army was recruited in the Newari Kingdom. Even King Prithivi Narayan Shah invited 100 families of Tirhutia Brahmin and gave large track of land to them because Tirhutia Brahmin were believed to be superior and purer than hilly Brahmins, whom King wanted to have for his religious duties[3]. Khas (called Parbatia) people also visited Nepal valley for their day to day purpose. Indian pilgrims used to visit Hindu lord Pashupati round the years. Pashupati used to get head priest from South India, a tradition continued since Shankaracharya days. Buddhist follower from different parts of world looked towards Swayambhu temple. After Firoz Shah Tuglak, a Muslim fighter, attacked and defeated last Karnat dynasty King Harisingh Dev, King, along with his many subjects fled from low land to Nepal

Valley, and was believed to have established rule, too. Since then many Malla kings invited Tirhutia (also called Maithil) scholars to Kathmandu for administrative reforms or religious discussions[4]. Newar Kings were themselves fluent in Maithili, a language of low land plain, and had written many poems and books too. There is hand-written manuscript of a collection of Maithili lyrical songs composed in a Newari script by King Jagatprakash Malla of Bhaktapur in 1662 CE. In the eastern hill, Sen Kings, who were culturally plain kings, were having joint rule with Kirâti people. The king was of low land origin and ministers were of hilly origin. The ease of access to Nepal valley can be understood from the fact that widow Kantivati (who later became queen of King Ran Bahadur. See box for more details), and her family had went to Pashupati temple walking on foot from Janakpur. Further it should be understood on the light that they went to Pashupati temple, which should have been too common a practice in those days, to complete a post-death religious ritual of someone dear.

However, the cordial relationship of hill-plain, which was deteriorating since King Prithivi Narayan Shah's accession to Kathmandu throne, almost stopped after Sugaolee treaty. Newars, who was fearful themselves after their native rule uprooting, were not allowed to interact with low land people and vice versa. Similar was the case with Kirati people, whose relationship came to an abrupt halt with low land people due to strict blockade imposed on Gurkha regime, who were new rulers in the land.

About Queen Kantivati

Queen Kantivati was born Kantivati Mishra, Maithil Brahmin, from Bindhi village; the village where we now have Janakpur Bus Stand, and lies 2 km South of Janakpur zero-mile in highway connecting Jaleshwar. Kantivati Mishra belonged to Jamindar family. In Mithila history Brahmin had long history of being Jamindar, including Darbhanga Maharaj. Kantivati first husband died untimely. Post her husband's death, it might be for her peace, she was on religious visit to Pashupati. It is said, King Rana Bahadur saw her on the bank of Bagmati and got infatuated by her Beauty. However, it should also be assumed, Rana bahadur, a cleaver and mighty, was already having prior information about her. King Rana Bahadur kidnapped Kantivati and kept her in captive for long time, persuading her for marriage. On this marriage proposal, there was a lot of politics within Royal family, within royal Durbar political players and from Kantivati family side.

Widow Kantivati was reluctant to marry King, because Maithil Brahmin culture don't permit re-marry, practiced even today. This denial lead her to permanent house arrest of her within Durbar. Finally, she put the hard condition, assuming not to be accepted by King, that the son to be born of her & King Rana Bahadur should be made King than only she can marry King Rana Bahadur.

Second queen Subarna Prabha was not in favor of this marriage because her two elder son's rights to become King was going to be denied. Whereas first queen Raj Rajeshwari Devi, who had no son, was favoring this marriage. Along the line of queens, the royal ministers/courtier were also divided.

General public and mostly Brahman of Kathmandu were opposed saying marriage was illegitimate and impure because (1) Kantivati was widow and (2) Kantivati was Brahmin and King was Chhetri.

Finally, marriage took placed in Gurkha and couple brought to Kathmandu. Kantivati was declared Maharani. Maharani Kantivati soon gave birth to Girvan Judh Bir Bikram. Soon, Kantivati was not feeling well, and she wished to have King's commitment fulfilled, to declare Girvan as King. While Girvan was just 2 years, he was made King in presence of then courtier. All the major courtiers then gave their approvals in writing. To further legitimize the Girvan as King, Rana bahadur invited powerful King Prithvipal Sen of Palpa to coronation, who put the crown to King Girvan. Rana Bahadur became guide to King also called regent. Maharani Kantivati health was not doing well, so she died soon. While she was ill, she donated a lot to get god's blessing.

The marriage of Kantivati to Ran Bahadur left many open questions. Political drama of Royal family, Royal courtier, and Kathmandu's people are well written. However the politics of Kantivati family is less discussed.

(a) How would King Rana Bahadur notice a person in the bank of Bagmati in the crowd of hundreds? Since centuries, predating Gurkha rule, plain people use to visit Pashupati on the occasion of Shivratri in thousands. Kantivati might have also been one of the pilgrimage along with families.

(b) Why would King marry a Brahmin and that too widow against the wish of then leaders following Hindu belief of having pure blood?

(c) Even if King was infatuated with Kantivati's beauty, why King would declare her Maharani, rather than keeping Kantivati as another simple queen, given the facts that King Rana Bahadur was very cruel, merciless and powerful king. King Rana Bahadur had around nine queens. Two were married already to Rana Bahadur before Kantivati came into his life.

(d) Why would Gurkha King marry a Madhesi people, despite his grandfather King P N Shah having contempt for the Madhesi people? We should remember that King P N Shah disbanded Tirhutia Army of King Jai Prakash after becoming King of Kathmandu. Also, queens married to King Rana Bahadur that had royal linkage to other states like (i) Maharani Raj Rajeshwari Devi was grand-daughter of Raja Shiva Shah, Raja of Gulmi (ii) Maharani Subarna Prabha Devi Subudhi Khadka Basniyat of Gorakhpur (iii) Lalita Tripura Sundari Devi, who ruled Nepal for almost three decades in collaboration of Bhim Sen Thapa, was from Thapa family.

(e) How can King Rana Bahadur, the king of Gurkha, listen 'No' from Kantivati for such a long time despite Kantivati being in captive in Kathmandu durbar? Kantivati took few months to accept the proposal after King agreed that their to-be born son will be declared King.

(f) Gurkha Kingdom believed in Dand-Vhed-Shaam-Daam, so why would powerful Gurkha King negotiate and Kneel down to Kantivati terms?

The answer to these questions is hidden in the fact that Kantivati was big landlord[5]. Additionally, she might have inherited her husband property. Together having value of tens of thousands in yearly tax in those days. Additionally, its high probable that negotiation power of Kantivati was very high as Kantivati family could have got support, if required, from Darbhanga Maharaj because both of them being Maithil Brahmin and physically Bindhi being close to Darbhanga. Thus we also find that to consolidate every chance to capture the Kantivati's property, King Rana Bahadur married Kantivati's sister Lakshmishvari after Kantivati's death. It could be that Lakshmishvari might have married to take care of King Girvan, who was just 2 years, however we don't find Lakshmishvari being King Girvan regent. Lalit Tripura Sundari became regent and remained in power for three decades. Kantivati was able to safely play this politics because of his father (Ganesh Dutt Mishra) support. It was Ganesh Dutt's idea to give counter proposal to King Rana Bahadur to accept the to-be born Kantivati's son as King, if King Rana Bahadur wanted to marry widow Kantivati.

Introduction of Passport and Blockade Against Plain People

Passport regulation was introduced in the January 1800 with the objective to "Maintain a constant watch on people, high or low, who come from the South, or go there"[6]. The regulative order was circulated among the officers of Makwanpur, Chitlang, Chisapani, Bhimphedi, Hetauda, Bichhakhori, and Parsa, which fell in the main route from Birgunj to Kathmandu. The regulation provided authority to detain any in coming person from southern territories. Only those persons were permitted who were allowed to pass after proper scrutiny. Another salient feature of Passport regulation was that even to leave Gurkha government territories valid passport was required.

On December 8, 1816 final memorandum was signed that crystalized the Sugaolee Treaty. A week after (Nepali date Poush Sudi 3, 1873) Kathmandu court sent order to regional officer Bhimsen Baniya in Sindhuli to "Remove all settlements from the area south of the Mahabharat Mountains, north of the Churia hills, west of Kawala and east of Pipaldanda. Close all tracks in that area and let it grow as a forest"[7]. On the same day orders were sent to junior officers in the Mahabharat range to "Close all tracks in the area and render them unusable by planting bamboo, cane and thorny bushes"[8].

Slowdown in Development

Much of the impetus for road building in the Sarun and Tirhut area came from "military and political objects," specifically the outbreaks of war with Nepal[9]. The impulse for developing a network of roads in Tirhut, as in the case of Champaran, came during the Nepalese war and was supported by the indigo planters. One road that attracted considerable official attention was the connection between Muzaffarpur and the cantonment of Mallai, located almost at the Nepal border.

The roads in north Bihar were as good as, if not better than, those found anywhere else in Bengal[10]. On the Gurkha side of the frontier, the policy was to adhere to protectionism and isolation, thus non-development became tool to enforce the formerly stated policy. On the eve of Anglo-Gurkha war, British noted, Nepalese had adopted the policy of using certain bad roads commonly and reserving better one for particular purpose or special season[11].

Till 1958, when bypass road was built by Indian Army in cooperation with Nepal, people had to walk from plain to reach Kathmandu.

In 1851 Jung Bahadur, when (British) pressurized to make a good road from the plains of India to the valley of Nepal, stated that the prejudices of his countrymen were very strong against this being done: they thought that while the roads remained in their present condition no invading army could make its way to the valley.

Similar was the response from Rana PM Ranodip Singh Kunwar. In 1880 a conference held at Faizabad, discussed the impact of road in trade with Nepal, and decided to bring pressure on Nepal Government to maintain and repair portions of roads on the Nepal side leading to marts to be traversed by carts. In fact, better road was boosting export from Nepal to India. The British resident in Nepal, Gridlestone, informed the Secretary of State, on the basis of Report prepared by Government of North Western Provinces, that export went from 215,199 mounds worth Rs. 258,731 (from April 1st 1875 to March 31st, 1880) to 220,878 mounds worth Rs. 927,688 (from April 1880 to March 31, 1881). Hence there was increase in both volume and value when the road was good[12].

It was calculated that there will be around 400 miles of road to connect principal Terai marts and each mile costing around Rs. 25 for maintenance. Thus total of Rs. 10,000 per annum. It was assumed to be wise decision to spend a portion of taxes for the maintenance of communication, which, in turn, will boost the trade and thereby both Durbar and its subjects will be benefitted. Rana Prime Minster, Ranodip Singh, was not inclined to meet the British request of having general improvement in road on plea of poverty and lack of labor. Resident Gridlestone rejected the PM plea of poverty and labor saying, thousands had been spent on temple constructions in Kathmandu and hundreds of coolies were employed to carry rice from Terai to Valley. Gridlestone further mentioned "a yearly expenditure of Rs. 10,000 would probably meet all reasonable requirements of Nepal to maintain the roads which equals to interest at 5 percent on Rs 2,00,000 that is half the sum (i.e. four lakhs of Rupees), which the Prime Minister is taking from the state treasury for expenditure on the tour in British India"[13]. The Prime Minister did not meet the terms of improvement of the roads and communications, and reason pushed forward was serious physical difficulties of maintaining the road throughout the year.

Tougher for Trader, Commerce, and Kashmiri House

The trade route between Indian plains and Tibet that was once flourishing and which had become root cause of dispute between the then Gorkha King Prithivi Narayan Shah and Kathmandu King Jay Prakash Malla, started declining after accession of Gurkha in Kathmandu. After defeat of Gurkha in Anglo-Gurkha war, the policy of Bhim Sen was to break direct link between Tibetan and Englishmen. Bhim Sen once said,

> *"If Tibetians and Firangis (i.e Foreigners or, in the contemporary context, Englishmen) meet and trade with each other, our ryots and trades will lose their employment and the results will not be good. Therefore, the native traders were strictly forbidden to deal directly with the English"*[14]

Government supported trade monopolies which were installed to act as intermediaries between local traders and English. Revenue appropriated through these sources increased the government income, however in long term this was killing the entrepreneurship capability of the people.

The age old Kashmiri House in Kathmandu was discouraged and most Kashmiri Muslim traders were expelled from Kathmandu valley. A Kashmiri commercial house was established at Patna about two centuries ago (prior to Anglo-Gurkha war). It had agents and depots in Kashmir, Nepaul, Lassa, Silink, on the frontier of China Proper and at Dhaka. The principal business of the branch at Patna was through minor agents to collect otter at Dacca and its neighborhood. These were transmitted through Nepaul Valley by Lassa to China and the return for each dispatch was made every two years principally in gold[15].

After King Prithivi Narayan accession to Kathmandu, Christian missionary, Gosains (Hindu merchants) were expelled and severe restrictions were imposed on the Kashmiri merchant houses. By 1774 only two such trading houses were functioning in Nepal valley. Two other Kashmiri trading houses opened branches in Bhutan after being expelled from Nepal valley, but as they were prohibited from trading in broad cloth and several other popular commodities, the volume of trade declined drastically[16].

On the eve of Anglo-Gurkha war, it was observed that any native of the British territories endeavoring to cross the mountains was subjugated by the Nepalese and especially a Muslim[17].

Around 1830, the main portion of the foreign trade was in the hands of the merchants from southern plains, who had been long domiciled at Kathmandu; and were well acquainted with the capabilities for increased trade, and had abundant capital and credit in the plains, to carry it on to the fullest extent, however they were under injudicious restrictions which retarded their progress[18].

On the southern border region, traders were subjected to trade restrictions. One of the instances of economic restriction of native Saptari people by the Gorkhali ruler is detailed by Francis Bauchanan from early nineteenth century. "In autumn 1809, for instances, there being at Nathpur a great demand for grain [rice] in order to send it to Patna, the merchants made large advances to the farmers of Suban Saptari, where there was a good crop, and agreed to give a rupee for two mounds (i.e 40kg) of rice in the husk, and for other grains in proportion. When harvest came, the Nepalese Collector issued an order that no grain should be exported, alleging that the Raja was afraid of a famine and would purchase whatever the tenantry had to spare. Large stores were erected and the grain was received; but the Raja gave only his own price, that is, one rupee for four mounds (i.e 40kg) of rice, and in proportion for the other kinds. The tenantry suffered a great loss, and of course will give over cultivating more grain than they can consume. Our merchants have lost all that they have advanced; and the Raja's profit is not likely to be great. The merchants of Nathpur have been invited to go to the stores, where they are offered the grain on cheaper rates, that is, for twice as much as it cost the Raja, but in August 1810 still declined to purchase, as their compliance would no doubt encourage the repetition of such enormities."[19]

Relocation of Tharu in West

Butwal was the epicenter of Anglo-Gurkha war of 1814-1816, which was native place of Tharu people. John Routledge, Collector of Gorakhpur in 1802, was impressed by the wealth of the principality of Butwal which lay between his Northern border and upland Nepal. He mentioned, Butwal to be well cultivated at par with Bihar or Benares, though [weather was] unhealthy[20].

However, due to the continuous conflict of Gurkha with British after 1803, the places started becoming desolate. On the other hand, the terms of East India Company was favorable that attracted Tharu to Indian side compared to the oppressive Gurkha side. Hence in 1804 a British officer reported "a considerable number of the inhabitants of Butwal lowlands have taken refuge within the Company territories in consequence of the oppression and tyrannical administration of the present government of Nepal"[21].

Immediately after Sugaolee Treaty, the Eighth regiment of English Cavalry was employed in destroying the crops and villages in the Terai from where the Tharus had agreed to migrate in the manner proposed[22].

Minor Border Skirmishes

Madhesis are native of the Indo-Nepal frontier, so any type of skirmish between the two government, minor or major, directly impacts them to take away their peace and stability. Though Sugaolee treaty fixed the border, which was once volatile, there has been cases of Border Skirmishes:

- o Around 1820, in the progress of demarcation, Gurkha advanced troops from Doti into the western Terai, forcibly ejecting the residence located there[23].
- o In April 1840, Subba Bhaktawar Khadka sent officials to collect taxes at a fair being held in the disputed area. There was a dispute between the British and Nepal on the question of the ownership of 18 villages in the Sahodara region of Parsa district. This confirmed the reports of Brian H. Hodgson and Lord Auckland sent Colonel Oliver with troops to that area. Pushkar Shah then transmitted the revenue collected there to Brian H. Hodgson and suggested that the border should be surveyed.

I have heard from my grandmother, who heard from her grandmother; in the preparation of war on Mahottari district frontier, local buffalos were collected from people by Gurkha officers, and their horns were wrapped with oiled cloths. On initiation of war, the oil clothed were lighted with fire, and buffalos were let go toward enemy camp. The angry buffalos and their horns acted like invincible weapon. The same account I have received from a friend, whose grand parents gave the account of frontier on Rautahat district.

Silent cry (Burden of More Rent)

There was assumption that mere increase in the land will self-fund the army expedition. The initial conquest in central Madhesh and Eastern Plain and Hills were on richest agricultural land. However, as the conquest moved westward hills into less fertile territories, the belief of self-funding was superficial. Cost outstripped revenue. Terai lands began to fill the deficit that resulted in the increased pressure on the villages. In 1809, the Westward expansion of Gurkha stopped[24], but immediately after that preparations for war with British East India Company began, which continued to put pressure on villages for economic demands. In addition to the economic demand, there was increasing demand for free labor service too. The mounting economic pressure on government treasury made them adjust the revenue system. The old revenue sharing (*bataiya*) system that was based on equal sharing (Adhiya meaning 50:50) of crop between government and tenant farmer was replaced by a contract (*Mankhap* or *Kut*) system which assured the government of fixed amount of cash[25]. Under Kut system, a farmer who was able to bid higher was able to get farm, to the disadvantage of former farmer who had already farmed it. In a letter from King Girvan Yuddha Bikram Shah to a Tharu Madhuram Chaudhuri of Saptari district, the land tax was doubled in 1804 compared to rent in 1801[26].

After signing of Sugaolee Treaty, the conquest of Gurkha army came to halt and in theory the economic pressure on the village should have reduced. However, for political reason, rather selfish reasons, instead of decreasing the size of army the number of army was scaled up, despite the fact that nation couldn't afford it, and he resisted the pressure after pressure to reduce the army size when it was clear that it was the very size of army that caused uneasiness to the English Resident. He adhered to the army to boost his own position internally vis-a-vis the competing Bhardars (state players) and externally, vis-a-vis the British government. With the increasing Army, the pressure on the village kept increasing.

In 1792, Nepal's standing army size was estimated to be 8,000; in 1816 post Anglo-Gurkha war the army size was estimated to be 10,000 that increased to 12,000 in 1819. In a decade size increased to 15,000 when estimated in 1831 and gradually standing regular army size ballooned to 18,000 in 1839. There were additional reserve army, 2 times the regular standing army, which means the total army size was around 54,000 in 1839[27]. The army men of the rank and file served, by rotation, one year on the roll and two years off the roll. During off the roll, they returned to land and farm.

Change to the Kut system added few more disadvantages to the individual farmers; (1) the risk of bad weather that was not a matter of concern in Adhiya system (2) Kut system added intermediary layers[28] above land tillers because Jagirdars who were living far away in Kathmandu or hill wanted to deal with one or two well to do intermediaries rather than many poor cultivators (3) Farmer had to deal with market to convert agriculture produce into cash to pay rent to government. The issue got further complexed with the fact that coins (liquidity) were a scare commodity at the village level. Throughout the whole country silver coins were in short supply and copper coins were practically non-existent[29]. There was enough copper in country to mint all the coins, however they were either not interested in using copper or it was used for ammunition production[30]. The coins received after selling agriculture produce to India was collected by government and artificial scarcity was created[31]. The few coins that village had tended to flow towards larger trading centers, and there were no way within the existing economic system to re-cycle them to the village. Thus requirement to pay even a small amount in cash then meant that farmer had to find some way to acquire coins. Farmers were obliged to sell grains to middleman. Lower class peasants, who lived at or near the subsistence level, were often compelled to sell their crop at lower rate as soon as it was harvested. Richer peasants, landlords, money lenders and jagirdars made most of this situation; they bought at lower rates and withheld the supplies until price was higher[32].

There is no reason to believe, central administration had no intention to oppress village. Ludwig Stiller asks in his book "Why did the central administration fail to realize what was going on in village"? There was Hulaki system maintained after war to collect the information for administrative purpose. However, no effort ever was made to understand the condition of villages. Even the voices that could go to Kathmandu elite door got unheard. In Bhadra 1847 (AD 1790), a delegation from Morang district, led by Chaudhari Dayaram, visited Kathmandu with the complaint. In AD 1794, delegation of farmers of Morang district went to King Ran Bahadur with the complaint of imposed compulsory Ijaras tax for each village in Morang district despite 3 years loss incurred by people. In Jestha, 1866 (May 1809) many farmers went to Kathmandu from Saptari and Mahottari with complaints of over-taxation and oppression. Jethraiyat [Elder Farmer] Raghkunath Rai and others of Mahottari district submitted a similar complaint on Kartik Sudi 10, 1866 (November 1809). In 1845, Sarlahi local people accordingly submitted complaints to His Majesty against contractor Hiralal Jha that they have been imposed fines and penalties in an arbitrary manner. During Jang Bahadur Rana's time (A.D. 1864), the raiyats [farmers] of the seven districts of the Eastern Tarai region went Kathmandu with complaints that the new tax rates were unduly high. In year 1934 after great earthquake, 103 raiyats of Kanchanbari submitted a petition to Prime Minister Judha Shamsher to reduce land-tax-assessment rates until the prices of agricultural commodities revived.

After war, there was personal ambition to raise military count in Nepal under Bhim Sen policy, thus it needed more resource from Terai, additionally, it should be understood in the light that After Anglo-war Nepalese state treasure was null. Thus the pressure on villagers was further aggravated.

Ludwig Stiller concludes in his famous book 'Silent Cry': "A reduction in the army, thus a reduction in salary (supported using jagir system) and encouragement of internal trade would have done a great deal to make life of farmers more rewarding".

Letter From King Rana Bahadur Shah,

To Kulachad Sahu.

We hereby grant you an Ijara (i.e. contract) for 5 maujas of virgin lands in Tappa Rautahat in Bara district, within the prescribed boundaries. These maujas are Badauliya, Bhikhna and Charhorwa-maidakhil in Tarf Panchrauta and Kudwa and Chhapdahiya in Basantapur Parganna. The Ijara shall be valid for a period of 7 years, from the harvesting season for Pachbirahi crops in 1856 (Vikrama) to that of Rabi crops in 1862 (Vikrama). The total amount of revenue payable during this 7-year period shall be 831 rupees and 2 annas, inclusive of Mal-Jahat, Sayer-Jahat, Kal, Hububat and Bahama-Jehati, and exclusive of Amilan levies.

Year (Vikrama)	Revenue Rs/Annas	Increment Rs/Annas	Total Revenue Rs/Annas
1856	25	-	25
1857	25	6/4	31/4
1858	31/4	15/10	46/14
1859	46/14	35/2½	81/12½
1860	81/12½	81/12½	163/9
1861	163/9	81/12½	245/5½
1862	245/5½	91/15½	337/5

With full assurance, promote reclamation and settlement of these maujas. Make payment of the stipulated land revenue and obtain clearance every year. Appropriate whatever revenue accrues in excess of the stipulated amount.

You shall not be deprived of these 5 maujas for a period of 7 years. You shall be exempt from the Bheti and Salami levies as well as the obligation to supply provisions (Sidha) and provide unpaid labor (Beth, Begar).

See that the water of rivers is not blocked in the northern (Sira) zone, thereby adversely affecting cultivated maujas in the southen (Bhatha zone. Do not promote settlement by rendering cultivated Raikar lands waste. Attrack settlers from Birta, Jagir and Nankar lands, as well as from India (Moglan), not from Raikar lands.

Marga Sudi 9, 1856,

Regmi Research Collections, Vol. 24, PP. 1-2.

From Autonomy to Colonization (Economy, Resource and People Resettlement)

Madhesh region, since Akbar's time, has been having claim and counter claim by both Makwanpur Raja and Indian rulers. In the most of the time period of the history, Makwanpur was collecting tax on Madhesh, and further they were paying tax to Indian rulers like Darbhanga Maharaj. Darbhanga Maharaj was Jamindar of the Indian Muslim rulers before they got transferred to British Jamindari. Sen Kings from East to West, including Makwanpur, Bijaypur, Palpa, Tanahu rulers were considered Madhesi on the basis of their following the marriage relation with the lowland plain counterparts.

Sen Kings having territory till Mahabharat Range had matrimonial relations with plain's Rajput families[33]. Palpa founder King Rudra Sen was married to a Rajput wife called Asanamala and their son was King Mukunda Sen I. Similarly, King Hemmira Sen of Tanahu married daughter of Purushottam Singh, a Rajput from Plain. Another Prince of Tanahu Dharmagada Sen had married Prince of Bansi, who was daughter of Raja Prayaga Shah, who became mother of Rukumangada Sen.

Hilly Kings in 18th century were having blood relationship within Hill. Hilly Kings of Lamjung, Kaski, Bhirkot, etc, whose frontier were within northern slopes of Mahabharata Mountains were not having blood relationship with Rajputs of plains.

Hilly Prince of Gurkha Prithivi Narayan Shah having relationship with plain's Makwanpur Princess Indra Kumari Devi was an exception in 1738 AD against the prevailing trend. The difference in cultures started the quarrel just after the marriage. The custom of allowing bride to remain at her father's place for some time further seems to be major reason of the dispute after marriage in addition to dowry demand of Navlakha necklace (value of Nine Lakh rupee) and an elephant[34]. At the age of fourteen, Prithivi Narayan was married with twelve years old Indra Kumari, the daughter of King Hemkarna Sen of Makwanpur. Queen Chandra Prabhavati wanted to have matrimonial relation with Makwanpur with a view to get some help of arms and ammunition from Makwanpur[35]. As per the Mithila elite caste rituals, just after marriage, the daughter is not sent to husband's house. Instead, both Bride and Groom are kept together at Bride's place for a few months. In Maithil Brahmin tradition, the wall of the house is painted white before marriage, in preparation to enable groom to use it for spitting the chewed pan (betel) that is red in color; the more they stay, the more the stains, the more the prestige to bride family. As per the prevailing custom, Hemkarn wanted to keep the newly married Indra Kumari Devi and Prithivi Narayan there for longer stay, and Digbandhan wanted to see new born to his sister in his own courtyard[36]. However, Prithivi Narayan was not happy and he returned Gorkha without taking Bride, and in the way visited the Chandragiri Mountain and had a look of Nepal Valley (Kathmandu, Bhaktapur and Patan) with the ill intention of conquering it, which he did later in 1765 AD.

Despite having long blockade to Nepal Valley, Gurkha King Prithivi Narayan realized that without conquering Makwanpur, his plan of ruling Nepal valley will not succeed. King Digbandhan Sen, son of King Hemkarna Sen, knew of the ill intention of his brother in law King Prithivi Narayan Shah, and also tried to build alliance with other hilly kings. However, it was late, when Makwanpur was attacked and captured in 1762. Initially, Digbandhan Sen and relatives fled to India, but later on Digbandhan Sen was arrested and kept in custody till death.

Transfer of Makwanpur to Gurkha did not solve the conflicting and antagonizing claim of Madhesh rulers. British, which owned Darbhanga

Jamindari, claimed Madhesh tax and Gurkha King obliged the previous arrangement and paid tribute to British via Darbhanga Maharaj year after year, till it was scrapped[37] in 1801 by British in the hope of getting business and transit to Tibet.

However, duplicity on the part of Gurkha to take as much as possible from British without giving any thing back eroded the remaining trust between them, which had already taken a dip after failure of 1792 treaty of commerce[38] signed after Abdool Kadir Khan Mission.

In early nineteenth century, Madhesh frontier was as fluid as before, additionally there was lack of trust. Throughout this period the situation in the eastern Tarai deteriorated. Both the Nepalese administration and the Company administration were indirect and ineffective in the border region. Their military forces were committed elsewhere and the malarial climate of the Madhesh restricted the visits of both the Gorkha and the English administrators except in the winter season. Unique climate condition overlapped with unique geographical location of being below the south slope of Himalaya. It attracts lot of direct rain water as well as comes under flow path of Himalayan rain water. From April to October the region was usually abandoned to the revenue collectors and Jamindars[39].

During the period both Gurkha and British were having same and mutually conflicting aspiration of expansion of territory. Thus, it is interesting to analyze the political situation, which was more autonomous, in the light of two expanding powers, both having imperial and colonial vision in center. We will analyze the expansion of imperial power and diminishing autonomy of Madhesh from two perspectives:

1. Hindu Politics, Abbot and King's Perspective
2. Commoner Tharu Perspective

Hindu Politics, Abbot and King

British idea of country's end point was in the form of well-defined border line both on paper and land. Gurkha's idea of country's end point was function of muscle power and influence. Like any other south Asian ruler, well defined line was unknown to Gurkha.

British people were cow-eating people and hence were untouchable for any die-hard Hindu of that time. The Abbot, which were many in those region, were believed to be protector of Hindu values. These Abbot established their relationship with early Kings and received huge land grants from Sen Kings of Makwanpur. Among them Matihani Abbotship was considered to be supreme, which was located 5 miles south of Janakpur. Others were Janakpur Ram temple Monastery, Janaki temple Monastery, Ratna Sagar Monastery, Kuwa Monastery, Laxman Temple Monastery, etc.

The grants called "Kusa Birta" received by them were autonomous in nature, allowing them all the rights devoid of any liability to King. After transfer of power from Sen King to Gurkha Kings, the land grants of these Abbot also got transferred to the existing abbots in their original form. The Abbot had huge track of lands, which they had -rented to common people and derived incomes that were used for daily maintenance of temple or Sthan in addition to feeding the Hindu ascetics and pilgrims who visited Janakpur on special religious days.

Kusa-birta Land Grant in 1812 at Sudiyahi, village a mile away from current Nepal-India border. Map taken from google map on July 29, 2016

Sensing the volatile nature of Madhesh, Gurkha king too granted additional "Kusa birta" to the Abbots, who were power leaders in the local regions. Gurkha King had declared that objective was to get blessings from Hindu gods for the prosperity of Royal families and his domination. However, the implied objective was to establish political influence upon the local population in addition to garner god's blessings in favor of their military expedition at the time of need. The largest grants of Kusa birta rights in land to local sadhus on behalf of the Shah Kings were the grant from King Rana Bahadur Shah to Pritam Das of Hanuman Nagar monastery in 1781 and the grant from King Girvan Yuddha Vikram Shah to the Abbot of the Ram Chandra monastery in 1807. In both the cases the recipient of the land was Hanuman worshipper, the god known for extraordinary muscle power who helped God Ram in searching Goddess Sita from the captivity of demon king Ravan and later fighting Ravan's army too. Year 1807 grants matches with the Gurkha's 1804-1805 attack on Garhwal and 1806 attach on Kangra[40]. Another reconfirmation of Kusa-birta comes on the eve of Anglo-Gurkha war on the closest point on frontier. In 1812, King Girvan reconfirmed the grant to Gopal Jha of the mauja of Sudiyahi on Mahottari parganna of Mahottari district, whose ancestors were granted Kusa birta by Sen Kings of Makwanpur. Sudiyahi is a mile away from border[41].

Gurkha king also provided land grants to these Abbots in deep hills and also in the then Nepal valley. In 1806, Matihani Abbot was granted residential property in Bhadgaon, Patan, and Kathmandu in the Nepal valley[42].

These big land grants from Kings stopped after Gurkha King became sure of fixed southern border having no threat from English East India Company. Smaller grants of land, from five to twenty bighas in area, were gifted to Sita Kund Kuti (1833), Ratna Sagar monastery (1834), and Agni Kund monastery (circa 1840). By 1843 the period of extensive royal gifts of land to Hindu ascetics in the district was over[43].

Sen Kings had also munificently granted Kusa-birta land to the established monasteries in the villages of Birpur, Birrak, and Barahi situated between 15 and 20 miles Southwest and West of Janakpurdham in the Muzaffarpur district of Bihar[44]. These monasteries also had branch monasteries established in Janakpur; main abbot living in main monastery. Main Barahi monastery, currently located in Sitamarhi district, half mile away from border, had direct connection with Shah Kings of eighteenth and nineteenth centuries, which received land grants at many places in Nepal, some of which even lied deep in hills[45]. Gurkha Kings might have cultivated relationship with Barahi monastery, lying on other side of border, for the strategic military reason. Barahi monastery is associated with development of Janakpur, which used surplus funds, after feeding visiting pilgrimage. The Abbot of Barahi monastery, for example, offered funds to the Ratna Sagar abbot for the construction of a brick and stucco temple and hostel at Ratna Sagar[46].

Barahi Sanskrit collage is established in western side of Janakpur near Ramanand chowk, on the land grant from Barahi monastery.

A survey of the monasteries near Janakpur brings to light that the Ram Chandra Monastery and Matihani monastery had also benefited from land grants from the King of Darbhanga[47]. The former monastery received in the name of Lord Ram Chandra the Seliheri mauja and the Narayanpur mauja and the latter monastery received in the name of Laksmi Narayan the Charaut mauja. These three maujas are situated in the Northern part of the Darbhanga and Muzaffarpur districts of Bihar in the territory which at that time was ruled by the King of Darbhanga.

The "Kusa" grants were sufficient but still smaller pie in the bigger track of land that Kingdom owned. Abbot wanted to extend their power and King wanted someone local to bring the track of land in use so that King can derive rental income from them. Under this scheme of thought, during Rana regime, these Abbots took additional responsibilities and became intermediaries of the revenue structure to collect rent from the farmers on behalf of the Kings.

These regions witnessed the autonomy in the following way:

A. The Abbot were local kings. As per the Kusa birta terms, the land observed autonomous power. Additionally, Matihani Abbot was granted constitutional authority from the then Rana Prime Minister Jang Bahadur Rana, under which that Abbot can pass judgment and settle dispute among the other Abbots (local kings), and collect fines after judgement. A Matihani abbot once declared during 1870's,"If there is my equal anywhere in Nepal, he can only be the king".

B. The Abbots were able to derive legislations suited for the local people as and when needed — such as rule to ban slaughter of animals in Janakpur.

The authority of Abbots and autonomy of Monasteries were stripped during King Mahendra tenure. This will be discussed in detail in next chapter.

A Middle Class Tharu Perspective

Tharu Characteristics in group behavior are different from other inhabitants of Madhesh. Tharus also formed the part of Low Land plain people which witnessed almost similar level of impact due to political change happening in the Indo-Gurkha frontier politics.

Tharus are mixed with the larger plain people for known historical time[48], and their culture overlaps the culture of other plain people. Today, Tharus are found in both side of border in sub-Himalayan Terai region from Jalpaiguri in East to Kumaon in the West[49]. Within the Gurkha realm, Tharus are scattered both in Eastern and Western Terai, and majority of them concentrated in five Western districts: Dang, Banke, Bardiya, Kailali and Kanchanpur.

On Indian side, large number of the Tharu is concentrated in Champaran district, geographically close to old Kingdom of Makwanpur from Indo-Nepal border. Based on the recently collected royal letters and published in a book Panjiar collection, it shows Tharu was actively integrated in the power Hierarchy of Sen Kingdoms of Makwanpur, Chaudandi and Palpa. During the Sen Dynasty in early Eighteenth century, Tharu contributed in military service. The benefits, in the form of large land grants, were hereditary passed in the family. In a letter written in 1838 AD by King Rajendra Bikram Shah, the pension land grant was reconfirmed to families of Bhupal Raya, who was killed while fighting with Muslim military on behalf of Makwanpur King, believed to be at the time of King Manik Sen[50]. Raya title signifies the Royal honor given to person of high regards in those periods. The families of Bhupal Raya located in Parsa district inherited a big track of 391 bigha land in 1838 as military pension having continuity since Sen King of Makwanpur. The military skill of Plain people corroborate with the historical event that King Jay Prakash Malla of Kathmandu valley trusted and hired people from plain (Tirhutia army) to fight on his behalf in 18th century.

In addition to Military officers, Tharu were positioned as regional head, entrusted with prospering the area, promoting the agriculture and collecting the tax; they were "little kings" whose power were hereditary passed in the family having complete authority over the land they were owning. There are many letters of Sen Kingdom time, showing the nature of their power sharing. Letter issued from (1) King Mahipati Sen of Bijaypur in 1726 AD (2) King Digbandhan Sen of Makwanpur in 1760 (3) Tax receipt issued from King Prithvipal Sen of Palpa in 1796 and (4) Tax exempt letter issued from Ratna Sen, son of Prithvipal Sen, in 1812. A letter issued in 1726 by

King Mahapatti Sen of Bijaypur, linked to the family of Makwanpur Sen Kings, reconfirmed the autonomous full authority rights to Ranapal Chaudhari of Patna village of Khalisa lying in Saptari district. The language of this letter is mixture of Bhojpuri and Maithili[51]. Next letter written by King Digbandhan Sen, last ruler of Makwanpur Kingdom, to Baliram of Tappa Basantpur have the similar mention of autonomous authority without paying any tax to Makwanpur kingdom and grant to be inherited from generation to generation.

In the late eighteenth century, when Gurkha replaced the Sen Kings, local elite retained the earlier privileges, however, simultaneously there was introduction of volatility in the relationship in terms of land grants, which was more stable during previous regime. Letter written by King Girvan in 1806 to Ganashyam Raut of Kolhabari village in Bara district reconfirms that the transfer of grants and privileges provided by Sen King of Makwanpur had already been granted earlier by King Girvan's great grandfather and grandfather. However, the relationship of old native elites with the new Gurkha power started crumbing in the same period while transitioning from eighteenth century to nineteenth century. Two letters of those period written to Hem Chaudhari of Saptari districts show the fluctuating power chemistry with Gurkha Kings. In 1776 a letter was written by King Pratap Singh Shah to Shri Hem Chaudhari of Saptari requesting him to come back from India, and reoccupy the village as Jamindar, that was bestowed to him by King Karan Sen of Chaudandi. Former Sen King's loyal people, like Hem Chaudhari, flew to India after Gurkha occupied Madhesh in 1765, either fearing prosecution or following the ousted former Royals. After Hem Chaudhari returns, in 1772, King Ran Bahadur reconfirms the Chaudhari post to Hem Chaudhari in 1772, however his designation was downgraded by new king compared to his former designation in Sen Dynasty. This time his title "Shri" was removed by Shah King. "Shri" denotes the honor associated with power hierarchy of royals; King in Kathmandu had 5 Shri before his name, similarly Rana Prime ministers had 3 Shri before his name. After four years, in the year 1782, King Ran Bahadur granted 2 more villages – Ekabarpur and Pakari – showing the increasing trust in relationship as well as eagerness on the part of Gurkha king to leverage the local power for expansion of income. Additionally, in 1783, Hem Chaudhary was awarded an elephant from Royal court. However, in a letter written four years after in 1787 indicates the adding of bureaucratic intermediary layer for the first time between him and King Ran Bahadur Shah, though there was expansion of two more villages under his management for agricultural revenue generation. After a gap of seventeen years, in 1800, the situation changed in the region dramatically. Gurkha king sent his close confident officer (of Hill origin) named Brahmanand Upadhyay (district administrative officer) and Mahima Khawas (military officer) to Saptari district for overseeing the activities on top of Chaudhuri. Hem Chaudhari's successor Madhuram Chaudhari passed through bumpy road, the Chaudhuri post was taken back in 1759-96. After a gap of 5 years, King Girvan Yuddha reinstalled Madhuram again as Chaudhuri in 1801. Later on in 1803, Madhuram was withdrawn from the Chaudhuri post for Khalisa parganna of Saptari district and Mahima Khawas was installed as replacement. Ten months later, Madhuram Chaudhari was reinstalled in Chaudhuri post of Khalisa parganna, however he had to pay price to King, his tax was doubled compared to year 1801. Slowly and steady Tharu elites lost their authority and was marginalized from power structure after emergence of Gurkha rule in Madhesh.

The early nineteenth century saw the business as usual, and letters suggest the successor of Madhuram Chaudhari named Kriparam Chaudhari could keep himself busy in the capacity of his designation as Chaudhari, additionally engaging himself as timber contractor, till 1842[52]. Though they had to maintain good relationship with Gurkha kings via some intermediary officers.

After the change of power from Thapa to Rana, there was change in policy. The Tharu families found themselves abruptly out of power structure as revenue collector. Two letters written in 1867 and 1877 during King Surendra's tenure, under Rana rule, assign Tharu responsibilities to manage elephant stables[53].

Institutionalization of Colonization During Rana Autocracy

Once the central and eastern Terai were restored to Nepal there was never any real danger that the state would fragment.

The family dispute of King Ran Bahadur's two wives for having their own sons as successor led to the rise of Jung Bahadur in the Durbar, which finally culminated into his accession as Prime Minister, in the after math of Kot massacre. The scope of Kot massacre is out of scope of current book and can be easily found from History books.

Plain People Pushed away from Power

Immediate aftermath of Jung Bahadur's becoming the Prime Minister, a few families from lowland plain, living in Kathmandu and having political reach, felt the heat. Kulanand Jha's and his son Hiralal Jha's power was curtailed and both were even put under detention. They paid a fine of a half million rupee at that time and their house were auctioned. Fearing more risk, they disappeared from politics of Kathmandu suddenly and went to India. It would be interesting to track the rise of Kulanand Jha in Kathmandu. He belonged to Rautahat and came from a moderate farmer family. After Anglo-Gurkha war, when border was fixed, Bhim Sen Thapa needed some trusted hands to raise money from fertile land of Madhesh, and Kulanand became the medium. Kulanand, soon saw his rise from village Ijiradar to Subba to Taksari (Master of the Mint) officer in Kathmandu. Based on available evidence it appears his career as an ijaradar stretched over to at least 25 years, from the beginning of the Nepal-British war in A.D. 1814 to the end of Bhimsen Thapa's Prime Ministership in A.D. 1837. Even thereafter, he was granted an ijara for the collection of revenue on jagir lands of Bhimsen Thapa in the eastern Tarai districts, which the government had resumed after Bhimsen Thapa's death. Kulanand was also granted Ijara for revenue collection in Bhadgaun as well as collection of customs duties in Naurangiya, Sidhmas, Chisapani, Hetauda, and Parsa-Gadhi. However, for most of the time, he was revenue collector in the Madhesh districts. His son Hiralal also found the favor and became Ijiradar, Subba and Taksari like his father during Bhimsen Thapa reign. Both father and son were definitely not the loveable elite among plain villagers, and many complaints were raised against them. The tyranny of father-son duo was also mentioned by Jung Bahadur in his letter written from London to his brother. Despite the fact that they were being hated in Madhesh, they were in the favored list of Bhimsen Thapa. It would be appropriate to say, Bhimsen was ruling Madhesh through Kulanand Jha and his son. When Bhimsen was ill, Kulanand Jha donated about 3,00,000 rupees to make three silver doors of Pashupatinath (which are still there). Kulanand also granted large land to create religious endowment, which is still present as "Jha Guthi".

The fate of Kulanand changed with the rise of Jung Bahadur Rana. An old land deal of 1823 came hunting them after 4 decades in 1862. According to the charge, in 1823 (1880 BS), Subba Kulanand Jha and Kaji Hiralal Jha had taken up on possessory mortgage 900 muris of rice-lands at Jarayotar from Ghatananda Padhya Khatiwada of Bungnam for Rs 6,601. Subsequently, arrears of payment to the government fell due to the government. Guhyalaxmi, Subba Kulananda Jha's wife, and Prithvilala Jha, his son, retained possession of the lands by falsely representing them as guthi. The mortgage-deed was recovered from among the papers of Subba Kulananda Jha. The mortgage was confiscated, and the lands were placed under the control of the Sadar Dafdarkhana. An order to this effect was issued in the name of Kharidar Bakabir of the Moth Tahabil Office on Aswin Badi 4, 1919 (September 1862). Subba Kulananda Jha owned a house at Kilagal in Kathmandu. This house too was confiscated by the government. On Jestha Sudi 14, 1934 (May 1877) an order was issued to register the sale of the house to Lt. Dilli Bahadur Thapa Chhetri, who had offered Rs 7,301 for it. He was permitted to demolish the house and build new one on the site.

Finally, Kulanand Jha and his family disappeared from politics of Kathmandu.

Another Jha that got linked to Jung Bahadur was Gopal Jha. He was hired by Jung bahadur's opponent to kill Jung Bahadur after Kot Massacre. One day while Jung Bhadur was praying, Gopal Jha went on the top of a house and fired gun. Luckily Jung survived, but Gopal Jha escaped and went to India, and no one knew it was Gopal Jha. After few years, Jha came back to Kathmandu while ill counting his last breaths and spilled the bin. People trusted his confession assuming no one will lie at last breath.

Another immediate blow to Madhesh people came directly or indirectly through the Alau Parva, associated with the King Rajendra Shah event. In the aftermath of Kot parva, Jung Bahadur went up the power ladder to become commander in chief and prime minister of Nepal. However, Jung was trying to help the younger queen in fulfilling her wish to make her son successor of thrown, which compelled Queen for next conspiracy. After finding Queen was involved in conspiracy to kill him, Jung Bahadur exterminated the queen to Banaras. Subsequently, King also offered to join her. On reaching Banaras, King wanted to return. But Jung was not interested to have queen back in Kathmandu. After multiple rounds of failed negotiations, King Rajendra was convinced by former elites of durbar and political opponents of Jung Bahadur, who had escaped to Banaras after Jung coming to power, to march towards Kathmandu. King Rajendra Shah's maternal side was also from Madhesh, so he also got support from Madhesh elites. King had tent in a place called Alau, where one night while people were sleeping, Jung's people attacked taking advantage of darkness. King's people couldn't react in confusion and ran away to India. Many people were killed and King was captured and brought to Kathmandu, where he was kept in house arrest till King died. Since Alau incident took place in Madhesh and many of the supporters were Madhesh natives, a great deal of loss could be assumed to native people, although there are little documentary evidences found to prove that.

By 1850, Jung Bahadur had eliminated his major enemies. He went on England-France tour in 1850-1851. On his return, he enacted 'Muluki Ain' in 1854, in which people of plains were put at the bottom of caste hierarchy, except Maithil Brahmin, who were again put below Hill Brahmin. In 1855-1856, Jung declared war on Tibet, and thus there was a big burden on the villagers (read low land Madhesh villagers) for funding the war, which distressed the government beyond expectation[54]. There was extended burden on Madhesh villagers to fund Army in 1857-1858, when Jung decided to support the British in the Indian Sipahi Mutiny. Gurkha army had also got complaints of looting in India during the mutiny.

Increasing Burden of Taxes

Rana tried to improve the tax rule of former regime based on contract and highest bidding price. Rana ensured that as long as farmer is paying land rent, they were not to be stripped off their holding, thus making the tenure more stable. This also opened door to the land ownership rights and transfer of land. However, Rana also had some of the new taxes that were burdening the villagers. Like water tax was levied on anyone who wanted to construct community drinking water source. Ox tax was collected from anyone owning ox used for farming, marriage tax if any individual decided to marry, and also if king decided to marry, etc.

During the time of Prime Minister Chandra Shamsher, a tax called grazing '*Chari*' was collected at the rate of eight annas on each buffalo grazed in the Char-kose (strip of 8 miles) forests. The new levy caused considerable hardship to the people, particularly because the Char-kose forests in Jhapa district were almost non-existent. The ryots [farmers] of Kanchanbari Jhapa therefore complained to Prime Minister Juddha Shamsher that the tax, along with the *Chari* tax, constituted a heavy burden on them. They pointed out that they did not maintain cattle farms in the Char-kose forests and prayed that the *Chari* tax, which had not been levied in any other district, should be abolished.

Contracts were issued by the government for the collection and disposal of hides and skins, bones and horns. Such contracts were previously operated by Muslims. They maintained warehouses in villages, and employed workers of the Mochi (leather-worker) caste to skin dead cattle. These Mochis resorted to various malpractices, such as poisoning cattle. The matter was referred to the government, which issued orders prohibiting Mochis from entering into village. Mochis were permitted to skin dead cattle only after the owners reported that their cattle had died.

This created another problem. People had to watch their cattle all through the night if they died in the evening, and continue to do so until Mochis became available. In case they failed to maintain such watch, and dogs and jackals damaged the skin as a result, the contractors extorted compensation on the basis of prices prevalent in Calcutta.

Drought, flooding, failure of seeds to germinate, and lack of agricultural labor were not deemed by the government to be sufficient cause for a remission of tax[55]. Only if productivity of land was permanently ruined, like flood covered the field with sand, the tax reduction was considered. When the crop failed, the tenant was tempted to harvest what remained of the standing crop and to abscond in the night[56].

There were rules that shaped the entrepreneurial opportunity and in turn expanded the market of Madhesh:

1. The tenancy was permanent as long as tenant pays the tax. Also, tenancy was transferable, thus it created value for the rights. It opened market for land buy-sell.

2. Jamindar were allowed to search plot in deep jungle, at 1 day walking distance, and invest in development. Once proposal was accepted by district officers, they can bring tenants, and enjoy five years of tax rebate or lower tax. After five years, landlord can still enjoy 5% of revenue.

3. Jamindar were allowed to provide loan advancement for initial settlement, building house, buying cattle, buying seeds. Government rate for loan was 10%. However, the actual rate of load, forwarded

by Jamindar, was much above the prescribed. In case crop failed, the tenant either foreclosed or ran away in night. Thus landlord can auction these lands titles, and get new tenant at better price. There were merchants in market ready to buy those titles. Nepalese from the hills who had retired from government service also came to the Tarai to purchase tenancy rights (posts in the customs and excise departments seem to have been lucrative and permitted savings).

4. Rana developed bazaars to attract merchants from across the border for exchanging commodity in the markets, and government collected sales tax, or sold permit to collect sales tax. These opened up avenue for local merchant to open shops in the local hat-bazaar. Marwari, migrant from Rajasthan, too opened and expanded these trading locations. Government benefited because, it attracted trades from across the border and helped in accumulating Indian currency. These currency helped Rana to (1) import luxury goods (2) invest surplus in Indian market.

The additional evidence of inhumanity of government in plain was presence of military form of government and the hardship it brought to people. A British officer James Inglis wrote "The government of Nepaul is purely military. All executive and judicial functions are carried on by military officers. With practically irresponsible power, and only answerable directly to his immediate military superior, an unscrupulous man may harry and harass a district pretty much as he chooses. Our old Major seemed to be civil and lenient, but in some districts the exactions and extortions by the rulers have driven many of the hard-working Nepaulese over the border into our territory."[57]

Acceleration in Wealth Transfer – a Way Towards Colonization

Rana established good relationship with British rulers in India after 1857 in the aftermath of Jung Bahadur providing help in curbing Indian Mutiny of 1857. British priority was the expedition of commerce between the countries. Madhesh was highly fertile land and was exporting a large surplus of rice to India. Additionally, Madhesh also had a large track of unexplored virgin woods, which had big demand in India. The Sal tree is the best among the timber in the world for Ship building, and at that time it had big demand in Calcutta for making commercial ships. Sal also found demand from London for making houses. Later when Railway was expanding in India in second half of nineteenth century, Sal was in great demand for railway track sleepers. All those needs were met from the vast Jungle in Madhesh – said to be stretching 12 km from East to West in 800 km. Janakpur Railway was established in 1928 with the primary purpose of transporting timber from interior of Jungle to Jaynagar station located at the border of India. Before railway road, Sal tree was transported to Calcutta by water way using elephants or just by using the water current that flows from Hill, meets Ganga and then finally merges in the Sea near Calcutta. Another wood of high value is *Khair* (Acacia catechu) that is used in the betel leaf for eating. Both these trees - Sal and Khair – were and are declared national resource, and planting on personal property is still offence. The export of the jungle and agriculture produce expedited during Rana regime. However, foreign exchange was going to the Rana's personal accounts, in the pretext of one or the other tax.

Also, it should be understood in the light that wealth spent on army was coming from Terai and salaries were taken to Hill, which catered the army recruitments. Thus as the plight of wealth from plain low land to hill.

Broadly, there were two types of revenue; (1) Land Revenue collected and sent to central treasury, also called crown land and (2) Land revenue used as salary and pension also called Jagir and Birta. Combining both the revenue, the Eastern flat lowland districts contributed more than 90% of total revenue of Gurkha Kingdom. In the year 1852, revenue contribution from Eastern Terai excluding revenue from Jagir/Birta was at whopping 89.3%.

Year	Total Kingdom Treasury Revenue	Eastern Terai Treasury Revenue	Eastern Terai Share (%)	Information Source
1793	500,000	244,104	48.8 %	Regmi, Mahesh
1852	729,230	651,563	89.3 %	Regmi, Mahesh
1853	926,273	722,956	78.04 %	Regmi, Mahesh
1854	1,012,678	758,063	74.8 %	Regmi, Mahesh
1855	1,570,994	696,814	44.4 %	Regmi, Mahesh
1856	1,398,611	749,836	53.6 %	Regmi, Mahesh
1857	1,254,628	785,219	62.5 %	Regmi, Mahesh
1858	1,005,130	567,723	56.4 %	Regmi, Mahesh
1861	3,109,181	1,865,509	60 %	Daniel Wright

Table showing Gurkha Kingdom Revenue from lands taxes, market duties; timber, export duties, and passturage tax.[58]

The revenue valuation of Jagir/Birta land was even more than the revenue sent to central treasury. The Jagir/Birta was segregated for people connected to ministers and Royal families of Gurkha Kingdom. In the year 1856 AD, the revenue valuation of Jagir/Birta land in Terai districts, Eastern and Western, was Rs 1.2 million.

District	Trikhandi Levy	Value of birta and jagir incomes
Morang	Rs 19,312	Rs 57,936
Saptari	Rs 51,511	Rs 154,533
Mahottari and Sarlahi	Rs 112,627	Rs 337,881
Rautahat	Rs 20,436	Rs 61,308
Bara	Rs 66,985	Rs 200,955
Parsa	Rs 22,561	Rs 67,683
Butwal	Rs 5,884	Rs 17,652
Total	Rs 299,316	Rs 897,948

Table showing revenue from Trikhandi Levy, 1856[59]*. Trikhandi means one-third of the income on Jagir/Birta. This was one time levy to finance the Nepal-Tibet war.*

Revenue figures compiled in the Eastern Tarai during the closing years of the nineteenth century are, of course, not available. Some idea of the amount of revenue may be obtained from the fact that in 1900 the chiefs of the revenue offices of Rautahat-Sarlahi, Mahottari, Saptari-Siraha, and Hanumannagar were ordered to transmit a total sum of Rs 1.2 million to the Tejarathi Adda[60].

The testimony of exclusive wealth in flat lowland Madhesh, rather than any other Gurkha domination, comes from Laurence Oliphant[61], who has written in 1851 thus:

> *"Terai is at present the only part of the Nepaul dominions which is profitable from the revenue yielded by its productions. Valuable timber and turpentine ivory and hides are shipped down the Boori Gundak, on which river Segowly is situated, to Calcutta. Still the cost of a government licence for cutting timber is so heavy, as in a great measure to deter speculators from engaging in an undertaking, in which so considerable an outlay is demanded exclusive of the expenses attendant on the felling and transport of the timber. Besides the Saul, the Terai*

contains ebony mimosa and other useful trees. The trade in hides is not as I have already remarked carried out to the extent it is capable of. But in spite of all these drawbacks the Terai alone of all the Nepaul dominions can be looked upon by the British as offering a profitable field for trade and commercial speculations."

Institutionalization of Madhesh Ethnicity

Pahari (High land people) and Madhesi (Low land people) have been there for long, even before King Prithivi Narayan Shah came to power in Kathmandu. They were different in the behavior and psychology. Rana government institutionalized the division through the country rule book. Rana created two central offices to govern Nepal along the same line; 'Madhesh Bandobast Adda' (Low land Plains Management Office) and Pahar Bandobast Adda (High Land Hill Management Office). Before physically creating two offices, there was promulgation of constitutional rule book for plain land. Madhesh was governed by 'Madhesh Mal ko Sawal' (revenue regulations for plains) and Pahar (revenue regulations for the Hills) was governed by 'Pahar Mal ko Sawal'. There were other Madhesh specific regulations like 'Madhesh jilla ko Jamindar Patuwari ka nam ko sawal' (regulations for Jamindar & Patwari of Various districts of plain)[62]. Bada hakim (High officer) used to sit in the Madhesh offices.

As per the 'Madhesh Mal ko Sawal' regulation[63], the districts belonging to Madhesh and their revenue assessment were (in proportion):

1. Jhapa – 5,000
2. Biratnagar (later renamed as Morung, and further Sunsari was carved out) – 7,500
3. Hanuman Nagar (now Saptari) – 6,000
4. Siraha – 5,000
5. Mahottari (later Dhanusha was carved out) – 7,500
6. Sarlahi – 5,000
7. Rautahut – 5,000
8. Bara – 5,000
9. Parsa – 4,000

10. Palhi – 4,000
11. Majhkhand – 5,000
12. Khajhani – 6,000
13. Sivraj – 2,000
14. Dangdeokheri – 2,000
15. Banke – 3,000
16. Bardiya – 3,000
17. Kailali – 2,000
18. Kanchanpur – 2,000
19. Makwanpur – 1,000
20. Udaypur – 1,000
21. Chitwan - 1,000
22. Surkhet - 500

There was separate tax law for the Madhesh (low land) and Pahar (high land). Madhesh had tax regulations as 'Madhesh Mal ko Sawal', and 'Madhesh Bando Bast Adda'. Seperate civil rule for Madhesi people was promulgated 'On Adultery and Slavery among the Madhesis of the Tarai' in 1870 AD[64].

The genesis for these Madhesh specific regulations come from regulation promulgated in 1861 regarding Madhesh. The promulgation appreciated and institutionalized "people of Hill" concept based on the ethnic and blood lineage in addition to the geographical origin. Section 42 and 43 of the 1861 regulation stated "Priority in the appointment of Jamindars and Patuwaris shall be given to hill people and respectable settlers, in that order", accordingly preference was given to people of hill origin while allocating land and appointing people for managing land and collecting tax in the lowland plain, and next comes the native ethnic lowland people[65]. Superimposition of the above concepts implies that traditionally hilly people dwellings are northern hill, and plain people dwellings are southern lowland. Additionally, in terms of economic benefits, Hill belongs to the Hilly people exclusively. And, when it comes to lowland plain, hilly people penetrated plains for economic activities and this phenomenon got official encouragement starting 1861 AD onwards from Rana rules.

Notes

1. Michael, Bernandro A. (2013), State Making and Territory in South Asia, Lesson from the Anglo-Gorkha War (1814-1816), 2013 PP 1
2. Letter from King Ran Bahadur to Karimullah, Rahimullah, Fakrullah and Bismillah in 1795 AD, Miscellaneous Land Grants And Endowments, Regmi Research Series Year 2, No. 9
3. Op Cite Lecomte-Tilouine , Marie (1998), On Francis Buchanan Hamilton's Account of the Kingdom of Nepal , European Bulletin of Himalayan Research, 1998, Number 14, Page 68
4. Chapagain, Prajwal (2012), Kathmandu ka Raithane Tirhutiya, Himal Khabar Kathmandu, Year 21 issue 18, 2012
5. Based on personal discussion with Mr. CK Lal, writer.
6. Passport Regulations, A.D.1800, Regmi Research Collection, Vol. 24, pp. 50-52
7. Regmi Research Collection, vol. 36, pp. 343-44
8. Regmi Research Collection, vol. 36, pp. 343-44
9. Yang, Anand A.(1998), Bazaar India : Markets, Society, and the Colonial State in Gangetic Bihar, University Of California Press ,1988, PP 41-43
10. Yang, Anand A.(1998), Bazaar India : Markets, Society, and the Colonial State in Gangetic Bihar, University Of California Press ,1988, PP 41-43
11. Bengal Secret letter 27 Dec 1814, Enclosure 38 in No 2, Letter from Mr. Moorcroft with Enclosures, PRNW PP 89
12. General A. January 1882 no 15. Charles Girldestone. British Resident in Nepal to Grant, Secretary to the Government of India, Foreign Department no 69 p. dated September 1881. As mentioned in Vijay Kuman Tiwary (2013) Indo-Nepal Trade Relations (1847-1947) pp 69
13. Political A. December 1880 No 38. Charles Girldestone. British Resident in Nepal to A.C. Lyall, Esq. Secretary to the Government of India, Foreign Department no 32 p, dated 25 September 1880. As mentioned in Vijay Kuman Tiwary (2013) Indo-Nepal Trade Relations (1847-1947) pp 69
14. Op.Cit, Pradhan, K.L (2012); Thapa Politics in Nepal: With Special Reference to Bhim Sen Thapa, 1806-1839, Concept Publishing Company, 2012, pp 35
15. Bengal Secret letter, 27 Dec 1814, Enclosure 37 in No 2 Letter from Mr Moorcroft, PRNW pp 85-86
16. Rose, Leo E.(1971), Nepal; Strategy for Survival, University of California, Berkeley., 1971, pp 25
17. Bengal Secret letter, 27 Dec 1814, Enclosure 38 in No 2 Letter from Mr Moorcroft
18. Political Consultation, A Campbell's Report on Political Transactions with Nepal, Camp, Court, and Politics of Nepal, 18 September 1837, as mentioned in Bikrama Jit Hasrat's History of Nepal (1871) PP 186
19. Hamilton, Francis Bauchanan (1809-10); An Account of the District of Purnea in 1809-10, pp-577
20. Bayly C. A. (1983), Rulers, Townsmen and Bazaars: North Indian Society in the Age of British Expansion, 1770-1870, Cambridge University Press, 1983, pp 222

21. Board Collection, India Office Library, F/4/185:7 as mentioned in the book The Kings of Nepal and The Tharu of the Terai by Gisele K and Pamela D.M 1998 pp 166
22. Attempts to persuade the Tharoos, a displaced tribe from Butwal in the Tarai, to settle in Gorakhpur District. IOR/F/4/548/1334 : Feb-Oct 1815 ; also in PRNW pp 743
23. Political Consultation, A Campbell's Report on A sketch of political relations with Nepal, 18 September 1837, as mentioned in Bikrama Jit Hasrat's History of Nepal (1871) PP 191
24. Stiller, Ludwing F (1979), The Silent Cry, Sahayogi Prakashan, Kathmandu, 1979. PP 291
25. Ibid. PP 292
26. Krauskopff, Gisele and Meyer, Pamela D (1998), The Kings of Nepal and The Tharu of the Terai, Panjiar Collection, 1998 pp 130
27. Political Consultation, A Campbell's Report on The supremacy of Bhimsen Thapa, as mentioned in Bikrama Jit Hasrat's History of Nepal (1871) PP 225
28. In turn of the nineteenth century in Mahottari. The cultivator obtained the cultivation right from the mauja collector who obtained the mauja collecting right from the divisional collector who, in turn, obtained the divisional collecting right from the district collector or district contractor. The district collector or contractor obtained the collecting right from the king. See Burghart, Richard (1978), History of Janakpurdham, Phd Thesis, 1978, pp 227
29. Stiller, Ludwing F (1979), The Silent Cry, Sahayogi Prakashan, Kathmandu, 1979. PP 294
30. ibid. PP 311
31. Political Consultation, A Campbell's Report on The supremacy of Bhimsen Thapa, as mentioned in Bikrama Jit Hasrat's History of Nepal (1871) PP 230
32. Regmi, M.C (1978), A study in Nepali Economic History, 1978. PP 88-89
33. Acharya, Baburam (1978), King Prithvi Narayan Shah, Regmi Research Series, Year 10, No. 5. Also see Rajbanshi, Shankar (1963), Sen Vamshavali, Ratna Pustak Bhandar, Kathmandu, 1963
34. Stiller, L.F (1968) Prithvi Narayan Shah in The Light of Dibya Upadesh, Chapter III, pp 38-39
35. Story of Prithvi Narayan Shah, downloaded on July 28 from http://mixnepali.blogspot.com/p/prithvi-narayan-shah-prithvi-narayan.html
36. Based on private group discussion with Historian Ramesh Dhungel in 2007.
37. Aitchison, C.U (1863), A Collection of Treaties, Engagements, and Sunnuds, Relating to India and Neighbouring Countries, Volume 2, India Foreign and Political Dept, 1863, PP 161-162

    Article 7 - So many elephants on account of Muckanacinpoor are annually sent to the Company by the Rajah of Nepaul and therefore the Governor General with a view of promoting the satisfaction of the Rajah of Nepaul and in consideration of the improved friendly connection and of this new Treaty relinquishes and foregoes the tribute above mentioned and directs that the officers of the Company both now and hereafter from generation to generation shall never during the continuance of the engagement contracted by this Treaty so long as the conditions of this Treaty shall be in force exact the elephants from the Rajah

38. Aitchison, C.U (1863), A Collection of Treaties, Engagements, and Sunnuds, Relating to India and Neighbouring Countries, Volume 2, India Foreign and Political Dept, 1863, PP 159

39. Burghart, Richard (1978), History of Janakpurdham, Phd Thesis, 1978, pp 218

40. Burghart, Richard (1978), History of Janakpurdham, Phd Thesis, 1978, pp 182

41. Letter from King Giraban to Gopal Jha, son of Tata Jha, Miscellaneous Land Grants And Edowments, Regmi Research Series Year 2, No. 9

42. Burghart, Richard (1978), History of Janakpurdham, Phd Thesis, 1978, pp 342

43. Burghart, Richard (1978), History of Janakpurdham, Phd Thesis, 1978, pp 165

44. Burghart, Richard (1978), History of Janakpurdham, Phd Thesis, 1978, pp 304

45. Based on local interview from native of Barahi

46. Burghart, Richard (1978), History of Janakpurdham, Phd Thesis, 1978, pp 421

47. Burghart, Richard (1978), History of Janakpurdham, Phd Thesis, 1978, pp 292

48. The earlier mention of Tharu people can be read in Muslim Scholar Alberuni's book written about 1033 AD : "Marching from Kanoj towards the east, you come to Bari, 10 farsakh; Dugum, 45 farsakh; the empire of Shilahat, 10 farsakh ; the town Bihat, 12 farsakh. Farther on the country to the right is called Tilwat, the inhabitants Taru, people of very black colour and flat-nosed like the Turks. Thence you come to the mountains of Kamru, which stretch away as far as the sea. Opposite Tilwat the country to the left is the realm of Naipal."

    Analyzing Alberuni's statement signifies, Tharus had been part of Tirhut (Tilwat) since long time and in 11th century they were a significant group of Tirhut, which has recorded history and culture dating at-least 2500 years old since the days of Buddha.

49. Bengal District Gazetteers, Volume 10, Part 1, 1907 pp 48-49

50. Krauskopff, Gisele and Meyer, Pamela D (1998), The Kings of Nepal and The Tharu of the Terai, Panjiar Collection, 1998 pp 159

51. Krauskopff, Gisele and Meyer, Pamela D (1998), The Kings of Nepal and The Tharu of the Terai, Panjiar Collection, 1998 pp 135-117

52. Krauskopff, Gisele and Meyer, Pamela D (1998), The Kings of Nepal and The Tharu of the Terai, Panjiar Collection, 1998 pp 132-139

53. Krauskopff, Gisele and Meyer, Pamela D (1998), The Kings of Nepal and The Tharu of the Terai, Panjiar Collection, 1998 pp 142-143

54. Daniel Wrights writes in his book History of Nepal, "To give an idea of the force which can be assembled I may mention that the troops employed in the last war with Tibet in 1854 amounted to 27,000 men with 29,000 partially armed coolies and camp followers and 390,000 unarmed baggage coolies; leaving about 7,000 fighting men at home. The utmost efforts however were made in this war and the country was reduced to the greatest distress the sole result being that the Tibetans agreed to pay an annual tribute of 10,000 rupees (Pound 1000)." See History of Nepal, Daniel Wright, Page 50

55. Burghart, Richard (1978), History of Janakpurdham, Phd Thesis, 1978, pp 400

56. Burghart, Richard (1978), History of Janakpurdham, Phd Thesis, 1978, pp 401
57. Inglis, James (1878), Sport and Work on the Nepaul Frontier, 1878, pp 217
58. Wright, D., ed. 1966. History of Nepal, translated from the Parbatiya by Munshi Shew Shunker Singh and Pandit Gunanand, pp 83. And Regmi, Mahesh C, (1979); Notes on the Revenues System of Nepal During the 19th Century, RRS, Year 11, No. 5, pp 66 and Regmi, Mahesh (1972, 57)
59. Mahesh C, (1979); Notes on the Revenues System of Nepal During the 19th Century, RRS, Year 11, No. 5, pp 67
60. Mahesh C, (1979); Notes on the Revenues System of Nepal During the 19th Century, RRS, Year 11, No. 5, pp 66
61. Oliphant, Laurence (1852); A journey to Katmandu .. with the camp of Jung Bahadoor, PP 173
62. Thapa, Shanker (2000); Historical Study of Agrarian Relations in Nepal(1846-1951), Pinnacle Technology, Feb 10, 2000, Chapter III
63. Madhesh Mal ko Sawal, number 105, updated on 1911 BS
64. Goverment of Nepal, Tarai Ka Madhesiya Ko: ''Aijan Ma Karni Garniya Masinya Ko Ra Namasinya Ko." (On Adultery and Slavery among the Madhesiyas of the Tarai). Ain (Legal Code), (1870 ed) as published in Regmi, Mahesh (1969); Regmi Research Series, Year 1, No. 2, Published December 1, 1969, pp 49
65. Regmi, Mahesh C (1969); Land Regulations in The Tarai, Regmi Research Series, Year 1, No. 2, Published December 1, 1969, pp 33. Also, an abstract translation of some of the provision of the Revenue Regulations of the eastern Tarai Districts of 1861 may be found in Regmi Research Series, 1, 1969, pp. 32-36.

6

Two Nations: Highland and Lowland

Two Nations and Their three Groups - Janajati, Khas and Madhesi

Janajati has been living in hills, mountain and Himalaya since thousands of years. Janajati in Hill consists of multiple groups: Kirâti, Lai, Limbu, Magar, Gurung, Sherpa, Newar, etc. The definition of Janajati is vague and is confused[1] with Newari and for the discussion in this chapter we will categorize Newari one among the Janajati group. Tharu, Rajbansi, Dhanuk, Mushar are identified as lowland plain's Janajati. National Foundation for Development of Indigenous Nationalities (NFDIN) has defined nine criteria for qualification of Janajati[2].

Each Indigenous Nepalese Nationality or Janajati has the following characteristics:

1. A distinct collective identity;
2. Own language, religion, tradition, culture, and civilization;
3. Own traditional egalitarian social structure;
4. Traditional homeland or geographical area;
5. Written or oral history;
6. Having "We" feeling;
7. Has had no decisive role in the politics and government of modern Nepal;
8. Who are the indigenous or native people of Nepal; and
9. Who declare themselves as "Janajati"

Tribal, the translation of Janajati, have been mentioned in the Hindu literatures. We are going to the start of Hindu literature. The story of Lord Shiva and Sati, the first wife of Lord Shiva, is very popular. Daksha, one of the sons of Lord Brahma, the creator of universe, was assigned responsibilities to create and grow the universe, as if like first king of the world. One of the daughters of Prajapati was Sati or Dakshayani, who wished to marry Shiva. Daksha forbade it, but Sati disobeyed him and did so anyway, finding in Shiva a loving husband. Daksha disliked Shiva intensely, calling him a dirty, roaming ascetic and he also reviled the great yogi's gang of spirits and ghosts. Lord Shiva's abode is in Kailash, beyond Nepal and India border in deep Himalaya, currently within Tibet border.

Prajapati Daksha was responsible to ensure 'Law of Divine', prescribed by Hindu poet, was followed. People followed Divine power to get protection for their homes, cattles and society. All those who infringed then established Hindu laws, mostly non-Aryan tribal, were called demons or ghosts. There were series of fights between Gods and Demons. Lord Shiva took the non-partisan stand, and supported demons as he supported Gods, when called for help. That could be the reason, Aryans associated Lord Shiva with Demons. If thought in depth, those demons having close relationship with Shiva would be someone close to his abode Kailash, who is rough, dirty, indisciplined and as destructive as Shiva himself. All this is pointer to the Hilly Tribal of Nepal Himalaya, who have been mentioned as *Mleccha* in the Hindu literatures. Kirati do not follow Hindu religion, however, they regard Lord Shiva as their god too. The Himalayan range and north Indian states have a large number of Shiva followers.

The Mlechha have been regarded as untouchable, indisciplined, violent, and destructive. Thus Hindus living in the plain of India always felt relieved knowing Mlechha land is far away. On the other hand, Mlechha felt relieved too, believing the people on the plain were always pushing them to fight, and both of them are good to be away. In this way, time went ahead for ages and those different races continued to flourish in their own world isolated by the inaccessible mountain ridge and thick Terai jungle which separated mainland Gangatic plains from the interior hill.

Around eleventh century, the attack of Muslim rulers escalated. The Muslims were violent and disliked Hindus. The staunch Hindus also equally disliked the Muslims, since Muslims were forcing impurity unto Hindus by way of cow killing, assaulting Hindu women and forcing Hindus to abandon idol worship.

According to Hindu definition, Muslims were also qualifying to be called Mlechha. Alberuni, the Iranian Muslim scholar who was in India when Ghazni conquered India, writes "All those who would not bear the yoke of the mlechhas fled and took up their abode in the neighboring Hindu empires." Kashmir was still independent Hindu state and was hermetically sealed to all strangers. King Anandapala of North-West, who tried to give some fight to Ghazni, had to flee to Kashmir.

Since then, the Muslim incursion in India increased, and thus increased the flights of ex-Hindu Kings, their ministers and Brahmin pundits in search of hide out places, which Himalaya range provided. The process of migration further escalated after sweeping of North Indian plains and Rajasthan Rajputana by Mughal army under Babur and Akbar during sixteenth century.

The migrating group of ex-Hindu Kings, their ministers and Brahmin pundits left behind their families. Queens and women along with Kids practiced Jauhar (or jowhar), a custom in which they jumped into well of fire wearing their wedding robes, with the intention of committing suicide or self-immolation, in case of their men getting defeated in war with Muslims and they sensed risk to their modesty or risk of being slaves under Muslim rule. In one of a major Jauhar, in the time of Maharawal Jait Singh, Alauddin Khilji besieged the fort of Jaisalmer, and after seven months, 24,000 women committed Jauhar[3].

The ex-Hindu Kings, their ministers and Brahmin pundits would enter hills in search of land away from Mlechhas (both Muslims and British were considered Mlechha). Few pundits of Banaras were also believed to have been expelled from boundary, who entered hill, on their conduct of high exploitation of pilgrims during reign of Aurangzeb[4]. They were young, polished, educated, and politically sharp. However, after entering the Himalayan hills, they found wild, barbaric tribes, 'without faith, but fierce and proud' and the women, who were attractive, were not declining the 'embraces' of the 'polished Brahmans'. Consequently the genetic cross of Brahmin males and Janajati females gave rise to a new race called Khas within Hindu order. Brian Hodgson writes[5] "They found the natives illiterate and without faith but fierce and proud" and further continues "Their object was to make them converts to Hinduism and so to confirm the fleeting influence derived from their learning and politeness. They saw that the barbarians had vacant minds ready to receive their doctrines but spirits not apt to stoop to degradation and they acted accordingly. To the earliest and most distinguished of their converts they communicated in defiance of the creed they taught the lofty rank and honors of the Kshatriya order. But the Brahmans had sensual passions to gratify as well as ambition. They found the native females even the most distinguished nothing loath but still of a temper like that of the males prompt to repel indignities. These females would indeed welcome the polished Brahmana to their embraces but their offspring must not be stigmatized as the infamous progeny of a Brahman and a Mlechha – must, on the contrary, be raised to eminence in the new order of things proposed to be introduced by their fathers. To this progeny also, then, the Brahmans, in still greater defiance of their creed, communicated the rank of the second order of Hinduism; and from these two roots, mainly, sprung the now numerous predominant and extensively ramified tribe of the Khas - originally the name of a small clan of creedless barbarians, now the proud title of the Kshatriya or military order of the kingdom of Nepal… Khas still insist that the fruit of commerce (marriage is out of the question) between their females and males of the sacred order shall be as Kshatriyas, wear the thread, and assume the patronymic title".

The remaining military tribes of the Parbatia are the Magar and Gurung, who refused to mix their blood with the migrant of plains, did not wear thread, and did not come under Hindu fold. Khas are intensely proud of their tradition, and look down upon Magars and Gurungs.

At this point, we can ask, was the migrated Brahmin powerful enough to add new caste order in Hindu establishment? The answer is twofold. (1) That was not first instance, and migrants had precedence from religious book, Mahabharata, to convince the religious orthodox and (2) Migrated group bothered least about the belief prevalent in the Hindus of plains, who were physically far away. The first point is linked to the story of Bhimsen, one among the Pandav brothers, of Mahabharata epic. The second point gave rise to the two groups of Hindus each claiming to be true Hindu in their own way.

Mahabharata is one among the two epics, immensely popular among Hindus, another being Ramayana. Story goes, Pandavas, all the five brothers along with their mother, were roaming in a jungle, where a man eater demon named Hidimb attacked Bhimsen. Bhimsen was strongest among the Pandavas and he fought intensely with Hidimb. However, the fight would turn into Bhimsen's favor, when Hidimba, the sister of Hidimb would tacitly support Bhimsen, finding him impressive handsome male. Hidimb got killed with the support of Hidimba to Bhimsen, and in return Hidimba proposed marriage with Bhimsen, which was accepted by Bhimsen's eldest brother Yudhisthira and mother Kunti. Bhimsen and Hidimba got married, spent long time together at Hidimba place (currently believed to be located in the hill of Manali in Himachal Pradesh or Latoli, Champawat of Uttarakhand of India). Their conjugation gave birth to son Ghatotkach, who had supernatural powers like his mother and religious virtues from his father, yet Ghatotkach and his mother chose to live in the Jungle rather than Aryan cities or Royal palaces.

Bhimsen temples are present in hills[6] and Bhimsen is believed to have ruled hills between Gangotri and Bhutan[7]. In some places, lower caste Hindus worship Bhimsen as their deity.

Probably, story of Bhimsen, Hidimba, and Ghatotkach would have helped migrating Brahmins to convince themselves and others on their engagement with hilly tribal girls. Khas were Hindus, and soon became committed to Brahmanical system, however they showed laxity towards the Hindu laws in regard to dietary obligations and sexual relationship possibly due to involvement in tantric practices. They would consume meat and follow not so strict diet schedule as Brahmins of plains. Similarly, their blood got mixed with Tribals and did not remain pure. Owing to these irregularities, Brahmins from plain were given high importance and were, from time to time, brought to hill for important religious purposes. King Prithivi Narayan Shah invited 100 families of Tirhutia Brahmins and gave large track of land to them because Tirhutia Brahmins were believed to be superior and pure than hilly Brahmins which King wanted to have for his religious rites and rituals[8] Plains Brahmans sometimes refused to call their Hill counterpart as Brahman (Sanskrit word), and only call them in vernacular Nepali term as Bahun Migrated ex-king (Thakuris) and Rajputs, were also regarded impure. The claim for being linked to Rajasthan Rajput by Rana Prime Minister was rejected by Mewar King in Rajasthan[9].

The descendants of migrated Rajput and Kshatriyas of the plains had less desire to mix their proud blood with that of the vile aboriginals compared to Brahmans. Hence Ekthariahs, the descendants of migrated Rajput and Kshatriyas of the plains, claim a vague superiority over the Khas. Thakuri differ from the Ekthariahs only by the accidental circumstances of their lineage being royal. The new race also came up with a new language, a kind of Hindi patois, which was called the language of the Khas, or Khas-Kura which is nowadays the lingua franca of Nepal, that was renamed Nepali somewhere in 1930s. Brian Hudgson writes "The Parbattia language is terse simple sufficiently copious in words and very characteristic of the unlettered but energetic race of soldiers and statesmen who made it what it is. At present it is almost wholly in its structure and in eight-tenths of its vocables substantially Hindee".

Over the period of time, the new breed of orthodox Hindu formed in the Hill and orthodox Hindu of plains started looking at other as inferior to themselves. The Hindu in the Hill had pride that Mlechha (read Muslim) couldn't rule over their Hindu body ever, and lived a life of an independent pure Hindu. They even felt proud that their Hill has never been subjugated by any Muslim ruler ever. They saw the Hindus left out in plain becoming impure due to the pollution of land by Muslim rule, and them compromising on the Hindu values under Muslim rule. However, the Hindus on the plain saw the migrated Hindus in Hill as impure, who compromised on the Hindu strict rules on food and marriage making their blood impure. Hindu of plain were proud that though Muslim conquered upon their body, however they couldn't win over heart and couldn't dictate terms on Hindu practice. Both of them lived happily in their own belief and were separated by hundreds of miles though hill terrain followed by jungle, even if they wanted to have influence over others' belief. To say in other way, two teams of Hindus flourished in last one thousand years, one in Himalayan range and other in north Indian plains, separated by Hill ridges and Jungle of Terai. The Hindus left out in the plains, located in the northern side close to the bottom of hills are the Madhesis.

Difference and Similarities

Religion

Let's start with the Royal documents written at the time of Sen Kings and Shah Kings, former representing plain king and later representing Hill king. Makwani King Digbandhan Sen document written in 1760 have document header as "Shri Ram" and its black seal saying "Shri Ishwar". Another Makwani King Mahipatti Sen of Bijaypur written in 1726 have header as "Shri Lakshminarayan Shri Barahji". It indicates, Sen Kings of plain were follower of Vaishnavism. The royal letters of Shah Kings from Prithivi Narayan Shah to King Gyanendra had header as "Shri Durga" and red-seal (famously called Lalmohar) saying "Jai Durga Bhawani" and having sword symbol within red-seal. This indicates, Shah Kings were follower of Shaivism. Vishnu and Shiva are two supreme lords of Hindu out of three, and other being Brahma. Vishnu symbolize someone who takes care of daily needs of living creatures in the world. Shakti and Shiva symbolize the power and destruction. Vishnu indicates love, and Shiva indicates violence.

The royal documents precisely represent the two cultures of plain and Hill.

Differences are found in religious practices too. In Kathmandu, Lord Ganesh is offered egg (which is a non-vegetarian diet), whereas in Madhesh Ganesh is offered sweets or flowers. In Hill districts, Holi- festival of color- is celebrated on full moon day (Purnima), and plain celebrate it a day after Purnima.

Plain has three days of Diwali festival whereas Hill has five days of celebrations. Hill people say Tihar rather than Diwali or Deepawali or Sukrati as said in plains. On the second day of Diwali, hill folks make groups and go around to the houses of neighbors, friends and family singing and dancing using traditional musical instruments. The hostess usually welcomes them with gifts, rice, fruits and a special type of roti called sel-roti. The group sings songs called dheusi-bhailo ("may your roof be of gold", "may Laxmi forever reside in this house", "may the earth you touch turn into grain", etc) which are thought to be auspicious and goes door to door. There is nothing similar in plains.

Hilly Hindus don't have Rakhi festival, in which sister worship brother. Hilly Hindus instead have sister worshipping brother on Bhai-tika, third day of Diwali. Plain Hindus also celebrate third day of Diwali as sister-brother day.

Hindus in plain are influenced by the Muslims, for example Daha (Tazia) are celebrated by both Hindu and Muslim. Another example is Hindu Suri caste worshipping Muslim Saint Mira as their deity, where Muslim priest Aulia comes for rituals. Hilly Hindu are integrated with Buddhism more, and good example being Swayambhu temple and Muktinath temple where both Hindus and Buddhists worship.

Caste System or Demographic Distribution

In plain lowland Madhesh, there is mix of different castes. Except Tharu and Yadav, no caste forms more than 5 percent of population. All other are in the range of one percentage or so. Indicating that Madhesh society is more homogenous. The caste structure in Madhesh is like a pyramid with Brahmins and Kshatriya smaller numbers at the top compared to the rest of the society.

Unlike Madhesi population, Hill demographic structure is one of an inverted pyramid, with the Khas Brahmins and Kshatriyas being more than 50% of the total Hilly population seating on the top. Dalits are about 12% at bottom of pyramid. Janajatis are also fragmented across different groups.

Marriage

Traditionally Plain people are strict in following the marriage practices, they follow practice of marriage between socially equal castes. Whereas, people from hill have some relaxed customs in terms of sexual relationships compared to the orthodox plain Hindus, and the hill population practice hypergamous (also called marrying up) meaning unions between high caste males and 'tribal' females. The relaxation in marriage relationship has given rise to multiple divisions[10] within Hill Hindu caste; Ekthariahs, Thakuris, Thapa, Bashnyat, Bhandari, Karki, Khanka, Adhikari, Bisht, Kunwar, Baniah, Dani, Gharti and Khattari. The offspring of a Brahman male and a Khas female was accepted as a Khas, with the result that many surnames (thar) were common to both Brahman and Chhetri. Similarly, the offspring of unions between Khas or Brahman male and a Magar or Gurung female were also accepted as Khas[11].

Marriage procession takes place during night time in lowland, and day is the preferred time for Hilly folks.

Marriage is an expensive affair in plains, especially girls family has to take loan.

Treatment of Women

Plain Hindu Males address their wife with equal honorific name as women will address their male husband. For example, Associate Prof Dr. Pramod Mishra of Lewis University say[12], "I never heard my father address my mother without the honorific '*aahaan*' (the highest of the three second person singular pronoun in Maithili)". Dr. Mishra further adds, "Whereas I have never heard a traditional Pahadi husband addressing his wife without '*tan*' (the lowest form of the five second person singular pronoun) or the wife addressing her husband without the third highest (*tapain*) or fourth highest (*hajoor*) in return".

Regarding menstruation related superstition, Dr. Mishra adds "Among the Madhesis, menstruation does not bring untouchability to women". But even now among the educated hill castes in towns and cities with running water and electricity, women suffer from menstrual untouchability every month"[13].

The festivals in plain are driven mostly by women. For example, Chhath, Jitiya, Bhai-dooj (also called Godhan), Sama-Chakewa are all women driven festivals. In terms of music and songs too, they are far superior to their male counterparts; DomKatch Dance, Jhijiya Dance, and marriage songs where they are free to have satirical dialogue upon males.

In survey result published in Nepal National Education Planning Commission 1956, people of plain gave more preference towards co-education, and indicates women are treated relatively better in plain[14]. Only 8% opposed co-education in plain compared to Nepal average of 13%, and 84% plain people favored co-education, compared to Nepal average of 70%.

Attitudes Towards Co-Education

Attitude	Kathmandu Valley	West Nepal	East Nepal	Terai	Average
Opposed	13%	7%	25%	8%	13%
Favour, in general	74%	67%	55%	84%	70%
Favour only in Primary School	61%	51%	51%	59%	56%
Also favour in Middle School	29%	36%	12%	19%	24%
Also favour in High School	12%	11%	20%	6%	12%

Though not practiced today, in the bygone era till twentieth century, Sati (volunteered immolation on fire pyre along with dead husband) was practiced by hilly Hindu people. Jung bahadur tried to control Sati practice with conditional rules, still his three wives out of five chose sati; Maharani Hiranya Garva Kumari, Antaree Maharani and Ramri Maharani. Sati was banned by Prime

Minister Chandra Shumshere Rana[15] on 28th June 1920 a century after practice was made illegal in India. However, Sati was not prevalent in lowland Madhesh, even though there was no rule to ban them. Robert Martin wrote in 1838 "The widows of the Hindus of Mithila are admitted to the same privileges in burning themselves with the bodies of their husbands as in Bengal but the custom is very rare. In many parts no one remembered ever having seen such a sacrifice", further he looked to benchmark Maithili culture for practice of Sati and added "It seems to be most prevalent towards the north east where the customs of Mithila are less prevalent".

In certain Hill Janajati groups, polyandry is practiced though not known in plain group. Polygamy was practiced extensively till three generations before both in Hill and Plain. The menace seems to be petering out from Hindu folds.

Another sensitive issue that is slaying Hill is prostitution. According to a survey, published in Human Rights Watch report[16], in Mumbai brothel, "Seventy percent are thought to belong to ethnic minority groups such as the Tamang, Gurung, Magar, and Sherpa. Women and girls from Nepal's Hindu majority communities comprise about ten to fifteen percent". The report attribute reason for demand in Indian town saying "fair skin and Mongolian features". The supply is linked to the poverty of girl's family and also to the social acceptance. In nineteenth century, ruling Rana families recruited Tamang girl from Helambu region of Sindhupalchok district, forty miles northeast of Kathmandu, to enjoy as concubines, which later became a mark of high social status. Though it looks to have escalated under protection of Rana ruler, prostitution was integrated into elite group since early days. Francis Buchanan Hamilton, on his visit to Kathmandu Valley two centuries back, has written in his book[17] "A female slave is called keti and costs about thirty Mohurs but, if young and handsome, she will bring ten Mohurs additional. A few have been degraded and sold by the raja on account of crimes alleged against them but by far the greatest part has been sold by necessitous parents. All the ketis, even those belonging to the queen, are prostitutes. The poor creatures are therefore forced to sacrifice their chastity, in order to procure clothings". Within plain group, prostitution is practiced by Badibadini community in western Nepal, who were earlier court dancers and musicians. However, plain towns like Birgunj[18], Nepalgunj, Jhapa, Kakarvhitta, and Bhairawa[19] are getting infested with prostitution recently on bigger scale due to increasing Hill Migrants involved in prostitutions[20].

Clothing

Climate and ecology are the great influencer of the clothing. Plain observes high temperature and high moisture in summer. Cold has not been so severe traditionally. Thus, lowland Madhesi wear light weight bare minimum cloths rather than heavier skin tight covering full body. Dhoti and Kurta had been traditional dress for male, and Sari being dress for women. Thin towel called Gamchha is substitute for the handkerchief to clean the high sweating body.

Hilly people wear thick and woolen cloths more often to protect themselves in the cold climate. Cap, chaubandi-surubal, and Khukuri are part of Hilly dress. They have started wearing a tweed coat of European pattern over the chaubandi that men wear with surubal. Plain people have migrated towards the modern paint-shirt combination. Pant-Shirt is also becoming popular in hills.

There are many ethnic groups in Hill, so is variety of dresses. Gurung, Magar, Kirâti, Sherpa, etc. each having their own traditional customs.

Forehead Tika: Madhesi people tikas are neat and well-drawn with Chandan or vermilion. Hilly people make their tika with rice, vermillion and yoghurt (used on most occasions) and are quite unstructured on forehead, while applied.

Women covering head: Hilly women have headscarf, a separate piece of cloth. Plain's women use Sari pallu (extreme side) to cover head and some part of face too (ghunghta).

Married Hilly women also wear heavy "tilahari" with the green pote (beads) which is a form of neck chain or neckless. There is no generalized accepted chain worn by Madhesi women.

Food

Food is also influenced by the climate, environment and productivity of the local land. Hill produces maize more than rice. Plain produces rice in plenty followed by pulses. Plain have favorable climate and plenty of water reservoir helping in fish farming. Whereas, Hill choice of animal protein is through poultry and big animal meet. Plain people would take meat, however will not go beyond goat or fowls. And the quantity of meat consumed by plain people is very less compared to the Hilly people. Plain people's primary sources of protein is milk, fish and pulses. Also, may be due to the cold weather, liquor consumption is more common in Hill compared to in plains, additionally cold climate give motivation to use more ginger and garlic in their food. All these food preferences over a long period of time have integrated into culture of each groups.

Society Culture: Collectivist vs Individualist

Lowland people are individualistic when it comes to public place and don't pay lot of importance on the group. They are more open to outsider in the public affair. Due to this trait, lowlands have become cosmopolitan immigration centers.

Highland people, who are collectivist, have more trouble accepting people from outside in their groups, even from similar neighboring group. For example, Khas don't accept Janajatis in group affairs. Also, it can be found, not a single politician belonging to plain people group has ever won a parliamentary seat from Hill constituency in direct election. On the contrary, the individualist lowland has elected extensive Parliamentarian belonging to Hill migrant group; former Prime Ministers like Girija Prasad Koirala, Bishweshwar Koirala, Madhav Kumar Nepal, Sushil Koirala, Pushpa Kamal Dahal (Prachanda), and Khadga Prasad Oli, they all got elected from plain with plain people's votes.

Newari of pre-Shah era was less collectivist compared to other groups, and had openly accepted varied groups from all direction into then Nepal Valley. Over a period two and half century, they have drifted little more towards collectivism. Still, they are less collectivist than other hill groups. Collectivist trait can be seen from their participation in Rato Machhendra festival - chariot-pulling festival, where whole city comes together, and without collective effort, the procession will not move even an inch. Compare this with famous Chhat festival of Plain people, where each will have their individual worship ghats (place) in a big pond, and there is no dependency on other to celebrate the 2 days of festival, even though it's celebrated in public space.

In Hills, a neighbor goes to other's agriculture field to help in rice planting or paddy harvesting, and other day the favors are returned in the same way. In plain, the labor required is exchanged for monetary exchange (or equivalent commodity like rice). This leads to next characteristic of

Individualistic traits; entrepreneurial and economically liberal. Plain peoples are on the top among the successful business personalities; like Dr. Upendra Mahato, Binod Chaudhary, Aditya Jha and business groups located in Plain like Golchha Group, Kedia Group, etc. There are a few successful business personalities from Newar communities, but then as mentioned, this is linked to their being more individualistic compared to other Hill groups. Khas are most collectivist group among the Hill group, and can be linked to their low ranking in successful business list. Shesh Ghale, a successful businessman, belongs to Janajati stock.

Collectivist Highlanders care more about personal ties, belonging to a group, feeling accepted and respected within the group. They are unfriendly to outsider and don't trust people outside their group. Additionally, collectivist Hilly Hindus care about their image and what plains Hindu think of them.

Not having trust impacts the communication, intransitively impacts the flow of information in the society. This can be linked to the time of British rule in India, when British were banned to enter Hills for fear of information leak. Still today, plain people are pariah in Hill lands for the same fear. I believe, the enforcement of Nepali, even the Mahendra's effort to move back to Nepali (from English penetratation) was to prevent flow of information. Inflow of information and communication was discouraged systematically.

Appearance

Hilly races are "decidedly Mongolian" in appearance, having high cheek-bones, almond-shaped eyes[21], flat noses, little eyes, and thick lips[22]. There are some variations observed in the Khas group whose ancestors are linked to Indian plains. To be tall in Hill brings no special admiration[23]. They are built strong and fair given to their exposure to cold climate, green mountains and fresh air. They are muscular which can be linked to their high intake of animal protein.

Skin of Plain inhabitant is mostly darker in complexion and there are a few with fair color too, which could be linked to their exposure to hot and humid weather. Lower caste exposed to field labor are darker. The hot weather does not support too much of metabolism, to add to that, preference for vegetarian food and burden of exporting agriculture commodity shape the plain people as lean and thin. The high intake of rice – the main staple – brings their tummy out. The facial look is mostly Indian, though have some shadow of Tartaric face – could be due to mixture of small amount of gene over thousands of years from Tibet side or being from aboriginal Dravidian. Especially low caste like Dusad face will look inclined to Tibetan face. The faces of politician Rajendra Mahato and Businessman Upendra Mahato also look slightly inclined to be like Tibetan. Bengalis of India also show somewhat similar facial trait, and they also are on equidistance level as Madhesi from Tibet. Tharu has facial more close to Tibetan, however the skin color and body structure are of Indian description.

Invisible Personality

Chinese traveler, scholar and a great Buddhist monk of that time Yuan Chwang - also known as Hiuen Tsang and Hwen Thsang - travelled from China to Central India in 629-645 A.D. He studied places, people, their behaviors, countries, and politics in addition to Buddhism. In his book there is an earliest account of Lumbini (La-fa-ni), Nepal Valley (Ni-po-lo), Khasghar (Ka-Sha), Vriji (Fu-li-chih) equivalent to today's eastern Madhesh including Darbhanga having Janakpur (Chan-shu-na) as capital of Vriji, neighboring Vaishali (Fei-shi-li) and sparsely populated ruined Kapilbastu.

Yuan Chwang describes: people of Nepal were "rude and deceitful"[24], Vriji People were "hasty-tempered"[25] which is different from the description of Vaishali people that he found were "honest, fond of good works, esteemers of learning"[26] and people of Kapilbastu as "genial"[27] implying friendly and cheerful.

Yuan Chwang further mentions, Nepal people insulted honesty, trust and moral values though they were skillful mechanics. In his own word: "good faith and rectitude were slighted by them; they had no learning but were skillful mechanics, they were ugly and coarse in appearance".

During the 1792 war of Gurkha-China 1792, the Gurkha were labelled as Thieves and the country as "Country of Thieves"[28]. This statement still recorded in a stone slab below Potala palace in the description of defeat of Gurkhas in 1972.

When British EIC started ruling in India, they came in close proximity with Hill people and gathered lot of information about the area and people. The process escalated during the period of British-Gurkha war of 1814-1816, the more detailed information were collected about the Gurkha ruler, Hilly peoples, lowland plain people and frontier peoples. Hamilton, who spent few years researching the Gurkha domination and is believed to be having detailed account of early nineteenth century writes about the Khas people "the Parbutties resemble entirely the Hindus of Northern parts of India: and delight in swaggering about fully armed, and in boasting of their warlike, and predatory adventures. They are however a diminutive race of men, but very active and hardy."[29] Hamilton continues saying Khas spend their morning in sleeping and remaining days in religious ceremonies thus hardly time left for business and learning "no time is left for business, nor for informing their minds concerning anything useful."[30] Hamilton also gives an insight into the criminal culture that was evolving in the plain lowland. Encouraged by Gurkha King Pratap Singh desired to increase revenue by attracting settlers from British India side "advances were made to poor wretch, who at home could not procure a subsistence. And all thieves, debtors and vagabonds were received with open arms."[31] To understand, how the Gurkha rules encouraged corruption of culture in plain land, Hamilton mention example of a Massun Row, a Mocuddams who was lower in rank than Suba, however, was valued more than Suba. Hamilton writes "Massun Row, had under his care three other villages. He was a man of considerable influence, being a very notorious and barbarous robber. On this account he was greatly feared by all his neighbours, who called him Sirdar, a title of much higher rank than that even of Suba, and to which he had in no manner any legal right. If we could credit the natives, his followers amounted to a thousand men able to bear arms. At convenient times he sends [his men] into the Company territory to steal cattle, or to commit similar depredations [criminal acts].... Such practices, it is said, are only allowed within the Terriany; and in fact, near the capital, we found the police tolerably good."[32]

In the collection of war papers, there is mention of these dacoits helping Gurkha army during British-Gurkha war. Massun Row (now spelled as Musun Rout) was killed during 1814-1816 war on 25 November 1814 in Burhurwa[33], while he was in Gurkha army camp along with Parsuram Thapa (Subah of the Bara, Parsa and commandant of the troops) and Chandra Shekhar Upadhyay (Vakeel of Rajah of Nepaul, who later signed Sugaolee treaty on behalf of Gurkha King Girvan Yudh). 3 sardars and 51 Gurkha soldier were killed in addition to Musun Rout.

British-Gurkha war papers collection have few insight into the characteristics of both Hill and Plain people. It mentions Gurkha commander as "subtle treacherous, faithless and avaricious to an extreme" and adds "after conquest and victory are bloodthirsty and relentless" and continues as "after defeat mean and abject". In the same letter that was written by Captain Hearsey to Secretary J Adams in London in Dec 1814 cautions, "No reliance can be placed" on any of Gurkha terms or treaties. Letter also give example of playing India against China and vis-a-versa in the form of deceits. Gurkha threatened Chinese dressing like British India Army "threatening countenance towards the Chinese Government pretending to be a part of our Government" officers and on the other side they were threatening British India, by writing them letter in Chinese style, and claiming to be part of Chinese rule "imitating the Chinese address and forms and wishing to inculcate in their minds that they were tributary to the Chinese"[34].

War paper collections also provide insight into plain peoples. A letter from Sarun magistrate[35] describes plain people fighting among families and neighbors rather willing to take up arm against outsiders, "although they are ever ready to resort to arms in their own private disputes concerning crops and boundaries yet they evince no such alacrity in the pursuit of decoits"[36]. The same letter indicates ordinary lowland peasant habit is to plunder neighbor property, rather defend their own from outsider "plunder the property of others than to defend their own". Similar observation was made by Magistrate of Tirhut C.J Sealy[37] in a letter, "cry of dacoit will strike such terror as to prevent the bravest from putting their heads even out of their doors although the common cry of thief only will generally produce the collection of the inhabitants of any village".

Two decades after Sugaolee treaty, Brian Hodgson and his assistance A Campbell were busy collecting information, as was mandated to them, and suggesting priorities for British government to engage Gurkha for permanent peace. Hodgson found the increasing Gurkha Army size as deliberate and politically motivated, though not sensible for larger benefit of country, having risk of flight of peace. Hodgson proposal was to engage Gurkha in commerce and recruit surplus Gurkhas into British Army, but he knew the challenges in the way. A Campbell has mentioned in a report[38] about the behavior of Gurkha people "the sway of a fierce and turbulent race, ignorant of arts and commerce, and devoted to war and plunder". Despite all those odds, Gurkha was able to retain high expense on Army because he found revenue coming from plains helping to finance Army as well as importing Army supplies. A Campbell appreciates the hardworking people of plain saying[39] "the entire population of the Terai is agriculture, there being no unproductive class whatever". The famous Nepal National Education Planning commission has underscored the similar fact in its 1956 report mentioning hardworking spirit of plain people: "Terai where the people have to struggle very hard for their livelihood and it is very difficult for them to spare even a few hours to devote to learning".

The arts of Nepal valley are contribution of Malla period and prior dynasties. Shah Kings and Rana rulers have hardly contributed in the enrichment and expansion of heritage, except few palaces built for their own use.

Heritage Site	Construction Period
Kasthamandapa	Early sixteenth century by King Laxmi Narsingha Malla
Taleju	Early Malla Period
Krishna	Built 1637AD by King Siddhi Narasigh Malla
55 Windows Palace (Pachpanna Jhyale Durbar)	By Malla King Yaksha Malla in 1427 AD
Kathmandu Durbar Square	Malla Period
Patan Durbar Square	Malla Period
Bhaktapur Durbar Square	Malla Period
Changu Narayan	Mandeva in 464 AD
Boudhanath Stupa	Licchavi Period
Ranipokhari	Built in 1670 AD by King Pratap Malla
Temple of Rato Macchindranath, Bungmati	Malla Period
Stone water taps "Dhunge Dhara"	Malla Period
Hanuman Dhoka Palace	First created by Pratap Malla
9 Storied Hanuman Dhoka Palace	Prithivi Narayan Shah
7 Storied Nuwakot palace	Prithivi Narayan Shah
Pashupati	Established long time ago. Last renovated during Malla King Ananta Malla period
Swayambhu	Established long time ago. Last major construction was done by Pratap Malla in 17th century. He built a temple and stairs.
Singha Durbar	Built in 1908 by Chandra Samsher Rana

Further below are given examples to link the Hidden Personality, which generally cannot be seen on face, and which were mentioned by different people of the period with regard to Hilly people (Khas/Parbatia and Janajati).

Treacherous, Faithless and Avaricious

- King Prithivi Narayan Shah married to Indra Kumari, the daughter of King Hem karna Sen of Makwanpur, because Queen Chandra Prabhavati wanted to have matrimonial relation with Makwanpur with a view to get some help of arms and ammunition from Makwanpur[40]. During marriage, King Prithivi Narayan demanded dowry of Navlakha necklace (value of Nine Lakh rupee) and an elephant[41], which added to the dispute in marriage.
- King Prithivi Narayan Shah did treaty with King Jai Prakash Malla of Kathmandu, with the assumption that on this pretext he will cheat him. Later Jai Prakash Malla was attacked and dethroned.
- King Prithivi Narayan went to the house of Bhaktapur King Ranjeet Malla and stayed there for long period, and Malla king regarded him as his son, due to family friendship between Bhaktapur and Gorkha. However, King Prithivi Narayan dethroned King Ranjeet Malla for no reason but greed.
- King of Tanahu, Tribikram Sen and Prithivi Narayan's father were friends. Guru Gaureshwar was their common teacher. Taking advantage of this relationship, through this Guru, Prithivi Narayan Shah called King Tribikram Sen to the bank of the Trishuli on the pretext of making friendship. Prithivi Narayan Shah had hidden arms in the sand of the bank of the river. When Tribikram Sen came, he was captured by the Gurkhas[42]. He was taken in chains to Nuwakot and was imprisoned there. By such a treacherous act, got hold of Tanahu and annexed it to the kingdom of Gorkha.
- In the year 1774 the Gurkhas attacked Bijaypur and assassinated as many of the legitimate family as they could seduce within their power by treachery and breach of pledged faith. The last heir aged only 5 years, who was then staying in Nathpur Indian with his mother, was destroyed by having a loathsome disease communicated to him by a Brahmin in place of the small pox inoculation. The Brahmin, disguised as medical specialist, went to mother and convinced he will help with Smallpox vaccination, however he instead injected another disease as planned, with the intent to kill the 5 years old, last royal successor. Soon after the boy died[43].

- As per the British-Gurkha treaty of 1792, both British and Gurkha would charge uniform import duty of two and a half percent. However this was never implanted by Gurkha government, though they enjoyed the two and a half percent import duty on their exports. Brian Hodgson raised this issue on 1st August 1834 asking, why were the additional duties levied by Nepal on Indian goods, while the Nepalese products were regularly charged only at the stipulated rate of two and a half per cent? The Nepalese government, on the contrary, habitually violated all its terms. Instead of two and a half per cent, almost ten percent duty was charged on the goods imported from India[44].

- After returning from Banaras, King Ran Bahadur sent marriage proposal to Palpa King Prithivi Pal Sen that he wants to marry sister of Palpa's King. Palpa king sensed something fishy, however still trusting, he sent his sister and brother to Kathmandu agreeing for marriage proposal. On their arrival at Kathmandu, King Ran Bahadur convinced his to-be brother in law that it would be honorable if King Prithivi Pal Sen, who is elder to Ran Bahadur, give sister by his hand. A Brahmin went to Palpa and convinced Prithivi Pal Sen saying King Ran Bahadur has given oath that no injury will be done to guests. Then Prithivi Pal went to Kathmandu, but Prithvipal had no sooner reached Kathmandu, with about 400 attendants, than these were disarmed, he and his principal officers were put in close confinement, and no more mention was made of the marriage. King Prithivi Pal Sen was later killed in cold blood by Bhimsen Thapa while in confinement[45].

- As per the treaty of 1801, the Tribute of Gurkha Kingdom to British was scrapped[46] by British in the hope of getting business and transit to Tibet. The Gurkha got the fruit, however, British never got the benefit.

- The initial Sugaolee treaty signed on 2 December 1815 was not accepted by Gurkha, until next military enforcement was started by British in 1816, when British captured land till Hetauda and was only 30 miles away from Kathmandu. Later on some modification on Treaty was suggested, and addendum was followed on 8 December 1816. As per addendum, government of Gurkha agreed "to refrain from prosecuting any inhabitants of the Terai, after its revertance to his rule, on account of having favoured the cause of the British Government during the war". However in reality, the people have become victims at the hand of state.

- Article 6 and 7 of 1950 Indo-Nepal Treaty of Peace and Friendship stipulates "national treatment" on a reciprocal basis, to the nationals of one country in the territories of the other the same privileges in the matter of residence, ownership of property, participation in trade and commerce, movement and other privileges of a similar nature. However in reality, Nepal broke these provisions by restricting Indians to buy land and get government jobs. India still allows Nepalese to get government jobs including Army in Gurkha Army that employ around 50,000 Nepalese.
- Nepal government signed two agreements with Madhesis in 30 August 2007 and 28 February 2008 to resolve Madhesi issue of Federalism, Proportional and inclusive participation in Government jobs including group entry into Army. However, a decade after, the issue is still hingering.

Bloodthirsty and Relentless

- After Makwanpur capture[47] (1762), Prithivi Narayan Shah focused on the blockade of Nepal valley focusing on Newar settlement specifically. The king of Gorkha, hopeless of his ability to get possession of Nepal Valley by strength, hoped to effect his purpose by causing a famine, and with this design, stationed troops at all the passes of the mountains to prevent any intercourse with Nepal Valley; and his orders were most rigorously obeyed, for every person who was found on the road, with only a little salt or cotton on him, was hung upon a tree; and he caused all the inhabitants of a neighboring village to be put to death in a most cruel manner (even the women and children did not escape) for having supplied a little cotton to the inhabitants of Nepal. Father Giuseppe writes "when I arrived in that country at the beginning of 1769, it was a most horrid spectacle to behold so many people hanging on the trees on the road. Demoralized by the blockade and bereft by any natural defences, the Kingdom of Nepal was finally overrun in September without a drop of blood being shed[48].

- After Kirtipur was captured by Gurkha Army in their third attempt in 1767, to take revenge with the citizens of people, and also to spread terror among the inhabitants, cut off the noses and lips of the defeated townspeople for putting up such fierce resistance[49]. Noseless people were seen by Colonel Kirkpatrick and Italian Capuchin missionary, Father Giuseppe. An estimated 865 commoner's nose were cut[50]. Kirtipur resident's house were put on fire.
- The Gurkha King put all small kids in mortars to death in short span of five years of war. Gurkha soldeirs segregated all pregnant women from other women and killed the sons in their womb (committed foeticide), thus leading to the death of the mothers as well[51]. This event is mentioned in detail in Brian Hodgson's collection[52].
- Gurkha King Prithivi Narayan Shah, after coquering Nuwakot, captured its commander Jayanta Rana and killed him by pealing the skin[53], so as to spread terror in the mind who could dare to challenge Prithivi Narayan Shah.
- On the morning of the 29th of May 1814, the principal police station in Butwal was attacked by a large body of the Gurkha troops headed by Munraj Foujdar, a high ranking Gurka officer surprised Company police and revenue stations, murdering 18 men[54]. The chief Thannadar escaped the massacre but was made prisoner and murdered in cold blood, with peculiar barbarity. Munraj Foujdar deliberately caused him to be tied to a tree and to be shot to death with arrows as an example to deter others from taking office under British against the will of the Gurkhas.
- Number of Court Parva (Massacres): In 1805 Bhimsen Killed many people in coldbood, on suspicion of King Ran Bahadur murder. In 1846, Jung Bahadur Rana instigated and led killing of many member of the Nepalese palace court. Later on, Jung Bahadur killed more people, who were political rival during Bhandarkhal massacre and Aul massacre.
- During Maoist insurgency period, around thirteen thousand people were killed in the conflicts between Army and Maoists.
- In Royal Massacres that happened on June 2001, whole family of then King Birendra were killed. Around more than 10 Royal member

of the family lost their lives, including King, Queen, Prince and Princess.

- Nepal police killed 48 peaceful protestors during 2015 Madhesh agitation[55], most of them were shot bullets above chest[56].

Mean and Abject

- After British-Gurkha 1814-1816 war, the entry restrictions of English people inside Nepal were strictly followed, though British resident was accepted through Sugaolee treaty. British had resident placed in Kathmandu, however resident staff were in virtual house arrest in Kathmandu till Bhimsen was in power. No one was allowed to meet or talk to resident staff while they were on road, and even their movements were restricted to minimal places. However, there was no reciprocal norms practiced by Gurkhas while in India at the time of visiting places of pilgrimages like Jagannath Puri, Banaras, etc. The similar situation was applicable to in respect of their blood relatives. This situation persisted to the extent that Gurkhas began availing British facilities while in India[57].
- Daniel Wright, who served as the Residence Surgeon, or chief medical officer, for ten years, 1866 to 1876 and also had collected largest number of Sanskrit manuscripts has written his observation saying[58] "Personally, the higher classes are overpoweringly polite and affable to European officials, or to anyone who is likely to be able to benefit them. Otherwise their bearing is rude and insolent in the highest degree. In fact, they seem to think rudeness a proof of manly independence. They are always ready to ask for favors, either public or private; but when any return is expected, the less that is looked for from them the better"[59].
- In early days of education planning after 1950-51 political change, a nationwide survey was conducted by Nepal government and in its report, Nepal National Education Planning commission has noted people's reluctance towards spending on education, but no hesitation in spending money on "beer and other intoxicating drinks, and on gambling". The report has not mentioned the group name, however the affinity towards beer and intoxicated drinks has been in Hill community more, so I assume, the observation was for the same.

The report further add "To them the acquisition of knowledge is a means of getting an official post or riches. Once they get through their studies and become officials, they think they or their sons can wear the gold badges like those of the Khardars, Dithas and Subbas, and make money". Here the report indicates corruption within government officers, and support with the previous trends saying "In times gone by, and even now, people serving in many places as Khardars for only a year have been found to have enriched themselves enormously and to be in no necessity of serving the Government again". Plain people had negligible access to Government Jobs, and the statement stands for Hill people[60].

Financial Behavior

As far as money is concerned, Highlanders love to earn and regard money as something that should be spent. Therefore, from money perspective, according to Northey[61], they are "Anglo-Saxon" in orientation.

Plain people love to earn money equally, however when it comes to spending they are miser. They love hoard money even when required for essential expenditure for health checkup, child education and self-clothing except when required to spend for extravagant marriage. Plain people are more in businesses for livelihood (compared to government employed highlander) and thus this has also given them better exposure to finance management.

Ethnic Group vs Indian: Proximity Map

All the three groups have direct relationship with India. Janajati today forms the largest group to benefit from the employment in Gurkha Army. Khas group has blood relation with the elites in India, also they are the migrant of India while Mlechha (Mughal and British) were ruling. Madhesh are on Indo-Nepal border and having family kins across the border.

The effort below is to summarize as to which group positions itself how closely with India.

<u>Culture Proximity</u> (India – Madhesi – Khas – Janajatis)

Today, Madheshis share more cultural events with Indians, more than other groups. Culture will include clothing, festivals, arts, language, food, etc. Janajati shares several traits with Indians on culture front. Khas having

Hindu heritage, have better closeness than Janajati, with Hindu majority India.

<u>Clothing</u> (India – Madhesh – Khas – Janajatis)

Madhesh is definitely close to India on clothing. Women from both sides prefer Saris and men's ethnic wear being Dhoti. We need to remember, it is Dhoti, which forms contempt in Hilly groups, though Bahun would still wear Dhotis. Similar to culture, Janajatis are less matching with India, and Khas has lot many closeness of clothing choice with Indians. For example, Daura-Suruwal was ethnic wear of Rajasthan, and is still found there.

<u>Geography</u> (India – Madhesh – Khas – Janajati)

In terms of geography, India is very diverse, and so is Nepal. However, for the discussion, we consider the center of India as reference point. Most of India has plain land, and as we go north, we increase height from sea level. Madhesh forms the border, so they are set close to India. However, among the other two, Bahun are also accessible from mid-range hills. Janajatis live in extreme far of Nepal, and can be found generally in less accessible places.

<u>Language</u> (India – Khas – Madhesi – Janajati)

Considering Hindi as base of India and Nepali (also called Parbatia or Khas) as base of Nepal, both the languages match with each other very closely. As Brian Hodgson has noted, 80% of the words of Nepali is similar to Hindi[62]. Awadhi, which is spoken in Western plains of Nepal and Bhojpuri, spoken in central plain has similarity with Hindi and they are considered to be dialects of Hindi. Maithili has commonality with Bengali. All these languages, Nepali, Maithili, Awadhi, and Bhojpuri have speakers in India too, in large number. Janajatis have varied languages which are unique. However the people of Janajatis have themselves switched to Nepali languages, and very few of them are still speaking Native Janajati languages. Tharu has multiple languages, and has speakers in India too.

<u>Political Connections</u> (India – Khas – Janajati – Madhesi)

Khas has closest political connection with Indian political group. Khas has been ruling class of Indian estates before they migrated to Nepal few centuries back. After coming to Nepal, they maintained minimum links among elite class whenever there was an opportunity. In a drive to establish political connection during 1839, Gurkha rulers initiated a drive, and this has been acknowledged in the 1839 British-Gurkha treaty article three "With the zemindars and baboos on this side of the Ganges who are connected by marriage with the Royal family of Nepal exchange of letters and persons shall remain open to the Nepal Government as heretofore". Even today, there still remain family connections between elites. Some of the high level connections are (1) Karen Singh of Kashmir having relationship in Nepal's Rana families. He married Yasho Rajiya Lakshmi, granddaughter of Rana Primeminister Mohan Shumsher JB Rana (2) King Gyanendra have family relations in Royal Indian families (3) Former Army Chief Pyar Jung Thapa married his daughter Pragyashree to Prince Pratapsinh Gaekwad of Baroda, grandson of the late Maharaja Pratapsinh Rao Gaekwad of Baroda, India, in 2006 (4) Pashupati Shamsher Jung Bahadur Rana married into Scindia family. His wife Usha Raje Scindia, daughter of Gwalior dynasty queen (late) Vijayaraje Scindia, is sibling of current Chief Minister of Rajasthan (India) Vasundhara Raje Scindia and former Indian cabinet minister late Madhavrao Scindia. Also, Pashupati's sister married to the same Scindia family.

<u>Strategic Significance to India</u> (India – Khas – Janajati – Madhesi)

India's strategic value in Nepal is in respect of the activities of China, and a few other foreign countries. India gives more value to Khas in terms of strategic significance. First Khas has sweeping control over the say of the country affair, and second, they also have the Hindu high caste connections with the most of the ruling people in India. Second strategic significance is given to Janajatis because of their having dwellings close to China/Tibet border. Last the Madhesis, who neither pose risk nor benefit to India, when it comes to China factor.

<u>History</u> (India – Khas – Madhesi – Janajati)

Khas has very recent ancestry link with Indian plains. Most Khas claims their blood from Rajputana of Rajasthan. Both King Rajendra Shah and Rana Prime Minster Jung Bahadur sent embassies to India to link their roots. Khas elites have time and resource to preserve and cherish their past history. On the other hand, Madhesis are peasant, and hardly get time to think on common history with India, so they never get the desired response from Indian counterpart too. There are some common History between Madhesi people and Indian people of Bihar and UP. Janajati 'Kirâti' shares little history with India, except few mentions in the Hindu epic Mahabharata, Vedic literatures and during the time of Chanakya.

<u>Religious Relationship</u> (India – Khas – Madhesi – Janajati)

In terms of Religion, Khas find stronger footholds in India, Hindu majority country, for their claim being progeny of two high castes of Hindus like Brahmin and Rajput. They together form one third of total population in Nepal. Madhesis have diverse Hindu caste, having pyramid structure, lower caste forming the larger base, and high caste forming very little. Most Janajatis claim themselves to be from outside of the Hindu system, except a few Newari Hindus.

<u>Fear from India</u> (India – Madhesi – Khas – Janajati)

Madhesis do not have sense of separate nationalism compared to India, thus doesn't feel threat of getting engulfed in Indian plain. On the other extreme, Janajatis have built separate Nationalism since Vedic age, and always feel threat from great Indian plain, having Aryan civilization. Khas is mixed race of Hindu blood and Janajati blood, and they feel inclined to both, as and when opportunity arises.

<u>Government Employment in India</u> (India – Janajati – Khas – Madhesi)

Most of Indian government jobs done by Nepalese are in Army. Janajatis, traditionally, have been choice in Gurkha regiment in India, since British days. Janajatis also choose the Army job in absence of other available opportunities. Khas are present in few well paid white-collar jobs in India. Today, they can be found in software industry, Bollywood, small businesses etc. In the private sector, in the field of unorganized jobs in India, Janajatis and Khas are equally found in menial jobs like house security, restaurant helper, house cook, etc. Madhesis are close to nothing in Indian government jobs, rather they can be found in a few seasonal jobs in the agricultural fields in Punjab.

<u>Physical Appearance</u> (India – Madhesi – Khas – Janajati)

Madhesis are having blood of Indian plain, and they look similar to north Indians in features. Janajatis are Mongolian in features; though there are many sub-groups within it. Khas has mix of both Indian blood and Janajati blood, thus their appearance bears mixed features.

Contempt Against Plain People

We read in the previous section, the independent existence of two civilizations, Aryan in Plain and non-Aryan in Hill, happy in their own space before Muslim arrival in Indian subcontinent. However, this was not sufficient to explain ambitions that were there in the minds of new Hindu migrants. These migrants (King, their ministers and purohits) had been rulers of Indian plains in past, so wanted to have similar privileges bestowed on them. The migrations of Hindus were not in a big group as army, or big enough to create suspicion in the minds of Native Hill people, Janajatis. Given acrimony between Hill and Plain since thousands of years, migrants wanted a strong story for them to be accepted in the Janajati group, when they entered Hill for the first time. This is when migrants used the story that was palatable to Janajatis – the rulers in plain are tyrants. Labeling, people left out in plain as tyrants, migrants were buying their acceptance among Janajati, and also opening a door of future alliance. The relationship between Janajatis and new migrants bloomed. Migrants, understood the people, politics in new land, and found natives to be devoid of any religion, naïve, and ignorant of politics. There were three tasks to be accomplished (1) Marrying female and establishing new caste "Khas" resulting into almost half of hill population (2) Converting other hill people into Hindu religion, those who didn't qualify for "Khas" Caste based on blood relationship, was labeled low caste Hindu (3) Occupying the highest political positions and opportunities of ruling Hills.

First and second steps didn't create so much of hostility between migrants and native Janajatis, than third. Over a period of time, Janajatis were slowly pushed to the corner by migrants, however it was already late by the time they realized it. Many of the old dynasties that ruled hills, where replaced by new Khas rulers. Most Janajatis were pushed from West to East. The migrant entered from western side, so they had their strong hold in the eastern hill, and manifested in ruling Baisi and Chaubisi Rajya (federation of twenty-two and twenty-four states).

Despite the differences among the Khas and Janajatis, both of them continued to have the common rival in south lowland plain, however, for different reasons. The Khas had rivalry with southern plain to claim who represents - *ashal Hindustani* - pure Hindu or true inheritor of Hindu culture. Janajatis continued the belief that down the hill in south lives tyrants who do not like their existence on earth. The belief that Janajatis nurtured had further received nourishment from Khas and made deep root in psychology on hill. Whenever a child would cry, mother would say keep quiet else there is big black ghost behind the big rock downhill that would come and take away crying child. If a plain people by chance reach street of hill, mother will caution child, do not go out else they would put you in sack bag and take away. And when an adult encounter with any Madhesi, they would say "it's Madhesi, not a man"[63] implying Madhesis were below human status.

It went from generation to generation, till ambitious King Prithivi Narayan Shah realized the gap between Khas and Janajati; and difference of both of them from plain peoples. King was ambitious, he had political skills, and he wanted muscle - which he saw among Janajatis - for his dream to become ruler of Nepal Valley and Makwanpur, which were having wealth and financial resources. He started thinking way to consolidate hilly people, which were segregated based on multiple states and Khas-Janajati division, to enable him consolidate state power. He knew the strength and weakness of each group. However the most vital was consolidating the contempt against lowland plain people, so in the tussle-between Hill Rulers, no plain people should come forward to interfere. King PN got opportunity to fan fire between hill-plain, while he was on his way to Banaras on pilgrimage, and en route met a party of hillmen from Parvat, Palpa and Pyuthan. He won them over by telling them that though they belonged to different states in the Hills - when we are in the plains (*madhes*), all hillmen (*pahari*) are one[64].

When Prithivi Narayan captured the Kathmandu Valley, he expelled the Plain's Businessman from Valley[65] to reconcile with the Newari mercantile community, as later was not happy with King Prithivi Narayan blockage that made the economy of valley collapse making it weaker and opening for political take over. Prithivi Narayan, also disbanded the twelve thousand Tirhutia Army[66] that formed the core of King Jay Prakash Malla[67].

Jung Bahadur Rana endorsed the difference in constitution "Muluki Ain" by defining "people of Hill" and also giving them priority in the Jamindari/patwari jobs available in plains. Gurkhas were proud of their independence, and further felt superior by mid-nineteenth century, due to their ability to stand prominent, when other Hindu Kingdoms had surrendered to British rule. The arrogance of superiority added to their contempt against Plain people. The plain Mishra/Jha Brahmins, who were considered superior to Hill counterparts by King Prithivi Narayan Shah for Hindu rituals, were demoted through Mulki Ain 1854. When the 1854 *Muluki Ain* (National Code) gave legal sanction to a single caste-hier-archy throughout Nepal, plains Brahmans were placed not only below the hill Brahmans but in a lower position than Thakuris and Chhetris[68].

English people noticed the behavioral difference between Hill and Plain people while preparing for the Gurkha-British war 1814-1816. British recruited Hill tribes into Nasiri regiment from the army, who had been defeated by British, in western frontier. However, it was Hodgson, who did extensive research of Hill people while staying in Nepal residency, and later built a case for more Hill tribe recruitment into British Army, in addition to political reason to absorb surplus armies than required by Gurkha Kingdom. Hodgson emphasized Hill groups have energy, love for military enterprise, unadulterated military habits, freedom from caste complexity and discipline. Moreover, he emphasized, group will be more reliable to British than ruling Indian plains, because he believed, Hill people have 'emphatic contempt of Madhesias (people of the plains)'[69]. The Hodgson's voice got priority among the British decision makers, when British East India Company faced the unprecedented challenge from 1857 revolution in northern India plain in Bengal, Bihar, UP, Delhi, etc – and Gurkha armies officially were sent from Nepal valley to suppress the 1857 mutiny under the guidance of Rana Prime Minister Jung Bahadur Rana.

How effective were Hill against plain people and how superior they compared to plain people is a different topic of discussion. Sam Cowan, a retired British general, believed 'Martial Races' is a myth created by British, and ongoing conflicts and presence of high number of Madhesi, Tharu and lower caste in the Maoist PLA ranks have broken the myth of 'Martial Races', and insists everyone can fight, as long as there is a cause, the right motivation, the right training and, above all, the right leadership[70].

Going back to the subject, many British of that time noticed the differences between Plain and Hill people. Bengal 1857 mutiny report states "They (Goorkha) speak with the utmost contempt of the Sepoys, whom they call the Kala-log, the black fellows, although they have been soundly thrashed by the latter alone."[71] In 1857, though British were having both Indian infantry and Gorkha infantry together to help suppress the mutineers, however, a British officer Macintyre reported that Gorkha wanted to pitch tents with those of the British soldiers, because they don't want to mix up with Kala log (black folk)[72]. Towards the end of nineteenth century, an officer (General Sale Hill) of Gurkha army was quoted "They hate and despise Orientals of all other creeds and countries and look up to and fraternize with Europeans whom they admire"[73].

It is open secret that one of the British strategies in Asia during colonial day was to divide and rule. In case of Hill-Plain divide, British acted as catalyst, and magnified the already existing differences[74] that could serve later purpose in the subcontinent. Anup Pahari, a native scholar of Nepal, emphasizes "anti-desi air in Gurkha regiments was a social, racial and strategic distance carefully cultivated by the battalions". After British left India, the most of the Gurkha army is left with India, and their count today is about 50,000 in Indian army. Though the scenario has changed in India, the country of *kala log*, the change is elusive for *Kala log* of Madhesh, analogue to British dealing within Gurkha country despite having British raj in India, that Sir Richard Carnac Temple has carefully stated "In their own country they are jealous of foreigners (British) and self-assertive"[75].

There are few accounts available to show, how Madhesh were treated in the Nepal political parties.

In the 1959 election, in a party meeting BP Koirala had tough task in selecting candidates for the constituencies in the plain districts. He was suggested by a few to select ethnic Madhesi for Madhesh based constituency for the chance to win. However, he did not like the idea based on the communal ground. In the same meeting, BP found the support from plain origin fellow, a Jha and to-be potential candidate Nirgun Yadav, to give ticket to Saroj Koirala, a hill origin person , to fight election from Siraha, a plain district[76]. Saroj did win the election. However, in the same election, BP Koirala missed the opportunity to put a plain origin candidate in Hilly district and get him/her selected, the trend that has not been broken till today by either Nepali Congress or any other political party.

After short period of armed struggle, BP Koirala returned to Nepal in 1980, and his agenda to reconcile with King was given name as "Rastriya Melmilap" (English translation "National Reconciliation"). During that time, many senior Madhesi leaders of Nepali Congress felt being sidelined in the Party and they established "Purbanchal Congress" as a pressure block within that party. Mahendra N Nidhi, Gajendra N. Singh, Rameshwar P. Singh, and few more prominent members of southern plain were part of that block[77]. Mahendra N. Nidhi also formed "Hindi Rakchha Samiti" in 1957 against Mahendra's Policy.

Harkha Gurung published a report titled 'Internal and International Migration in Nepal' in 1983 suggesting strict ban on Indo-Nepal people movement along with few more stringent measures counterproductive to plain people. Gajendra Narayan Singh, then Nepali Congress member, wanted strong reaction from Congress on this report, in addition to the traditional issue of language. Singh's voice was subdued, and he resigned from Congress to form Sadbhavana Parishad ("Goodwill Council") in 1985 along with Ram Janam Tiwari, Shyam Lal Mishra, Balram Nayak, and Sankar Kediya[78]. This council became Sadbhavana Party after 1990 revolution and restoration of democracy.

Maoist party led by Prachanda and Bhattarai went through the same churning. Jay Krishna Goit, the head of Madhesi Mukti Morcha, a sister arm of underground Maoist Party, resigned and formed Janatantrik Terai Mukti Morcha (JTMM) around 2005 saying, plain people are discriminated against inside party structure, and in the nine years of Maoist insurgency (revolution), only one member of Terai region got included in central committee[79].

Next wave of Madhesis to desert Nepali Congress party was after 2005's political uprising. Madhesis leaders were not happy with the NCP leadership for its handling of Madhesi issue raised through 2007's Madhesis Protest, and Mahanta Thakur resigned from Nepali Congress and under Girija Prasad Koirala formed TMLP (Terai Madhesh Loktantrik Party) in 2008 along with few other Madhesis from other parties. Mahendra Yadav joined TMLP after abandoning Nepal Communist Party.

Ethnic Collaborative Space

Pre-1770

The Sen kingdoms were able to garner support of Janajatis to run the administrative units. In the eastern region, Sen was King and his ministers were mostly Rai and Limbus. Similarly, the Makwanpur state was taking help of Basnets and few other ethnic groups to run the state.

Malla Kings used to welcome Tirhut Brahmins into their court, and they even were open to recruiting plain people in the army. Jay Prakash Malla had 12,000 plain people from Tirhut recruited in his army.

Political Revolutions 1770-1950

Madhesis were active in the labor movement and Satyagraha to overthrow the Ranas. On 4 March 1894, the laborers of the Biratnagar Jute Mill and Morang Cotton Mill in the South-East started their labor agitation, the first of its kind in Nepali history. Madhesi leaders such as Dinesh Dubey, Munnilal Chaudhari, Panchanand Das and Puran Singh were at the forefront of the movement. Many Madhesi youths of Biratnagar, Birgunj, Kathmandu and Lumbini intensified the movement.

Madhesi people also contributed to the nationwide protests and campaigns to have the despotic Rana regime overthrown and to establish democracy in the country. At this juncture, on 4 June 1936 Nepal Praja Parishad came into being. Many were arrested following the formation of this party; many were hanged, exiled or deprived of their properties.

Under the leadership of Pandit Ramakant Jha twenty-two Madhesi youths took an oath in Janakpur to end the Rana rule by signing their pledge with their blood. Jha formed a Service Committee with the aid of Kanwar Jha, Ramanand Thakur and Pandit Surya Kant Jha. In his poetic work, Sudama Charitra, he depicted the public as Sudama. The anthology was recited in villages to arouse the people against the Ranas. Ramakant Jha was also founder member of the Nepali Rastriya Congress. He was imprisoned in 1949 and released in 1951. He thereafter became president of the Nepali Congress in Mahottari district. Panchanand innovated handmade grenades and tractors combined to resemble tank-like armored vehicles, which helped defeat the Rana Royal Force in Biratnagar. Many became martyrs in Biratnagar during the rebellion.

When the Nepali Congress decided to launch an armed struggle against the Ranas and the Mukti Sena was formed after the meeting at Bairganiya, a border town in India, Matrika Prasad Koirala became commander-in-chief of the armed movement. In this struggle, many Madhesis were his associates and supporters. Kashi Prasad Srivastava was given the responsibility for the procurement of arms and ammunition from India. Under the leadership of Kulpati Mishra and Yamuna Devi, a Revolutionary Force of men and women was organized. Laxmi Narayan Adhikari, Vashudev Tripathi, Premchand Agrawal and Bhagyanath Dubey formed the Krishak Sena in Kathmandu. On 17 November 1950, the Mukti Sena captured Rangeli Bazaar and Bara and Rautahat districts.

In 1951 anti-Rana movement, workers in Biratnagar used a tractor as "tank". Biratnagar Jute Mills was locked at the end of the Rana Regime. Laborers were expelled from their work, but they did not stop waging protests. Devi Paswan, an Indian by birth, is an inspiring personality to Nepali workers. Born in 1918, Mrs. Paswan worked for 37 years, from 1949-1986, in Biratnagar Jute Mills. In this period she actively participated in many movements. She is presently known better by "Hadtali-ki-ma", than by her name, Devi Paswan. Mrs. Paswan, who presently lives at Tikule, Jogbani, says that during her 35-year working life, she took part in many movements and faced the suppression of reactionaries. Devi Paswan said, "Women participated in 1951 movement carrying kitchen utensils with them. They also participated in other forms of the movement, including donation collection. Devi Paswan gave birth to a son while she was on a strike. She is thus known as the "Hadtali-ki-ma," because the son was named Hadtali meaning Protest in English. Three of the women laborers working in the Jute Mills-Nanda Devi Nepal, Rukmani Acharya and Radha Devi Poudel staged a hunger strike for 27 days. It forced the management to reopen the factory. Everyone returned back to work following a decision to reinstate all the expelled laborers[80].

It was a year of mass movements that gradually turned into general armed struggles. As a result, on 8 January 1951, under the mediation of the Indian government, Prime Minister Mohan Shamsher signed an agreement in New Delhi for ushering democracy in Nepal[81].

In the 1959 general election, the Nepali Congress Party introduced a slogan '*Jamin Jotneko; Ghar*

Potneko' (land belongs to tillers and houses belong to the one who smears it)[82]. This slogan became very popular among poor peasants and land-poor people, winning the Congress Party a majority of parliamentary seats, and most of them were from plain low lands.

Political Revolutions 1960-1990

The Madhesi people then launched their agitation and denounced the king Mahendra's arbitrary rule. The revolutionary people of Saptari, Dhanusha, Mahottari and Sarlahi districts were organized and mobilized by leaders such as Rameshwar Prasad Singh, Sukhadev Singh, Saroj Koirala, etc. In 1962 Sukhadev Singh was killed in a military barrack. In Rautahat, Bara and Parsa districts, the Mukti Sena was headed by Seikh Idrish, Tej Bahadur Amatya and Bhagwat Prasad Yadav. Accused of leading the Mukti Sena, Nepali Congress leader Vishwanath Prasad Yadav was shot at in Raxaul and was seriously injured.

On 22 January 1962, a student leader, Durganand Jha, lobbed a grenade at King Mahendra in Janakpur. He was later sentenced to death. In the same incident, another youth Arbinda Thakur was arrested and was released after spending sixteen years in jail. A similar incident took place in Birgunj, in which Dukhi Sahani, Kapleshwar Jha, Dilip Thapa Magar and Kapleshwar Lal were implicated and given life sentences. Many Madhesi leaders were killed or exiled in connection with citizenship and land reform issues. Students such as Shiva Chandra Mishra and leaders such as Rambilas Ray Yadav, Suleman Miyan and Bhola Jha, who were involved in the armed struggle led by the Nepali Congress for the restoration of democracy, were either killed by the Royal Nepal Army at different places or were imprisoned. The final aftermath of this people's movement was the restoration of democracy in 1990, some thirty years later.

In the early 1970s, security personnel killed two school students near Janakpur —known jointly as Kameshwar-Kusheshwar now—for their political beliefs. After Durganand Jha, these two teens became martyrs to the cause of democracy in the long-drawn fight against Panchayat for freedom.

Protest happened in Janakpur, Rajbiraj, Biratnagar, Gaur, Birgunj, Nepalgunj etc.

During the People's Movement of 1990, three rural women (Janaki Devi Yadav, Muneswori Yadav and Sonawati Yadav) and two men from Yadukuha, near Janakpur, embraced death and succeeded in igniting the fire of imagination of every freedom-loving Nepali in the country and abroad. The People's Movement had begun to lose momentum—the blood of martyrs from Yadukuha rekindled embers of liberty that finally spread like wild fire and consumed the autocratic Panchayat system.

People's Revolution 2006

The 2006 protest was in collaboration of Maoists and seven parties after their 12 points agreement in Delhi. In Kapilbastu's Taulihawa 11 people including civilians and Maoist were killed in overnight clashes between government forces which started at 10PM on Friday evening. Nine others also died in clashes in Rupandehi's Butwal where the Maoist rebels began attacking the security force base at 8 PM last night. Ashok Thapa, a civilian from Jyotinagar was among those killed in Butwal. The rebels freed 110 prisoners from the Kapilbastu jail during the attack. Two army personnel, two police personnel, one civilian and six rebels were known to have died during the attack[83].

In the declared street protest, Sadbhavana Party was party of seven party coalition and they took part in all the protests. Protests took place in the Madhesh towns too.

After successful conclusion of protest, new government officially declared 21 people as martyrs of 2006 revolution. Many of those Martyrs were from plains; Horilal Rana Tharu of Dhangadi, Darshan Lal Yadav of Rajbiraj, Bishnu Prasad Pandey of Parasi, Hiralal Gautam of Bara Nijgarh, Setu Bishwakarma of Nepalgunj and Suraj Biswas and Rajan Giri of Chandragadhi.

Notes

1 Rai, Hemlata (2000), Are Newars janjati ?, Nepal Times, Issue #12 (04 OCT 2000 - 10 OCT 2000)

2 National Foundation for Development of Indigenous Nationalities (NFDIN) An Introduction, 2013, pp

3 Beny & Matheson (1926); Khooni Itihaas, Arya Prakashan Mandi, Bikaner,1926, Page 149

4 Lal, CK (2016); Contempt of familiarity, myrepublica, published on 29 May 2016

5 Hodgson, Brian H (1874); Essays on the Languages, Literature, and Religion of Nepal and Tibet, 1874, pp 37

6 Though there is another belief that the Bhimsen, who protected traders, was different and not the one among Pandav brothers.

7 Crooke, William (1894); An Introduction to the Popular Religion and Folklore of Northern India, Printed at the government Press, North-Western Provinces and Oudh, 1894, pp 55

8 Op Çite Lecomte-Tilouine , Marie (1998), On Francis Buchanan Hamilton's Account of the Kingdom of Nepal , European Bulletin of Himalayan Research, 1998, Number 14, Page 68

9 Brian Hodgson, 'The Miltary Tribes of Nepal', in Essays in the Languages, Religion and Literature of Nepal and Tibet (New Delhi: Manjushri, 1972, reprint of 1974 edition), p.38

10 Hodgson, Brian H (1874); Essays on the Languages, Literature, and Religion of Nepal and Tibet, 1874, pp 42

11 Whelpton, J. 1993. 'Being Nepali: The Construction of a National Identity in South Asia, Paper presented to the 34th ICANAS, Hong Kong, August 1993

12 Dr. Mishra, Pramod (2015); Not quite what it seems, Kathmandu Post, published on: 24-12-2015

http://kathmandupost.ekantipur.com/news/2015-12-24/not-quite-what-it-seems.html

13 Editorial (2016), Reform begins at home, The Kathmandu Post, Published on Dec 2, 2016 Downloaded on Dec 2 from http://kathmandupost.ekantipur.com/news/2016-12-02/reform-begins-at-home.html

14 Nepal National Educational Planning Commission, 1956, p. 52

15 Rules on Abolition of Sati issued on 1944 B.S, By Bir Shumsher Junga Bahadur Rana, Lawcommision of Nepal, downloaded from http://www.lawcommission.gov.np/en/documents/2015/08/rules-on-abolition-of-sati-issued-by-bir-shumsher-1944-b-s.pdf

16 Rape For Profit, Trafficking of Nepali Girls and Women to India's Brothels, Human Rights Watch/Asia, Vol. 12, No. 5 (A), October 1995

17 Buchanan, Francis Hamilton (1819), An Account of the Kingdom of Nepal: And of the Territories Annexed to this Dominion by the House of Gorkha, 1819, pp 234

18 Rape For Profit, Trafficking of Nepali Girls and Women to India's Brothels, Human Rights Watch/Asia, Vol. 12, No. 5 (A), October 1995

19 Hausner, Sondra L (2007), Border Town In The Tarai: Sites Of Migration, Occasional Papers in Sociology and Anthropology, TU, Kathmandu, Volume 10, 2007

20 Menyangbo, Pradeep (2017); *इटहरीमा किशोरीहरू यौन श्रमको जो* (Girls under risk of Flesh Trade in Itahari), Kantipur Daily, Published January 31, 2017 . Downloaded from http://kantipur.ekantipur.com/news/2017-01-31/20170131143521.html

21 Northey, William Brook (1937); The Land of the Gurkhas or The Himalayan Kingdom of Nepal, Cambridge: W. Heffer & Sons Ltd, 1937, pp 95

22 The mutiny in the Bengal army, Volume 8, Bengal Army, 1857, pp 22

23 Northey, William Brook (1937); The Land of the Gurkhas or The Himalayan Kingdom of Nepal, Cambridge: W. Heffer & Sons Ltd, 1937, pp 95

24 Watters, Thomas and Smith, Vincent Arthur (1905); Yuan Chwang's Travels in India, Volume II, Royal Asiatic Society, 1905, pp 83

25 Watters, Thomas and Smith, Vincent Arthur (1905); Yuan Chwang's Travels in India, Volume II, Royal Asiatic Society, 1905, pp 81

26 Watters, Thomas and Smith, Vincent Arthur (1905); Yuan Chwang's Travels in India, Volume II, Royal Asiatic Society, 1905, pp 63

27 Watters, Thomas and Smith, Vincent Arthur (1905); Yuan Chwang's Travels in India, Volume II, Royal Asiatic Society, 1905, pp 1

28 Rose, Leo(1971), Strategy of survival, 1971, pp 73 and Bell, Charles (1924), Tibet Past and Present, 1924, pp 276

29 Op Cite Lecomte-Tilouine, Marie (1998), On Francis Buchanan Hamilton's Account of the Kingdom of Nepal, European Bulletin of Himalayan Research, 1998, Number 14, Page 67

30 Op Cite Lecomte-Tilouine, Marie (1998), On Francis Buchanan Hamilton's Account of the Kingdom of Nepal, European Bulletin of Himalayan Research, 1998, Number 14, Page 66

31 Op Cite Lecomte-Tilouine, Marie (1998), On Francis Buchanan Hamilton's Account of the Kingdom of Nepal, European Bulletin of Himalayan Research, 1998, Number 14, Page 55

32 Op Cite Lecomte-Tilouine , Marie (1998), On Francis Buchanan Hamilton's Account of the Kingdom of Nepal , European Bulletin of Himalayan Research, 1998, Number 14, Page 57

33 Paper Respecting Nepaul War, NAMES of Nepaulese Sirdars killed and taken in the Attack on their Post of Burhurwa on the 25th November 1814, pp 482

34 Paper Respecting Nepaul War, pp 48

35 Paper Respecting Nepaul War, pp 416

36 Paper Respecting Nepaul War, pp 416

37 Paper Respecting Nepaul War, pp 417-418

38 Political Consultation, A Campbell's Report on Political Transactions with Nepal, A Sketch of Political Relations with Nepal, 1 September 1837, as mentioned in Bikrama Jit Hasrat's History of Nepal (1871) , pp 173

39 Political Consultation, A Campbell's Report on Political Transactions with Nepal, The Supermacy of Bhimsen Thapa, 1 September 1837, as mentioned in Bikrama Jit Hasrat's History of Nepal (1871) , pp 231

40 Story of Prithvi Narayan Shah, downloaded on July 28 from http://mixnepali.blogspot.com/p/prithvi-narayan-shah-prithvi-narayan.html

41 Stiller, L.F (1968) Prithvi Narayan Shah in The Light of Dibya Upadesh, Chapter III, pp 38-39

42 Baral, Leelanatheshwar Sharma (1964), Life and Writings of Prithvinarayan Shah, Unpublished PhD dissertation, University of London, 1964, pp 202-205

43 Buchanan, Francis Hamilton (1819), An Account of the Kingdom of Nepal: And of the Territories Annexed to this Dominion by the House of Gorkha, pp 141-142

44 Ramakant (1968), Indo-Nepalese Relations, pp 118-120

45 Buchanan, Francis Hamilton (1819), An Account of the Kingdom of Nepal: And of the Territories Annexed to this Dominion by the House of Gorkha, pp 176

46 Aitchison, C.U (1863), A Collection of Treaties, Engagements, and Sunnuds, Relating to India and Neighbouring Countries, Volume 2, India Foreign and Political Dept, 1863, PP 161-162

Article 7 - So many elephants on account of Muckanacinpoor are annually sent to the Company by the Rajah of Nepaul and therefore the Governor General with a view of promoting the satisfaction of the Rajah of Nepaul and in consideration of the improved friendly connection and of this new Treaty relinquishes and foregoes the tribute above mentioned and directs that the officers of the Company both now and hereafter from generation to generation shall never during the continuance of the engagement contracted by this Treaty so long as the conditions of this Treaty shall be in force exact the elephants from the Rajah

47 Regmi, Mahesh, A Study in Nepali Economic History, 1768-1846, New Delhi: Manjusri Publishing House, 1971, pp 11

48 Regmi, Mahesh, A Study in Nepali Economic History, 1768-1846, New Delhi: Manjusri Publishing House, 1971, pp 7

49 Wright, Daniel (1990). History of Nepal. New Delhi: Asian Educational Services. Retrieved 16 October 2012. Pages 18-19

50 Sharma, Balchanda (1969), ***काठमाडौं उपत्यकाको एक राजवंशावली*** (A history of Kathmandu Valley), Ancient Nepal, Number 6, 1969, pp 15

51 Chemjong, Imanshing (2014); Kirat History and Culture, pp 190

52 MSS EUR HODGSON/85 Limbu manuscripts: texts of religion and culture 1846, British Library, London

53 Âsâ, Esa. Pî (2003) and Paodel, Prabha Krishna; The Founder of Modern Nepal Prithvinarayan Shah, Vaani Prakashan, 2003, pp 182

54 Adam. J, Sec to Govt, The Gentleman's Magazine (London, England), Volume 118, 1815, page 361

55 Sangroula, Sangeet (2016), DPM Nidhi agrees to 'Madhesi martyrs' list of 68, Myrepublica, August 15, 2016. downloaded from link http://www.myrepublica.com/news/3838

56 Human Rights Watch Report (2015), Like We Are Not Nepali, Protest and Police Crackdown in the Terai Region of Nepal, Human Rights Watch, 2015

57 Political Consultation, A Campbell's Report on The supremacy of Bhimsen Thapa, as mentioned in Bikrama Jit Hasrat's History of Nepal (1871) PP 224

58 Wright, Daniel (1990). History of Nepal. New Delhi: Asian Educational Services. Retrieved 16 October 2012. Pages 18-73

59 Wright, Daniel (1877), History of Nepâl, Cambridge University Press, 1877

60 Nepal National Educational Planning Commission, 1956, p. 59

61 Northey, William Brook (1937); The Land of the Gurkhas or The Himalayan Kingdom of Nepal, Cambridge: W. Heffer & Sons Ltd, 1937, pp 143

62 Hodgson, Brian (1828); Notices of the Languages Literature and Religion of Nepâl and Tibet, Asiatic Researches pp 2

63 Lal, CK (2006); NRIs in Nepal; Madhesi.wordpress.com , extracted on Dec 2016 from https://madhesi.wordpress.com/2006/07/13/nris-in-nepal/

64 Baral, Leelanatheshwar Sharma (1964), Life and Writings of Prithvinarayan Shah, Unpublished PhD dissertation, University of London, 1964, pp 146, Also quoted in John Welpton paper , Being Nepali: The Construction Of A National Identity In South Asia, Paper presented to the 34th ICANAS, Hong Kong, August 1993.

65 Regmi, Mahesh (1978), A study of Nepali Economic History, 1768-1846, pp 11

66 Goait, J K (2007); History of Terai in Nepal, Nepalese Rule in Terai, https://madhesi.wordpress.com/2007/04/04/history-of-terai-in-nepal/

67 Surya Bikram Gnyawali, Prithvi Narayan Shah's Conquest Of Nepal, Regmi Research Series, Year 6, # 1, 1974, pp 9

68 John Welpton paper , Being Nepali: The Construction Of A National Identity In South Asia, Paper presented to the 34th ICANAS, Hong Kong, August 1993

69 Brian Hodgson, 'The Miltary Tribes of Nepal', in Essays in the Languages, Religion and Literature of Nepal and Tibet (New Delhi: Manjushri, 1972, reprint of 1974 edition), p.41

70 Cowan, Sam (2012); Colonial dogma, The Kathmandu Post, Kantipuronline, Nov 26, 2012

71 The mutiny in the Bengal army, Volume 8, Bengal Army, 1857, pp 22

72 Op cite in Farwell, Byron (1990); The Gurkhas, W. W. Norton & Company, 1990, pp 41

73 Temple, Sir Richard Carnac (1887); Journals kept in Hyderabad, Kashmir, Sikkim, and Nepal, Vol II, 1887, pp 232

74 British used Parbatiya language, rather than Hindi or English' to communicate within Gurkha Camp. Their food canteen was separate too.

75 Temple, Sir Richard Carnac (1887); Journals kept in Hyderabad, Kashmir, Sikkim, and Nepal, Vol II, 1887, pp 232

76 Koirala, Bishweshwar Prasad (2001); Atmabrittanta: Late Life Recollections, Himal Books, Jan 1, 2001, pp 184

77 Based on Private discussion with Rakesh Mishra.

78 Joshi, Sushma (2004); Goodwill Hunting: Sadbhawana Party, 2004. Downloaded from http://sushma.blogspot.com/2004/02/goodwill-hunting-sadbhawana-party.html on 28 Jan 2017

79 Goit, J.k (2007); History of Terai in Nepal, Nepalese Rule in Terai; downloaded on August 2016 from https://madhesi.wordpress.com/2007/04/04/history-of-terai-in-nepal/

80 Pandey, Binda (unknown); Women Participation in Nepali Labour Movement, GEFONT-Nepal, pp 24

81 Upendra Yadav 2003, Upendra Yadav 2004, as quoted in Amaresh Singh PhD thesis.

82 INSEC (1995) Nepal Human Rights Year Books 1995, INSEC: Kathmandu, pp 155-164

83 News, Government declares curfew - parties defy orders, Nepalitimes, issue #293 (07 - 13 april 2006)

7

Encounter with Racist State: Mahendra's Nationalism

Rise of Mahendra

Mahendra was Prince in 1950, when King Tribhuwan was struggling to get back power from Rana families. Politics was not new to them, but definitely forgotten area for Shah Kings. Shah Kings were out of direct power, and were acting merely as a rubber stamp for a century. Jung Bahadur Rana made the ascendency to throne through Kot massacre in 1846 followed by transfer of power to Rana prime minster through royal decree in 1856 that formalized the dominance of the Rana family.

Mahendra had an ambition and supported by luck he bumped back. First, the natural disaster proved "good omen" to King, second the international politics was changing after Second World War where new powers were trying to establish themselves, and third both the Nepal's neighbors were going through transformation.

Rana was thrown out of power in 1951 by King riding on the People's movement led by Congress Party. After that there were power struggle between different groups. Two groups having favor from Kings were led by Matrika Prasad Koirala and Tanka Prasad Acharya respectively and third Congress group was led by Bishweshwar Prasad Koirala. While political bickering was going on, a natural disaster struck the kingdom. In the July 1954, there were heavy rain falls recorded throughout the Hills primarily around Kathmandu including few places that witnessed the cloud bursts. Another heavy rain followed a month after. There were losses and causalities reported from Hills. However, the worst hit region was Central Madhesh, when the water current reached the plains.

Flood of 1954 AD (July) was worst in 100 years. As per Government estimate 1000 people died and crores of assets were destroyed[1]. Flood created havoc for almost 200,000 people in the Terai and damaged huge areas. The flood brought sand/silt and for next seven years there was severe droughts. Among them were almost 10,000 people whose land was covered completely by sand, and had become landless. Flood had washed away almost 200 villages in the Eastern Tarai. The most affected area was the central Tarai, particularly Bara, Parsa, Rautahat, Sarlahi and Mahottari (and Dhanusha too). The flood had hit Rautahat the worst, particularly due to the increased flow in the Bagmati River.

Flood provided the opportunity that they were looking for since 1952, to push politics behind the humanitarian cause[2]. US who were already worried of expanding China communist tentacle, were now also worrying if Nepal could also come under the influence of communists, which encroached Tibet in 1950. India was perceived by US as neutral, and was not ready to take proactive role in containing communist. India-China had just signed Panchsheel Treaty (Five Principles of Peaceful Coexistence) with China in April 1954. In this scenario on political stage, US got the opportunity in the guise of flood. Dr. Alexander Langmuir arrived in Kathmandu on 19 September with some medicine and relief material, had different consultations for signing agreement and returned on October 6. This was followed by an agreement signed between Government of Nepal and USOM in Calcutta on 23 October 1954. Prime Minister MP Koirala and USOM Director Paul Rose signed the agreement. India was not happy with the agreement, which did not want to have foreign player in Nepal, and Nepal felt happy assuming US can be played against India's omnipresence.

Flood mayhem was followed by series of drought and water scarcity in the central Tarai, particularly in Bara, Parsa, Rautahat, Mahottari and Saptari, right after the downpour. The drought was felt particularly in November 1954, when crops were drying up. The Advisory Assembly (AA), which had mix of Royal and political representations, was entrusted for relief of flood and drought.

After the flood, US gave the first major donation to Nepal of 2 Million USD in 1954 (then forex conversion was 1USD = 5 NRs and a primary and secondary school teacher salary was NRs40 and NRs125 per month). As per agreement, which would be terminated on 30 June 1955, the fund would cover food and clothing relief to disaster victims, emergency supply line to Kathmandu, road rehabilitation, farm rehabilitation and medical assistance. India also gave fund, however not as big as US, as India was herself engaged with the same flood that impacted Bihar province in northern India.

There was huge corruption in the relief materials given by internationals, particularly by USA. The relief material couldn't reach the needy people, rather it was sold or lost. There was criticism from everywhere. B.P. Koirala criticized the government failure. There was fissure in government coalition by January 1955; Tanka Prasad Acharya criticized government's inability to utilize the foreign assistance. Few people compared relief work with India, which was able to distribute cash to victims. Vedananda Jha, a member of AA would also criticize the government. King Tribhuwan died and Mahendra got the authority in March 1956. Mahendra dissolved the government and began the direct rule to run the country until January 1956. All this happened in the context of the flood crisis[3].

The total amount allocated for relief was remained unspent until the end of the agreement period. US was determined to push the Rapti Valley project further on the pretext of flood, which was conceptualized before 1954 flood. The flood fund of two million was reallocated for Rapti Valley rehabilitation project. There was severe drought till 1956, which further attracted 2 million additional commitments from USOM. Nepal and USA planned rehabilitation for flood impacted people in Rapti valley. However, on the pretext, a large number of hilly people were migrated to Rapti valley instead of flood-drought impacted Terai people[4].

Initiation of Foreign Aid Politics

Initial US donation to Nepal was via India. During 1950s, US would sell surplus agriculture commodities to India and the generated money would be used to finance local development projects in India. India projects would not absorb the entire amount. In 1954, US would channel money to Nepal for flood relief, and later impetus grew to channel surplus PL480 (Food for Peace: Public Law 480) to finance US projects in Nepal. Nepal HMG (His Majesty Government) heavily relied on the US donated Indian rupees to meet regular expenditure, development expenditure, and recurrent budget expenditure which delayed reforms (Tax, monetary and Trade). USAID not only paid for its own new projects, it financed the operations of a majority of Nepalese ministries[5].

Mahendra was hooking up to the taste of donation, a new term in International politics. After the death of Stalin in 1953, Russia (USSR) saw a general shift in Africa-Asia strategy, and wanted to have focus on Nepal. Having Control of newly formed UN (United Nations) was becoming important tool in international politics. Powerful nations were looking for smaller nation's vote which was deciding UN election process. USSR soon removed the veto to allow Nepal to be UN member expecting vote in UN elections. At that time Russia was facing criticism for his army intervention in Hungary, and was looking for non-aligned bloc members. USSR became first country to invite King Mahendra for an official tour in 1958. The return visit was paid by President Voroshilov in February 1960. In the meantime, Nepal signed agreement to receive $7.5 million aid from Russia. Even though, Russia's help was smaller in scale and size compared to US and India, it affected Indian position adversely, as it was principal foreign power in Nepal. Tanka Prasad Acharya was favoring communist Russia relationship, as he was pro-communist. Tanka Prasad also favored China, another communist country. While he was Prime minster, T.P Acharya gave statement in Kathmandu that government is open to "aid without strings" and "equal friendship", which was direct opposite to India's "Special Relationship". PM Tanka Prasad Acharya visited Beijing in May 1956, and both nations signed a new treaty terminating the Treaty of Thapathali of 1856 and Nepal recognized Tibet as a part of China; agreeing to give up all privileges and rights it had enjoyed in the Tibet under the treaty of 1856. As per 1856 treaty, Tibet had to pay tribute of 10,000 to Nepal each year. In 1957, there was reciprocal visit from Chinese Chou-En-Lai to Kathmandu and during his five day stay, his effort was to remove fear about China's expansionist design and to get strong foothold of Tibet gain. Nepal celebrated its new found relationship with China, because it gave a sense of freedom from India's omnipresence and also got all its wish fulfilled from generous China for its concession over Tibet rights. US was not happy though with Nepal being close to communist bloc, especially it was a shock for US to see King visit to Russia in 1958. Nepal was pitting Russia against US, similar to what it did while pitting US against India. To put Russia out of education and aviation sector, Nepal extracted a huge aid from US in 1959[6]. Nepal-US went ahead with understanding and opened embassies in each other's countries, followed by King Mahendra visit to US in May 1960. By 1965, America has provided more than half of the aid. India ranked second with 33% aid contribution. The other donors and UN contributed about 14% of the aid.

FOREIGN AID COMMITTED TO NEPAL
AND ACTUAL EXPENDITURES TO END OF 1963

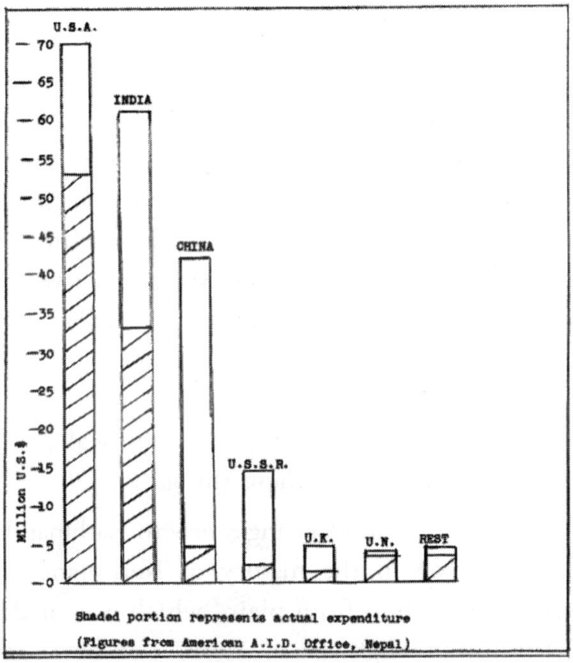

Source: Oldham, C.H.G (1964), Nepal and Foreign Aid, Institute of World Current Affair, 1964, pp 3

King Mahendra found out international donors are more interested in Nepal to see India getting sidelined. However, he needed Indian money as well, so his take was to show as if Nepal is different than India. Thus he created symbols different than Indian; time Zone 15 min apart India, different currency exchange rate between Nepali-Indian currency, Nepali language, Ranjana font[7], dress as Daura-Suruwal, National symbols like cow as national animal, Rhododendron as national flower, Lophophorus as national bird, etc. Nepal was busy drafting constitution, while India-China were fighting war, and as soon as India got defeated in late November 1962, Nepal promulgated a totally transformed constitution on December 16, 1962, scrapping the just 3 years old constitution of 1959.

By distancing away from India, Nepal got generous foreign money poured in especially from the India-unfriendly block. Then, King Mahendra wanted to show to the world, he genuinely hated India and Indians, and expected reactions from India as a proof. Thus he created a game of vilification that was common during Prince Surendra (1840)'s time. The incident reminds the madness that Surendra used to play in his room. Prince Surendra hated British, so as entertainment he was fond of seeing fictitious battle scenes between the Nepalese and the British armies, particularly scenes wherein the Nepalese soldiers beat the British Army[8].

Two incidents linked to Madhesh happened around 1960, which had direct relationship with King Mahendra's personality. First, his political opponent B. P. Koirala led congress got thumping vote in Madhesh which enabled him getting selected as first elected Prime Minister of Nepal in 1959, to be soon followed by dismissal from Mahendra a year after. Secondly, while Mahendra was visiting Janakpur in 1961, a Madhesi Brahmin, linked to Congress Party and frustrated with B. P. Koirala dismissal, threw bomb on his car with the intention to kill him. After these political incidents, political leaders crossed Indian side to escape political prosecution. King Mahendra saw hand of India in all these things.

Additionally, there were two more changes new to Kathmandu and favorable to plain people. First time in the history of Kathmandu Valley, a four wheeler could reach Kathmandu from plain, which was made possible after construction of Tribhuwan Highway in 1956. The first regular daily bus service on the highway was operated by Nepal Transport Service in 1959. Secondly, the requirement for Visa was abolished in 1958. Before 1958, plain people and Indian required Visa issued by Gurkha officer to enter Kathmandu valley from plain. These two changes propelled other change; educated people from Madhesh entered Kathmandu in search of employments primarily in education sectors, which was coming from projects completed by donor money.

Foreign power presence in Nepal were becoming stronger, however India was expanding in Nepal like never before through its project initiatives as well as people connections. King was not happy with the India's omnipresence, though he needed India's money for development projects.

King Mahendra could not touch India directly fearing loss in financial aid from India, so he brought Madhesis in bilateral game, and started victimizing them. The constitution of 1962 introduced the concept of Citizenship for the first time, unlike the 1959 constitution, in addition to the symbols of Nepali State. The situation became tougher for plain people through language policy. On other hand, King was appeasing Hill population with state initiatives like (1) Resettlement (2) Land Reform (3) Guthi Regulations and (4) East-West Highway.

To counter any Indian reaction, he took help of Hill people constituency. Thus started involvement or inciting of people against India, via victimization of Madhesi. India did not have to bear the physical pain, rather it was Madhesi getting the hurt.

Mahendra tactic of creating ground in Nepal for foreign powers to pit one against another, through foreign financial aid, paid off. The quantum of foreign aid during the two decades (1951/52 -1969/70) totaled more than 178 million dollars[9]. Foreign aid inflow rose from 3.5 million dollars in 1958/59 to over 21 million dollars in 1968/69, indicating a seven-fold increase within a decade. In the five year period between 1965 and 1970, the contributions, in terms of percentage, by major donors were as follows: India - 53.7, U.S. - 25.7, China -16.0, U.S.S.R - 1.3 and others - 1.3. Also, it was significant to note that since 1964/65, Indian and Chinese aid amounting to 90.6 million dollars together account for nearly 70 percent of the total foreign aid over the next five year period.

Discrimination as State Policy

Resettlement Company (1957)

US wanted to have more connections with people than just remaining money donors. They thought this was happening through Malaria eradication project, which would put them at the door of each citizen, also through Rapti Valley Settlement Project will help them understand the community better.

After 1934 flood and ensuing droughts, the US gave priority to the Rapti valley resettlement Project (in Chitwan district) and reallocated the unspent amount from flood relief to resettlement project. There was additional two million commitment from USOM in guise of drought. The first success came to them in 1958 by eradicating Malaria in the Chitwan valley, which was a major deterrent to migration of hill people. USOM's first road-building endeavor was the 87-kilometer link road between Bharatpur and Hetauda, part of the Rapti Development Program, constructed with flood relief funds and completed in 1959. However, on the pretext, a large migration of hilly people was brought to Rapti valley instead of flood-drought impacted Terai people[10]. To promote migration from Hill, individuals were provided with a piece of land and few cash rewards too. Initially the project was under the relatively tight control of the joint Rapti Valley Cooperative Service, administered by USOM and HMG co-directors. When this organization was dissolved on orders from Washington in mid-1958, its functions were dispersed to various ministries, which meant USOM and HMG project managers effectively lost control of the project. As a result, some Kathmandu politicians were able to acquire large tracts of land and ignore project conditions requiring use of improved technology[11]. Many of the new small landholders quickly became indebted and were forced to sell, becoming tenants again. Traditional cultivation methods were quickly re-adopted, and the model effort to a large extent failed, mainly because the area was settled too rapidly and without effective enforcement. There was flood of people more than the allocated settlement plan. The surplus people started haphazard deforestation of jungle.

Realizing the devastation of forest resources and lack of social equality, government established an autonomous body to run resettlement program, learning lesson from Rapti Valley resettlement project, the planned resettlement program began in 1964 with Israeli aid, based on a survey in the Tarai led by Israeli Dr A Kadem as Advisor which suggested possible resettlement areas as Nawalpur, Banke, Bardia, Kailali and Kanchanpur Districts. The Nepal Resettlement Company was established in 1964 under the Nepal Company Act with His Majesty's Government as the shareholder. The main objectives were:

- To reduce population pressure on land in the Hills and give Hill people economic opportunity[12]
- To bring fallow and uneconomic forest land under cultivation through resettlement
- To remove forest encroachers from protected forest and resettle them in an organized way elsewhere
- Political sufferers from Rana period
- Gurkha ex-servicemen both of Nepalese, Indian and British armies[13]
- To resettle Nepalese returning from Burma and India. A large number of Nepalese returned to Nepal from Burma following the enactment of the Burmese Citizenship act in 1964. However, a large number

of Nepalese were returning from India and Burma before that period[14]. A large number of ex-Gurkha army families from British period, who were settled in north-east India, started returning, after frictions between Nepalese people and native people started, following Gurkha role in suppressing the uprising of Mizo and Nagas[15].

Nawalpur was followed by resettlement projects in Dhanewa (Nawalparasi District), Prithvinagar (Jhapa), Kajura (Banke), Jamuni (Bardia), Parsan (Kanchanpur), Jugeda (Kailal.), and Nawalpur (Sarlahi).

The massive Hill people response forced government to establish objective of organizing land resettlement on a massive scale. Department started its early resettlement programs in Sijuwa (Morang District), Murtia (Sarlahi), Sindhureghari (Rautahat), Nijgarh (Bara), and Dhanewa (Nawalparasi). Later as these settlements grew and forest encroachment began, the Department had to establish offices at Jhapa, Morang, Parsa, Rupandehi, Dang, Nepalgunj, Dhangadi and Mahendranagar[16].

As of 1981, officially 6,85,000 people migrated from Hill to Terai. Unofficial and unaccounted figure is very high. Despite the resettlement of farmers from Hills, many remained landless or lost land later due to indebtness. It maintained social harmony in hill by reducing the population pressure there, and the migrated hilly people offered political support to government[17] once they settled in plain.

Migration to plain was promoted before by Rana government through the 1861 regulation that gave priority to Hilly people in assigning land in Jamindari system. There is little information on how many hilly people were there in plain districts earlier, however taking Nepali language, which was mostly spoken by Hilly caste in 1951, as indirect measure, plain lowland had only 6 percent of the people speaking Nepali[18]. King Mahendra's active state promotion resulted into rapid migration of hilly people to plain, and as of 2011 census, the percentage share of hilly people in plain districts (including inner Terai) has jumped 6.7 times in five decades to touch around 40%. In some of the plain districts, the migrants have changed the demography entirely; the natives have become minority in their traditional dwelling. As of 2011, Jhapa, Kailali, Kanchanpur, Morang, and Nawalparasi have migrants forming about 70%, 54%, 69%, 51%, and 58% of district population. All the interior plain districts, called inner Terai, are today dominated by hilly people. On the other way round, Plain people have negligible presence in

Hill/mountain, and this figure becomes dreadful if we exclude their presence in Kathmandu valley. Kathmandu valley has around 6% plain natives. Another two districts Baitadi (5.65%) and Kaski (3.18%) have some presence of plain's natives. In remaining hill districts, plain natives form about 1% of district's total population. Similarly, plain natives form about 1.21% of mountain district's total population.

		Geography				
		Hill	Mountain	Terai	Terai (Inner)	Total
Ethnicity and Social Groups	**Hill Natives**	**97.53%**	**98.79%**	**32.82%**	**85.34%**	**66.69%**
	Hill's Hindu Caste excluding Dalit	42.59%	51.83%	18.05%	35.45%	31.25%
	Hill's Dalit Caste	12.68%	12.55%	3.90%	11.39%	8.51%
	Hill's Janajatis	42.17%	34.28%	10.87%	38.50%	26.89%
	Others	0.08%	0.12%	0.00%	0.00%	0.04%
	Plain Natives	2.47%	1.21%	67.18%	14.66%	33.31%
	Plain's Hindu Caste excluding Dalit	0.98%	0.66%	30.43%	1.59%	14.56%
	Plain's Dalit Caste	0.05%	0.14%	9.96%	0.47%	4.66%
	Plain's Muslim	0.50%	0.02%	8.99%	0.70%	4.39%
	Plain's Janajatis	0.59%	0.31%	16.42%	11.69%	8.91%
	Others	0.34%	0.07%	1.38%	0.21%	0.79%
	Total	100.00%	100.00%	100.00%	100.00%	100.00%

Table showing distribution of Ethnic groups in each geographical region as of 2011 census. About 55% of Nepal's population lives in Terai. *Compiled by the Author.*

Resettlement projects had a devastating impact on lowland Plain peoples. Let's take case of Tharu people, who were on the frontier to get devastated in Rapti Valley (Chitwan).

Tharu's land ownership system changed. Before resettlement, they had free access to land and forest, but many uneducated Tharu families lost land because of Hill people's cunning. They were forced to become landless squatter and bonded labors.

Tharu were no longer allowed into national parks, which was once their village and home. Tharu ceased to use the natural resources after government declared Chitwan national park. In a field study, Joanne McLean of Australia narrates the story of Amiliya village, which was designated as National park, people became landless and poor with no compensation from government. The quality of life was lost in addition to the loss of human dignity. Soldiers forcibly removed all the villagers located inside the boundary of Park. Houses were burned down, fields and houses were trampled by elephants, men, women and children were threatened sometimes at gun point[19].

The other village had litter better, though not less painful story. Padampur Village, did not succumb to the force of the army. There were many conflicts between the villagers in Padampur and soldiers. The soldiers seized some village land, but the people continued to resist. When the soldiers seized the land the local people tried to plough their fields, but were badly beaten by the soldiers. Padampur were able to resist, because they had proof of permanent residence in the form of land registration papers. Over time the people of Padampur gradually suffered from increased wildlife depredation on their crops, restricted access to traditional resources and grazing grounds and constant surveillance by the army.

Few additional notable impacts on Tharu were[20]

1. The traditional territories were lost, and it resulted in the loss of inherited knowledge of the land and cultivation that were passed from generation to generation.
2. The new place, where people were relocated, were in the higher altitude and rocky place. The irrigation facilities were not available. There were insufficient supply of drinking water, limited education and medical facilities. Insufficient irrigation changed their crop production from their staple rice to maize. Many people do not know traditional knowledge to grow maize compared to rice, thus suffered economically. Their food habit changed from rice to maize, and impact was on their health.
3. Demography and sociology changed among the Tharu. They were allocated land in such a manner that, one house is Tharu, another is Hill people, and another is another caste. There is no unity, and getting help when needed has become difficult.
4. Their rituals changed. A villager narrated, "in Jayamangala we used to worship our own village god, but here nobody is worshipping our god. In fact, here there is no god. It is not possible that all the gods be here, because those places were the gods' places but how can we

bring those gods here? Now we do not have even the village god to protect the crops, animals and the family. We do not have any gods here now".

5. Tharu traditions were missing. They found out there was no place from where to collect water snails because there were no rivers in New Padampur. The snail was very important food for them to get protein. Festivals were charmless, because they were not able to collect resources for the festivals from traditional forest.

Ecologically, settlement has impacted the geographical structure and increased the flood problem. Study of geographical data pattern, over the years of 1976-2010 with the help of satellite imagery maps on the flooding problems of Eastern Chitwan, revealed that due to the rapid degradation of the vegetative cover in the upper catchments of its rivers has resulted in increasing occurrence of flooding events[21].

Land Reform (1964)

Dictionary meaning of land reform is, any program, undertaken by a national government, involving the reallocation of agricultural land among the landless. On paper objective of the Nepal government was the same, for which people have been voicing since 1950-51. However, behind the scene desire of elite group was to do acting of Land Reform, and misinform Land Reform to the foreign donors, who were more interested in the project. During the early 1960's, pressures were brought on the government by foreign aid donors to implement some land reforms. Among the foreign development agencies, US Agency for International Development and Ford Foundation pressured more. In 1962, Wolf Ladejinsky, of Ford Foundation, wrote letter to King Mahendra to emphasize that foreign aid was a futile gesture if not accompanied by land reform. Two years after Ladejinsky wrote in an article more emphatically: "Important through the other ingredients [technical assistance, cooperatives, credit, etc.] are, unless those who work the land own it, or are at least secure on the land as tenants, all the rest is likely to be writ in water." This message was not lost on the Nepalese Government. It needed to attract foreign aid and therefore it went through the motions of enacting land-reform legislation[22].

However, making use of the opportunity, government representative of Hill elite had two things in mind; (1) land-reform program could be used as vehicle for transferring to Hill people the landholding of plain people. At that time around 50 percent of rich land was under large landowners of plain origin. (2) Legally formalize the landowner's large holding instead of land redistribution to landless people.

Sensing the conspiracy, Indian Government raised the land-reform concern on first point. Indian government made it clear that it would not tolerate the disposition of plain people in this manner. Elite were successful in the second agenda. The land reform act prescribed limit of 40 acre (25 Bigha in Nepali measurement) per person, and further granted relaxation to own land in the name of each son (over sixteen years old) and each unmarried daughter (over thirty five years old). In those days, family planning was less priority and family size used to be bigger. Additionally, there were out of office setting with officers to layoff surplus lands through financial transactions. As a result, by mid-1968, only 146,000 acres of excess land was acquired by government, out of which only 56,000 acres were redistributed by mid-1972.

Land reform did not talk about the absentee landowner and landowner holdings in multiple locations. Kathmandu based Hill elites used to have land in plain, and simultaneously they held land in Hills, though there were not much big sized lands in Hills.

The land reform had repercussion on common plain origin people creating another set of problems; (1) beneficiary of the land (2) eviction from farming and (3) citizenship issue.

As mentioned in the previous section, the official policy of resettlement was to migrate hill people to plain. Thus, despite all the shortfalls in collecting excess land, the distribution of 56,000 acres of land did not benefit plain peoples. So in a sense, land got transferred from landlord of plain origin to the landless of Hill origin. Secondly, the poor land tenants (land lessee), were evacuated from the land they were previously cultivating, because landowner did not want former to claim any legal rights, as much as possible, till landlord had capacity to digest land under 40 acre limits within family members or through selling. These small land tenants were illiterate and powerless to act legally. The evicted small farmers had no basis to prove legal residence once their landlord denied, thus they became illegal migrants, in front of Hill nationalism, ignoring the fact that people can be native landless and their historical dwelling had been plain. Thus it culminated into the citizenship issue.

The problem of eviction and related citizenship issue became severe in mid-western Madhesh, especially in Nawalparasi, Rupendehi and Kapilbastu districts, where abolition of Ukhada Land Tenure System created law an order problem. The 1964 Ukhada Land Tenure Act states that title to Ukhada lands in excess of land-holding ceiling shall be transferred from Jamindars to their tenant cultivators, unless the tenants are proven to be alien. And in case, tenants could not provide citizenship card, then land will not be registered in their name. This implies, person having no citizenship did not run the risk of losing land, but land owning rights. The rules add: "Land of the following categories shall be retained by and registered in the name of the landowner in the following circumstances:(a) Ukhada land cultivated by any peasant who is proved to be an alien in accordance with the particulars submitted by the landowner under Rule 3, or, (b) land registered under these rules in the name of any peasant who is proved to be an alien"[23]. By providing landowners the license to accuse their tenants of being alien, government benefitted the landowners directly, thus conflict of interest, where landowner would be motivated to tag everyone aliens and retain the lands. The discontent was evident and government presented the first amended Ukhada Land Tenure in 1965. It stated "In case such peasant is, or is subsequently proved to be, and alien, the Ukhada lands cultivated by him shall be registered in the name of His Majesty's Government, which shall sell or distribute such lands to landless."[24] 1965 amendment was little improvement, and was not providing incentive to landlord, if tenant is declared alien. Thus in 1965, landowner did not declare someone alien. Now it was turn of landowner to take advantage of Citizenship controversy. Over a period of time, landowner transferred title to family members, without giving any share to local families[25]. And common poor farmers were rendered without citizenship.

Legal gap in Ukhada land tenure shaped the unfortunate consequences. The Landowners rushed for transferring land to either family member or sell to someone. This action evicted many former tiller of the land and this situation culminated into citizenship issue. Legal actions initiated by landowners and government officials threatened many tenants, leading to an outburst of violence in Nawalparasi districts in September 1966. A crowd estimated around 4,000 came around the district administrative center in the village of Parasi. In the police firing 9 persons were killed and 12 were injured. Government suppressed the news, actual reason for agitation became speculation, and many Kathmandu based people accusing poor landless poor farmer as Indian[26].

Citizenship

There was no definition of Citizenship in 1948 constitution that was pushed at late occasion by Rana Prime Minister Padma Shamsher Jung Bahadur Rana. Citizenship was first distributed in 1952.

King Mahendra first published constitution in 1959, believed to accommodate the people's aspiration of 1950-51 revolution. The 1959 constitution has one line definition of Citizenship: "Citizen means a person who is a citizen of Nepal in accordance with the provisions of the law". 1959 constitution was basis for election of first democratic government that selected B. P. Koirala as Prime Minister of Congress Government.

Three years after, the political condition changed drastically; King had control of the affair, democratic government was dismissed. International politics was also changing drastically; there was war between India-China in 1962 (October 20 to November 21) in which India's position was compromised. A month later, December 16, 1962, King Mahendra promulgated constitution.

As per 1962 constitution, Citizenship of Nepal was defined as

Every Person who has his domicile in Nepal and-

a) Who was born in Nepal; or

b) either of whose parents was born in Nepal; or

c) Who, as a woman, has any kind of relation with a citizen of Nepal constituting matrimony in accordance with the laws and customs of Nepal; or

d) Who has already obtained a certificate of citizenship in accordance with the laws of Nepal; shall be a citizen of Nepal at the commencement of this constitution.

The close look at above provision indicates, definition has subjective and objective component. Having certificate of citizenship is objective criteria. However points a, b, and c brought subjective judgment to be disposed by district officer, of which, almost all of them belonged to Hill origin. At that time, most of the births took place in house, and there was no practice of birth registration record.

The citizenship certificate was worthless for the common people in 1962. Large mass of people were illiterate, most people were either independent farmers with small land lease or agriculture labors. There were Jamindars having control over plain lands, however they were mostly of Hill origin. There was no pre-condition to either pursue economic activities or get land lease or join government employment. However, significance was soon to get changed; Nepal introduced land reform act in 1964 that required land tenancy to be granted to citizen only. The mandatory citizenship certificate for land acquisition pushed people to queue in front of district government office, and then common Madhesi faced the Citizenship eligibility criteria, which was frustrating to them.

As per 1962 constitution, the eligibility criteria to acquire Citizenship were

(a) one can read and write the national language (i.e. Nepali language);

(b) one is engaged in an occupation, resides in Nepal;

(c) he has taken steps to renounce the citizenship of the country of which he is a citizen;

(d) such person as defined by law, has resided in Nepal for a period of not less than two years in the case of a person of Nepalese origin, after renouncing the citizenship of her country in the case of female married to a Nepalese citizen and for a period of not less than fifteen years in the case of other persons; and

(e) Whatsoever stated in clause a, b and d, if person internationally recognized apply for the Nepalese citizenship or whatsoever stated in clause a, b, c and d, to provide Nepalese citizenship to honor somebody with high goodwill.

The 1964 citizenship eligibility criteria assumed, individual is foreigner, if not citizen of Nepal. However, the reality was in between. First Citizenship certificate is modern concept based on State concept that evolved in western countries in last 2-3 centuries. Second, people living in Madhesh were not Indian (a state concept). Rather, people have been living in the land for generations and many of them even before Shah King occupied the land. Nepal definition of citizenship was derived from Hill nationality perspective, and ignored the plain nationality. Historically, plain had been inhabited by Plain people. Plain people have controlled and prospered the Nepalese plain land for thousands of years, and are well recorded in ancient epics of Ramayana and Mahabharata. In the recorded history since Buddha time too, plain people have controlled the land, and has been recorded as Vriji Republic, Tirhut, Videha, Kapilbastu, or Mithila civilization.

The challenge was even bigger. A person had to learn Nepali language, in addition to prove through paper that he/she has been staying in Madhesh. This became a big hurdle given learning new language was close to impossible for illiterate people and most of the people were agriculture labors, hardly having access to papers.

In case of women marrying Nepalese men, there was different challenge. They had to prove, they surrendered the Indian citizenship certificate, whereas, in fact, India herself was not having concept of citizenship card. Till today, there is no citizenship card as such in India, similar to citizenship certificate in Nepal, though there are other certificates in India; Birth registration certificate, Passport, Aadhar Card, Ration Card, Pan Card, Driving License, Voter Card, and Land Registration. So, how can women surrender the thing, that doesn't exist? This opened up another bigger loop of running to the doors of local officers.

There were a few foreigners who received citizenship very easily due to their high skilled service to the Nepal government, which Nepal needed badly, when it opened country in 1950 driven from foreign donations.

All these culminated into millions of stateless citizens, having no citizenship certificate. In absence of citizenship certificate they could neither buy land nor can they join government employment (citizenship card for employment was enforced during 1980s). In absence of citizenship card they can neitheropen bank account nor can they get license to start any commercial business nor can they get passport to fly gulf countries as labor migrants.

In 1965, King Mahendra promulgated Citizenship act 1965, with the objective to accommodate the returning expatriate Hill people driven out from Burma, North-eastern Indian states and other places. 1965 citizenship act was extension of 1962; it defined "son, daughter, or descendant of any Nepali national" and their eligibility to acquire Nepalese citizenship certificate. The constitution of 1990 was in line with citizenship acts of 1962 and 1965.

The citizenship of 2006 interim constitution was liberal from its predecessor in the sense, it allowed inheritance of citizenship from either of the parents.

It states "any person whose father or mother was a citizen of Nepal at the birth of such person".

Citizenship act of 2015 constitution is more convoluted than 2006, and is intended to create more confusion than simplicity. Thus, the first draft of constitution which was released few weeks before official promulgation on Sep 20, 2015, created more controversy than any other provision of the constitution. Marginalized Madhesis, who have historically being victims of contempt, were further subjectedto marginalize.

The draft version on constitution had provision that Child's both parents should be citizenship provision "Any person whose father or mother was a citizen of Nepal at the birth of such a person". The "and" in the provision attracted United Nation's attention[27], in addition to Madhesis and Women groups. The United Nation even lobbied in capital to make the necessary change in the citizenship provision. Nepal government was pressurized internally and internationally to accommodate necessary changes to as per international standard.

Still, the first constitution promulgated on September 20, 2015 has convoluted provisions that impacts (1) the child who is getting born out of parent, whose one of the parent is only Nepali (2) the child who has only one known parent and (3) male who is getting married to Nepali female. The Citizenship act of 2015 constitution saw protest from the women of Kathmandu Valley too[28] and its prominent leading face was Mrs. Sapna Malla.

Immigration is a reality. What if a women goes to foreign county, gives birth to a kid and also stay there for substantial long time? Isn't this conflict with provision 11.5 that mandates to have "A person born to a Nepali citizen mother and having his/her domicile in Nepal but whose father is not traced, shall be conferred the Nepali citizenship by descent." The provision also overload the process with the onus to prove domicile and non-traceability of father. How long is the acceptable domicile? And how to prove domicile when transactions are mostly paperless in informal setting. To prove someone is traceable is easier, however, to prove someone is not traceable, in this big world, becomes a task as big as world.

Another provision on citizenship act states to get a new citizenship a person is eligible if "a person whose father or mother was a citizen of Nepal at his or her birth". However what if his/her parents received citizenship while the kid was in school going age? Doesn't this provision suggest, a person should be citizenship holder before giving birth to kids, else even if he/she can get citizenship somehow, however their kids will not get citizenship? This is not hypothetical scenario, rather a living case reported during UN field report[29]. Sanjeev Sajahi did not apply for a citizenship certificate during the 2007 campaign because he thought he would be able to obtain citizenship by descent, as his mother had hers by descent and his father obtained his on the basis of birth. Along with his father he went to the Sub-district Administration Office with the certificates of both his parents to inquire how to obtain his own. He was told that there is no provision to issue citizenship certificates under the Citizenship Act in his case. Similar issue was faced by Kumar Murmu of Jalthal-6, Jhapa belonging to Santhal community[30]. The interpretation of provision denies citizenship to children from parents by either descent or birth.

It is estimated that about 20% of the population does not possess a citizenship certificate and the numbers are growing[31]. Majority of the stateless are plain's people, and some of them also include people from Hills like Chepangs[32] and Mahakali residents[33].

The recent constitution of 2015 creates multiple levels of citizens; Citizenship by birth, by naturalization, by descendent, Non-residential citizenship and honorary citizenship. Also, there are few people who have only voting rights, but they are not citizens.

Additionally, government creates one more category of citizenship, Non-PR (Permanent Residency), targeted toward the seasonal immigrant works who have received PR in foreign countries while still holding Nepali citizenship. The last category is a cheating to the hard work and contribution of the migrant workers on whose money elites are getting their salary, economy is getting liquidity and country is maintaining balance of payment. Nepal's remittance as % of GDP accounted 29.2 percent in 2015, which is third highest in the world[34]. As per the provision 289, the immigrant will not be eligible for any government post and key appointment or fighting election; they have to wait for cooling period after showing residency in Nepal. It reiterates the old phrase of Nepal, "Brta Basne Haami, Falahaar garne Kami" meaning we do the fasting and someone else does the breakfast. Similarly, as per provision 291, all except naturalized citizens will be debarred from key post like Prime Minister, Chief Minister, etc.

Language Policy (1956)

Discussion on Language is complex and interesting. The language discussion is linked to the historical evolution of three groups (1) Khas (2) Hill Janajati and (3) Plain people.

As we discussed in previous chapter, the Khas groups are the migrants stock from plain of north India. These people primarily came from Banaras and surrounding, or passed from these places while reaching the hills. These migrating people brought their plain language and mixed with the hill natives to produce language called "Khas Kura" also called "Parbatia" or "Gurkha Bhasha", and over a period of time got renamed to Nepali. As Brian Hodgson noted, 80% of the words of Khas Kura was similar to Hindi[35]. He explains the mix of Hindi with local language during the formation of Khas language in this way: "The Khas language became a corrupt dialect of Hindi retaining not many palpable traces (except to curious eyes) of primitive barbarism"[36]. During 1930s, "Khas" language name was changed to "Nepali", a confusing term, given Khas was not native to Nepal Valley, and "Nepal Language" (Nepal Bhasha) nomenclature is used for Newari, a language of natives of Nepal Valley. Orthodox Khas group opposed the renaming of "Khas" or "Gurkha" language to "Nepali Language" and also renaming of country ruled by descendent of Gurkha King Prithivi Narayan Shah to "Nepal", instead of saying "Gurkha"[37]. Probably, they hijacked the name Nepal and its derivation Nepali name for "Gurkha" because of the rich history and culture linked to Nepal. Additionally it also enabled people to hide the barbaric history of "Khas".

Janajati are having different language groups. So, when they were recruited by British EIC, the officer wanted a common language to communicate with all of them, collectively called Gurkha. British chose the Gurkha court language "Khas Bhasha" rather than north Indian language Hindi, because it also enabled British to build a strategic difference between the two groups in army camp; highlander and lowlander. During late nineteenth century, British found the language was rapidly expanding to become lingua-franca in hill. It was observed that, the British Gurkha army returning to village from British camp was agent of change. Anyone knowing Khas language was regarded as superior, and language itself became status symbol within Janajati people. However, the interesting insight was, these Gurkha army was not allowed to learn English and any attempt by Gurkha soldier was punished by British officers[38]. The written communication was done in Khas language in Roman font. The policy has continued till late twentieth century[39].

The Elite Ranas were progressive in respect of language. After Jung bahadur returned from England, he opened Nepal's first school, Durbar High School, for kids of Rana families. The medium of education was English language till 1950s. Even the Trichanda collage, which was open to accommodate the graduates of Durbar High School, had language of instruction as English[40]. Tribhuwan University was established in 1959, before that all the collages in Nepal, including Trichanda Collage (1918) and Law College (1954), were affiliated to Patna University of India. These collages continued to run Hindi medium curriculum[41].

The first emphasis of Nepal language came while Rana allowed opening school for common people around early twentyeth century. The language of tenth class examination was decided as Nepali through the language law of 1934 and same law defined the official language as Nepali[42].

The major change in language policy came after 1950-51 political change. Vedananda Jha led Terai congress, advocating more political power for plain people, advocated for greater autonomy of plain lower land and promotion of "Hindi" as national language. Hindi had been lingua-franca for the plain people in the lowland Madhesh. The movement of Terai congress was able to get traction, and was followed by "Save Hindi" campaign. The "Save Hindi" campaign was initially supported across all political parties of that time; Communist party of Nepal, Nepali Congress, United Democratic Party, and Praja Parishad. At the same time, two factors were shaping the decision (1) the Cultural Revolution in favor of protecting "Khas" identity, initially started in Banaras by the expat, who were bonded together by sense of Rana's political suppression and common identity of Hill. After political change of 1950-51, these people moved to Kathmandu. (2) Need of education, which was almost none till 1950, due to Rana's fear of political uprising coming from educated class, thus suppressed opening up of schools during Rana rules.

In 1953, Nepal government constituted Nepal National Educational Planning Commission, a group of Nepali civil servants advised by University of Oregon Professor of Education Hugh B. Wood developed an overarching educational plan. The commission went to different places to survey the then existing education facilities, the opportunities and collection of people's preferences. As per the survey finding, published in 1956, plain people had preference for the "Hindi" as medium of instruction, across all level of school educations; primary, middle, and secondary[43].

	MEDIUM OF INSTRUCTION DESIRED				
	Kathmandu Valley	West Nepal	East Nepal	Terai	Average
Primary School					
Local	71%	48%	75%	79%	68%
National	38%	44%	13%	16%	28%
English	12%	17%	75%**	4%	27%
Middle School					
Local	18%	22%	25%	51%	29%
National	81%	69%	50%	50%	63%
English	26%	25%	12%	16%	20%
High School					
Local	20%	22%	5%	54%*	25%
National	68%	67%	75%	45%	64%
English	52%	35%	73%	26%	46%

* "Local" language for the Terai area means Hindi in most sections.

** This reflects the influence of the missionary English schools in the Darjeeling area

Source: Nepal National Educational Planning Commission, 1956

However during the survey itself, people of plain started feeling a sense of discrimination on Hindi language. In an interview published in 1954, Dr. Wood gave his opinion in favor of having one language in the country as medium of instruction. When the final report was published in 1956, the decision was to push for the single language across all level of education, and it was Nepali.

The advantage listed by Nepal National Educational Planning Commission 1956 were

(1) If the national language is made the medium of instruction, [it would avoid] preparing text- books in many languages....

(2) It will be imperative to adopt a general policy to give status to a language which is spoken by the majority of the people...

(3) The national language will be easier to learn than Hindi. No truly Hindi speaking people inhabit any part of the country.

(4) As an official language for a long time, Nepali has been current everywhere and therefore is not difficult for the local people to understand.

(5) ...The different communities of Nepal, easily understand the language and express their thoughts to one another through its medium....

(6) Nepali bears a closer affinity with Hindi than any other local language and both Nepali and Hindi are unlike Maithili, Newari, and Tibetan, using Deva Nagari script.

(7) Bond of language has been the greatest factor in determining the frontiers of our country. Garhwal and the other conquered parts of Nepal broke away because of different languages prevailing there. To solve the problems of multiplicity of language, stress and importance will have to be laid on one language, if the integrity and sovereignty of Nepal is to be maintained.

Argument 1 is certainly valid, however still doesn't justify which language should be the winner. Point 6 is a fact appreciated earlier by Brian Hodgson, however the mention in the report is confusing; if Nepali and Hindi have close affinity then, how does that make case for Nepali and not Hindi? Point 3 is similarly overloaded statement if it assumes both Nepali and Hindi having close affinity. Justification 4 and 5, escaped the fact that Hill Nepalese class too was exposed to Hindi via their connections in plains; Khas having pilgrimage to Banaras, and also having government jobs in Madhesh, Janajatis having army jobs in Indian army and Indian plains since the Kingdom of Ranjit Singh in Lahore (and thus migrants are also called Lahure), Hill elites having blood relationships with Indian elites. Point 2 was a deciding factor, given Nepali (i.e. Khas) language was spoken by Khas community, which formed one-third of population and even almost cent percent of government structure. Even bigger deciding factor was justification 7, which banked upon Hill nationalism, supported by foreign aids and filled by international politics of that time.

Government decided to enforce Hindi, and declared all teachers to produce proficiency in Hindi, as well as Nepali Citizenship card. This was blow to plain people, because schools were having curriculum based on Hindi as medium of instruction (till 1980s), supported by Hindi speaking teachers, who had received education in close by Indian schools, and also Hindi was lingua-franca of the plain. After government decision to introduce Nepali as a medium of instruction, a large number of teachers were suddenly rendered jobless[44]. For example, despite government discouragement, even after a decade in 1967-68, seventy five percent of Nepal's primary-school teachers were of plain origin[45]. Due to the lack of teachers, the schools were on the verge of shutdown. Taking this frustration, initially, Vedananda Jha led the "Save Hindi" campaign, and later congress member Mahendra Narayan Nidhi led the campaign in 1957[46]. There was support from Terai Congress, Communist Party of Nepal, Nepali Congress, United Democratic Front and Praja Parishad to the save Hindi movement[47]. There were street protests in Biratnagar, Gaur, Rajbiraj, and Janakpur. There was street fight in Biratnagar injuring twenty-five[48], when processions led by local Save Hindi Committee and Nepali Pracharini Sabha clashed with one another. By the end of 1957, discussion on language assumed the shape of politics, and it was challenging rise of monarchy aspiration of King Mahendra. First he showed softening of stand on 14 November 1957 by removing the PM K.I Singh, an anti-Hindi icon. Then on January 1958, coming under the pressure of political protest, whose primary agenda was election and secondary was language, King declared the national election date for February 1959 against his desire (not to give political freedom), with the intention to divert public attention from language movement. Language movement then changed to raise political topic, whether the election would befor parliamentary body or to a constitution assembly. Pro-Hindi supporters and few among Front favored constitution assembly, where as King declared it is going to be parliamentary election. Pro-Hindi supporter believed constitution drawn up by Palace would not fulfill people's desire[49].

After the Nepali Congress assumed power as a result of 1959 election, status of Hindi was restored as a medium of instruction from Primary to University level. In addition to Hindi, Maithili and Newari were also taught in the schools. Hindi was used in the deliberations of the Parliament.

However, after the introduction of Panchayat democracy in 1960, not only was Hindi abolished as a medium of instruction but was also declared as a foreign language[50]. In April 1965, Radio Nepal terminated its daily ten-minute news broadcasts in Newari and Hindi. A number of Newari organizations reacted indignantly, but not a note of protest was heard from Terai. The Marich Man Singh Government derecognized the degree of MA in Hindi, Newari and Maithili as a basis of promotion. Except Nepali and English, the Public Service Commission (PSC) recognized no other languages".[51]

In early 1970s a participant from Nepal participated in Hindi international conference held in Nepal and explained about state imposed marginalization of Hindi in Nepal. This story was covered alongside the news of coronation (Rajyabhishek) of King Birendra in "Dharmayug" a popular Hindi magazine of that time. Dr. Krishna Chandra Mishra, then head of Hindi department in TU and a renowned academic figure in Nepal published a booklet called "Sambidhan Saabdhan" in which he elaborated the proposed Language planning in new (1990) constitution. He also wrote a book named "Nepal me Hindi ki Durdasha" after few years. After 1990 GON (HMG then) participated in all the Hindi international conferences organized in Canada, Trinidad and USA[52].

Interestingly, King Mahendra used English as medium of communication with plain people, and King Birendra did the same[53].

The Nepali language was pushed with argument as tool of unification. However it would turn out, the argument was false, rather the logic was to create hurdle for the development of plain region and an excuse to deny the access to education opportunities. Today, the people of plain speak equally good language, score high marks, and some even choose to switch to Nepali as mother tongue for their Kids. However, speaking Nepali doesn't qualify them to be accepted in mainstream, and one of the reasons provided is language itself. Today, they will be humiliated in terms of accent and style of speaking Nepali[54]. In radio programs, plain people speaking in Nepali language have become a medium of comedy. A plain people will find, in two way communication, plain people will speak in Nepali and hill people will return call in Hindi. Today, Hindi movies, TV serial, stage programs are more popular in Nepal than programs in Nepali.

Even interesting is the fact that India sees language in broader perspective than as defining state identity. Nepali is one of the national language of India as per Indian constitution, and Nepali imprint is one among the 15 languages found in the language panel of Indian banknote.

Picture showing reverse side of Indian Banknote Rupee Ten. See language panel on left side

After restoration of democracy in 1990, Government enacted freedom of language. 1990 constitution (Article 6) states "All the languages spoken as the mother tongue in the various parts of Nepal are the national languages of Nepal", however would add rider "The Nepali language shall be Official language". The Hindi controversy would hit in the first session of parliament itself. After viewing heated politics, on July 7, 992, Mahant Thakur, Deputy Speaker of the house of representative, gave a historical ruling saying "Constitution has allowed full freedom for the parliamentarians to use their respective mother tongues except for the ministers, who will use national language, and for the government purpose and parliamentary notices". Using this decision, Seikh Idris, Member of Parliament from Nepali congress, would use Urdu and Padma Ratna Tuladhar, Member of Parliament from Communist party of Nepal (UML), would use Newari to express views in parliament. Later Gajendra Narayan would give speech in Hindi in Nepal Parliament. After interim constitution of 2007, Vice-President Paramanand Jha, a native of plain, would hit the controversy by taking oath in Hindi language. Later constitution was amended to include oath taking in mother tongue however signature will be put on two copies of oath; one in mother tongue and other in Nepali language. The constitution of 2015 would define language in two categories; Languages of the nation (all language spoken in Nepal) and Official Languages (Nepali and state language to be adopted by federal state).

Cultural Policy

Culture was part of King Mahendra's policy of one language, one dress, one code, one country. Interesting, however, it is, there is no written constitutional provision for the uniform; may be due to the physical form and the cost associated with it, poor might have asked government to provide cloth, if government wished them to dress like gentle man. Also, there is challenge of enforcing it into numerous Janajati groups within Nepal. Pictures given below show traditional dresses of different groups.

Picture showing different tribal groups of Nepal in their traditional cloths.

The uniform formed the core of King Mahendra policy as part of his culture movement, especially in the days of "Back to the village campaign", when China initiated Cultural movement was hitting Nepal that was making Government unhappy. The program was conceptualized to counter three political events (1) The banning of political party created unhappy mood within village, and political party started working in villages as underground entities (2) The land reform was creating discontents within village (3) Influence of China cultural movements in Nepal.

King Mahendra introduced the programs in May 1967 saying "The majority of the people of the country live in the villages. Accordingly, we must go back to the villages to achieve the fundamental objectives of the [panchayat] system."[55] He further added "The problem is complicated because educated people who provide leadership have tendency to leave the village.... Now everyone should concentrate his entire attention upon village activities in order to fulfill the objectives of the [panchayat] system... and they can be achieved only through cultivation of the qualities of nationalism, patriotism, honesty, discipline, and diligence."[56]

King gave 10 point guideline to meet his objective of "Back to the village campaign". Interestingly they all represent his personal interest rather improving quality of life in villages[57]

1. Consolidation and expansion of the spirit of nationalism and national unity.
2. Dissemination of the fact that the nation needs the partyless panchayat democracy, the fact that it has no alternative in Nepal, and fact that "partyless feeling" should be developed.
3. Cultivation of behavior in accordance with Nepal's non-aligned foreign policy.
4. Introduction of a campaign to eliminate corruption, injustice, oppression, and unnecessary administration inefficiency.
5. Infusion of consciousness and dynamism in the village society.
6. Further strengthening the implementation of the land-reform program, the new legal code, social welfare programs, and nationwide reconstruction activities.
7. Propagation and extension of co-operative programs and feelings.

8. Imparting of knowledge about the significance of forest and wild-life protection and afforestation.
9. Emphasis on agricultural production.
10. Arousing of consciousness regarding the need for cottage industries.

Close look at the above 10 points gives no direct benefit to the poor villagers, whose day is spent only in making two ends meet. Neither these programs directed volunteers of "Go back to village" to contribute physical labor in improving roads of village or planting trees or providing labor service in health sector or education sector. There was no concrete village development programs. There was no target given to dug wells, or trees to be planted, or roads to be built. These all points were intangible to the villagers and volunteers did not have to do anything except offering lip service. They were like religious preaching with political objectives to protect an individual monarchy.

As part of program, the educated people (including government officers and elected representatives) had to spend some time in the village to teach village about history and heroes (who were none other than warriors in last 250 years); encourage Nepali language; distribute Nepali flags; spread message against political party and in support of partyless panchayat system, etc.[58]

The primary focus of the program was on plain, because political party had more network in plain, filling the gap against the discontent against the government. Plain people were not only physically away but culturally away from the ruling elites of Kathmandu. Thus, in Frederick H Gaige assessment, plain people felt threat of "Nepalization" drive by government[59].

The symbol of Nepalization practiced among common people, and were taken as measurement while entering a government office for certain service were (1) Language as Nepali (2) Cap as Dhaka Topi (3) Body Dress as Daura Suruwal, also called Labeda Suruwal, and (4) appreciation for National Anthem. If anyone where found to be adhering to these, their file clearance would be smooth, else the work would be pending. In the street too, flashing the Nepalization symbol added status symbol to any person linked to the state structure. Language is discussed in detail as separate topic. Below is an effort to discuss the other symbols.

Dhaka Topi: Topi means Hat or Cap in English, and Dhaka is local name, which derived its name from capital of Bangladesh. It is believed,

Dhaka used to supply fabric for cap, and thus it derives its name. However, it is not understood why Khas people (concentrated in mid-west of Nepal) would not go to nearby places like Banaras which had been famous for fabrics. Secondly, there is no cap endorsed in local Bengali culture, except for religious Muslim Skull cap that is different from Dhaka Topi. Topi is popular in cold places as protective measure for head. Thus, we find cap included in daily attire in Hilly place like Kashmir. Additionally, the Nepal Dhaka Topi closely resemble to that of Kashmiri Cap Karakul. Afghanistan also has similar cap structure, except that it is thick compared to Dhaka Topi. Pakistani also wear a similar cap, and is today famous as Jinna cap a name derived from Muhammad Ali Jinnah, Founder of Pakistan. The linkage of cap from Afghanistan to Kashmir to Kathmandu, also corroborate with the history of migration, which indicates the initial Khas aboriginal people entered hill of Nepal from top eastern side which is physically closest to Kashmir. Phonetically too, Khas is linked to Kashmir. Topi is accustomed to cold place to help head. In plain, heat is problem, and people do not wear Topi as usually, and even if they do it then it is to protect against sun radiation and structure of such cap is different.

King Mahendra of Nepal in Nepali Cap (Dhaka Topi)	*Founder of Pakistan, Muhammad Ali Jinnah in Cap (now called Jinnah cap)*	*Hamid Karzai, Former President of Afghanistan in Afghani cap (Karakul)*	*Dr. Farooq Abdullah, Former CM of J&K in Kashmiri Cap (Karakul)*

Daura Suruwal (Labeda Suruwal): It is two piece dress. Daura worn on top of body, and Suruwal in the leg. Suruwal is common across South Asia and both male and female wear it. In north India it's called Salwar or Pajama. Daura (or Labeda) is not a unique dress of Nepal. It has been in use since centuries, and was popular with Mughals too. Today, it's popular with all class of Rajsthani people and within Hindu ascetic. It's being reintroduced in fashion world, both males and females dresses are designed on this pattern and Shah Rukh khan can be seen wearing in Hindi movie Paheli. The reason for having different names can be analyzed with the word Daura, which is close to Maithili word Dauru (means Running) and similarly Hindi word Daud (meaning Run). As running is easier in this dress, compared to other traditional dress Dhoti-Kurta, thus it might be related with running, which was lifestyle of the migrants entering Hill from Indian plain, who ran away from aggression of Muslim rulers. Also, in hilly terrain, where we have too much of tree bushes and narrow passes, it's easier to walk in fit dress like Daura, compared to flying Dhoti-Kurta. This might also indicate, the fit dress was more suited to warriors than other traditional dress. Indian people call it Angarkha or Angrakha, which means Body (English for Ang) Protector (English for Rakha).There has been change in the style of Daura since King Prithivi Narayan days. The lower part of Daura is now tighter than before. However, Daura is not suited for plains temperate climate, especially in Madhesh, where we have high humidity. People prefer loose dress that keeps the wind going inside body and keeping the body cool. Interestingly, King never pushed for national dress for women, could be he calculated, there is no difference among Khas women attire and plain's women attire, both of them wearing Sari, thus giving no advantage to Nepalization movement.

Portrait of King Prithivi Narayan Shah in Daura Suruwal (Nepali for Angarkha)	*Portrait of Raja Ranjit Singh of Sikh Dynasty in Angarkha*	*Portrait of Akbar, great Mughal ruler of India, in Angarkha*	*Hindi movie Actor Shahrukh Khan in movie Paheli wearing Rajsthani dress Angarkha*

National Anthems: There were two songs we had to sing in school during panchayat days. Though only one of them was national anthem, however both were equally treated. Both had praise of Kings. Both of them were intended to infuse the loyalty for King. They also praise Sovereign and preach gallantry of hill race. No where there is mention of plain icon, neither there is mention of Buddha, the Global symbol of justice, peace and equality who was born in southern plain of Nepal. Neither there is mention

Nepali Version	Translation in English (unofficial)
श्रीमान गम्भीर नेपाली प्रचड प्रतापी भूपति श्री ५ को सरकार महाराजाधिराजको सदा रहोस् उन्नति राखून चिरायु ईशले प्रजा फैलियोस पुकारौं जय प्रेमले हामी नेपाली साराले ।	May glory crown you, courageous Sovereign, You, the gallant Nepalese, Shri Panch Maharajadhiraja, our glorious ruler, May he live for many years to come And may the number of his subjects increase. Let every Nepalese sing this with joy
हट्ने होइन डटी लड्ने नेपालीको बानी हुन्छ कहिले नझुक्ने शीर उभेको स्वाभिमानी नेपाली हुन्छ विश्वको कुना काप्चामा खोज नेपालीको मुटुमा खोज (त्यहाँ सिङ्गो नेपाल हुन्छ त्यहाँ राजारानी हुन्छ (2 श्रीपेचको नवि रङ डाँफे चरीले बोकेर उड्छ एकता अनि वीरताको गाथा सारंगिले गाउँदै हिंड्छ खुकुरीको डोवभित्र वीरहरुको पाइला हुन्छ पर्वतराजा हिमाल मुनी गुराँस त फुलेको हुन्छ गुराँसको रङ हेर त्यो पनि त रातो हुन्छ हाम्रो मुटुको रगत हेर त्यो पनि त रातो हुन्छ रातो रङ्ग सिम्रिक रङ्ग चन्द्र सुर्य झण्डाको रङ्ग त्यो पनि त रातो हुन्छ त्यहाँ सिङो नेपाल हुन्छ त्यहाँ सिङो नेपाल हुन्छ त्यहाँ राजा रानी हुन्छ हाम्रो मादल शान्तिको लागि मरुभुमिमा परेड खेल्छ स्वयम्भुको दुइटा आँखाले न्याय अन्याय छुट्याइ हेर्छ बाँच र बचाऊ भन्ने छाती भित्र कुदिएको हुन्छ	Fight rather than retract Is behavior of Nepali Never surrendered, heads up Proud is Nepali Search anywhere in world Search in heart of Nepali There will be single Nepal There will be King and Queen – 2 Nine colors of Crown Danfe bird fly carrying then Unity and bravery songs Sarangi keeps singing Inside Khukri sheath Footprint of braves are there Below the Himalaya, King of hill Gurash flower is there See the color of Gurash It is also red See our color of heart It is also red Red color is of Vermilion (Simrik) Moon, sun, and Flag color Are also red There will be single Nepal There will be King and Queen – 2 Ours drum for Peace Parade on desert Svayambhu's two eye

of Sita and her father, symbol of freedom of women and knowledge in Hindu society. Nor there is mention of green color, which symbolize plain's vegetation that feeds the country. So, in absence of the related symbols, the songs had meaningless impression on the Children of Plain, who had to sing these in Nepali making it further difficult to comprehend the lyrics.

Guthi Regulations (1964, 1976)

Guthi are land endowment given by individual or kings for the religious purpose. The tradition of Guthi is recorded since Licchavi kings of 5th century. Most of the Guthi land was granted by ruler Malla Kings of Kathmandu and Sen Kings of Makwanpur, and thus region ruled by them have concentration of Guthi lands. The initial Shah Kings, after the occupation of these regions did not make any change of Guthi orders.

These grants were issued for a religious purpose to a deity to be managed by an ascetic who was the deity's devotee. These lands were rented by ascetic to the cultivator for agriculture purpose and the collected incomes were used by ascetic for day to day running of religious monastery devoted to deity. Monastery used the collected income for running charity kitchen (bhandara), running hostel (Dharamshala) for pilgrims, making bathing pond, running religious school, donating to visiting ascetics and offering worship to the deity. The religious monastery was led by Mahant, who inherited the powers to the successor selected from monastery disciples. The ascetic was granted the powers of inheritability but not the powers of divisibility or transferability.

The land grant in the Janakpur region was categorized as Kusa birta grant. The sadhus who benefited from these Kusa birta grants, were exempted from forwarding to the king's revenue collectors and revenue contractors, all of the rents, levies, and duties which constituted the revenue system of the Kingdom of Nepal. In particular, the king's intermediary revenue officers were not entitled to collect from the ascetics who managed the tract of land, the rent on cultivated land (mal) and on the supplies of firewood and water.

In sum, with regard to the income from the Kusa birta land the ascetics who managed the land gifted in the name of a deity were completely outside of the purview of revenue system of the Kingdom of Nepal.

In 1852 Jang Bahadur formed Temple Trust Arrangement (Guthi Bandobast Adda) to examine the grants and compile the records in order to ascertain whether any recipient of these land grants who was appropriating the surplus income, had not been specifically entitled to do so. In Guthi Bandobast office it ensured that the recipient, after having fulfilled the conditions of the grant, was not entitled to appropriate the remaining income from the land, then Jang Bahadur awarded the management of that land on a contract basis to the person who offered to manage the tract of land according to the terms of the grant and yet submit to the government the greatest amount of the remaining income. The government office which compiled the records of these Kusa bitalab birta, Kusa birta, and Guthi rights over land and which maintained the accounts of the contractors.

King Mahendra dissolved Temple Trust Arrangement and erected Temple Trust Corporation (Guthi Sansthan) in 1964 with new regulation for religious and charitable endowment of the Kingdom. There was follow-up regulations introduced in 1976.

After 1964, however, the Temple Trust Corporation introduced changes which did disrupt the monastic organization.

1. The autonomy of the monastery was lost. Government behind the Temple Trust Corporation began to interfere in the operation of the monastery. The board members of Temple Trust Corporation are (i) Government of Nepal Government representative (ii) Home Ministry representative (iii) Law Ministry Representative (iv) Education Ministry representative, etc.[60]. The district officers were made local in charge of the monasteries[61].
2. The land of Guthi was either allowed to sell or forced to sell to different entities. The government entities who got hold of Guthi lands then became new authority replacing the ascetics. Much of the land in Janakpurdham was purchased during 1960s from Temple Trust Corporation by various departments of government which had established district offices in Janakpurdham[62].
3. The Corporation downgraded the importance of the charity kitchen thereby reducing the number of resident and iterant ascetics to whom the abbot could offer hospitality. Moreover, the Corporation reduced the number of ascetic officers of the monasteries whose functions they recognized. The Corporation chose to remunerate the services

of the abbot, the worshipper/cook, and a householder kitchen servant. In a larger fortress the Corporation sometimes remunerated both a worshipper and a cook. These persons then became employees of the Temple Trust Corporation and, like other employees, these ascetics had to sign the daily attendance book (hajiri form) indicating the number of days per month that they were on duty. The Temple Trust Corporation also remunerated the service of householders to sweep the fortress, guard the temple, keep the accounts, and so forth, but the ascetic officers of the monastery, such as the ascetic executive, the ascetic storekeeper, and the ascetic sergeant-at-arms did not have their functions recognized by the Temple Trust Corporation. If the abbot wanted to retain these officers in his monastic organization, the abbot was obliged to remunerate them himself from his own salary. The abbot's own salary, however, was not sufficiently munificent to enable him to recreate the elaborate monastic organization of the past[63].

4. Most of the valuable possessions of the monastery, such as the gold and silver ornaments used in the worship of the deity and the brass cookware used in the kitchen, had been gifted to the monastery by devotees or purchased by the abbot with the surplus income. The possession had not been personally gifted by the king and they were thought to be owned by the abbot. According to the Temple Trust Corporation Act of 1964, however, His Majesty's Government assigned the right to manage the monastery possessions to the corporation. Also, after 1965 the abbots lost their ownership rights over the monastery building and the monastery moveable property[64].

5. The most important change introduced by the Temple Trust Corporation lay in the mode of recruitment to the abbotship. Formerly the abbot of a fortress designated his successor from among his disciples. After 1964 the Temple Trust Corporation began to recruit abbots in the same manner in which other Government Personnel were recruited to their posts. This also mandated abbot to have Nepali citizenship – a concept enforced during King Mahendra rule - to be recruited by Temple Trust Corporation. In Past, irrespective of citizenship status and place of birth, disciples of abbot was able to become abbot of temples[65].

The Temple Trust Corporation regulations impacted the already marginalized groups: Newari and Madhesi. Most of the charitable land endowment to temple or monastery are located in the districts ruled by Newar Malla Kings and Madhesi Sen Kings; Kathmandu Valley and region between Gandaki and Koshi. Guthi has 70,647 acres (5,61,990 Ropani) land in hilly region and 1,11,102 acres (66,330 Bigha) land in lowland plains[66]. The district wise asset distribution of Guthi can be estimated from Guthi Sansthan branch offices and numbers of employees in the corresponding offices are as below.

Guthi Branch Office	Region	No. of Employees
Kathmandu	Hill	21
Lalitpur	Hill	13
Bhaktapur	Hill	14
Pashupati Goswara office, Pashupati	Hill	7
Central Guthi and Archival, Bhadrakali	Hill	16
Kavre	Hill	6
Janakpur, Dhanusha	Plain	17
Jaleshwar, Mahottari	Plain	10
Birgunj, Bara-Parsa	Plain	11

Table showing employee and branch offices of Guthi Sansthan (Temple Trust Corporation) as of 2016. Source: Guthi Sansthan Website[67]

The Temple Trust Corporations created deep impact on the Newari and Madhesi society. Due to a conspiracy between the bureaucracy and the land mafia which has never understood local culture and tradition, the sustainable institution of the Guthi, which ensures the continuity of Newar religion, tradition and culture, is gradually vanishing[68]. For example, the state of Trishul Festival of Pashupati God (Deopatan) has not been held for the past 23 years because the Guthi in charge of organizing has no money. Similarly, in Janakpur the Swing festival (jhulan) is not observed in the way it was few decades back. There has been decline of visitors to Janakpur as government is reducing importance of Charity Kitchen and Monastery Hostels (Dharamshala)[69] . The Vaisnavite ascetics who have developed Janakpurdham into a great pilgrimage center came from diverse regions of the subcontinent. There was Narayan Das (of Ratna Sagar monastery) from Bihar, Mauni Baba (built parikrama road) from Madhya Pradesh, Rasik Ali (Rasik Niwas Monastery) and Avadh Kisor Das (Ramanand Ashram) from Gujarat, Sur Kisor (Janaki Temple) from Rajasthan[70]. Present Janaki temple was built in

1911 by Queen of Tikamgarh from Madhya Pradesh and Rasik Niwas Monastery was built by King of Tikari from Bihar[71]. The regulations of Temple Trust Corporation has severely limited the development of Janakpurdham as devotional center. The neutral identity of Janakpur based temples are maligning, after Temple Trust Corporation enforced Citizenship for selection of Abbots in plain's religious places, which has large numbers of followers from India. But surprisingly, the citizenship criteria for Abbot's appointment is not enforced in Pashupati, the favorite temple of Nepal's ruling class – Khas Hindus. Pashupati temple selects it's abbot from Sringeri Peeth of South India and its abbots are not on Government payroll[72] unlike Janakpur Temple's abbot. After Temple Trust Corporation of recruitment process, the hilly origin people are appointed in Abbotship in important monasteries of plains. The increasing control of Temple Trust Corporation in monasteries gives them deciding control over the monasteries' huge pool of land assets through their appointments. Monasteries lost authority over lands, after they were forced to lease large pieces of monasteries' lands to Government offices[73] or private businesses[74]. Small lands get awarded, as sell or lease, at favorable conditions to grease palm of powerful peoples[75]. In 1970s, when lease for monasteries' lands was vacated by plain origin cultivators, these Guthi lands in plains were leased to hill origin people's in line with King Mahendra's resettlement drive.

East West Highway (1963)

East West Highway is another example where hill ego prevailed over sensible scenario. Plain already had the Hulaki Road (Postal Road in English), that was conceived during early nineteenth century during the days of Anglo-Gurkha War. There was similar postal road in mid-hill region. The objective of postal road was to have communication links between different strategic centers, collect information, and forward to center for updates. Those road network was optimized in terms of time to reach two places. People were dedicated during pre-Rana and Rana period to maintain the postal road and transfer information from places to Kathmandu. Hulaki roads were useful in times when communications were manually carried through writings or messengers.

King Mahendra was different than his predecessors who hesitated to invite any foreigner to Kathmandu; Mahendra invited all the possible foreign powers in Nepal who were willing to pay price. In the competition to surpass other in showoff game, each country was giving more than expectation.

East West highway was the good example, where King played each country against other to extract the financial benefit. King Mahendra first conceived of east-west highway in plain after 1960 Royal coup. He went to Gaidakot, a place in Nawalparasi district, about 110 miles South West of Kathmandu, inaugurated the earthworks by heaving a silver pick-axe. In a nationalism fever, he declared, the road would be built by Nepalese for Nepalese. However, the drumbeat of nationalism could not be sustained in the absence of funding, equipment and technical expertise. Despite his commitment, he could not show anything for the first two years. King approached US for foreign aid in 1964, and they declined saying, why do Nepal need white elephant of $70 million, whose yearly maintenance cost would eat up almost all of budget resources? Nepal budget was financed eighty percent through foreign donations[76]. Probably US might have thought, maintenance might again come on US soldier. It was a sensible assumption on the part of US, because till 1965, US contributed about 70mm USD forming more than fifty percent of total foreign aid. The 1964 Country Assistance Program noted "USAID/N feels that the East/West Road is not economically justified at the present time, but applauds this concrete manifestation of Nepalese self-help."[77] King then approached India for assistance. However, India couldn't be convinced because the road objective was to undermine India's influence in the plain region. Then King approached to Russia. Russia showed reluctance too.

King approached China, and China jumped at the opportunity to woo Kathmandu. In 1964 they agreed to build 17- kilometer Biratnagar-Janakpur section of Highway. Russians reacted and offered to build 109 kilometer Pathlaiya-Dhalkebar section. India was not happy about China's entry into plain that is few miles away from Bihar border. Indian Ambassador of that time, Sriman Narayan used feverish diplomacy and Kathmandu agreed to send the Chinese packing, but for a price. India would build road from Janakpur to Biratnagar and then to Mechi River.[78]

East-West was a rape on environment. Jungle was cleared for building road. Later people migrated from Hill, and they started encroachment into the lands on both sides of Highway. Today, there lies a large Hill community migrated after 1962, and it has also contributed in inorganic expansion of many plain cities like Lahan, Bardibas, Chandranigahpur, Lalbandi etc.

The postal highway remains neglected as before, with most part having sand on the road. At max, the good section will have gravelling.

Why State is Failing?

In a state we have two groups (1) Government and (2) Happy People. If people are not happy then, either they will change the domestic government or runaway to another government. They both see economy as a space where both can collaborate to generate fruits/profit; Happy People invest (Finance, Labor) and State facilitates (through infrastructure) to produce fruits or Profit. State natural resource might help as catalyst to enlarge the fruits. The economy fruit (i.e. profit) is shared roughly in 70:30 ratio, between Happy People and Government. Government employee gets salary (and perks) out of the tax, and reuse surplus tax into infrastructure. Happy People buy means of happiness from the economy and thus remain happy, and the saving makes way to economy again as reinvestment. In this system, everyone has incentive to increase economy size, thus increase in profit, which directly benefits both Happy People and Government.

Let's narrow down to each actors. People are Happy People, if they get good share of (1) profit (for investment) or Salary (for labor) and (2) Good service (Health, Education and Governance) from government in return for the tax paid. If government cannot provide Health service and Education, people can still be happy; they can buy them from economy, provided they have good share of profit; a characteristic of capitalistic government compared to socialist government which provides Health service and Education. The minimum people expect from Government is governance. If they do not get it, they will become sad. If people have to buy governance as if in monopolistic market, instead of getting free, this is bound to give impetus to corruption.

Government has control on Infrastructure (Development &Maintenance) and Natural resource. That can become place of corruption, as people do not have direct control on those rather they are at receiving ends. That money does not come to Public economy and this does not help in creating Happy people. Corruption money goes into black economy, making few powerful people happy who are close to Government.

Outside the system, the two acts can be dependent through social relationship and community for emotional needs, which are next level needs within Maslow Hierarchy of needs. If members of a community are distributed in both government and among Happy people, and they also share social space, then social setting ensures, all members of society are happy, thus division of profit is in amicable way, proportional to the invested labor. However, if they do not share social space, then there is negligible emotional pressure to member who is part of government to (1) ensure equitable extraction of tax (3) provide governance to the people and (3) proper use of remaining tax. Thus giving rise to Sad People.

Note, in this system, everywhere there is physical movement of money from one entity to another.

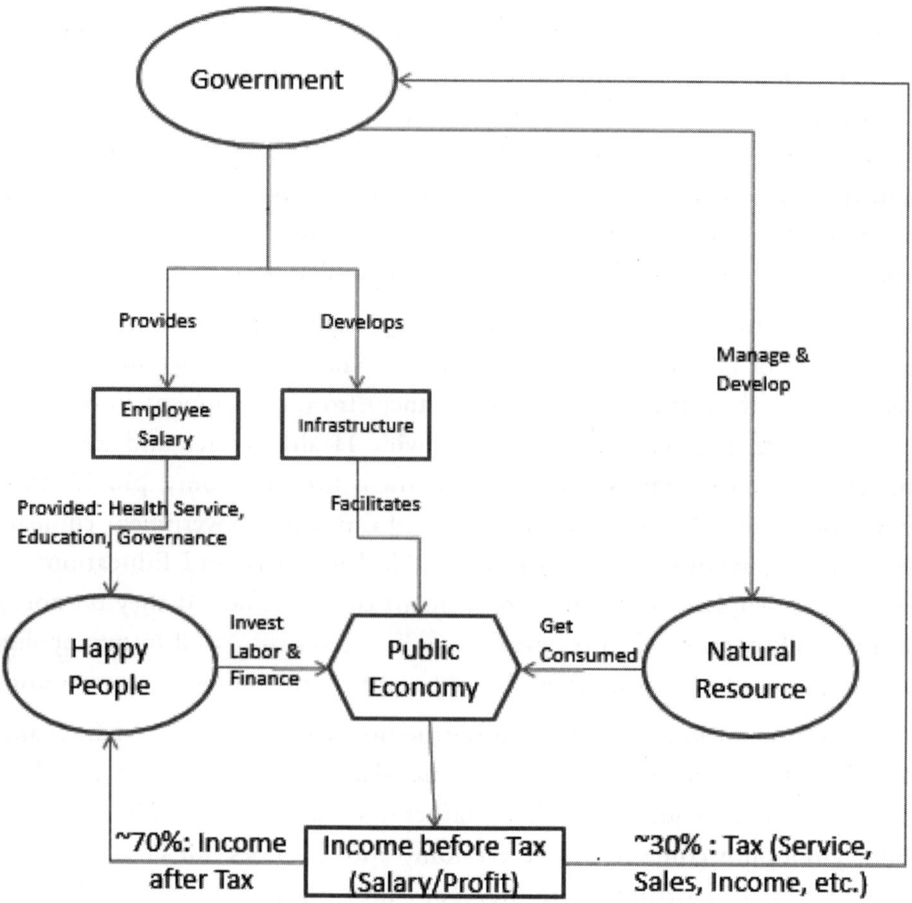

Happy People Model: Showing responsibilities of Government towards "Happy People" and Public Economy. It also shows role of economy in maximizing Happiness of both "Happy People" and "Government". The solid line and direction represent the physical money movements and direction.

After Second World War, there is evolution of this system, and foreign donation through donor has become factor influencing the Happiness of people.

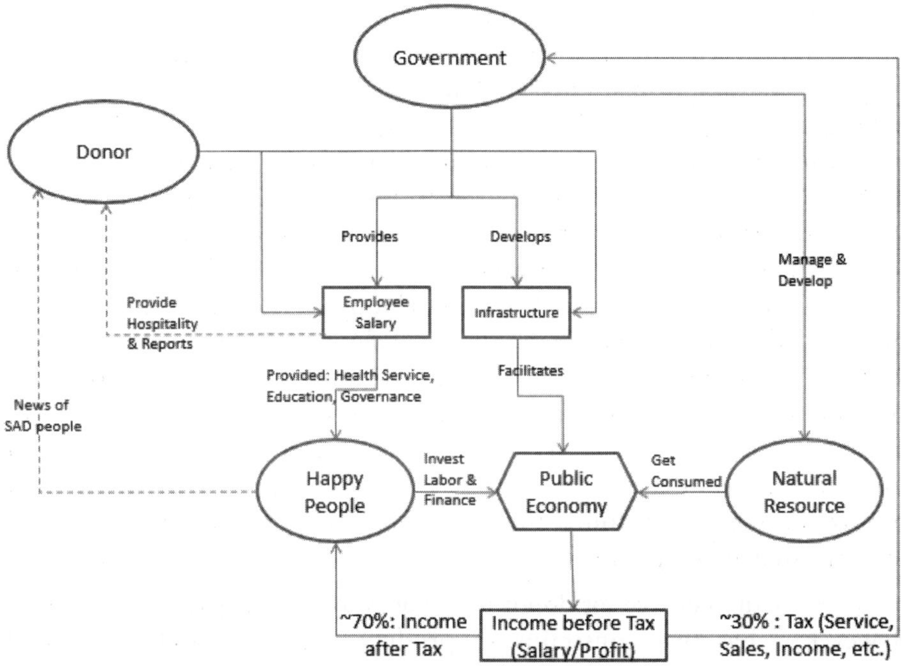

Modified Happy People Model (Unhappy People Model): Showing interaction between Donor, Government and "Happy People". The dotted line shows no physical movement of money to donor. The solid line and direction represent the physical money movements and direction.

Donor has physical relationship with the government, whereas it's one-way emotional relationship with people (see dotted line). One way relationship because Happy People hardly interact with Donor, but Donor proactively believe world as one system, and this universal concept is against the concept and interest of Government. However, if they accept Government existence, then Donor independent role doesn't really produce "Happy People", as the system without Donor does.

The motivation for Donor to contribute finance or labor comes from the assumption that there exist "Sad People", else Donor cannot justify their charity in their home country. So, when Donor provides Labor and Finance in the form of "No String Attached" or "Free Money", Government does not have to wait for long to get the economic cycle completed to derive their salary or perk. Rather Government has easy source of money, with no string attached, to derive the salary. Government feels, they are accountable to donor rather to people and government does not seek consent of people for development projects; slowly contract between people and government vanish, a prerequisite for people oriented development[79]. So, we end up in the scenario, where Government becomes "Yes Man" to donor, and presents the plans that emotionally makes donor instantaneously Happy rather that making the "Happy People". In the long run too, it is in Government interest to produce "Sad People" rather than "Happy People", because news of "Sad People" motivates donor to keep providing financial contributions. Donor can support in Infrastructure or to the "Government Employee Salary", however there has to be fine distinction, if it is investment or Donation? If it is investment, then the line between "Happy People" and "donor" will be solid, and this undermines the meaning of donor. This indicates, the donor changes its role and becomes part of the "Happy People", whose purpose is to invest and get profit. Government allows those conversion from donor to "Happy People" for some fees. However, if donor is giving money for infrastructure as donation, then there is room for corruption, and it again follows the same dichotomy, the more "Sad People", the more donor will be motivated in long run.

There is another role for donor too, that is to become pseudo-Government. However it has two constrains to produce "Happy People" as pseudo-Government; first donor has to build emotional relationship with people, else it will become skewed relationship and second donor derives physical benefits from the system. The example of this transformation from donor to pseudo-Government can be seen in US role in India, where US is getting Indian human resource for its support, and US is also having social relationship with Indians living in US where different Indians are at the helm of US society; Sundar Pichai of Google, Vikram Pandit of Citi, Attorney Preet Bharara, and millions of software professionals. India is having similar role in Nepal. India derives labor from Nepal, and also gets share in profit through exports (sales tax goes to Indian Government). Thus, it is in Indian interest to keep investing in Nepal. A close look at Indian projects indicate, India puts money in (1) Building roads, (2) in improving education sector by building schools and donating school bus, (3) in improving Health service by donating ambulances, by building and running B.P. Koirala Health institute, etc. These are projects fitted into public service that citizens expect from government.

China as such has smaller trade with Nepal, however with the increasing trades it is slowly changing from Donor to pseudo-Government role. However, it is still far away compared to India. China has physical benefit in supporting

Nepal in terms of security it needs on Nepal-China border considering Tibet political perspective. Thus China supports government employee perks through different means like opening Police academy, army, etc. However, China's other donations to Nepal like opening factories or providing street lights or running hospital is contributing towards "Sad People", because China does not derive any benefit out of these freebies. There is negligible social connection between "Happy People" and China, which indicates, there is negligible emotional connections between them.

British has role as pseudo-Government, when it derives benefit from Gurkha employment, it invests in those programs linked to Gurkha families. However, British donation to support Nepal Police, through salary is creating "Sad People", as it is seen from the recent human rights violations records linked to Nepal police[80], including during Madhesh Protests. US has lately been deriving benefits, as talents are migrating to US. There are around 200k Nepalese in US at different levels. However, US 1960s role in Nepal have created tremendous "Sad People", especially in plain people through projects like resettlement, land reforms, etc.

There are other countries, whose role are limited to pure donor, and their contribution is producing "Sad People" rather than "Happy People". For example Switzerland or Japan or Russia, who derived no physical benefit. South Korea has chosen to contribute in a different way; it sources Nepalese human resource through Government-to-Government channel[81], and this is helping in creating "Happy People" through Win-Win situation where South Korea is acting like pseudo-government in generating employment.

Donor can choose following four approaches to produce "Happy People" people in host countries.

1. Do not transfer perks to government through shortcut means, in which there is no return of physical benefit to donor from domestic country.
2. Foreign government should put pressure on domestic government to ensure fruits are distributed in 30-70 ratio both in policy and action. Any attempt to change ratio in favor of government by government without justification, should be discouraged internationally.
3. Provide finance to people (based on some form of credit score), who can use those to invest into economy, and earn the spread. That is,

donor becomes part of the people. And donor gets the cost for its capital from the "Happy People".

4. Donor becomes part of pseudo-Government.

Road Ahead

Hydropower projects (and other projects) are being built under BOOT model. The situation of exclusion is going to be more complex and worst in the next 3 decades due to BOOT model after the transfer of ownership to domestic government. After transfer, the asset will be in the hands of government employees (around 0.1% country population), who will consider them as private asset to fund their salary. This will be same like Panchayat rule before 1990, where factories were under Government control, like communist country model. We all saw, those factories were underperformers, became sanctuary of corruption and finally had to be closed (see table below). Nepal was ranked 15th most corrupt countries in the world in 2015 survey[82]. If BOOT model wins in coming days, the situation of governance delivery will change from bad to worst and the exclusion of Nepalese will be more than it is today, almost will touch to the level of Rana period, which derived its revenue by cutting the jungle, exporting them and income going to private bank account of Rana family members.

Nepal can attract the foreign investor, however, the model need to be modified into BOOST (Build–Own-Operate-Sell and Transfer), rather the BOOT. First three phases Build, Own and Operate would be same in BOOST model like BOOT. Instead of Transfer to Government, the foreign company should be obliged to sell the share to public in open financial market, and transfer ownership to the shareholders. Government should limit to Tax, which they are entitled to. There is so much of surplus liquidity in Nepal, primarily from remittance, that would be ready to take the share of those production plants in the last two phases of BOOST model.

There are few advantages of BOOST model. (1) The cost of financing project would go down, because Initial Investor have maturity amount to withdraw at the end of project through sell of equity share. Thus the production cost of electricity would be lower. (2) It will develop strong domestic financial secondary market that would finance the projects. Thus further decreasing the cost of capital, and which, in turn, would decrease production cost of electricity (3) It will give a democratic representation to common people in the financial system, to those whoever wants to buy a share in secondary market (4) Government would focus on core governance delivery rather than managing a power company.

In the improved BOOST model, foreign investor should have phased approach to Sell and Transfer ownership; say for example if a project is of 20 years period then, at the end of 15 years their ownership should be decreased by X%, then at the end of 16years, the ownership should further decrease by Y%, so on and so forth, until at the end of 20th year, the ownership of foreign investor becomes 0%. To provide more control to the foreign investor in the initial phase of the project, they can rely on convertible bonds rather than the common stock for crowd funding.

Enterprise Name	Year	Country	Status as of 2012	Profit/ Loss 2009/ 10	Profit/ Loss 2010/ 11	Profit/ Loss 2011/ 12
Agricultural Input Corporation						
Agricultural Tools Factory Limited	1968	USSR	Privatized and Closed within 6 months			
Bansbari Leather and Shoe Factory	1964	China	Privatized in 1992 thru Asset and Business Sales			
Bhaktapur Brick Factory, Limited	1974	China	In 2004, Asset and Business Sales			
Dairy Development Corporation	1956/ 1969	Switzerland, New Zealand, Denmark	Government Holding	258	849	(796)
Hetauda Cement Industry, Limited	1976	Financing	Government Holding	1,170	389	71
Hetauda Textile Industry	1974	China	Liquidated in 2002 to minimize loss			
Himal Cement Company, Limited	1966	Germany	Liquidated in 2002 to minimize loss			
Janakpur Cigarette Factory	1964	USSR	Government Holding	(5,009)	(2,181)	(3,813)
Nepal Food Corporation	1974	WB, FAO, UNDP	Government Holding	149	10	166
Raghupati Jute Mills, Limited			Privatized in 1996 (Share sales)			
Nepal Drugs Limited	1972	Great Britain, UNIDO, WHO, and UNICEF		(758)	(740)	-
Udaypur Cement Industries Limited	1987	OECF-Japans		(879)	(1,989)	(2,484)
Lumbini sugar Mill		China	Privatized in 2006 thru Asset and Business Sales			

Table showing the status of the foreign donated factories. Most of them are either closed or in loss. Source: Annual Performance Review of Public Enterprises 2012, Government of Nepal Ministry of Finance, pp 32 and 45

Madhesh – Further Victim of Foreign Aids and Extractive Institution

Plain people consist of thirty percent of Nepal's total population. Hill people consist the remaining sixty six percent. Hill Group is equally divided into Hill Caste and Hill Tribal, also called Hill Janajatis or Nationalites. Tribal groups are differentiated if a person follows Hindu caste system or not, and if they have their own ethnic uniqueness.

The representation of Plain people and Hill Nationalites in the state structure is disproportionate, and if we consider women the situation becomes further worse. Dalits consist another smaller though prominent group within Hill caste people and plain people having the exclusion issue at its extreme.

So ideally, 15% of the people – Hindu Upper Caste Hilly – filling most of government job vacancies. Among the plain people, most find themselves in school teaching and among Janajatis, most find themselves in Police or Army jobs.

According to the Nepal National Human Rights Commission, there are 16.83% women and 24% indigenous nationalities in civil service. Likewise 3.55% women, 27.35% indigenous nationalities, 6.14% Madhesi, 3.11% Dalits, 2.46% PWD (person with disabilities) and 3.14% persons from backward regions in Nepal Army. There are 5% women, 29.4% indigenous nationalities, 2.2% Madhesi, 6.3% Dalits and 2.5% persons from backward regions in the Armed Police Force. There are 29.28% women in Constituent Assembly, and 12.05% women, 16.66% indigenous nationalities and 12.5% Madhesi in the Council of Ministers[83].

Ethnic Group	Jobs in Army Count	Jobs in Army %	Population %	Inclusion Ratio (% Jobs/ % Population)
Plain Origin People	7,412	8.056	33.31	0.241849
Plain Tribal	5,667	6.161	8.9	0.692247
Plain Excluding Tribal	1,745	1.895	24.4	0.077664
Hill Origin People	84,586	91.944	66.69	1.378677

Table: Showing Inclusion Ratios as a measure of disadvantage of Plain people in Army Jobs compared to Hill origin people. Source: Author's calculation based on the Nepal Census CBS 2011 and Army Inclusiveness data 2016. See appendix for full data for Inclusion within Nepal Army.

Scanning through the Nepal's history, we find army was able to expand since mid-eighteenth century because they could extract resource from the southern plain. Army officers were allocated lands in Plain, which they rented out to the plain farmers, and the income so extracted was used to maintain the army. Post retirement too, the army officers were allocated lands as pension which continued till mid twentieth century. After Mahendra's land reform, the income from those lands are collected as state tax, which fund the state institution including armies. Despite being financial source of state treasure, plain people have never been included in the state jobs. State has followed the caste preference policies for different appointments since King Prithivi Narayan Shah Days. After 1950s, country has expanded other sector of government, and there too, the past culture of caste preference has continued till date.

Nepal Army in a candid confession has acknowledged the plain people under representation saying "only 6.26 percent are seemingly serving in the army."[84] At the high level posting involving decision making, the situation becomes worst for plain people. As of July 2010, out of 19 posts in Nepal Army, including two technical, in the rank of Major General and above, the current representations are- 9 Chhetri, 2 Brahmin, 4 Gurung, 2 Thakuri, 1 Rana, 1 Newar and none of the plain people.[85]

Army tries to throw the ball outside it's court for the lower representation of Plain people, and gives hypothetical reasons as "seems to be the lack of interest on the part of Madhesi communities to join military services" and further justifies stating there is "no representation of Madhesis in the British or Indian Gurkhas."[86] The argument is manufactured having no ground for institution like army, which is deriving resource from state treasure for its running. Closure look at the history and recent facts shows the different image of plain people.

1. During King Ratna Malla reign (1482 – 1520AD), Tirhutia Brahmans had brought plain people troops from Raja of Palpa, to assist Ratna Malla driving off the Bhotiyas. The place where Bhotiya were defeated became known as Kuku-syana-jor. Tirhutia Brahmans were rewarded[87]. There is another mention of valor in history, by none other than King Salhesh, a revered god of Dusad people, and worshipped by all. In 7th century, he defended Tirhut from Tibetan attack[88], thus his name Salhesh, meaning King of Mountain.

2. Prithivi Narayan Shah had brought 12000 Tirhutia army in the initial days of his struggle against Kantipur[89]. His opponent Jai Prakash Malla had also brought Tirhutia army to defend Kathmandu[90]. The loyalty of Tirhutia Brahmans to Jai Prakash Malla was appreciated by King Prithivi Narayan Shah too[91].
3. Prior to Shah King usurpation, there were independent kingdoms of plains people from east to west, mostly under two branches of Sen Kings. First branch ruling East of River Gandaki till Morang, second branch ruling West of Gandaki. First branch had three kings each ruling between (1) Gandaki to Kamla river (2) Kamla to Morang and (3) Morang till Sikkim. There is record that plain people have defended Sen kingdoms[92], where Muslims were attacking them.
4. Shah Kings had grabbed plain lands from plain Kings without fights. All the plain kings – Bijaypur, Makwanpur, and Palpa - were killed by treachery rather than in open declared war. The remaining formality of land rights were established with treaty of British EIC in eighteenth century. This indicates, there was no test to show Plain people's valor, and plain people were labelled coward and defeated without reason.
5. During British-Gurkha war of 1814-1816, plain people, mostly Bengal natives, were fighting on British side under leadership of British officers that defeated Gurkha Army. The plain people in Madhesh and Bengal have close genetic link, and culture, as such they have similar capability. The contribution of plain people from Madhesh, based on available records, was not so great, however there is mention of protecting plain people rights under Sugaolee Treaty.
6. Today Indian army derives its large portion of recruitment from Bihar, Bengal and UP. These states border Nepal and have cultural and genetic relationship with plain people of Nepal.
7. During the last 15 years, around 1,500 plain peoples (Madhesi and Tharu) have died, knowing the risk that they would die. Around 1300 people, of which 50 percent were Tharu, died during Maoist insurgency for being on Maoist army. Kailali, Dhanusha, Siraha and Rautahat were the most impacted districts. There was plain people uprising in 2007, in which around 45 people died facing police guns face to face. In 2015-2016 plain people's uprising, another 52

> people died facing police bullets. During 2008-2009, there were uprising of underground armed groups in plain in support of Madhesh politics; the prominent among them were Goit and Jwala Singh led Janatantrik Terai Mukti Morcha (JTMM). During the police covert operations, around 100 people were killed in encounter. Although there was never official acknowledgement, Human rights organization conducted independent investigations. All these political killings do indicate, plain people are willing to face death, but they are not coward as Nepal Army wants to depict them.

The discussion above gives ample proof to reject the Coward theory. This is not more than prejudice of state decision makers against the plain people. Further to the extreme side, we have 'Martial Race' theory, as conceived during British Era. Nepal army in another argument tries to hide behind this 'Martial Race' theory putting the analogy of British and Indian army having recruitment from Hill people. There are three counters to this (1) Is Nepal independent sovereign country or part of India, British state? If Madhesis are paying tax to Nepal government to fund Nepal army Salary, then why shouldn't it ask Nepal army to be accountable? Yes, it is question for British and India to explain the discrimination, as mentioned by Nepal army, however there is no excuse for Nepal to justify the race theory in Government recruitment. (2) British and Indian Gurkha regiment do not have Brahmin and Chhetri in the preference list of recruitment because they have mix of Indian plain blood rather than the original hill blood, however in Nepal, army has maximum ratio of these two castes. So, is really Nepal Army having parity of following British and Indian policy? (3) Is the Martial Theory really valid? British relied on plain people. In early nineteenth century, three quarters of the Bengal Native Infantry were "high caste" men from Awadh, mainly Brahmans[93]. The same group of plain people defeated Nepal in 1814-16 war, and also invaded Sikh state in 1845 and 1849 war. Even after 1857 revolt, British relied on Bengal recruits, though there was focus on wider social base through Army reorganization. There was policy change in 1870 to increase Gurkha because British feared Russian attack via China and Tibet. The policy was based on Gurkha familiarity of terrain leading to Tibet. That's when Lord (as he later became) Roberts hypothesized Martial race theory, who can take on Russian fights. The recent British Gurkha fight for 'Equal Pay'[94] indicates it is the cost which is putting Gurkha in the preference list of British recruiter than anything else. The hardship of life, poverty, tough hilly terrain and state discrimination leave few choice to Janajati group than to become Gurkha mercenaries. The recent uprising have also shown, few thousand Maoist fighter, which drew sizeable recruits from plain people, were able to take on Nepal army. Sam Cowan, a retired Gurkha Army officer, summarized well saying everyone can fight provided they have "the right motivation, the right training and, above all, the right leadership".

After interim constitution was implemented, there was pressure to Army to become transparent. Army disclosed a result of the recruitment process. Army accepted, "bulk of the [plain people] applicants" failed in the written tests. Success ratio of Brahmin and Chhetri community in written tests were reported relatively high i.e., 85.47 percent. Whereas success rate of Madhesi / Tharu, Dalits and Janajati communities were much less; 0.54, 1.36 and 12.60 percent respectively. Nepal army also realizes, though in veil, that there is something wrong with the government system, and wrote in the report "Why the latter three communities are relatively weaker in written tests is a matter of research in relation to their education quality and social opportunities that fall beyond the responsibilities of the Nepalese Army itself and an area of concern to the state as a whole."[95]

Next in the discussion, we are focusing on education, to peel the mystery of government exclusion policy towards plain people.

Division	District	Population	Schools	Teachers	Ratio: Popu/ School	Ratio: Popu/ Teacher	Literacy Rank
Hill Far-Western	Achham	257477	502	3393	513	76	61
Hill Far-Western	Doti	211746	381	3041	556	70	58
Hill Far-Western	Baitadi	250898	554	3224	453	78	45
Hill Far-Western	Dadeldhura	142094	263	2151	540	66	41
Hill Mid-Western	Jajarkot	171304	430	1671	398	103	56
Hill Mid-Western	Rolpa	224506	423	2269	531	99	53
Hill Mid-Western	Rukum	208567	391	1614	533	129	51
Hill Mid-Western	Dailekh	261770	508	2412	515	109	48
Hill Mid-Western	Salyan	242444	454	1907	534	127	44
Hill Mid-Western	Pyuthan	228102	373	2434	612	94	35
Hill Western	Gorkha	271061	553	3769	490	72	36
Hill Western	Lamjung	167724	424	3344	396	50	22
Hill Western	Myagdi	113641	273	1617	416	70	20
Hill Western	Baglung	268613	594	4255	452	63	19
Hill Western	Gulmi	280160	615	4610	456	61	18
Hill Western	Arghakhanchi	197632	451	2693	438	73	16

Hill Western	Parbat	146590	369	2911	397	50	14
Hill Western	Tanahu	323288	650	4856	497	67	11
Hill Western	Palpa	261180	496	4723	527	55	8
Hill Western	Syangja	289148	637	5983	454	48	7
Hill Western	Kaski	492098	645	8597	763	57	3
Hill Central	Nuwakot	277471	521	2813	533	99	54
Hill Central	Ramechhap	202646	492	3018	412	67	50
Hill Central	Dhading	336067	634	4647	530	72	46
Hill Central	Kavrepalanchok	381937	696	7580	549	50	27
Hill Central	Bhaktapur	304651	355	5724	858	53	4
Hill Central	Lalitpur	468132	488	7110	959	66	2
Hill Central	Kathmandu	1744240	1370	18827	1273	93	1
Hill Eastern	Okhaldhunga	147984	368	2272	402	65	42
Hill Eastern	Khotang	206312	484	2972	426	69	31
Hill Eastern	Bhojpur	182459	404	2472	452	74	30
Hill Eastern	Panchthar	191817	436	3298	440	58	17
Hill Eastern	Dhankuta	163412	340	2261	481	72	13
Hill Eastern	Tehrathum	101577	253	1764	401	58	12
Hill Eastern	Ilam	290254	494	3695	588	79	5
Mountain Far-Western	Bajhang	195159	457	3230	427	60	62
Mountain Far-Western	Bajura	134912	262	2312	515	58	60
Mountain Far-Western	Darchula	133274	361	2053	369	65	40
Mountain Far-Western	Humla	50858	135	636	377	80	72
Mountain Far-Western	Mugu	55286	152	701	364	79	69
Mountain Far-Western	Dolpa	36700	121	723	303	51	66
Mountain Far-Western	Jumla	108921	155	1123	703	97	64
Mountain Far-Western	Kalikot	136948	288	2149	476	64	57
Mountain Western	Mustang	13452	70	506	192	27	38
Mountain Western	Manang	6538	32	223	204	29	10
Mountain Central	Rasuwa	43300	113	702	383	62	67
Mountain Central	Sindhupalchok	287798	556	3707	518	78	55
Mountain Central	Dolakha	186557	431	3166	433	59	47
Mountain Eastern	Solukhumbu	105886	290	1601	365	66	43
Mountain Eastern	Sankhuwasabha	158742	414	2622	383	61	29
Mountain Eastern	Taplejung	127461	339	2439	376	52	21
Terai Far-Western	Kailali	775709	605	5498	1282	141	37
Terai Far-Western	Kanchanpur	451248	430	3506	1049	129	24
Terai Mid-Western	Banke	491313	436	4026	1127	122	49
Terai Mid-Western	Bardiya	426576	350	3369	1219	127	39

Terai (Inner) Mid-Western	Dang	552583	512	4942	1079	112	26
Terai (Inner) Mid-Western	Surkhet	350804	581	3469	604	101	15
Terai Western	Kapilbastu	571936	511	4253	1119	134	63
Terai Western	Rupandehi	880196	597	9081	1474	97	28
Terai Western	Nawalparasi	643508	706	6502	911	99	23
Terai Central	Rautahat	686722	487	2531	1410	271	75
Terai Central	Sarlahi	769729	745	3064	1033	251	74
Terai Central	Mahottari	627580	415	2801	1512	224	73
Terai Central	Dhanusha	754777	397	2850	1901	265	70
Terai Central	Bara	687708	418	3225	1645	213	68
Terai Central	Parsa	601017	392	3282	1533	183	59
Terai (Inner) Central	Sindhuli	296192	581	3838	510	77	52
Terai (Inner) Central	Makwanpur	420477	597	5079	704	83	34
Terai (Inner) Central	Chitwan	579984	543	6745	1068	86	6
Terai Eastern	Siraha	637328	469	2952	1359	216	71
Terai Eastern	Saptari	639284	484	2973	1321	215	65
Terai Eastern	Sunsari	763487	745	5120	1025	149	33
Terai (Inner) Eastern	Udaypur	317532	472	3190	673	100	32
Terai Eastern	Morang	965370	707	5375	1365	180	25
Terai Eastern	Jhapa	812650	684	10191	1188	80	9
Total		26494504	34361	275682	771	96	

Table showing Population, Schools and Teachers, and their relationship with district literacy. Literacy ranking 1 represents best. Tabular representation compiled by Author based on 2011 Nepal census data.

There looks definite pattern in the education infrastructure (School counts), teacher counts and literacy ratio (see Table showing Population, Schools and Teachers, and their relationship with district literacy). In Hill and Plains cluster, the number of teachers is more prominent factor for the literacy ranking compared to the school number; the more the teacher, the better ranking. Based on the same observation, we find Terai region having worst hit due to lower number of teacher appointments. The country average for Teacher is 1 teacher per 96 population. However for the districts having Madhesi people are having teacher to population ratio less than half times the country average, meaning 1 teacher for more than 200 people. The worst affected districts are between Koshi and Gandaki Rivers; Saptari having

2.2 times (1 teach per 215 people), Siraha having 2.25 times (1 teacher per 216 people), Mahottari having 2.33 times (1 teacher per 224 people), Dhanusha having 2.76 times (1 teacher per 265 people), Sarlahi having 2.61 times (1 teacher per 251 people), Rautahat having 2.82 times (1 teacher 271 people), Parsa having 1.9 times (1 teacher 183 people), and Bara having 2.2 times (1 teacher per 213 people). Saptari, Siraha, Mahottari, Dhanusha, Sarlahi, Rautahat, Parsa and Bara have worst literacy ranking in the 75 districts: standing at 65, 71, 73, 70, 74, 75, 59 and 68 respectively. Compare these with Manang and Mustang, which have 1 teacher per 29 and 27 peoples respectively, which also contributed in better national literacy ranking of 10 and 38 respectively.

The next in the worst off group, though better than central Terai, are the Tharu majority western Terai districts having Population to teacher ratio; Kailali having 1.46 times (1 teacher per 141 people), Kanchanpur having 1.34 times (1 teacher per 129 people), Banke having 1.27 times (1 teacher 122 people), Bardiya having 1.32 (1 teacher per 127 people), Dang having 1.17 (1 teacher per 112 people) times the country average. Except 5 districts of Hill Mid-Western cluster, all the remaining districts are either hovering around 96 people per teacher or better statistics. This reflects pattern in budget planning discrimination.

There is an exception within Terai district; Inner Terai districts and three eastern districts, namely, Jhapa, Sunsari and Morang are having better in terms of literacy. To understand the reason for variance within Terai and Inner Terai, an analysis of 70 years of literacy records is required, which is given in table (showing pattern for the literacy ranking for past 70 years).

Division	District	1952 - 54	1961	1971	1981	1991	2001	2011	Population increase 1961-2011
Hill Central	Kathmandu	1	1	1	1	1	1	1	676%
Hill Central	Lalitpur	2	2	2	2	2	4	2	222%
Hill Central	Bhaktapur	3	3	4	9	3	5	4	239%
Hill Central	Kavrepalanchok	33	20	45	23	34	12	27	76%
Hill Central	Dhading	54	55	71	59	48	53	46	66%
Hill Central	Ramechhap	45	51	49	50	52	62	50	64%
Hill Central	Nuwakot	55	47	59	45	49	40	54	210%
Hill Eastern	Ilam	16	4	17	7	8	8	5	377%
Hill Eastern	Tehrathum	37	28	15	5	6	20	12	-76%
Hill Eastern	Dhankuta	29	16	19	12	12	11	13	141%
Hill Eastern	Panchthar	16	4	29	25	21	29	17	201%
Hill Eastern	Bhojpur	34	41	35	27	26	30	30	-12%

Hill Eastern	Khotang	34	41	40	30	30	43	31	19%
Hill Eastern	Okhaldhunga	39	45	46	51	36	46	42	67%
Hill Far-Western	Dadeldhura	12	29	26	34	40	39	41	72%
Hill Far-Western	Baitadi	19	30	27	40	41	38	45	142%
Hill Far-Western	Doti	47	60	61	68	60	54	58	52%
Hill Far-Western	Achham	47	74	68	60	70	71	61	69%
Hill Mid-Western	Pyuthan	38	43	31	54	46	50	35	7%
Hill Mid-Western	Salyan	59	65	54	64	53	48	44	101%
Hill Mid-Western	Dailekh	65	63	55	43	54	49	48	110%
Hill Mid-Western	Rukum	59	65	63	63	57	60	51	154%
Hill Mid-Western	Rolpa	59	65	64	61	62	64	53	62%
Hill Mid-Western	Jajarkot	59	65	73	72	69	61	56	132%
Hill Western	Kaski	4	8	3	4	4	2	3	286%
Hill Western	Syangja	13	15	11	17	10	7	7	-15%
Hill Western	Palpa	5	11	5	16	16	9	8	51%
Hill Western	Tanahu	6	13	12	20	11	15	11	153%
Hill Western	Parbat	55	48	14	10	9	25	14	127%
Hill Western	Arghakhanchi	14	36	22	21	23	27	16	80%
Hill Western	Gulmi	14	36	16	11	18	23	18	46%
Hill Western	Baglung	21	38	28	29	29	16	19	75%
Hill Western	Myagdi	21	38	32	33	33	28	20	121%
Hill Western	Lamjung	10	24	13	8	17	26	22	35%
Hill Western	Gorkha	32	44	41	46	22	31	36	79%
Mountain Central	Dolakha	42	59	52	53	43	41	47	41%
Mountain Central	Sindhupalchok	63	57	58	58	55	59	55	54%
Mountain Central	Rasuwa	55	48	65	74	72	69	67	378%
Mountain Eastern	Taplejung	29	16	25	15	19	36	21	139%
Mountain Eastern	Sankhuwasabha	29	16	30	19	15	32	29	121%
Mountain Eastern	Solukhumbu	39	45	34	35	37	51	43	40%
Mountain Far-Western	Darchula	19	30	23	32	27	45	40	141%
Mountain Far-Western	Bajura	47	60	75	71	67	70	60	161%
Mountain Far-Western	Bajhang	47	60	53	67	63	66	62	114%
Mountain Mid-Western	Kalikot	71	69	60	75	75	63	57	1435%
Mountain Mid-Western	Jumla	71	69	66	47	66	73	64	0%
Mountain Mid-Western	Dolpa	71	69	70	70	71	67	66	116%
Mountain Mid-Western	Mugu	71	69	72	73	73	74	69	141%
Mountain Mid-Western	Humla	71	69	67	66	74	75	72	93%
Mountain Western	Manang	10	24	74	39	24	18	10	-1%
Mountain Western	Mustang	21	38	10	28	14	37	38	-44%
Terai (Inner) Central	Chitwan	70	21	6	6	7	3	6	754%
Terai (Inner) Central	Makwanpur	46	50	37	24	38	13	34	165%
Terai (Inner) Central	Sindhuli	58	54	51	41	45	42	52	184%
Terai (Inner) Eastern	Udaypur	52	52	50	42	39	33	32	255%
Terai (Inner) Mid-Western	Surkhet	65	63	48	36	25	14	15	318%

Terai (Inner) Mid-Western	Dang	64	12	47	37	32	21	26	460%
Terai Central	Parsa	51	33	24	38	47	56	59	337%
Terai Central	Bara	24	19	43	49	61	55	68	175%
Terai Central	Dhanusha	26	22	38	44	51	47	70	206%
Terai Central	Mahottari	26	22	44	55	65	68	73	159%
Terai Central	Sarlahi	44	32	56	57	64	65	74	372%
Terai Central	Rautahat	41	34	57	69	68	72	75	214%
Terai Eastern	Saptari	18	9	21	22	42	44	65	113%
Terai Eastern	Siraha	43	35	36	52	58	58	71	203%
Terai Eastern	Sunsari	7	6	9	13	20	17	33	451%
Terai Eastern	Morang	7	6	8	14	13	24	25	416%
Terai Eastern	Jhapa	36	10	7	3	5	6	9	579%
Terai Far-Western	Kanchanpur	67	75	42	26	28	19	24	2290%
Terai Far-Western	Kailali	68	56	62	56	50	35	37	764%
Terai Mid-Western	Bardiya	69	58	69	62	56	52	39	530%
Terai Mid-Western	Banke	25	14	33	48	44	22	49	416%
Terai Western	Nawalparasi	53	53	20	31	35	34	23	304%
Terai Western	Rupandehi	28	27	18	18	31	10	28	298%
Terai Western	Kapilbastu	9	26	39	65	59	57	63	1427%
	Nepal								-179.8%

Table: Showing pattern for the literacy ranking for past 70 years. The district wise literacy data is enriched with the migration data to understand the impact of migrants in influencing the literacy. There were 55 districts reported in 1960 census and numbers were 54 in 1952-54 census. In 1971, the new districts were formed by reorganization of old district. Tabular representation compiled by Author based on Nepal census data. Statistical modelling was used to adjust the 1960 and 1952-54 ranking number for newly created districts.

Notes: Colored table - Heat Chart is in appendix

In the table, showing pattern for the literacy ranking for past 70 years, we have following observation

1. Between 1952 and 1961, a decade when there was maximum freedom for plains people in terms of state policy, the literacy ranking improved for Terai region; almost all the plain districts showed improvement in literacy ranking and outer Terai showing better ranking than Inner Terai; also note the green grading of districts between Koshi and Gandaki in 1952. The improvement trend collaborate with the duration when there was more political freedom for Terai people between fall of Rana (1951) and rise of King Mahendra(1960). The education was in Hindi medium. During this period, Terai Congress led by Vedananda Jha was able to raise Plain people issue. Plain people were able to get share in ministry, though low in percentage.

2. Comparing the period of 70 years, the big swings in literacy ranking are localized in Terai districts. Other districts' current ranking remains more or less in the same range as it was 7 decades before. The trend in Terai districts are of two types; one group showing the continuous rank sliding trend and second cluster showing continuous improving trend. Migration of hill people has changed the demography substantially.

3. After 1960, the ranking has been slowly decreasing year after year in Central Terai, Eastern Terai and Western Terai; Siraha, Saptari, Mahottari, Dhanusha, Rautahat, Bara, Parsa, Banke, Kapilbastu. Strikingly inner Terai districts along with Jhapa, have shown tremendous improvements, and those showing improvement have coincidentally higher rate of migration since 1970. These migrations were state sponsored during King Mahendra time under (1) rehabilitation projects and (2) land reform projects. It was in this tenure that Hindi was replaced by Nepali as education medium. The Hilly migrant were of socially higher caste profile, able to take the leadership position in collusion with officer – who were of hilly origin too – suppressing the political activities of native people. All these combined together promoted "Nepalization" of Terai, especially in places where we have high migration percentage of Hilly people.

The complex nature of migration and literacy ranking is difficult to understand on the face value, unless we bring the state inclusion factor and foreign donation perspective together, as discussed in "Why Nation Fails" by Daron Acemoglu and James A. Robinson. The understanding becomes even better, if we see the things in the light of foreign aid, as mentioned by 2015 Economics Nobel prize winner Angus Deaton.

The first step of discrimination happens there in allocating resource for school infrastructure development and teacher assignment. Center manages these high level budget decision, and central bureaucracy, located in the Kathmandu, are full of hilly peoples. Then there is central policy of using Nepali as education medium ignoring the challenge of learning in non-native language.

In the second level, there is local administrative officers having lukewarm response in development of local education system. Plain districts are native land of Plain People, however, like any place, the plain district offices are also controlled by Hilly people. The policy of Hilly state is exclusion of plain people from decision making body. The district officers, superintendents of police are sent from Kathmandu and all of them are of hilly origin. Mid rank, low rank and every officer of some importance are of hill origin in plain districts. This indicates, basic human interest of the local people from the government school is not served, and wherever there is need of district officers' intervention, they ignore their responsibilities as officers, and because officer do not share the social space with local people, there is neither social incentive for Hilly officer nor social pressure. For example, the exam cheating is not controlled by district officers, and, in fact, in turn, it is helping the Hilly people because the competitiveness of plain people is compromised through loose examination system. The aid makes the system further looser, because aid money is mostly unaccountable and native people are disconnected with the money due to its foreign origin. This gives uncontrolled access to foreign aid for officers to use their discretion, rather than put the money where it will give marginal return. As we discussed before, aid weakens the feedback mechanism and it does not have to rely on consent of local people for development projects, rather these officers are accountable to foreign donors.

US provided $19 million during 1954-1975 period, which US AID categorizes as "massive", accounting for as much as two-thirds of the Ministry of Education budget[96]. Money were used for construction of buildings and facilities and other local costs for support of salaries to teachers'.[97] For Financial year 1991/92 the expenditure of Tribhuwan University was estimated at Rs. 1,028,469,500 of which Rs. 501,146,500 (48.7%) was born by foreign assistance[98]. The Basic Primary Education initiative also peg the foreign donation at 40% of the total budget of $211mm for year 1997-2002[99].

Financing of BPE Budget
Sources of Financing BPE Expenditure 1997-2002

Rs. Million

Description	Amount	%
1. Total BPE Expenditure	30119	100.0
2. Financing Sources		
Internal	18045	59.9
Foreign Aid	12074	40.1
3. Foreign Aid (US&in million)	211	-

* Conversion rate US$ 1 = Rs. 57.3

The recent report, see table below, from Ministry of finance gives distinct picture of the foreigners' contribution in plain districts[100]. The lowest 10 districts receiving the foreign funded projects are the same plain districts, which rank lowest in the literacy. The projects are of different types including education, however the assertion in this chapter is to find the co-relation of inclusion in state structure, foreign donors and impact on the well-being of populations. The co-relation indicates, if a population is excluded from state structure then the foreign aids (and related projects) which comes via state structure will also be tainted with the same virtue of exclusion. The Ministry of finance report accepts, foreign aid disbursements have co-relation with the level of poverty[101].

District	Estimated Disbursement FY 2012-13 in USD $	Population 2011	Per Capita Disbursement USD $	Ranking (low to High)
Dhanusha	5,316,059	754,777	7.04	75
Siraha	4,575,084	637,328	7.18	74
Saptari	4,916,003	639,284	7.69	73
Bara	5,354,559	687,708	7.79	72
Mahottari	5,317,584	627,580	8.47	71
Rautahat	6,056,736	686,722	8.82	70
Nawalparasi	6,314,809	643,508	9.81	69
Parsa	5,985,477	601,017	9.96	68
Morang	9,647,276	965,370	9.99	67
Sarlahi	8,399,165	769,729	10.91	66

Table: Estimated foreign aid disbursement per target district: top 10 lowest (nationwide projects excluded) . Source: Ministry of finance, Development Cooperation Report, Fiscal Year 2012-2013

Kathmandu Valley had best technologies till Malla dynasty, which can be seen in the architecture of hundreds of temples and natural stone-water-taps "Dhunge Dhara". Similarly, Madhesh had the best Sal wood resource in the world. Madhesh exported the rice to Britain via Patna traders. The Malla era trade route connected Lhasa with Patna which housed Kashmiri business establishments through which Nepal Valley was deriving business till 1760s. The political and economic problems in Kathmandu started with the rise of Shah Kingdom primarily due to prejudice, contempt and exclusionary politics. However foreign donors are made to believe that Nepal has technical problem and it is used as cover to push billions of dollars in foreign donation. Officially, foreign donor would neither have mandate to change politics nor to change people. The organization setup of INGO informally conforms to government bureaucracy and political parties' structure, which gets favorable rules/policy to run these organization from government. Thus, the chronical issue of people and inclusion are also reflected within foreign aid dependent INGO (International Non-Government Organization) (see table below for inclusion data in INGO).

Ethnicity	Professional Level					Total
	Senior Management	Middle Level Management	Officer Level	Assistant Level	Support Staff	
Brahman	60 35.5%	132 35.0%	254 28.3%	73 20.2%	63 133%	582 25.7%
Chhetrl	28 16.6%	66 17.5%	172 192%	86 233%	109 23.4%	461 203%
Dalit	4 2.4%	8 2.1%	47 5.2%	28 73%	38 82%	125 5.5%
Janajati	24 14.2%	62 16.4%	208 232%	99 27.4%	190 40.8%	583 25.7%
Newar	49 29%	81 21.5%	169 18.9%	64 17.7%	54 11.6%	417 18.4%
Muslim	**10.6%**	**20.5%**	**40.4%**	**103%**	**102%**	**9 0.4%**
Other Madheshi/ Terai Caste Group	2 1.2%	6 6 1.6%	38 4.2%	6 1.7%	6 13%	58 2.6%
Other Caste/Ethnic Minority Group	1 0.6%	19 5%	3 0.3%	1 0.3%	4 0.9%	28 1.2%
Person with Disability (PWD)	0 0.0%	1 0.3%	1 0.1%	3 03%	1 02%	6 0.3%
Total	169 100%	377 100%	896 100%	361 100%	466 100%	2,269 100%

Table: Distribution of Personnel by ethnicity and professional level. Source AIN, 2012[102]

These analysis bring us to adopt the finding of Angus Deaton, the 2015 recipient of the Nobel Prize in Economics that "Aid money going to governments can cause more harm than good"[103]. Foreign aid has exacerbated the issue of ethnic conflict and exclusion rather than help bridging the difference. Education sector and literacy that we analyzed above is one of the visible symptom. We should also remember the foreign aided resettlement plan, land reform and East-West high has also increased the ethnic conflict.

Holistic development, prosperity and wealth distribution as a function of inclusion of group member in government decision making can be derived adopting the concept of Inclusive-Extractive institution as discussed in book "Why Nation Fails"[104]. The institute becomes Exclusive, worse than extractive, if country has external donation (without string attached) and lacks representation of all groups within a country. The donation without string is like mad ox which does not know where to stop. It promotes corruption, unaccountability, exclusion and kills entrepreneurship. Especially in the country where ethnic discrimination issue is prevalent, the donation aggravates the issue. Nature of development, prosperity and wealth distribution is summarized below in the diagram (ISEE Model).

The situation of Nepal with respect to Madhesi is in left bottom quadrant, where donation is high and representation of Madhesis in government jobs are less compared to the population percentage. The shape of the development, prosperity and wealth distribution is in the shape of wine glass. Bottom flat shape representing poor people with low income making the foundation of country economy. Extractive class people are present above the root level poor people, however the nature is like Leptokurtic curve. These, first two groups in the bottom, are native people dependent on the domestically generated economy. The imbalance comes from the foreign financing like donation "without string attached", which creates a reverse normal distribution curve trend. Wealthy people trying to push money to the poor people in the form of donation, however money getting distributed in bell shape and reaching at maximum to somewhere in the middle of social hierarchy. The money nature is like bubble in the water. It goes from bottom to top naturally, however the forced money packed in donation (like balloon) cannot reach bottom, and will remain floating on top.

The two economies – donation based and native economy - existing simultaneously in a country, creates a shape of hour glass (top left hand side quadrant). Bottom half of hour glass representing domestic production based economy and upper half of hour glass representing foreign aid dependent economy. However in Nepal, where country is infected with exclusion - where wealth distribution is questionable and the social justice is elusive - the shape of economy becomes Wine Glass; the bottom half representing domestic production based economy with thinner peak and upper half of glass representing foreign aid dependent economy, who also have administrative power over both the economies. The relationship between two economies is connected through thin layer of extractor, and the thinner it becomes the weaker the bond between two economies. And it connects to the question, why Nation is failing? The topic that we have discussed in detail in previous section.

Connecting this to Madhesi education trend, the base of education in Madhesh is depleting year after year, whereas the people of ruling class is having upward trend in literacy. The ecosystem of education has been built on foreign donation, rather than tax and entrepreneurship, thus it is becoming zero sum game to fight for the state budgetary resource. Madhesis loose because neither they have political power nor representation in state structure, thus their interests are getting ignored at the table where budgets are allocated. The foreign donation in education is under control of central government, thus further supporting ruling class rather than improving literacy in Madhesh districts. Finally contributing to the increasing literacy gap between Hilly population and plains population, each year.

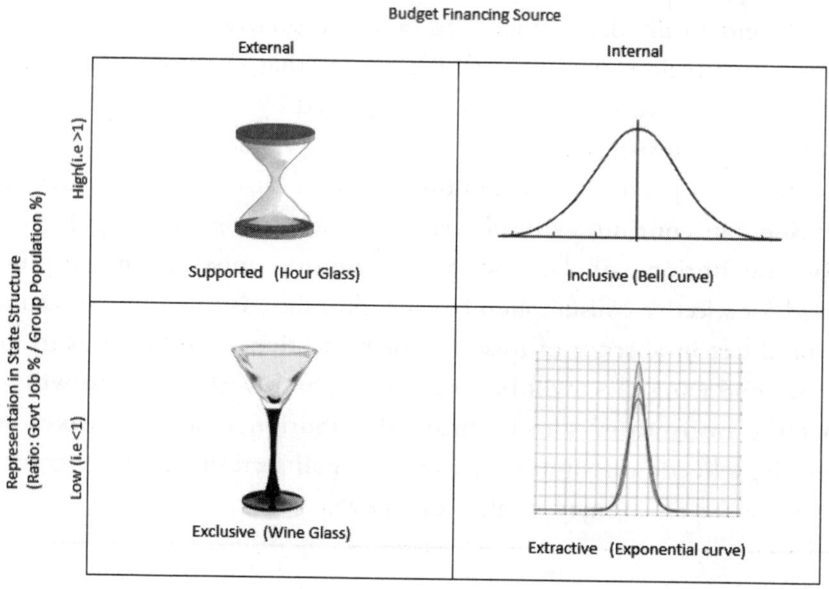

Diagram shows enhancement of model presented in the book "Why Country Fails?" suggested by Daron Acemoglu and James A. Robinson. In this ISEE model, X axis represents source of government budget funds; external from donors or internal from Taxes. Y axis represents group participation in government structure; the ratio of group's employed percentage and group's total percentage. Each shape characterizes, how economy will take shape; high income people are on top of shape, and shape area represents Development (Health, Education, Wealth, etc.) distribution.

Insight into Wealth Distribution in ISEE Model

Inclusive political institutions provide all (or at least most) with a voice in the political decisions; this makes it more difficult for elites to rig the rules in their own favor and therefore results in more inclusive economic institutions (e.g. concerning property rights and contract enforcement) that encourage innovation and investment. This institution promotes the property right, encourages innovation, protects intellectual property right, and fosters constructive destruction. Thus, there is incentive for all to protect and re-invest in the economy. The incentive distribution model is bell shaped (normal distribution), enabling large population to share the fruits of system.

Extractive political institutions are ones where a tiny elite hold the power and put in place mechanisms to ensure that this continues to be the case e.g. by systematically disenfranchising others in society. Similarly, extractive economic institutions are those which ensure that the lion's share of the country's wealth and annual output is captured by elites, with the rest of the population subsisting on a much more meagre income. The institution has incentive to protect the common people to bare minimum such that institution can continue with golden egg; else if goose laying golden egg is dead, institution will fall too. Since peasants' most of the surplus is extracted for selective consumption by elite, thus there is minimum investment from producer in absence of incentive or protection of right. Thus in long run, the producing class will become weaker and weaker, and so will also impact the institution. The incentive distribution model is peaked bell shaped (leptokurtic distribution), where a small section of people controls the large share of country wealth and power.

Supported political institutes are the ones which think they cannot do anything without the help of foreign or external donations. More people are encouraged to make voices in public space suiting the taste of donor agencies, and also masses are encouraged to participate in funded projects to build statistical figures that form basis for the next cycle of donation. In this institution, donor is physically far from the ground, and also away from ground reality. Thus, many layers get added to the institution, starting from funds donor to the target, and funds get distributed at each layer, making very small pie to trickle down to target. The donation is on the top of the domestic economy, thus the shape of the economy is hour-glass, lower half representing domestic economy and upper half representing donation economy. The incentive distribution model is hour glass shaped, assuming the institutions are inclusive, still their wealth distribution is not even. Because the economy supported by the pure donation base is isolated from the rest of the economy. Since we assume the institution is inclusive, so the domestic economy will take bell shape. However, the pure donation is top down, having many donating agencies competing with each other, and there is no incentive for fruit generation, thus the sole purpose of donated money is consumption. Money trickles down from top to bottom, thus the number of beneficiary will decrease as well as amount of money will decrease too. The donation economy is seasonal having high risk, compared to domestic traditional economy, thus only way people will be attracted to donation economy is by high gain. So, donation economy forms the upper part of the hour glass model. In the long run, donation economy will kill the domestic economy, and there will be less talented people left to support domestic economy, compared to the free money economy of donation world.

Begging institution (i.e. supported institution) has incentive to protect the vicious cycle of poverty and donation, because once donor feels people are well off, the donation flow will stop. At the same time, institution misuses the emotion of western nations, because citizens of many Western nations feel guilt and unease about the economic and humanitarian disasters around the world and foreign aid makes them believe that something is being done to combat the problems. Thus, stopping the foreign aid is impractical and would likely lead to additional human suffering. In the long run, it paralyses the local production, and country would rely on import of even basic things of life. Having long bureaucratic procedures is characteristic of this institution where top to bottom institution will have so many layers of government and many departments. The donor will never get to understand the labyrinth of bureaucracy and the privacy will get protected under the mask of sovereign right. Another characteristic of the supported institutes is they will avoid being linked to one donor or to have over reliance on one donor. And as network of donors compete and rivals each other to be on preference list, the question of fund utilization takes back seat. However point missed by both institute and donor is that they are hospitalizing polio ridden country on bed and running saline water rather than encouraging self-confidence and let country walk a step, one at a time.

Incentive of Beggar Model (Example): In India, there are many organized begging networks, operated illegally. These networks kidnap kids and make them handicapped by making them blind or cutting legs. It serves two purposes, the kid cannot runaway and, second, these handicapped kids make good begging business by garnering more sympathy from the donors. Thus, more income motivates more kidnapping to increase the begging network size.

Exclusive political institutes ignore the relevance of the substantial population. This looks possible when discrimination is practiced by institutions towards the people. Institutions need resources to run, and they are getting support from either (1) one section of population sufficient enough to run the institution or (2) institution has natural resources under institution's full control which is sold in market for funding the salaries and other office expenses or (3) Institutions have Foreign Aid, which acts as substitute to the source that was being extracted before from people.

In case of extractive institutes, they still have some dependency on people and thus obligation to protect. However in case of Exclusive institution, institution wants to deny the share of country wealth and annual produce. These excluded people might feel economically relieved in the short run as their produce goes out of institution's focus since institution found economic substitution. However, in the long run, these people would get deprived of the facilities that elites would be enjoying at the expense of national wealth and annual produce. However, in absence of government promotion, the financial market would be missing that could have expanded the market for common people's produce. Thus, there would be disconnect between the groups; elite and excluded people; and the group or region belonging to excluded people would be lagging behind in development, modernization and growth opportunities.

Example of disconnected groups: Villagers in a remote district in the central valley of Afghanistan heard a radio announcement about a new multimillion-dollar program to restore shelter to their area. After a while, a few wooden beams, carried by the trucking cartel of Ismail Khan, famous former war lord and member of the Afghan government, were delivered. But they were too big to be used for anything in the district, and the villagers put them to the only possible use, firewood. So what had happened to millions of dollars promised to the villagers? Of the promised money, 20 percent of it was taken as UN head office costs in Geneva. The remainder was subcontracted to an NGO, which took another 20 percent for its own head office costs in Brussels, and soon, for another three layers, with each party taking approximately another 20 percent of what was remaining. The little money that reached Afghanistan was used to buy wood from western Iran, and much of it was paid to Ismail Khan's trucking cartel to cover the inflated transport prices. It was a bit of a miracle that those oversized wooden beams even arrived in the village.

Notes

1. Ghimire, Sharad (2014); Flood of 1954: The beginning of a developmental state, New Angle: Nepal Journal of Social Science and Public Policy Vol. 3(1), December 2014
2. Ghimire, Sharad and Robertson, Tom (2015); Disaster geopolitics, The devastating flood of 1954 first exposed Nepal to the geopolitics of natural disasters, Nepali Times, 24-30 July 2015 #768, 2015
3. Ghimire, Sharad (2014); Flood of 1954: The beginning of a developmental state, New Angel, Volume 3, Number 1, December 2014
4. K.C, Ram Bahadur (1983); Land Reform: Progress And Prospects In Nepal, HMG-USAID-GTZ-INROCK PROJECT, STRENGTHENING INSTITUTIONAL CAPACITY IN THE, FOOD AND AGRICULTURAL SECTOR IN NEPAL, pp 5
5. Isaacson et al (2001); Half-a-Century of Development, The History of U.S. Assistance to Nepal, 1951-2001, pp 88
6. Singh, Raj Kumar (2009);Global Dimensions of Indo-Nepal Political Relations: Post Independence, pp 134-137
7. When King Mahendra applied for entry to the UN. in the 1950s he sent them Devanagari as the Nepali script; this was refused by the UN because it had already been submitted by India, so he sent the Newar (i.e. Pracalit) script instead as the

national script. As mentioned in: Language, caste, religion and territory: Newar identity ancient and modern, European Journal of Sociology, Cambridge Univ Press, Publication Date: Jan 1, 1986

8. Acharya, Baburam (2013); The Bloodstained Throne: Struggles for Power in Nepal (1775-1914), Penguin UK, 2015
9. Dr. Gurung, Harka (1970), Economic Implications Of Foreign Aid, technical assistance and development, The Harry S Truman Research Institute, The Hebrew University of Jerusalem, 1971, pp 263
10. K.C, Ram Bahadur (1983); Land Reform: Progress And: Prospects In Nepal, HMG-USAID-GTZ-INROCK PROJECT, Strengthening Institutional Capacity In The, Food And Agricultural Sector In Nepal, pp 5
11. Skerry, Christa A (1991); Four Decades of Development, The History of U.S. Assistance to Nepal, 1951-1991, United States Agency for International Development (USAID) in Kathmandu, Nepal, 1991
12. K.C, Ram Bahadur (1983); Land Reform: Progress And: Prospects In Nepal, HMG-USAID-GTZ-INROCK PROJECT, STRENGTHENING INSTITUTIONAL CAPACITY IN THE, FOOD AND AGRICULTURAL SECTOR IN NEPAL, pp 5
13. Kansakar, Vidya Bir Singh (2001); s Nepal-India Open Border: Prospects, Problems and Challenges, seminars organized by the Institute of Foreign Affairs and FES in Nepalgunj, Birgunj, Biratnagar and Kathmandu. 2001
14. L.A. Kosinski, K.M. Elahi (2012); Population Redistribution and Development in South Asia, Springer Science & Business Media, Dec 6, 2012, pp 114
15. L.A. Kosinski, K.M. Elahi (2012); Population Redistribution and Development in South Asia, Springer Science & Business Media, Dec 6, 2012, pp 114
16. K.C, Ram Bahadur (1983); Land Reform: Progress And: Prospects In Nepal, HMG-USAID-GTZ-INROCK PROJECT, STRENGTHENING INSTITUTIONAL CAPACITY IN THE, FOOD AND AGRICULTURAL SECTOR IN NEPAL, pp 5
17. Sugden, Fraser and Gurung, Ganesh (2012), Absentee landordism and agrarian stagnation in Nepal: A case from the Eastern Tarai, Nepal Institute of Development Studies, Jul 1, 2012, pp 15-16
18. Gaige, Frederick (1975); Regionalism and National Unity in Nepal, Univ.of California Press, 1975, pp 120
19. McLean, Joanne (1999); Conservation and the Impact of Relocation on the Tharus of Chitwan, Nepal, Himalaya, the Journal of the Association for Nepal and Himalayan Studies, Volume 19, Number 2, 1999
20. McLean, Joanne (1999); Conservation and the Impact of Relocation on the Tharus of Chitwan, Nepal, Himalaya, the Journal of the Association for Nepal and Himalayan Studies, Volume 19, Number 2, 1999
21. Singh, Achyut Man (2013), An Integrated Approach for Long Term Solutions of Flooding: A Study of the Eastern Chitwan Valley, HYDRO NEPAL ISSUE NO. 12 JANUARY, 2013
22. Gaige, Frederick (1975); Regionalism and National Unity in Nepal, University of California Press, 1975, pp 172

23. Gaige, Frederick (1975); Regionalism and National Unity in Nepal, University of California Press, 1975, pp 96

24. Gaige, Frederick (1975); Regionalism and National Unity in Nepal, University of California Press, 1975, pp 97

25. Gaige, Frederick (1975); Regionalism and National Unity in Nepal, University of California Press, 1975, pp 97

26. Gaige, Frederick (1975); Regionalism and National Unity in Nepal, University of California Press, 1975, pp 174

27. Pokhrel, Rajan (2015); UN lobbying for amendments to draft constitution, The Himalayan Times, published on July 13, 2015

28. Malla, Sapana Pradhan (2016); Citizenship provisions discriminate against women, The Himalayan Times, Published on September 21, 2015

29. UN (2011); People without citizenship certificates in Central Tarai: the unregistered next generation, United Nations Resident and Humanitarian Coordinator's Office, Issue No: 15; August 2011

30. UN (2011); State of stateless citizens: A case study on citizenship and landlessness issues of the Santhal community, United Nations Resident and Humanitarian Coordinator's Office, Issue No.: 5, May 2011

31. Care Nepal (2016), HOUSING, LAND AND PROPERTY ISSUES IN NEPAL and their consequences for the post-earthquake reconstruction process, CARE Nepal 2016

32. UN (2012); Chepangs' Struggle for Survival: Views from Makwanpur and Chitwan Districts, United Nations Resident and Humanitarian Coordinator's Office, Issue 51, January 2013, p 3

33. UN (2013); 2013: Potential risks to peace and development, Issue 47, September 2012, pp 6-7

34. Nepal Rastra Bank (2016); विप्रेाण प्राप्त गर्ने धरपरिवारको बचत तथा लगानी प्रवत्ति (Saving and Investment trend in immigrant families), Nepal Rastra Bank, published June-July 2016, p 9

35. Hodgson, Brian (1828); Notices of the Languages Literature and Religion of Nepâl and Tibet, Asiatic Researches pp 2

36. Hodgson, Brian Houghton (1833), Origin and Classification of the Military Tribes of Nepal, Journal of the Bengal Asiatic Society, vol ii,1833, p 37

37. Sijapati, Lalitjung (1955); *Nepâla Ki? Gorashâ* (Nepal or Gorkha?), published by Kumari Mitthudevi Sijapati, Banaras, 1955 downloaded from http://eap.bl.uk/database/overview_item.a4d?catId=184765;r=18337 on 26/8/2016

38. Interview of Major (Ret'd) Satya Bahadur Pun, MBE, Gurkha Stories, downloaded from http://gurkhastories.com/portfolio-view/satya-bahadur-pun/ on 26/8/2016 .

39. Pariyar, Govinda (2012); For Empire And Friends: Nepali Gurkhas In Britain, 2012. Downloaded from https://gpariyar.wordpress.com/2013/09/05/gurkha-veteran-my-fight-for-justice/ on 26/8/2016

40. Weinberg, Miranda (2013); Revisiting History in Language Policy: The Case of Medium of Instruction in Nepal, Working Papers in Educational Linguistics 28(1): 61-80, University of Pennsylvania, 2013, pp 68-69
41. Tribhuwan University Anniversary Special - 2015 AD, Published on July 25, 2915 by TU, Kathmandu
42. Weinberg, Miranda (2013); Revisiting History in Language Policy: The Case of Medium of Instruction in Nepal, Working Papers in Educational Linguistics 28(1): 61-80, University of Pennsylvania, 2013, pp 68-69
43. Nepal National Educational Planning Commission, 1956, p. 53
44. Pattanaik, Smruti Smita (2015); Migration and ethnic politics in South Asia with reference to Nepal and Bhutan, PhD Thesis, Jawaharlal Nehru University, Delhi, India, 2015, pp 98
45. Gaige, Frederick (1975); Regionalism and National Unity in Nepal, University of California Press, 1975, pp 114
46. Mahendra Narayan Nidhi headed the "Hindi Rakchha Samiti" (English tranlation "Save Hindi") formed to oppose government's move to ban Hindi text books before 2015 elections. He was also instrumental in formation of "Purvanchal samiti" within Nepali Congress, which was virtually a "Madhesi Caucus" within Nepali Congress.
47. Gaige, Frederick (1975); Regionalism and National Unity in Nepal, University of California Press, 1975, p 111
48. Gaige, Frederick (1975); Regionalism and National Unity in Nepal, University of California Press, 1975, pp 112
49. Gaige, Frederick (1975); Regionalism and National Unity in Nepal, University of California Press, 1975, pp 113
50. Pattanaik, Smruti Smita (2015); Migration and ethnic politics in South Asia with reference to Nepal and Bhutan, PhD Thesis, Jawaharlal Nehru University, Delhi, India, 2015, pp 98
51. Dr. Dahal, Ram Kumar (2000); Language Politics in Nepal, Professor, CEDA, TU, February 2000
52. Based on conversation with Rakesh Mishra from Pipra Mahottari.
53. Based on personal interview with Dr. Ram Mohan Mahato, who was private English tutor for King Mahendra's Kids, and Dr. Hari Bansh Jha, who was in touch with King Birendra.
54. Read about Gopal Thakur in Chapter two. His writing apperead in Esamata online Magazine, Ab Malai Nepali na bhana (Now Don't Tell me Nepali), June 2015
55. Gaige, Frederick (1975); Regionalism and National Unity in Nepal, University of California Press, 1975, pp 178
56. Gaige, Frederick (1975); Regionalism and National Unity in Nepal, University of California Press, 1975, pp 178
57. Gaige, Frederick (1975); Regionalism and National Unity in Nepal, University of California Press, 1975, pp 178-79

58. Gaige, Frederick (1975); Regionalism and National Unity in Nepal, University of California Press, 1975, pp 179

59. Gaige, Frederick (1975); Regionalism and National Unity in Nepal, University of California Press, 1975, pp 181

60. Guthi Santhan Ain (1976), http://www.guthisansthan.org.np/images/pdf/guthi-sansthan-ain.pdf

61. Burghart, Richard (1978), History of Janakpurdham, PhD Thesis, 1978, pp 493

62. Burghart, Richard (1978), History of Janakpurdham, PhD Thesis, 1978, pp 507

63. Burghart, Richard (1978), History of Janakpurdham, PhD Thesis, 1978, pp 502

64. Burghart, Richard (1978), History of Janakpurdham, PhD Thesis, 1978, pp 502

65. Burghart, Richard (1978), History of Janakpurdham, PhD Thesis, 1978, pp 502

66. Amatya, Meera Rajbhandari (2015); Facing extinction, The Kathmandu Post, Published on 2015-12-15. Also see Guthi Introduction booklet, Guthi Office. Downloaded on Dec 2016 from http://www.guthisansthan.org.np/images/pdf/guthi-introduction.pdf

67. Guthi Introduction booklet, Guthi Office. Downloaded on Dec 2016 from http://www.guthisansthan.org.np/images/pdf/guthi-introduction.pdf

68. Amatya, Meera Rajbhandari (2015); Facing extinction, The Kathmandu Post, Published on 2015-12-15.

69. Burghart, Richard (1978), History of Janakpurdham, PhD Thesis, 1978, pp 502

70. Burghart, Richard (1978), History of Janakpurdham, PhD Thesis, 1978, pp 502

71. Burghart, Richard (1978), History of Janakpurdham, PhD Thesis, 1978, pp 303-304

72. Shrestha, Rekha (2006); Pashupati Guthi lands in PAC bad books, The Himalayan Times, Published: November 22, 2006

73. Burghart, Richard (1978), History of Janakpurdham, PhD Thesis, 1978, pp 507

74. Shrestha, Rekha (2006); Pashupati Guthi lands in PAC bad books, The Himalayan Times, Published: November 22, 2006

75. Janakpurdham's land as Prasad, जनकपुरधामको प्रसाद 'कट्ठा र धुर ', Haal Chal, published on June 4, 2016, http://www.haalchal.com/madhesh-news/land-mafia-of-janakpur-selling-and-buying-janki-mandir-land-and-guthi-land/

76. Oldham, C.H.G (1964), Nepal and Foreign Aid, Institute of World Current Afair, 1964, pp 2

77. Isaacson et al (2001); Half-a-Century of Development, The History of U.S. Assistance to Nepal, 1951-2001, pp 147

78. Shrestha, Bijaya Lal (1990), East to West, A Highway to the Future, Tarai: Backwater or New Frontier, Himal, Alternative Bi-Monthly Magazine Vol. 3, Sep/Oct, 1990

79. Deaton, Angus (2013); The Great Escape: Health, Wealth, and the Origins of Inequality, Princeton University Press, Sep 22, 2013, pp 295

80. HRW (2010); Indifference to Duty, Impunity for Crimes Committed in Nepal, Human Right Watch Reasearch Report, December 14, 2010

81. South Korea agrees to hire Nepali workers, Governments to sign an MoU by month end, The Himalayan Times, published on 13 March 2007, http://thehimalayantimes.com/business/south-korea-agrees-to-hire-nepali-workers-governments-to-sign-an-mou-by-month-end/

82. Chalise, Kuvera (2016); Nepal third most corrupt country in S Asia, 15th globally, Myrepublica, Published on 28 Jan 2016, http://admin.myrepublica.com/politics/story/35955/nepal-third-most-corrupt-country-in-s-asia-15th-globally.html#sthash.agAAIMXS.dpuf . There is also increasing awareness in Aid provider amout the corruption in Nepal. Taking note, a parliamentary committee of UK government said, Britain should cut its 86 million pound ($128 million) aid budget for Nepal unless the country acts to combat poor governance and "endemic" corruption. See Reuters News, Fri Mar 27, 2015, UK should cut aid to Nepal if "endemic" corruption persists: report

83. The NHRI Nepal Joint Submission for The Second Universal Periodic Review of Nepal, National Human Rights Commission, National Women Commission, National Dalit Commission, Submitted March 22, 2015, PP 12

84. The Nepalese Army, Directorate of Public Relations, Nepalese Army Headquarters, 2010, pp 71

85. The Nepalese Army, Directorate of Public Relations, Nepalese Army Headquarters, 2010, pp 71

86. The Nepalese Army, Directorate of Public Relations, Nepalese Army Headquarters, 2010, pp 71

87. Wright, Daniel (1990). History of Nepal. New Delhi: Asian Educational Services. Retrieved 16 October 2012. Pages 201-202

88. Dr. Thakur, Prem Chandra (2012); Mithila State, The International Journal's, Research Journal of Social Science and Management, Volume 01, Number 10, 2012

89. Balchanda Sharma (1969); History of Kathmandu Valley (काठमाडौं उपत्यकाको एक राजवंशावली), Ancient Nepal, Number 6, 1969, pp 13

90. Gnyawali, Surya Bikram (1974); Prithvi Narayan Shah's Conquest Of Nepal, Regmi Research Series, Year 6, No 1, 1974, pp 9

91. Sharma, Balchanda (1969); History of Kathmandu Valley (काठमाडौं उपत्यकाको एक राजवंशावली), Ancient Nepal, Number 6, 1969, pp 15 . Also see Dibyopadesh of King Prithivi Narayan Shah

92. Krauskopff, Gisele and Meyer, Pamela D (1998), The Kings of Nepal and The Tharu of the Terai, Panjiar Collection, 1998 pp 158-159

93. Omissi, David (2016); The Sepoy and the Raj: The Indian Army, 1860-1940, Springer, Jul 27, 2016, pp 4

94. Gurkhas lose equal pay appeal, BBC, Thursday, 9 October, 2003 downloaded on Sep 7th from http://news.bbc.co.uk/2/hi/uk_news/3177152.stm

95. The Nepalese Army, Directorate of Public Relations, Nepalese Army Headquarters, 2010, pp 71

96. Aid and Education: A Sector Report on Lessons Learned, US AID, 1984, pp - 14

97. US AID to Education in Nepal: A 20 year Beginning, US AID, May 1981, PP 4

98. Report Of The National Education Commission, National Education Commission, Keshar Mahal, Kathmandu, Nepal 1992, pp 52

99. The Basic and Primary Education, Master Plan for 1997 – 2002, His Majesty's Government Ministry of Education The Master Plan Team, Kathmandu, 15 May 1997, pp 273

100. Development Cooperation Report, Fiscal Year 2012-2013, Government of Nepal Ministry of Finance International Economic Cooperation Coordination Division (IECCD), Singhadurbar, Kathmandu, March 2014, pp 11

101. Development Cooperation Report, Fiscal Year 2012-2013, Government of Nepal, Ministry of Finance, International Economic Cooperation Coordination Division (IECCD), Singhadurbar, Kathmandu, March 2014, pp VII point 8

102. Staff composition and Diversity Management among the AIN member, Baseline Study, Association of International NGOs in Nepal, June 2011, pp 18

103. Angus Deaton on Foreign Aid and Inequality, C. Peter McColough Series on International Economics with Angus Deaton, February 18, 2016 downloaded on Sep 30 from http://www.cfr.org/economics/angus-deaton-foreign-aid-inequality/p37546

104. Acemoglu, Daron and Robinson, James A. (2013); Why Nations Fail: The Origins of Power, Prosperity, and Poverty, Crown Publishers, 2013

8

People Opposition

Pre 1950 - Dark Age

Golden age was flourishing in the region during mid of eighteenth century, both in terms of social harmony and economy. Gangadhar Jha was minister[1]of King Jay Prakash Malla of Kathmandu within Nepal valley, whose currency was official denomination in Tibet and currency of exchange for trades between India and Tibet. Long before that, Maithil scholars, Raghunath Jha and Ramanatha Jha, had worked with King Jayasthith Malla in 14th century to reform Nepal valley's civil laws regarding house, land, castes and dead bodies[2].

Arrival of Prithivi Narayan Shah, or Barbarian age, not only spread terror in the region by cutting nose, killing kids in womb, or punishing Sen Kings supporters but also witnessed collapse of regional economy, which was initiated by five years of blockade of Kathmandu valley[3]. The economic influence diminished after Tibetan rejected contaminated currency circulation in Tibet. Downhill in the plain, the economic order underwent volcanic change, which was primarily based on land and agriculture.

In the late eighteenth century, land was excess, compared to the population, thus there was no value to the land as such. However there was still challenge for common people to manage living because land virtually belonged to the state, rather than common people. Thus, any economic activity on the land has to get permission from state actors, and the cost of getting permission was the tax/rent people paid for using the land. When the asked rent/tax exceeded the economic output of the land, common people were directly impacted. Big farmer, who could afford, took the grievances to rulers, however most people, silently used to leave one state and move to other state[4]. This phenomenon was not hypothetical but real, and has been mentioned in Gurkha's Administrative Regulation of 1793: "Our Tarai region is desolate since large areas are given on Ijira to one person, as there was no Jamindars. If tenants want to lodge complaints in Kathmandu, they will have to spend 10 or 20 rupees as travel expense. Those who get lands give 2 or 4 rupees more to the revenue collector to keep him happy. Those who do not get (lands) become homeless and migrate abroad". Records are found that mention people and village leaders crossing the border when the economic burden on people increased during eighteenth century[5] and early nineteenth century[6]. A royal letter to officers of Mahottari(1810 AD) asserts "Persuade all Chaudharis, Mokadams, and ryots[tenant farmers] who have left the districts to come back and reoccupy their lands, and pay your taxes through the Subba"[7]. Another royal order dating back to 1780 AD states "Chaudharis, Kangoyes, Mokaddams, and ryots who have fled to the Moglan (i.e India) shall be persuaded to come back. Partial remission may be made in arrears of revenue due from them"[8]. Records also show local residents of Rautahat disobeyed Gorkhali ruler, "We have now received reports that you do not obey the orders of the jagirdar, but do what you like. If you want to stay on in that mouja, pay land tax at the rate of Rs 12½ per bigha"[9].

Some people, who could afford, grouped togetherto register protestagainst the rulers. In Bhadra 1847 BS (1790 AD), a delegation from Morang district, led by Chaudhari Dayaram, visited Kathmandu with the complaint. In 1794 AD, delegation of ryotsof Morang district went to King Ran Bahadurwith thecomplaint of imposedcompulsory Ijarastax for each village in Morang district despite 3 years loss by people. In Jestha, 1866 (May 1809) many ryotswent to Kathmandu from Saptari and Mahottari with complaints of over-taxation and oppression[10].In the same year, another delegation led by JethraiyatRaghkunath Rai and others of Mahottari district submitted a similar complaint on KartikSudi 10, 1866 (November 1809)[11].

During 1814-1816 War, after British victory, there was British EIC rule in Madhesh for about 2 years. It is no surprise, that Madhesi People,oppressed under Gurkha rules, welcomed and supported the British system in Terai[12]. British gave the Madhesh to Gurkha with the agreement that native Madhesi people will not be tortured.

The extraction continued. In October 1844, three decades after Sugaolee Treaty, three hundred Tharus visited Kathmandu to complain of the oppression by tax collector Hiralal who held the revenue contract for the region[13]. A year later in 1845, Sarlahi and Mahottari residents submitted complaints to KingRajendraagainst tax contractor that they were imposed fines and penalties in an arbitrary manner. Many people had already fled to India. In January 1846 King appealed to people who had fled to India because of tax harassment, "You are there directed to come back and reoccupy your lands and homesteads. We shall not permit any harassment or oppression in the future"[14]. In September 1846 Jung Bahadur established himself as Prime Minister after Kot Massacre. During Jang Bahadur Rana's time (A.D. 1864), the ryots of the seven districts of the eastern Tarai region went Kathmandu with complaints that the new tax rates were unduly high. In the year 1934 after great earthquake, 103 ryots of Kanchanbari submitted a petition to Prime Minister Judha Shamsher to reduce land-tax-assessment rates until the prices of agricultural commodities revived.

1950 to 1960 - Beam of Light

The scenario of the 1950 was ugly for the plain people. Almost 90% of the land was monopolized by large and absent landholders—mostly hilly people from Kathmandu. More than 50% of these were gifts to individuals. Some of the birta (gift) landlords owned over 10,000 acres—one of them owned about a million - all tax free. Only 10% of the Terai lands were smallholdings, varying from 10 to 15 acres each, held either by migrants from the hills or from plain[15]. However, most of the population was landless farmer, working as labor for their landlords or renting lands from absentee landlords or middlemen.

Yet, even given those disparity between holdings in 1950s, the high percentage of untaxed lands, and the low taxes which varied from Re 1 per acre to Rs 6, revenue from the land formed the major share of the Terai's contribution to the Central Exchequer of Nepal. Earnings from agricultural revenue alone were estimated at Rs 107 lakhs annually, slightly less than half the annual budget[16].

In the background of above mentioned discrepancies, different agrarian movementssprouted in the plain. Leaders of many of those agrarian movements were of limited reach and remains unknown today. Few of the agrarian movements were led and organized by political parties. These movements were in addition to, and separate from, the political movement against Rana that led to the fall of Rana regime in February 1951.It is a different topic all together that even BP Koirala led movement, to dethrone Rana, was mainly fought from plain towns[17]: Birgunj (November 12& 20),

Bhairahawa(November 15 & 20), Gaur (November 19), Rangeli (November 16), December (December 11-20), Jhapa (December 14), Lauki (January 3), Bandipur (January 14) and etc.

Below are the summaries of different agrarian movements between 1950 and 1960

1952 - Tamsuk Fatta Movement (Rautahut)

TamsukFatta Andolan (English transalation 'Destroying of Bondage Papers) in Rautahat was movement of poor and landless peasants. They attacked feudals landlords and merchants, who charged high interest on loans, and destroyed the loan contract papers. They also attached district offices to destroy land records called BhogBandagi (land mortgage papers). Police crushed the movement resulting in arrest and suppression[18].

1952-1953- 'Re Nahi, Ji Kaho' Movement (Rautahut and Bara)

*Re Nahi, Ji Kaho*Andolan (English Translation 'Say Hello with respect, not Hey you') started in Rautahat and Bara district and played an important role in the history of peasant movements in Nepal. In its protest against the use of humiliating language and bullying by landlords over small farmers and landless

Peasants, this movement not only struggled for land rights but also for social dignity, prestigeand self-pride[19]. In a movement in Birgunj, procession with slogans in Birgunj, 5 were killed and 125 were injured[20]. In 1953's Peasants' movement of Rautahat, AsarfiSaha was murdered[21].

1952 - Western Terai Agrarian Agitation

In the western Terai Region agitation started in May 1952, ledby Dr. K.I Singh supporters, who wereinfluenced by Chinese Communists. These people were later joined, during June 1952, by the communist sponsored All Nepal Peasant conference (association), which has been mainly responsible for the present large-scale unrest in lowland[22]. In Bardia during movement of peasants, tillers and cattle herders, 9 were killed and 27 injured by police[23].

1953 - All Nepal Peasant Association Rally (Bara)

Main demands were to 'let the land of big landlords and big Birta owners be confiscated and distributed to small farmers and landless people and middle class peasants' and to stop the socio-economic exploitation of small farmers and landless people by feudal landlords. The feudal landlords kept hatching conspiracies to suppress the struggle. A huge gathering of protesters counter-attacked, when a troop of armed police, led by the regional administrator, arrived on 22 January 1955 to arrest peasant leaders Madhu Singh, Comrade Ran Vriksya Chaudhari, Nanda Kishwar Chaudhari, Mohan Singh Mahato, NandanAryal, Dev Narayan Kalwar, Ram Lal Tharu, Rama Kanta and Nathuni. During this struggle, police fire killed 19-year-old peasant Mukha Lal Mahato, tortured several others and the movement was suppressed immediately.

1953 - No rent Campaign (Biratnagar-Saptari-Janakpur-Birgunj)

The Nepal Congress Party (NCP) launched a no-rent campaign in Biratnagar on 15 may 1953, when BP Koirala, the leader of NCP, addressed a public gathering of about 35,000 people asking them to defy the government's lockout order (regarding Biratnagar Jute Mill). During the first week of June the peasants' agitation spread to the Saptari-Mahottari area. Ram Narayan Mishra along with Saroj Koirala toured the area organizing peasants meetingasking them not to pay their land rents[24].

1953 to 1955 Khamar Roko Andolan (Jhapa)

The andolan was started in Jhapa, and moved to other Terai regions too[25].KhamarRoko (English translation 'Stop proprietor's private property) seems to have been influenced by communists in Bangal. Khamar in Bangali means '*nij-jote*' land, which is equivalent to '*Jirayat*' land[26].

1956 to 1958 – Peasant Movement (Siraha, Saptari)

In Peasants' movement of Saptari saw the murder of Aghori Yadav in 1958. Similarly, 1955/56 Peasants' movement of Siraha saw the murder of Bahadur Saha[27].

1959 to 1960 – Land Right Struggle (Dang - BeluwaBanjari Peasant Movement)

In December 1959, a movement against landlords began in Dang District with the participation of the Tharus, the indigenous people in the locality. The movement took a new height in 1960. In an effort to contain the movement, the then Nepali Congress government murdered peasant Gumraha

Chaudhary. Women had an important role in this movement in which Lahani Chaudhary and Somati Chaudhary had a leading role. Police arrested Ratna, Kalu and Lahani and released them after a weeklong torture.

"When the landlords came to loot mustard in 1959, all of us except old and children, went out to defend the land-lord atrocity with sticks in our hand. Lahani suffered injuries on her back. But we were not hopeless, we did not leave the ground for the landlords. Rather, we could chase away their servants. They came again, next morning, we chased them again"[28], says Somati Chaudhary. Commenting on the movement, she adds, "They came back to fight again in 1960. The fight continued throughout the month of June/July. Police assisted the landlords, they haunted regularly to look for our people. One day, Ratna and Kalu were arrested. Gumraha was murdered. We had to struggle hard to save the village people from the Jamindars and police."[29]

The struggle was against the landlords who were evicting the farmers from their land. During struggle, Gumraha Tharu, a local peasant, lost his life in the movement- which further aggravated the struggle. The movement had genesis from Nepal Congress Party's 1959 election slogan saying "*JaggaKasko? Jotneko. GharKasko? Potneko*" which meant Land belongs to the tillers and Home belongs to the tenants. Asa backslash, the conflict between farmer and landlord escalated[30].

The declaration of election of 1959 had interesting episode. King Mahendra was interested in escaping the constitutional election, promised by his father. At the same time, Pro-Hindi movement was at its peak, which was initiated in protest of 1955's Nepal Education Planning Commission Report that advocated education in Nepali language only. The movement, which had support of many parties including Nepali Congress and Communist Party, was led by Vedananda Jha, the leader of Terai Congress. When language issue increased the heat on the street, King issued Royal Proclamation in December 15 1957 announcing the election date to February 1959 to divert the attention of people from the language issue. Pro Hindi supporter felt that the constitution drawn up by a constitutional assembly would give them more power than the one drawn by King Mahendra and his advisors. This agreement wasmore for election than continuing institutionalization of the Pro Hindi language demand[31]. Later in February 1958, the King issued another directive saying the election would be for Parliament seat rather than Constitutional assembly. Pro Hindi supporter was doubtful of the revised election objective, however other reluctantly accepted the proposed election.

Terai Congresswas founded originally in 1951 under the name Terai Newasi Sangh (Association of Terai People) by Kulanand Jha, Ram Janam Tiwari and Shyam Lal Mishra after they failed to get assurance from Nepal Congress leadership of provincial model in future government setup.In 1954, Terai Congress party command went to Vedananda Jha, a journalist, after his elder brother Kulanand Jha became ill due to old age[32].In 1953, the party claimed having membership of 60,000 and accordingly demanded adequate representation of the Terai in the proposed Advisory Assembly.

The Principal objectives of the Terai Congress, which was leading the Pro-Hindi movement, were following[33]

- establishment of an autonomous Terai state
- adequate employment of the Terai people in the Nepal civil service
- recognition of Hindi as a state language

The political exclusion of plain people in 1950s from the state organ can be assessed from the writing ofMaharajakrishnaRasgotra, an Indian diplomat and former Indian Foreign Secretary and a recipient of Padma Bhushan award, "I criss-crossed virtually Terai virtually the entire Terai three times in 1954 and 1955. The East-West highway and some roads were built years later, more of less along the dense jungle tracks I had walked on in those two years. The Terai were governed then, as it is now, by the ruling elite of Kathmandu as a colony. Throughout my travels I never met a Teraian high administrative or police officer or even a petty official - they all came from Kathmandu"[34]. MaharajakrishnaRasgotra,was in Terai on mission, on behalf of Government, to stop epidemic of Malaria, Cholora, and other diseasesappeared after the worst flood of June-July 1954. Later he served in Kathmandu Indian embassy and also became good friend with King Mahendra.

At the end of the decade, there were few lights emerging from the awakening of the plains people. The period saw highest growth of education and educational institute (see chapter 7 for detail data) achieved till date. Visa restriction to the plain people to enter Kathmandu valley or hill were removed in 1958. The opening of Tribhuwan Highway road to Kathmandu from Amlekhgunj, in support of Indian government, educated saw entry of plains people into Kathmandu valley for jobs. The Pro Hindi movement forced the Government to back-off on its earlier directive. The January directive dropped the citizenship requirement for teachers, which was lifeline to keep running the school in Terai. The new directive also postponed the immediate enforcement of Nepali in primary school. This period also saw Madhesis fraternality, from across the border, finding space in Kathmandu elite circle. The most prominent personalities were Dr. Jogendra Jha[35] from Darbhanga and Professor Dr. Ram Mohan Mahato[36] from Madhubani, both remained the trusted man of King Mahendratill end.Bhadrakali Mishra was appointed minister (Communications, Public Works, Transport, and Law and Parliamentary Affairs) in 1950s, and Vedanand Jha also got appointed as Minister (Home, Development, Industry, Commerce) beginning 1961 and later became Ambassdor to India in 1977, though he was not believed to be closer to Royal Palace[37].

1960 to 1979 - Confusion Era

This period saw change in the form ofagitation in plains, which was directed towards the central state'snewly introduced policies, compared to the fully agrarian movement directed towards the local landlords. The clear political support was missing during panchayat regime, unlike the last decade where there were political banners on the street. This time, state was trying to impose its new rules on people and plain peoples were reacting with protest.

Brief descriptions of movements in this periods:

1966–Ukhada Tenants Uprising (Nawalparasi)

In the shadow of land reform program there was rush of land title transfers in collision with officials. In many cases, tenants were being replaced by owner-cultivators, and in some cases Ukhada[38]tenants were replaced by daily paid laborers. This trend was common in mid-western plain districts. The collision of landlord with government officials was threating many tenants, thus leading to the violence in Nawalparasi District in September 1996. A crowd estimated at around 4,000 encircled the district office administrative center in Parasi. Government reacted with the gun, killing 9 persons (by official figure) and injuring 12 other people[39]. The official investigation was never carried out. Kathmandu based media, as always, linked this with India. Gorkhapatra, government paper, reported "certain elements had misguided the peasants on the issue of land reform, and they should not be left unpunished"[40].

1969 – Agitation Against Imposition of Compulsory Saving Scheme (Kapilbastu, Rupendehi)

According to the blueprint of the compulsory-saving scheme initiated in 1965, every farmer was required to deposit a small percentage of his crops with the government each year. Most farmers viewed this as another form of taxation, despite the government promise to return their deposit with interest at the end of five years[41]. Many small farmers obliged.However, many landlords having power to resist avoided making deposits. It was natural for people to suspect the government intention, who had lowest credibility left from the past and the government officials were suspected of corruption. During 1967 and 1968, the Nepalese press reported frequently that officials were not keeping adequate records of saving collected, and influential people were mis-appropriating the farmers' savings. Savings were collected by intimidation from villagers living at a subsistence or near subsistence level[42]. The resistance to payment was growing and finally in April 1969 protest against the compulsory saving turned to violence.

The protest started in Taulihawa, capital of Kapilbastu district, where a crowd of village women surrounded and attacked officials attempting to collect compulsory savings. Violence quickly spread across Kapilbastu district and into Rupandehi district. Compulsory-saving deposits were looted and burnt. Looting and police firing occurred in a thirty villages over a three-week period, in which at least 33 persons died, hundreds were injured and many other arrested[43]. The violence forced the government to suspend the collection of saving throughout the country[44].

1978 - Bhakariphor Andolan (Janakpur Zone)

At the beginning of 1978, poor peasant and landless people started themovement popularly known as Bhakariphor Andolan (Break theGranary Movement) and confiscated the granary of Justice Prakash Man in Dhanusha. However, these uprisings were shortlived and were immediately suppressed by brutal military operations[45].

The rise of Mahendra was filled with both excitement and disappointment. On one hand, though controversial, he pushed for land reform that was core of plains issue. On other hand, King was disenfranchising plains people from civil rights through introduction of unfavorable Citizenship acts. King was reluctant in power sharing with plains people, and had made skewed constitution arrangement of electing, at the same time seeing Madhesi Minister, though hand-picked symbolic, was definitely a big leap compared to Rana regime. Roads were being built in the lowland plains, prominent of which was east-west highway. However, people were naïve to understand then, the adverse impact of ecological destruction and political consequences. Postal High-way (Hulaki Rajmarg) would have benefited plain people most. Plain people were also not able to understand the rapid change that was being brought through the Hilly migrants were detrimental to the native people. People were able to vote, however the weight of each vote in plains was penny. For example, Manang with a population of 10,000 was sending one representative to National Panchayat, whereas Dhanusha with a population of 330,600 and Saptari with a population of 312,500 sent two representatives each[46]. King Mahendra started direct rule in 1960 and died in 1972, and in these twelve years, things were changing too fast for common people, to be able to understand, due to the lack of freedom of media. After King Birendra came to power, he had benefit of doubt for initial few years. In this period, plain people were in confusion questioning, whether state belongs to them or not?

1979 to 1999–Reaction Era

It was almost close to two decades since King started direct rule. Both internal and external people had understoodby then, what the Panchayati system can do and cannot do? The discrimination of state against Southern Plains people was out and open, leaving little confusion in the mind of Madhesi people. For example, Rice sale and export was banned by individual rather monopolized through Government's Rice Corporation. This was having direct impact on the Southern plains people, which had only agriculture produce to meet their economy. Additionally there was different rules in Hill and different in plains, similar to rules observed during Rana regime. For political reasons, poor man's favorite parboiled rice was sold [by Government Rice Corporation] at a cheaper price in Kathmandu Valley (Rs 0.85 per mana) than in the Terai (RS. 1.15 per mana) where it is produced. In the year 1975, numbers of people walked to Kathmandu from areas outside the valley to take advantage of the lower prices[47].

Communistswere active within Panchayati system, under the same banner of 'Nationalism', like a hidden disease inside Panchayat system, slowly expanding and waiting for right time to come out. The growth of communismwas ringing alarm in the US establishment, at the time when cold war was at the peak. In a bilateral meeting King agreed with US diplomat that "communists appear to have made substantial gains in Nepal during 19 years of partyless panchayat system"[48], and thus wantedto check the communist expansion through "political liberalization"[49]. The US and King became more impatient and announced National Referendum after strong student protest followed by unprecedented southern plain agitation.

1979 - Student Protest followed by Widespread Madhesi Protest

On April 6 a group of students demonstrated in the capital Kathmandu, protesting against the execution of Zulfikar Ali Bhutto, former Prime Minister of Pakistan. As the manifestation came nearer the Pakistani embassy, the student procession was stopped by police at Lainchour. In the following days, there were wide spreadstudent agitation in Terai colleges. Although the agitation began with students it quickly took a different turn. As per a secret US intelligence report, "the differences were recognized by the authorities in their manner of dealing with the two situations. In effect, Kathmandu was recognized and treated as the political key to the country and the demonstrators here were ultimately accepted as valid interlocutors, Nepalistyle, while the Terai was dealt with as a rebellious stepchild"[50].

Protest in the Kathmandu area differed significantly from the Terai in both form and causes. Kathmandu's demonstrators were chiefly students, and the police, after their early blunders, avoided the use of force or other provocations and stayed away or stood tamely by. The demonstrators had their processions, made their speeches, and dispersed. Their demands had been precisely formulated, and the purpose of their demonstrations was to call upon the authorities to fulfill these demands. Their actions were coordinated, up to a point, by a committee including representatives from the various political student groups involved (principally "democratic," i.e. Pro-nepal congress party, "pro-soviet" communist and "pro-Chinese" communist). Student agitation was centered on educational grievances, asking for more freedom to operate Independent student union rather than student union favored by Panchayat system.

In theTerai, on the other hand, it appears that students, after providing the spark, were quickly overshadowed by people having economic grievances, especially factory workers and farmers opposed to higher land taxes. Others included group protesting discrimination in state organs. The major contribution was exploitative, repressive and corrupt administration. In Janakpur, which was the main storm center in the Terai, all of these elements appeared, where both the chief district officer (CDO) and the zonal commissioner (*Anchaladhis*) were suspended.

In the second week of May, situation in Kathmandu was calm, however Janakpur was burning. There were major clashes in and around Janakpur which left five dead according to government reports. A Home-Ministry report released on May 19 indicated serious disturbances in the East-Central Terai—specifically in Dhanusha district where Janakpur is located, Siraha district and places west of Janakpur. The ministry report noted four separate incidents between May 17-19, in which one policeman and four demonstrators were reported to have been killed and a number of others injured. The report spoke of a series of mob attacks on customs posts and government godowns, including burning of buildings, as well as attacks directed against government officials and aimed at disrupting traffic on the East-West highway. On May 20, news from Janakpurreported removal, from a government office and the subsequent destruction of portraits of the King and Queen and even burning of their effigies. Agitators also set on fire railway terminus to put Nepal's only railroad out of operation.

The independent daily, Motherland, carried a home ministry report that, six persons were killed when police fired on May 20 in Sarlahi district, between Janakpur and Birgunj[51].Government claimed Janakpur was silent on May 21, however, the neighboring district Mahottari was on boil, police again fired on a crowd, with one resultant death and another wounded. Another shooting incident took place in the western Terai in Nawalparasi district. In Nawalparasi district in Lumbini zone, the car of assistant Minister of Education was stoned and the CDO (chief district officer) was attacked. Security forces fired on the crowd and four were reported injured[52].

Across the southern plain, burning, thrashing, destruction of bridges, barricading of Roads took place. In dealing with situation, the authorities treated it primarily as a law enforcement problem, as distinct from the political approach taken in Kathmandu. Although some egregiously offensive local officials were removed, and arrested students were released as in

Kathmandu, firm suppression of people was applied at a relatively early stage, with the army sent down to control the border and to suppress the agitation. Police were given shoot at sight order to suppress the agitation.

The US intelligence report concluded saying "Unless the government pays attention, this distinction will merely feed the Terai's long-standing resentment of its palpably second-class citizen status"[53].

1983 – Birth of Sadbhavana Parishad

As discussion for election for referendum was going on, King Birendra was preparing blueprint of restricting people of plains from the political participation. In a meetingof one of theUS diplomat with King Birendra on 17August1979 in Kathmandu, the top two issues wereprioritized by King before election: (i) preparation of voters' lists and (ii) resolving Nationality problems in the Terai.

In 1979's discussion, MEA Joint Secretary (East Asia/Nepal) C.V. Ranganathan had expressed similar opinion. Ranganathan expressed some apprehension that if large numbers were excluded from voting there, on grounds that they were not Nepalese, there could be serious repercussions in Bihar political circles. He suggested that this could develop into a problem in Indo-Nepalese relations. Here it should be noted that being non-Nepali doesn't mean being Indian. There are native plain dwellers who has been living in plain even before hill dweller occupied the plains, and many of these people are without legal citizenship paper introduced since 1960's. The last resort to get safety for plain dwellers in Nepal is to cross border when pressure increase due to ethnic conflicts.

In the referendum that followed, King was winner amid the allegation of rigging, however the point got noted in Palace that the opposition party led by BP Koirala had huge support in Terai. In fact, BP Koirala was unpopular choice among Kathmandu elite even in 1950s due to his huge following in Terai. Palace, making note of the BP Koirala support, appointed a Task Force "National Commission on Population" under Harka Gurung. The report was published in 1983 August, which suggested strict ban on Indo-Nepal people movement. Report mentioned plain people responsible for numerous ills affecting the country. The report suggested that Madhesi people had major allegiances to India, and therefore should only marry within Nepal. Report also suggested "work permits" to the people of plains, and a ban on Hindi films, songs, and magazines[54]. India was obviously concerned with the idea and saw them as no issue for Nepal. In a private discussion in 1974, Indian Ambassador Rasgotra claimed that "100,000 Nepalis each year migrated permanently to India. Under the circumstances he thought the Nepalese press was completely unreasonable in criticizing the very limited migration (perhaps 5,000 to 6,000 in the year 1974) which might have taken place into the Terai"[55]. American scholar Dr. Myron Weiner had similarly mentioned in 1971 that India has helped Nepal by acting as "safety valve" for surplus Nepalese Hill population by providing employment in India[56].

Gajendra Narayan Singh, then Nepali Congress member wanted strong reaction from Congress on Harka Gurung report, in addition to the 1950's issue of language. Singh went to Kolkata, where Congress leaders were meeting after the defeat in the referendum election. Singh'sdemand was rejected, and he resigned from Congress to form Sadbhavana Parisad ("Goodwill Council") in 1985, along with Ram Janam Tiwari and Shyam Lal Mishra[57]. Gajendra Narayan Singh and team publicly opposed the Harka Gurung's report. Singh was arrested on this. Mr Singh's political activism led him to spend seven years in prison.This council became Sadbhavana Party after 1990 revolution and reestablishment of democracy. Since then the Party has sent many seats in parliament and has also seen multiple splits.

1983 - The Situation Assessment of Terai by CIA

The panchayat system remains inherently unrepresentative. Reputable scholars have noted that, under the Constitution, participation in the National Panchayat is weighted heavily in favor of the sparsely populated hill and mountain districts—the traditional backbone of support for the monarchy and the panchayat system—and against the teeming Terai belt adjacent to northern India. This disparity grew out of a conscious palace effort in the 1960s to disenfranchise the Terai region, Which knowledgeable observers consider a breeding ground for Indian-financed political discontent and occasional underground activity aimed at the monarchy. Failure to integrate the Terai into the national main-stream could seriously jeopardize Nepal's political and economic future, yet Governing elements in Kathmandu are not interested in righting the balance. The region comprises 17 percent of Nepal's land and about 40 percent of its population, yet it contributes wellover half of the country's GDP and its domestically generated government revenue. We believe widespread political unrest in the Terai could prove ruinous for Nepal's fragile economy. Some scholars conclude that, socially and politically, the plains people of the Terai feel alienated from the hill-dominated government in Kathmandu and closer to India. Tensions in the region are being further aggravated by overcrowding, which stems from a continuing influx of hill peoples from the north and Indians from the south seeking economic opportunity. According to Nepalese Government studies, the population growth of the Terai is almost double that of the hill and mountain areas, and we believe it will continue to surpass them through the end of this century.Source: CIA (1983); Nepal: Continuity and Change in a Himalayan Monarchy, An Intelligence Assessment, Declassified Document # CIA-RDP84S00927R000200030003-7, NESA 83-10307, November 1983, pp 9, downloaded from https://www.cia.gov/library/readingroom/docs/CIA-RDP84S00927R000200030003-7.pdf

Post 2000 – Expansion Era

Democracy was reestablished in 1990

2000- Riots against Madhesi (Popularly known as Hrithik RoshanRiot)

This riot was outburst of historical contempt against plain people on frivolous triggering reason. A rumor started in Chitwan that Indian Bollywood actor had mentioned in a Star TV interview with Simi Garewal that he hated Nepalese people. Some student protested on street and local newspaper published the news on December 15th 2000. On reading the news, the president of an all-Nepal students union issued a statement in Biratnagar, condemning Hrithik's alleged remarks and calls for a boycott of the actor's films[58]. The situation worsened when said secretary repeated the statement in Kathmandu. The fire on street was already high. Hilly people targeted plain people in a violent manner. The statement was reported in all major Kathmandu newspapers on 25th December[59]. The Indian TV channel distribution was closed. Plain people were being beaten on the street of Kathmandu[60] and in southern plains towns. Kushilal Yadav of Rajbiraj died in police firing[61]. In Kathmandu, the car of Sadbhavana Party was put on fire, and many business stores of plains people were vandalized. The students and people living in Kathmandu were terrified with the target of black faced people. Total seven people died in the riot and it even threatened the government survival. On one side G.P Koirala Government was facing no-confidence motion from democratic force, on other King was questioning the democracy and lastly communist forces weresiding Maoistsand weretaking advantage of fluid situation. The impact and scale of violence did curse the Garment Industry in Kathmandu, which employed most of the plains' people, and is reflected in the drastic decline of readymade garments from NRs133 million to NRs804 million in 2001 (see table below). Since the violence year, the skilled people have slowly and steadilyleft Kathmandu for other places like Gulf.

The unique thing in 2000 was, Hill mass was opening against the plains people on street. This was shift from earlier instances, where either State had acted against the interest of plains people or Hill People had mass protested againstIndia for perceived encroachment on sovereign independence.

Year	Total Export	Export TC*	Export RMG RMG	Share TC	Share RMG
1993/94	19293.4	5943.2	5943.2	30.8	30.8
1994/95	17639.2	5390.8	5139.3	30.6	29.1
1995/96	19881.1	5612.8	5374.8	28.2	27.0
1996/97	22636.5	6281.3	5955	27.7	26.3
1997/98	27513.5	7582	7032.5	27.6	25.6
1998/99	35676.3	10231.4	9744.7	28.7	27.3
1999/00	49822.7	22134.4	13987.7	44.4	28.1
2000/01	55654.1	23046.3	13316.8	41.4	23.9
2001/02	46944.8	12408.6	8046.5	26.4	17.1
2002/03	49930.6	16692.8	12289.3	33.4	24.6
2003/04	53910.7	16201	10176.7	30.1	18.9
2004/05	58705.7	14988.41	6490.5	25.5	11.1
2005/06	55812.5	14922	6505.7	26.7	11.7

Table: Contribution of textiles-clothing (TC) and readymade Garments (RMG) in export[62]. Figure are in NRs. in million.

2004 – Iraq Riot

This riot would look awkward, however this would help to understand the level of insanity. On 1st September 2004, thousands of irate agitators set fire to Nepal's biggest mosque in Kathmandu, destroyed offices of job recruitment agencies and clashed with policemen in protest against the killing of 12 Nepalese laborers in Iraq.A day earlier, a video posted oninternet showed militants slitting the neck of one Nepalese worker and shooting 11 others in Iraq after militancyeruptedfollowing fall of Saddam Hussein. Iraq militancy or politics was in no way connected to Nepal or plains people. However, like Hrithik Roshan riots of 2000, though it was another laughing stock of the world, the riot created great damage to the plain people. About 97% percent of muslimsbelong to plains[63]. It was not Hindu-Muslim riot, rather few hilly people leading the unrest. Mobs, belonging to Hilly community, clashed with the police in various places in Kathmandu, including Ratnapark, Jamal, Chabahil, Kalimati, Bauddha, Maharajgunj and Lainchaur.Besides the capital city, demonstrations were also held in Jhapa, Gorkha, Dhanusha, Dhankuta and Lamjung districts[64].At least 3 people died in the riot[65]. Anything with a connection to the Middle East was attacked. The offices of Qatar Air and Gulf Air were set on fire. Besides the 110 or so recruitment companies, the targets were Nepali Muslims in the capital and Terai towns[66].

2006 - Riot against Madhesi in Nepalgunj

Exactly six years after Hrithik Roshan riot, plains people were again victim of riot by Hill people. Tensions had risen following a scuffle that ensued on 25th December 2006 between Madhesis (people from Terai region) and Paharis (people from Hilly region) during a Madhesh banda (general strike) called by Nepal Sadbhavana Party (Anandidevi) (NSP-A). The NSP (A), which was an ally of the seven-party government, had called the bandh expressing dissatisfaction overdraft interim constitution[67]signed two weeks earlier and alleged that the interim constitution failed to address the demands of Madhesi people. The party demanded that election constituencies for the constituent assembly polls be determined on the basis of population. The party had also demanded land reform.Nepalgunj riot left death of a 15 years boy, Kamal Giri[68], and business sectors worth millions damaged.[69]A foreigner, Anne Elisabeth, who was in the city wrote "Many burnt down shops and furniture and motorcycles on Surkhet Road drew a clear picture of a town that had been through 2 days riots. End result was 150 looted and burnt down shops, one dead and 20 wounded"[70]. The riot ended on Dec 28, however the damage was captured in visual technology. What was seen on video was another big shock. Video recordings showed 200 police officers watching a handful of people looting a tv-store and carrying the goods pass the police. This happened on the 26th of December – a day there was curfew in Nepalgunj, which the police – obviously – was unable/ unwilling to enforce. Whoever, and whatever motive was there, it turned out to be Madhesi-Pahari riot, and authorities didn't act at all[71]. Crowds were seen chanting contemptuous slogans against plains people, and rioting crowds were even found to be cheering on arrival of police. The video found way to Internet, which was slowly penetrating the houses.

2007 – Madhesi Mass Uprising

The Nepalgunj riot opened door to the Madhesh mass uprising a month after. The video (in DVD) of Nepalgunj was widely circulated, guessed to beprobably by King's supporters, to introduce volatility in politics which was marginalizing King. However 2007's uprising was different from 2006's riot. A month earlier Sadbhavana Party (NSPA), which was also in government, had called general strike in Nepalgunj and Hilly people reacted with violence. In January 2007, Madhesi Janadhikar Forum (MJF), an unknown group under leadership of Upendra Yadav, were arrested in Kathmandu while burning copies of the interim constitution. Three days later, MJF activists protesting the arrests in Lahan, Siraha district, clashed with Maoists, who shot dead Ramesh Kumar Mahato, a young MJF activist. On 20 January, as the MJF demanded action against the perpetrator and compensation, Maoist cadres seized his body and cremated it. The MJF stepped up protests against both the government, for inaction, and the Maoists. In some places, Maoist cadres were behind police patrol teams, and Maoist leaders, having PLA army, had offered Home Minister Sitaula to help in controlling Madhesi protesters. Maoists labelled the Madhesi protest as the conspiracy of the royalists who were inciting violence in the name of the Madhesis[72]. The protest lasted for 21 days January-February 2007, and established MJF as major political entity for plains people. MJF filled the political vacuum that NSP left after its inability to stand with Nepalgunj riot victim's sympathizers in addition to also being part of Koirala Government at that time.

Mahato's killing was the spark for prolonged agitation. The protests initially centeredaround Lahan and Janakpur but soon spreadall other major Tarai towns. The protests were spontaneous or organized by local groups, as MJF was virtually having no organizational structure to carry such a big protest, never happened in history. Participation in the protests cut across political divides; activists of other groups, from Nepali Congress and Nepal Communist party (UML) to both Janatantrik Terai Mukti Morcha (JTMM) factions, played a major role. Madhesis' longstanding grievances, aggravated by exclusion from the peace process, even spurred Communist Party of Nepal (Maoist) cadres to join in, despite the anti-Maoist theme of many protests.

The escalation of protest to such an extent surprised even those who led the movements. MJF, NSP, Nepal government, Indian diplomats who followed events closelyall failed to read the intensity of popular support[73].These mobilized people, provided support to the injured and helped coordinate protests. Malangwa, Birgunj, Lahan and Biratnagar saw major clashes[74].

Madhesi activists called for a general strike in the Tarai and organized widespread protests; the government responded with curfews and an increased police presence. On 25 January, the MJF announced it would continue the protests indefinitely until the interim constitution was amended. Activists looted government offices, police posts, banks, mainstream parties' district offices, media organizations and they vandalized statues of Pahari political leaders. The blocking of Kathmandu's key supply routes had a more direct impact, leading to travel disruption, price rise andpetrol shortage. Terai unrest incurred an estimated loss over Rs 18 billion to Nepal as transport, industries, bazaars, customs and revenue collection, academic institutions and other sectors of mid-Terai and eastern Terai were shut for thethree weeks.Although there were sporadic attacks on Terai-based paharis, communalism was not a defining feature of the unrest. The state response was harsh[75]: police shot dead more than 30 to 45 people and wounded 800.

On January 31, a week after start of protest, Prime Minister Girija Prasad Koirala addressed on TV, inviting protesting groups to negotiation promising to increase electoral seats in the Tarai and announced a commitment to federalism.MJF-led protestors rejected the offer and complained he did notsympathiestheir movement. Many Madhesis felt that the speech was high-handed and unilateral and did not recognize Madhesi demands as rights that were due to them. Koirala made a second address a week later expressing regret over the loss of lives and promisingelectoral representation and inclusion of marginalized groups in state bodies on a proportional basis. The MJF cautiously welcomed this announcement and suspended its agitation for ten days to allow the government to implement its promises but setting preconditions for talks: the home minister's resignation, action against those responsible for the killings and a judicial commission to examine the government's behavior. The JTMM(JS) conditionally agreed to talks but the JTMM(Goit) (then the much stronger faction) rejected the offer[76].

Many Kathmandu residents vociferously opposed the movement, believing it had been stirred up by King Supporters or was an Indian conspiracy to undermine Nepal's sovereignty. Human Rights organization, having heavy presence of Hilly people, were blamed in plain region for biased opinion. Similarly, media groups, which have major control in Kathmandu, were targeted in plain region for their lack of transparent news during the protest.

Indian political and social groups, especially in Jogbani and Raxaul, organized camps to give shelter and medical care to the injured[77].

The promised judicial commission was only formed months later and dominated by establishment figures, including the police chief, whose own force's actions are under investigation[78].

Two months later, there was direct confrontation between Maoist-MJF which turned violent in Gaur on 21 March, when the Maoist affiliated Madhesh Rastriya Mukti Morcha (MRMM) organized a mass meeting at the same time and venue as the MJF. MJF activists allegedly destroyed the MRMM stage, provoking a similar response. After initially fleeing, MJF partisans attacked the outnumbered Maoists, killing 27 people[79]. UN Office of the High Commissioner for Human Rights, Nepal in its field research report mentioned "CPN-M action in organizing a rally at the same time and place as the MPRF [MJF], as it has done in other locations, was provocative"[80].

The after effect of Madhesi mass uprising circulated positive confidence in plains. Madhesis from Nepali Congress and Nepal Communist party (UML) initially put pressure on their parties to address Madhesh issues, and later resigned to form TMLP (Terai Madhesh Loktantrik Party) on December 27, 2007. Mahant Thakur came from Congress and Mahendra Yadav came from Nepal Communist Party. On December 31, 2007, a Central Working Committee of the party was formed, chaired by Thakur. In India, Madhesi students started mobilizing people and had a conference in Bangalore having presence of more than 200 students under leadership of Surendra Yadav, Vijay Sah, Lokendra Yadav and Sujit Thakur. A Madhesi group was formed in United Kingdom, and a Madhesi group was formed in United States in 2005, ANTA, lobbied for MJF chief Upendra Yadav's visit and acceptance in United States.

Given below is the list of people died during protest

1. Ashish Ali Mikrani - Malangwa, Sarlahi
2. Babunarayan Yadav - Janakpur, Dhanusha
3. Bechan Yadav - Dhodhna-5, Siraha
4. Bhagwati Mandal - Inaruwa, Sunsari
5. Bijay Sahani - Mahadeva-3, Siraha
6. Binod Ray - Madanpur, Sarlahi
7. Birbal Mukhiya - Bardiya
8. Dilram Yadav - Bardiya
9. Dindayal Mandal - Hatkhola, Morang
10. Dinesh Ray Yadav - Gamhariya-6, Sarlahai
11. Dipendra Sah - Birganj, Parsa
12. Hari Lal Mehta - Inaruwa, Sunsari
13. Jitendra Marwaita - Saptari
14. Jivdharai Yadav - Malangwa, Sarlahi
15. Kari Thakur - Janakpur-14, Dhanusha
16. Kashiram Harijang - Behari, Banke
17. Khahre Goriya - Puraina, Banke
18. Koili Koiri - Puraina, Banke
19. Mahabir Sah - Birganj, Parsa
20. Manish Jha - Saptari
21. Manjil Alam Ansari - Kalaiya, Bara
22. Mataprasad Barma - Belhari, Banke
23. Md. Anish Rain - Charrapatti, Siraha
24. Md. Mudasin - Siraha
25. MulramTripathi - Khajura, Banke
26. Nirmal Kumar Rajbanshi - Hatkhola, Morang
27. Pawan Kumar Sah - Janakpur, Dhanusha
28. PramodSada - Mahadeva-3, Siraha
29. Rajesh Thakur - Parkauli, Mahottari
30. Rajesh Yadav - Saptari
31. RajkumarKamat - Biratnagar, Morang
32. Ram Ekwal Ray - Sirpur-6, Sarlahai
33. Ram Narayan Sah - Salempur-3, Sarlahi
34. Ram Swarup Mehta - Inaruwa, Sunsari
35. Ramanand Mehta - Inaruwa, Sunsari
36. Ramesh Mahato - Majhaura-5, Siraha
37. Sadanand Yadav - Biratnagar, Morang
38. Sanjay Kumar Yadav - Jamuniya, Sarlahi
39. Shekh Abdul Asarf - Dhanusha
40. Shiv Shankar Yadav - Dharapari-14
41. Shyam Sundar Mehta - Inaruwa, Sunsari
42. SunitaMahato - Govindapur-8, Siraha
43. TalluHarda – Hemram - Hatkhola, Morang
44. ZamirAlam - Kalaiya, Bara

2008 – Madhesh II Uprising

On 8 February 2008, a new alliance of three Madhesi political parties, the "United Democratic Madhesi Front" (UDMF)[81] announced that it would call a Terai-wide bandh from 13 February to support their demands to the Government. The UDMF bandh was called off on 28 February following agreement with the Government and the others were terminated a few days later following similar agreements. The imposition of the bandhs paralyzed daily life in most of the Terai and led to violent confrontations between bandh supporters and both the Nepal Police and Armed Police Force (APF). All Eastern, Central and Western Region Terai districts except Chitwan were affected[82]. In the Far-Western region, a bandh called by the United Tharu National Front (UTNF) was partiallyobserved. The restrictions on daily life were also compounded by the imposition of curfews, for example, in Biratnagar, Birgunj, Nawalparasi and Nepalgunj. OHCHR investigated the deaths of six civilians, all males, who died during the protests; in Nepalgunj on 17 February, Siraha district on 19 February, Saptari district on 25 February (two persons), Nawalparasi district on 26 February and Sunsari district on 27 February. Five died as a result of police fire and one as a result of injuries sustained when he was hit by lathis; Mohammad Riskutmiya (died Feb 27, Duhabi),Idris Ansari (d. Feb 27, Duhabi),JagadishPashi (d. Feb 26, Maheshpur, Nawalparasi), Kalbari Paswan (d. Feb 26, Maheshpur, Nawalparasi), Gulten Das (d. Feb 25, Rajbiraj, Saptari), Rajesh Thakur (d. Feb 19, Lahan), and Gulzar Khan (d. Feb 17, Nepalgunj). OHCHR report concluded that the use of lethal force was not justified and live ammunition was used directly against protestors by the police. Of the five persons who died as a result of police fire, three were found not to have been actively participating in protests and could not have presented any kind of threat to life.APF personnel forcefully entered homes and physically assaulted inhabitants in Gaur, Birgunj, Janakpur and Nepalgunj. Several students were also allegedly taken out of a nearby school hostel and beaten with lathis and the butts of firearms. In Banke district, a 60-year-old woman was shot in the hip by APF, reportedly while trying to stop them from looting money from her house[83].

Six point demand put forward by United Democratic Madhesi Front (UDMF) to government before start of the Madhesi movement on February 13th (unofficial English translation):

1. An autonomous "One Madhes, one province" with a republican order and right to self determination
2. Immediate implementation of constitutional provision regarding proportional representation of the Madhesi, Indigenous, Dalits, women and all marginalized groups in all organs of the stateImmediate en-mass recruitment of Madhesis youths in the Nepali Army on the proportion of their population
3. A status of martyrs to 45 persons killed in the course of the previous Madhes movement, and adequate compensation and free medical treatment to those injured and/or physically disabled in the course of the agitation.
4. A provision that allows the parties, which have filed less than 50 percent of candidacy for the CA elections, not to field candidates for proportional representation system.

5. Genuine efforts to bring armed outfits of Madhes to a negotiation table
6. All past agreements (with MPRF) should be enforced before holding the CA elections

The UDMF bandh was called off on 28 February following agreement with the Government. Indian embassy under the leadership of Shiv Shankar Mukherjee mediatedthe agreement between Girija Prasad Koirala and UDMF.

Eight points agreement between UDMF and Government done on 26th Feb 2008 (unofficial translation)

1. The government will declare martyrdom for those killed during the Madhes agitation and provide proper compensation for the injured who haven't been compensated yet. Similarly, expenses will be provided for treatment for those injured during the agitation, one million rupees will be provided as compensation to the family of those killed during the agitation and those arrested will be released immediately.
2. Nepal will be a federal republican democratic state by accepting the wish of the Madhesi people for an autonomous Madhes state and wish of people of other regions for an autonomous state with federal structure. There will be distinct power sharing between the center and the region in the federal structure on the basis of list. The regions will have complete autonomy and authority. The elected Constituent Assembly will devise a way to apply the formation of such states and the rights attributed to the region and the center while keeping national sovereignty, unity and integrity intact.
3. The current 20 percent legal provision mentioned in Article 7 (proportional representation in election), sub-article 14 of the Constituent Assembly Member Election Act-2054 will be increased to 30 percent.
4. The government will compulsoryappoint, promote and nominate Madhesi, indigenous communities, women, Dalits, backward areas and minority communities to ensure proportional participation in security bodies and all organs of the state.

5. The entry of Madhesi and other groups into the Nepal Army will be ensured to give the army a national and inclusive structure.
6. The government along with the UDMF urged all armed agitating groups in the Terai to join the peaceful political process and come to talks to resolve all problems. The Nepal government will take immediate steps to create a favorable environment for the same. We appeal everyone to conduct the April 10 elections in a peaceful, fair, non-violent and terror-free manner.
7. The Nepal government will immediately implement the agreement reached with the Madhesi People's Rights Forum (MPRF) on August 13 last year including releasing those under police detention, dismissing cases against MRPF leaders and activists.
8. All the agitation programs called by the UDMF will be immediately withdrawn.

Like the first Madhesh agitation (2007), which successfully changed the interim constitution to a federal one, the second Madhesh agitation (2008) resulted in proportional representation and identity-based quotas in the electoral system[84].

2012 – Jaleshwar-Janakpur Agitation against Government Offices Relocation

In January 2012, people in Jaleshwar, a southern town, started agitation to protest Nepal Government decision toopen a government Internal Revenue Office (IRO) service center in Bardibas (Mahottari District) by reducing power in the district office in Jaleshwar. The protest widened the rift between Madhesi and Pahari communities in the Central Terai[85]. Industrialists, supported by local political parties and civil society organizations, padlocked the IRO in Janakpur (Dhanusha District) and enforced a bandh in the area for several days in early January to protest against the decision. Due to these protests, the Ministry of Finance decided to withdraw its decision to establish another IRO in Bardibas. However, in reaction to this reversal, a strike was held by local industrialists and entrepreneurs in Bardibas, a place established by Hilly migrants in 1970, from 15 to 22 January, which only ceased after the Mahottari Chief District Officer (CDO) inaugurated the IRO service center in Bardibas, having received instruction from the government. Although this move assuaged protestors in Bardibas, the industrialists of Janakpur felt this was a continued “deceit” against Madhesi people by the government and enforced a new bandh in Janakpur on 24 January and begun planning further actions. Locals and industrialists in Jaleshwar (Mahottari district headquarters) also sided with protesters in Janakpur, not only demanding the withdrawal of the IRO from Bardibas but also the relocation of a number of government offices (i.e. Land-Protection Office, Drinking Water and Sanitation Office, District Forest Office and District Traffic Office) from Bardibas back to Jaleshwar. The protestors from Janakpur perceived the decision by the government as “anti Madhesi”. They argued that the establishment of various government offices along the highway and previous removals of key government offices from “south of the highway” were moves to weaken a future Madhesh province and a continuation of stripping Madhesis of government services and resources[86].

2014 – Agitation Demanding Road Maintenance (Simraungadh)

The tragedy of Simraungadh is representation of whole plains. Simraungadh has richest archaeological site of Sen Kingdom from 13th century. Simraungadh never fellunder Government excavation and preservation planning because the archeological and historical richness of Simraungadh would establish plains people's heritage among world's best archeological sites.

People of Simraungadh started agitation on 10th Oct 2014 demanding repair of the 25 Kilometer Kalaiya-Simraungadh road along the Gandak canal. Kalaiya connects with Birgunj, the southern business hub. Demonstrators approached the police station for talks. But Armed Police Force (APF) responded with force instead. Armed Police Force (APF) indiscriminately charged batons and lobbed tear gas canisters and even fired in the air. People responded with stones and batons. A 42-year-old man, Jayanarayan Patel, of Hariharpur -7 was killed while Shah Mohammad Hawari, 28, of Hariharpur-5 and NageshhworKushwaha of Amritgunjsustained injuries. Patel was shot in the chest[87]. After opposition parties obstructed Parliament on October 15th, the major political parties agreed to form a parliamentary panel to probe the killing in Bara. Home Minister Bam Dev Gautam told parliament that the government would form a parliamentary probe panel and make efforts to announce Jayanarayan Patel, who was killed in police firing, a martyr. He also said it would implement other demands, including blacktopping of the road section from Simraungadh-Kalaiya to Birgunj within three months as demanded by locals[88]. However, the road condition is bad in 2017 even after 3 years[89] have passed since government assurance.

2014 to 2016 - Agitation Demanding Road Repair (Jaleshwar)

Janakpur-Jaleshwar road, which runs till Bhittamod, had been in pathetic condition since 2005 and becoming worse day by day. The road was modernized by India in 1970s while building East-West Highway, however this road is historical, as it connected religious town Janakpur with Muzaffarpur of India. Captain Kinloch used this road to reach Janakpur from Patna with his army, while on his way to help King Jay Prakash Malla of Kathmandu. Millions of pilgrims use this road to visit Janakpur from India year after year. Unlike spontaneous protest in Simraungadh for road maintenance, the people in Jaleshwar formed a protest group under banner "Sundar Abhiyani" meaning Beautification Drive. Between2014 and 2016, they organized protestswith the help of locals and government made agreements with them multiple times in past to take care of the road. In June 2015 the protest slogan was "build the road or hang us to death rather than dying each day in installment"[90] due to dust related diseases, such asTuberculosis, Asthma and road accidents (see image below).

Image showing protest banner in Jaleshwar demanding 14 miles road reconstruction between Bhittamod and Janakpur.

2014 – Protest in Janakpur to Welcome Indian PM Narendra Modi

Indian PM Narendra Modi had planned to visit Janakpur on 25th November 2014, a day ahead of the formal inauguration of the 18th Saarc Summit. He had promised to visit Janakpur when he was in Kathmandu in August 2013. An advanced Indian security team had given him a security clearance for a Janakpur visit. Modi wanted to address the public gathering in Janakpur, similar to he did last time in Kathmandu by addressing the parliament. However, Communist parties, who werepartners in Sushil Koirala Government was ambiguous on the response. Initially, Modi wanted to enter Janakpur through Bhittamod-Jaleshwarborder by road[91], instead of directly landing in Janakpur by helicopter. This plan put Nepal government into awkward position, because the road was in dilapidated state, despite an assurancefrom Indian government of funding to build the road. Additionallygovernment put pressure that Modi should also visit Muktinath, a temple located in Mustang if he is visiting Janakpur. Later, Deputy Prime Minister Bam Dev Gautam mentioned to a House panel that the Indian premier will not address the public gathering in Janakpur, but will receive civic reception at Ram-Janaki Temple. The Nepal government's highhanded plan to changeModi's scheduledvisit to Janakpur saw widespread protest from Madhesi parties and local people. Finally, Modi's visit was cancelled by Indian government to preempt any controversy[92].

2015 - Gaur-Kalaiya-Inaruwa Agitation Against Government Offices Relocation

Like the 2012's agitation in Jaleshwar-Janakpur, there were again agitations in 2015at three different places; Gaur-Kalaiya-Inaruwa. These agitations were spontaneous and localized without any top political support.

On 16 March 2015, peoplestarted protest led by Rautahat chapter of Federation of Nepali Chamber of Commerce and Industry (FNCCI) demanding,fromthe government, to revoke its decision to establish branches of the District Land Revenue Office and the Survey Department Office in Chandranigahpur[93]. National Human Rights Commission (NHRC) found through the monitoring that the police allegedly entered into the house of local residents and thrashed them, the media persons deployed to collect the news and human rights workers involved in monitoring endured unprecedented violence, common citizens were thrashed and the local community and women were rebuked with abusive words[94]. The protest was withdrawn on April 8th after local administration agreed to(i) withdraw its decision to move service center of the Land Survey and Land Revenue Offices[95] and (2) declare Ram Asish Thakur of Gaur municipality-10, who was killed in course of the protest, as martyr, and provide suitable employment to one member of his family.

Similar protests were staged in neighboring Bara district in February. Kalaiya, the headquarters of Bara, saw protests against the government's decision to relocate the land revenue and survey offices to Simara. After protests raged, the government rolled back its decision, only to rouse the ire of Simara locals, who took to the streets demanding that the offices be relocated as planned[96]. The same thing happened in Inaruwa, the headquarters of Sunsari district. Government shifted Land registration and Land Measurement offices to Dharan in the midnight of 5th June 2015, when people of Inaruwa protested[97].

The government claimed that the relocation and expansion of services to centres outside of the district headquarters was purely an administrative decision. The locals saw it otherwise. In many districts of the Terai, the East-West, or the Mahendra, Highway acts as an unofficial boundary. North of the highway are relatively newer settlements of Pahari migrants, who have established communities and business hubs, benefiting from their proximity to the vital road. South of the highway generally have a greater concentration of Madhesi communities, who saw the shift in government offices as part of a long-term political ploy to move administration to the north, benefiting Paharis at the cost of Madhesis[98]. On the extended logic, Madhesis ask, "if government objective is to provide better service then, why neither Government has opened service center in Simraungadh nor it has built good road connecting Simraungadh with Kalaiya?"[99]

2015 - Hunger Strike Against Power Cuts (Janakpur)

In the second week of June, businessmen Bijaya Kumar Sah, Surendra Bhandari and Ful Dev Pandit among others started a hunger strike against longer power cuts in Janakpur, which they said went beyond the load-shedding schedule published by the NEA.Beside longer load-shedding hours, low-voltage problem has also affected industrial activities. The Federation of Nepalese Chambers of Commerce and Industry on 12th June 2015 expressed its solidarity with the hunger strike. The strike ended on June 14thfollowing a five-point agreement with the Nepal Electricity Authority.

2016 – Hunger Strike Demanding Reform in Hospital (Rajbiraj)

Chairman of the Nepal Sadbhavana Party (Gajendrabadi), Bikas Kumar Tiwari, staged hunger strike starting 23rd November 2016 at the premises of Rajbiraj-based Gajendra Narayan Singh Sagarmatha Zonal Hospital from

Wednesday putting forth various demands.Sagarmatha zone has population of more than 2 million. The demands of Tiwari were to make the hospital children-friendly, provide healthy and nutritious food to the patients, arrange fresh drinking water at the hospital premise, construct main entrance gate, availability of doctors for eye, nose, neck, skin, among others, availability of radiologist, construction of maternity building among other under-construction buildings, stick a list of medicines to be provided by the government in hospital premises, among other demands[100]. Tiwari ended the strike on 18th day after he reached a four-point agreement with the government in presence of Minister for Health,Gagan Kumar Thapa. The agreement paper read that works for construction of maternity center would start within 15 days and posting of specialized doctors in all the departments of the hospital would be made within one month. Likewise, an agreement was reached to purchase all the necessary equipments for dialysis, surgery, digital x-ray among others immediately and to form a high-level committee to investigate alleged corruption at the hospital among others[101]. Tiwari's strike was motivated by similar protest of DrGovinda KC, who was staging fast-unto- death in the Capital demanding reforms in the medical education sector[102].

2015 – Madhesh III Agitation

The first Constituent Assembly was elected in 2008, but it failed to complete the new charter, in large part due to differences over the delineation of federal provinces. A second Constituent Assembly elected in 2013 was also deadlocked for over a year[103]. However, in the aftermath of the devastating earthquake which struck Nepal in April 2015, four major political parties reached an agreement to complete the charter by a "fast track" process[104], in an expectation that stable political environment would motivate international donors[105]. On 8 June, in an atmosphere of political panic, Nepal Congress, Nepal Communist party (UML) and the opposition UCPN-M signed a sixteen-point deal to fast-track the constitution, saying it would enable amore effective earthquake response. The signatories of sixteen point agreements[106] on (i) Parliament and Electoral System (ii) Forms of Government (iii) Judicial System and (iv) Local Body Election did notconsult UDMF (United Democratic Madhesi Front).

Soon after the sixteen-point agreement, the protest started building. Sixteen-point agreement was challenged in court by Rita Sah, a women Madhesi Civil Society activist and Vijay Kant Karna, a Madhesi former ambassador.The court ruling noted "if attempts are made to frame the new constitution by bypassing the existing constitutional provisions, they could make the new constitution controversial, pose threat to peace and order and can create fear of another conflict"[107]. The court ruling implied federalism issues have to be resolved by the CA and their resolution cannot be left for the transformed Parliament as stated in the 16-point agreement[108]. Court also further said the agreement violated articles of the 2007 Interim Constitution, including 138 (1a): "Provinces shall be autonomous and vested with full authority. The boundaries, number, names and structures, as well as full details of the lists of autonomous provinces and the center and allocation of means, resources and powers shall be determined by the Constituent Assembly"[109].

Street was warming to protest the sixteen point agreement, including the protest in Kathmandu, who were mostly against the unequal citizenship provisions that were designed to restrict the ability of single woman or women married to non-Nepali to pass the citizenship on to their children. Plains streetswere prepared for wider protest. Public meetings had provocative speeches, and effigies of national leaders were burnt[110]. Protest got spiked in July during the public consultation on draft constitution. People were not allowed to meet the constitution feedback collecting team. Additionally, there was very short time window for collecting feedback; timeframe for collecting public opinion and redrafting based on analysis of this opinion from over two months to under ten days[111]. The feedback collecting centers were heavily guarded by the Nepal Police and paramilitary Armed Police Force (APF), thus discouraging Madhesis and Tharus. People challenged the restrictions on feedback collection which resulted in conflicts[112] and close to 130 were wounded in clashes with the police and APF in five Terai districts[113] including Janakpur, Biratnagar, and Saptari[114]. Additionally, the fast track constitution process reduced the time for constitution assembly members to read and debate the draft.

On 5th August, the four parties issued a map with proposed state boundaries without formal consultation with Madhesi, Tharu, Janajati or Dalit groups and despite cautions from Madhesi and Tharu leaders that it would spark major unrest[115].

On August 17, the protest erupted in Bhardah of Saptari district. The protesters would not allow vehicle to run on the highway during theday timeas a result,about 150 vehicles were stranded in the area.This hold-up would ease around midnight and vehicles would start moving. Police started pressing to open the vehicle strikes. On August 18, protesters began to erect a tent at 8 am on the road with the intention to block the road to enforce general strike. Police came and started beating the protesters. The locals who felt humiliated by police aggressive behavior calledpeople from the nearby villages to protest against the brutality of the police. A large number of people gathered from the villages and some of them threw stones at the police.Then a Nepal police, without giving any warning, opened fire with live bullet at the protesters. Rajiv Raut, who was killed in the police firing, was half a kilometer away from the protest place[116].

Western plains, the strong hold of Tharu, was boiling in the August. Tharus were angry that Kanchanpur and Kailali districts would become part of hill-based state number six instead of autonomous Tharu state. They were protest marching in large number on the street of Tikapur and elsewhere. Tikapur, the district capital of Kailali, has become hotspot of migrant hilly people and turned to become dominated by hilly people. Tikapur is surrounded by Tharu villages. Tharu protesters clashed with AkhandaSudurPaschim (the undivided Far-West), a group against the Tharu autonomous region. The Akhanda movement enjoys the blessings of powerful national leaders from this region in all major parties. Since it gained prominence in 2011, its supporters have often been clashingwith Tharu groups[117]. There was third group protesting the merger of Mid-Western region with the Far-Western region to form state number six. On August 10th, two protesters were killed in police firing, which forced four parties on August 21 to split state number six and carving out state number seven with much of the hill territories of the mid-western region[118]. However, August 21st re-organization again left the Tharu and Madhesi demand unaddressed rather made plains people enraged that hills people demands were getting fulfilled quickly, and their old protest were ignored.

On August 24, protesters gathered in Gaur of Rautahat district to protest against the proposed seven-province model. A large number of women were also participated in the demonstration carrying fake swords (made of wood). The protest was peaceful till 4pm, when Police started firing without warning. Over 65 protesters sustained injuries from rubber bullets and baton charges, including 5 women protesters who suffered bruises and cuts. Raj Kishor Thakur, who was not among protesting group rather a bystander, was hit by police firing and fell on the ground. Police then encircled Thakur and repeatedly kicked him with boots. Thakur died in the hospital[119].

The protest intensified in Tikapur. Two days later, on August 25th, there was a big mass marchpast rally organized by Tharuhut/Tharuwan Action Committee, and people joined in thousands from neighboring villages. To contain the Tharus protest, which was peaceful, police applied force. In the after conflict, eight persons including Senior Superintendent of Police (SSP) LaxmanNeupane and security personnel were killed by the use of home-made weapons in Tikapur incident of Kailali. The National Human Rights Commission investigation team found that "protesters went out of control and resorted tocounterattack after the police shot teargas shells and opened fire at them"[120]. In the next days, despite a curfew and virtual national media blackout, there were multiple systematic attacks by local hill-origin communities on Tharu homes and businesses in and around Tikapur, and over four thousandsTharus were estimated to have fled to India[121].

Protests escalated, and agitators and security forces engaged in confrontations that frequently resulted in excessive use of force by the latter.

Dilip Chaurasiyawas killed in police firing in Birgunj on August 31, when police tried to disperse around four thousand protesters demonstrating at Radhemai Chowk and marching towards GhantaGhar (Clock Tower) through postal road[122]. Next day, September 1st, was more difficult for Birgunj people, which saw four deaths. Sohan Sah was killed by police firing in front of Naguwa Police Post while protesting against the killing of DilipChaurasiya. Jay Prakash Sah and Dinanath Sah entered a deserted residential area (Pratima Chowk), where locals had run away from police terror, on bicycle without knowledge of local conflict, when they became victim of police firing. Hifajat Miya, who was deliberately killed by police, fell down after he sustained a bullet injury whileprotesting in Kalaiya Chowk. Then police encircled him while he lay seriously injured and one officer shot him twice in the chest[123].

On September 9th, another person, Ram Krishna Raut, was killed in Portaha village in Saptari district. Ram Krishna Raut was a 62 years old man, who was visiting his brother-in-law, Parmanand, house located near Hanuman temple on the Bhardaha-Hanuman nagar road. While he was chatting near the house with friends, clash erupted between police and protesters near police post, located about 500 meters away. Seeing disputes between protesters-police, Raut and friends fled towards Parmanad's house.

As Ram Krishna Raut entered the house, a member of the armed police force fired a shot in his back[124].

On the same day, September 9th, five people were killed in Jaleshwarinindiscriminate firing by police. When crowd of around eight thousandgathered at Mahendra Chowk (now called Durga Chowk) in the middle of town, police fired a dozen of teargas canisters to disperse protesters. All of a sudden the security personnel started to fire shots indiscriminately at Mahendra Chowk and moved towards Shankar temple while firing. Birendra Bichchha was close to Mahendra Chowk when police fired teargas. While Bichchha was sprinkling water in his eyes to get relief from the burning sensation caused by firing of teargas canister, he was suddenly hit on his right temple by a bullet fired by police. The police then shot Rambibek Yadav, part of protesting group, at around 3:30pm near Rastriya Banijya Bank (National Commercial Bank) between Mahendra Chowk and Shankar Chowk. However the surprising killing was of Rohan Chaudhary, a student, who was on his way home from his tuition walking through the street that connects Mahendra Chowk and Malpot (Land Revenue) office. Similarly, Amit Kapar was shot dead by police firing at Shankar Chowk[125].

Police terror returned in Jaleshwar again two days after on September 11th. On September 11th people had been protesting since the morning. The situation became tense around Mahendra Chowk at around 12pm as the news of the killing of ASI Thaman BK spread in the area. Police officers came out aggressively after the news. Protesters and police clashed with each other near Shankar temple. Police fired teargas canisters to disperse the crowd. Although the protesters had left the area, the police continued to fire indiscriminately. In the meantime, a police bullet hit Ramshila Mandal, woman member of RastriyaPrajatantra Party, Nepalon her forehead, who was standing at the gate of a beauty parlor located near the temple at around 2pm. At around 5pm, in the outskirts of Jaleshwar, police killed Ganesh Chaudhary, who had gone to buy vegetables and tobacco in the local markets, Raniratbara, located few miles north of Jaleshwar. Ganesh Chaudhary was on bicycle almost 40 meter away from the road when a bullet fired by armed police force out of the van hit him in his left eye. Unfortunately, Ganesh Chaudhary, a member of local Red Cross, was grandfather of Roshan Chaudhary killed two days before[126].

On the same September 11th, police firing was on in Janakpur, a town 10 miles north of Jaleshwar[127]. Local administration had imposed curfew in different parts of Janakpur to prevent UDMF from organizing a large protest in the city. Over three thousand protesters marched defying the curfew. Police used teargas and opened fire on a group of protesters who were walking through the Mills Area neighborhood on their way toward the center of Janakpur, a town in southern Nepal. Fourteen-year-old Nitu Yadav was among the protesters. He attempted to hide from the police in some bushes, when police started chasing him. In front of onlookers he was dragged from his hiding place by police officers, thrown to the ground, and, while an officer stood on his legs, shot him in the face at point-blank range[128]. Another protester, Sanjay Chaudhari, a member of Sadbhavana Party, was hiding on the veranda of a nearby resident's house. Police firedashot at his back moments later, as he attempted to flee after seeing the Nitu Yadav being shot by police[129]. A police bullet also killed 13 years old Dilip Yadav who happened to be passing by while returning home on his bicycle near Pidari Chowk.

By this time the movements of vehicles on the road were almost zero. If needed, police was escorting the vehicles. On September 15, police were escorting 112 trucks loaded with goods from local factories. A group of around 40 protesters tried to stop the last three of these vehicles at Bethari Chowk, about two kilometers west of Bhairahawa. Police used teargas canisters to disperse the protesters. After half an hour around 5:45pm, additional 150 APF (armed police forces) arrived, and started indiscriminate firing from Tinau Bridge towards the local market. Six people got killed in the firing[130]. Nandani Pandey, who was trying to close her grocery store was hit with a bullet on her left thigh. Ranjana Singh was hit by bullet in her grandparents' house, while she was preparing tea on first floor. Bindu Kumar Lacaul, a local hotel worker, started running with crowd, after police firing started. Bindu was hit with a bullet in his right eye. Raj Kumar Barai, who was buying vegetables in the market at the time, sustained bullet injuries in his neck when police fired shots indiscriminately. SahwatiMurau, who had gone to sell vegetable, was killed in the same incident. The most tragic was the killing of four years old Chandan Patel, who was with her mother in the market[131]. None of the killed in Bethari had anything to do with the protest other than they happenedto be there at that moment.

By mid-September, about 40 people had been killed in clashes with police and APF. Madhesi Tarai Human Rights Defenders Alliance (THRD Alliance) in their report[132] found that a number of those who died had been shot in the back or the chest, and in a few cases, some distance away from the protest sites. The movement was becoming very personal; everyone knew someone who died or was injured.

As the death toll rose, there were calls from different places to halt the drafting process and negotiate with the protesting parties. India, the U.S. and UN publicly and privately urged the government to bring dissenters on board[133]. A week before the constitution was passed, India sent Foreign SecretaryJaishankar as special envoy on September 17 to meetwith top political leaders and officials of Nepal, including Prime Minister Sushil Koirala and President Ram Baran Yadav, during his two-day stay[134]. Jaishanker also held meeting with Madhesi parties[135]. On this, Prime Minister Sushil Koirala press advisor accused Delhi of meddling in internal affairs[136]. United States of America released a press statement saying "The United States is closely following the debate as Nepal approaches the final stages of drafting and promulgating its constitution. We hope that the document that emerges embraces the creativity, inclusiveness, and flexibility that will build a peaceful and prosperous Nepal. The constitution should have the broadest possible support and the outcome should honor fundamental rights such as gender equality and basic freedoms"[137].

Two days before the September 20th deadline, three major parties announced they were "pausing" the process to try talk with Madhesi parties. In reality, it was a pretended move, in which a day was religious holiday in plains and September 19 was Saturday, an official weekend. No groundwork had been laid by informal contacts or agenda discussion, and security forces, including the army, were still deployed in parts of the Terai[138].

The night of 20 September, the day constitution was promulagated,was a deeply divided Nepal between Hill and plains.Hill observed the day like "Dipawali celebrations", after the festival of lights, and plains celebrated the day as Black night, with the lights off. People have realized by then that no matter how many Madhesis died or how large the protests were – Kathmandu just did not listen[139]. And more importantly, the people in plains were terrorized by unabated intentional shooting by the police forces.

Hours after Nepal promulgated the constitution, Indian government press statement read "We note the promulgation in Nepal today of a Constitution. We are concerned that the situation in several parts of the country bordering India continues to be violent. Our Ambassador in Kathmandu has spoken to the Prime Minister of Nepal in this regard. We urge that issues on which there are differences should be resolved through dialogue in an atmosphere free from violence and intimidation, and institutionalized in a manner that would enable broad-based ownership and acceptance. This would lay the foundation of harmony, progress and development in Nepal"[140]. On September 21st, United Nations Secretary-General Ban Ki-moon voiced concern and requested "all political leaders to act in the broad national interest and with continued flexibility and inclusivity"[141].

The supporters of UDMF continued their protest in several Terai districts as the new constitution was promulgated on Sunday. On September 21st, Satrughna Patel of Pakhamainpur died due to bullet injuries while two others were seriously injured in police firing in Birgunj, Parsa[142]. Around a dozen protesters, former CA member KarimaBegam, were hurt in a scuffle with police.

On 23 September, the United Democratic Madhesi Front (UDMF) announced blockading of all customs points bordering India. Mahant Thakur, the leader of UDMF said in an interview "We were not allowed to protest on streets. We were shot at during sit-ins. The police even intervened during peaceful sit-ins at border. The problem remained the same when we used Indian soil to protest. Hence, we chose to launch sit-ins on no man's land. This was the only option left for us. Then we realized that the blockade could be effectively carried out from the no man's land"[143]. The immediate impact was the reduction in the death by police firing.

Within days, cargo and container trucks were in ever-lengthening lines at some crossings, notably Birgunj, Nepal's busiest transit point for import of fuel, cooking gas and other goods. Protesters occupied a transit bridge on no-man's land between Birgunj and Raxaul in India and clashed often with police in the early weeks, as the government continued an aggressive approach. In mid-November, when security forces tried to clear the route by force, protesters moved to the Indian end of no-man's land to enforce the blockade. The occupiers were a mixture of party activists, ordinary Nepalese and some Indians who said they were there to show support[144]. In Birgunj, the protests started with an almost festive air, having different types of public programs from drama, dance to political activities. Hundreds of thousands people joining from nearby villages in shifts. Indian citizens and civil society groups from Raxaul across the border organized one big meal, a light snack and tea for the protestors every day[145].

Even if the blockade was indigenous, there was moral support from India. Indian government on September 21stissued a press release saying "We are deeply concerned over the incidents of violence resulting in death and injury in the regions of Nepal bordering India following the promulgation of Constitution yesterday. Our freight companies and transporters have also voiced complaints about the difficulties they are facing in movement within Nepal and their security concerns, due to the prevailing unrest"[146]. Madhesi protestors' efforts were bolstered from the Indian side by bureaucratic foot dragging, new complications for transit and customs procedures and suddenly absent officials[147].

As per the pre-agreement between Nepali Congress and Nepal Communist party (UML), Sushil Koirala resigned from Prime Minster post. The UDMF was confused and went ahead to vote for Sushil Koirala to re-elect him as PM instead of UML, who had contemplated Madhesis protest multiple times. Former prime minister Jhala Nath Khanal of UML used the term 'Dhoti Pradesh' in his interview[148] with Reporter Club's Rishi Dhamala about the Madhes province in September first week, which intensified the protest[149]. Party Chairman KP Oli had mentioned on September 9ththat "a few mangoes are bound to fall from the tree"[150] in reference to opposition to the constitution when people were getting killed during the protests by police[151]. KP Oli with the support of Maoist, and tactical backing from Chinese became new Prime Minister. The UML-led government felt it had the upper hand and could not give into a blockade it described as imposed by India; the UDMF was confused, unable to agree on the blockade, a negotiating strategy and acceptable compromises. All actors dug in, waiting for opponents to tire[152].

Before leaving the government, Congress government registered the amendment of constitution on October proposing to replace the phrase "based on geography and population" with "based on population and geographic convenience and uniqueness" and replace phrase "while taking population and the geography as the bases for representation" with "while taking mainly population as the basis"[153]. The amendment was unilateral effort of ruling parties without agreement of UDMF[154].

KP Oli, the communist Prime Minister, started playing China Card from the very moment he became Prime Minister on Oct 12th. China, on other hand, assured Madhesi political leaders that they were not Anti Madhesis[155]. The blockage was impacting the fuel supply in Nepal including plains. However, the priority for PM Oli was to take this as a pretext to establish contact with China and assure Kathmandu population that he was capable for teaching a lesson to plain peoples including India. On October 25th, China government announced the donation of 1.3 million litres of fuel to Nepal[156] which reached Kathmandu in second week of November[157]. Through thisa small amount of Nepal's consumption of less than a week, was to be met.Thissymbolic significance was immense in Kathmandu, which had relied on India exclusively for fuel supply. Nepal further went ahead and signedmemorandum of understandingagreement with China to import gasoline, diesel and cooking gas[158]. The cost of bringing the oil from China was challenged by longer distance and trans-Himalayan hilly terrain, where road connectivity was costly affair.

China's move created panic in Madhesh, and people started feeling China was against the Madhesis movement[159]. Indian government was not worried about the China Card initially[160], but the domestic pressure in India started growing against the government move fearing China's stronger penetration into Nepal[161]. Oil tankers were entering Nepal via Jogbani in first week of October[162], where UDMF was not able to put strong protest like Birgunj.

The protest and police suppression continued. On Bhairahawa border, police in collision with local hilly people clashed with the protesters on first week of October. By second week, hilly people living in plains were seen supporting Madhesi people through rallies in places like Malangwa of Sarlahi[163] and Rajbiraj of Saptari[164]. On the October 14th, another protestor, Sheikh Mahinuddin, was shot in Gaur, almost after a gap of one month.

The negotiation between UDMF and Government was moving at snail pace. In the talks, Madhesi parties wanted all deaths investigated, the army withdrawn, compensation to the recently victim families, free medical treatment to injured people. The political issues with discussion of the significance of past agreements on state boundary, proportional electoral representation, proportional government employment, and citizenship issues[165].

The talk initiative got another frustration, when police again crack downed on protester on 2nd of November. The UDMF group, led by RajendraMahato, had been staging a sit-in on the Birgunj-Raxaul border entry point for days. At around 4:30 in the morning, some 400 members of Nepal police and Nepal Armed forces swarmed to the MaitriBridge and began baton charge on the protestors. The police set on the tents and mattresses on fire forcing the protestors to flee. Around 300 trucks that were stationed in the Nepali territory entered Indian side after police evicted the protesters from the border entry point. At around 8 am, a large number of protesters again gathered and blocked the border point. Protesters also gathered in the city to protest. Police responded with teargas and bullets. At around 12:30 Ashish Ram was killed in police firing.

On November 21, Birendra Ram was killed by police in Bhardah of Saptari when protestors were obstructing the highway. Next day on Nov 22, Nagendra Yadav was killed by police firing at around 11:30 pm at Rupani of Saptari, again on the highway obstruction protest. On the sameday, Dilip Sah was killed in police firing in Hatiya Line in Rajbiraj, who was participating in protest for killing Birendra Ram. Another protestor, Shivshankar Das, was killed by police while protesting near district administration office of Rajbiraj.

The political activity suddenly went up in December first week. The foreign minister of Nepal, Kamal Thapa, presented a four point formula to Indian foreign minister in Delhi, without consulting the Madhesis parties. Indian External Affairs MinisterSushma Swarajgave three pages Statement on Calling Attention Motion on "Situation in Nepal and State of Indo-Nepal Relation" in Rajya Sabha on December 03, 2015. The statement mentioned, "Yesterday, I had another good meeting with the visiting Deputy Prime Minister and Foreign Minister of Nepal, Shri Kamal Thapa. He assured me that there has been progress in the dialogue on the contentious issues with the agitating parties". Seeing the development in Delhi, UDMF leaders got into action and reached embassy to find more about the four point formuladiscussed between Indian and Nepalese foreign minister. Unofficially four-point formula commitment of Nepal to India were guessed to be following[166]

1. To make changes to the boundaries of the provinces through a constitutional amendment
2. In making changes to the boundaries, the ruling alliance shall take the demands of the Madhesis into account
3. The changes to the boundaries will be made by forming a political committee on the basis of political consensus, within three months
4. Ambiguities related to citizenship provisions to be addressed

Madhesi leaders were not happy with the hijacking of core issues and their role. On December 6th, four Madhesi leader landed in Delhi[167]: Upendra

Yadav, Mahanta Thakur, RajendraMahato and Mahendra Rae Yadav. The UDMF leaders met Indian Foreign Minister Sushma Swaraj and put forward their perspective[168]. They also had an interaction program in JNU (Jawaharlal Nehru University) with students and intellectuals. Sushma Swaraj,while replying to a debate, again spoke on Madhesi issues on Dec 7 in Rajya Sabha (upper house of Indian Parliament). She said, "We can push the supplies either by firing at the protestors or crushing them under the trucks. Both are not desirable" and added "Nepal had suddenly adopted the Constitution in two days without any debate, making two amendments in the interim Constitution of 2007, which made the Madhesis to feel that they have lost all rights in that country"[169]. Indian side continued to pursue the Kamal Thapa's commitment through-out December, even though Madhesi leader were not convinced with the proposed solutions[170].

On December 20, Mohammed SamsTabrez was killed in police firing at Gaur of Rautahat in protest of Students against the arrest of student leader Lalan Yadav on previous day. Around 3000 students had gathered in city to express their solidarity with the student leader.

On January 21st, three protestors were killed in police firing at Rangeli Municipality of Morang District. Dropadi Devi Chaudhary, MahadevRishidev, and ShivuMajhi were killed in police firing on January 21. On that day, the youth force, a sister organization of CPN-UML, had organized a programme at 1pm, which had attendance of some seniors UML leaders. In the same area 1,000 members of Nepal Police and Armed police force were deployed in riot gear. On the other side of the location, almost three thousand UDMF protestors gathered shouting slogans such as – "Down with Oli", "Our Madhes Movement is continuing", "we are demanding our rights and our movement is not against any community". By 1:45pm a group of UDMF cadres led by their leaders arrived at the Kali temple, which was close to the programme venue of UML. Following the arrival of UDMF cadres, the police started to fire indiscriminately at the crowd. Dropadi Devi and MahadevRishidev received the bullets in firing. At around 3:30pm, a group of around 200 hilly youth gathered in Dainya and started abusing plains people verbally and physically. Local plains people came out in thousands to protest these assaults. Hilly youth ran away and got police protection, who took them to Rangeli in police vans. A groupof Madhesi people had thrown stones at the police van alleging them of playing double standard. In the meantime, one armed force officer fired at the crowd, hitting ShivuMajhi, who died in ten minutes[171]. Similar people to people conflict was in sight in Belahi Bhairahawa on August 20th where three Madhesis were killed.On August 20, a few thousand people went to shut down Belahiya customs. As they walked through the market areas, they tried to shut down shops in Belahiya market. Suddenly, over 200 unknown people from hill origin, which opposed UDMF's protest, started to beat the protesters. Around 50 to 60 people in civil clothes with short hair, suspected of being members of Nepal police and Armed Police Force, were seen beating the protestors with iron rods, baton and attacking them with Khukuris (Knives used as Arm). The attack resulted in death of three persons; Durgesh Yadav, Sunil Yadav and Rameshwor Pasi[172].

In late January 2016, the talks collapsed. The major parties unilaterally passed constitutional amendments on constituency delineation and quotas that the UDMF and Madhesi civil society activists felt were inadequate. In the Terai, the protestors were tired, their numbers were falling and disillusionment with the UDMF was widespread. There was growing anger on both sides of the border about lost economic opportunities even as the blockade's tactical utility was undermined by the quick rise of a thriving fuel black market. India's sympathy for the blockade was waning, because of the stalemate and domestic criticism of what some saw as the government's botched or bullying policy towards Nepal[173].

During the agitation period, people level support came from border side Indian peoples, independent of Government of India. Most notable was the support of people in Raxaul, who hosted lunch/dinner for protesters. DrRaghuvansh Prasad Singh, a former Indian MP from Lalu Yadav's RJD party, organized programs in many places[174] including Delhi in support of Madhesi agitation, under the banner of Bharat Nepal MaitriYatraSamwad (India-Nepal Friendship Dialogue).

Dr. CK Raut's group, who started Independent Madhesh movement around 2014, was passive during Madhesi mass agitation. On 24 October 2015, they mentioned, their participation in agitation would give political scapegoat to both UMDF and Government to reach any political solution[175]. On December 29, Dr. CK Raut reiterated[176], (1) Will the change in constitution ensure Plains people are employed in Army and deployed in plain instead of Hilly people? If not any change in constitution will be temporary (2) Will the change in constitution ensure none in plain is stateless? (3) Will the constitution guarantee local government jobs go to local people? (4) Will the constitution give local people priority rights over land, water and jungle?

The protest which started on July 21st 2015 continued till the first week of February 2016. On 6 February, traders from both sides of the border reportedly vandalized the protestors' camps and forced them out. Two days later, the UDMF called off the blockade; which had lasted 135 days. The protest ended without any agreement after six months. However, the protest had a far reaching impact on the people of Madhesh building foundation for stronger society. In the early months people were more likely to join a rally if it was not explicitly associated with a Madhesi political party. Women, college students and elderly people joined the agitation, and in some areas, parties and mobilization networks both competed and cooperated to organize support[177]. Over the following months, the increasing death counts contributed to the radicalization of younger protestors.

Initially it appeared as if Madhesi Muslims and Dalits were reluctant to participate in the mainstream Madhesi protests, whose leadership at all levels tends to be dominated by men of a few influential castes. That changed after the constitution was promulgated.In some areas, Dalits and non-Dalits were protesting – and eating – together, breaking what for many is the ultimate caste taboo[178].

People holdingeach other's hands, formed human chain on October 1st. People from all groups, Students-women-elders, were seen standing in water, on street, atagricultural fields, for hundred and hundreds of kilometers as sign of solidarity to the protest. Volunteers were collecting helps for the victims. Immigrants were sending donations for the treatment of injured peoples. Immigrant Madhesis were found protesting in India infront of Nepalese Embassy in Delhi, in Australia infront of Parliament house, in Britain in front of parliament house, in US infront of United Nation Building and also in front of Whitehouse of US president.

The most important change came in the perception of world community to break the type casting of Madhesis as coward caste of world who would not stand for themselves instead wouldrun away if Gurkha fighter fires bullet in the air.

Notes

1. Baral, Leelanatheshwar Sharma (1964); Life and Writing of King Prithivi Narayan Sah, PhD thesis, 1964, pp 216
2. Wright, Daniel (1877); History of Nepal, Cambridge University Press, 1877, pp 183
3. Regmi, Mahesh Chandra (1971); A Study in Nepali Economic History, 1768-1846, Manjuúrî Publishing House, 1971, pp 11
4. Hamilton, Francis Bauchanan (1809); An Account of the District of Purnea in 1809-10, pp-257
5. Appeal to Runway Chaudharis, FalgunSudi 15, 1856, Regmi Research Collection, vol. 24, pp. 146-47. Also see Land Reclamation in the Eastern Tarai Region, Regmi Research Series, Year 10, No. 9, September 1, 1978
6. Regmi, Mahesh (1982); Saptari and Mahottari Affairs, A.D. 1810-11, Regmi Research Series, Year 14, No. 8, Kathmandu: August 1982, pp 123
7. Regmi, Mahesh (1982); Saptari and Mahottari Affairs, A.D. 1810-11, Regmi Research Series, Year 14, No. 8, 1982, pp 128
8. Fouzdars And Munsiffs In Saptari And Mahotari, Regmi Research Series, Year 4, No. 9, 1972, pp – 168
9. Royal Order to Modi Mishra, Baisakh Sudi 9, 1867, Regmi Research Collection, vol. 39, pp. 185-86. Also see Bara, Parsa, and Rautahat in A.D. 1810, Regmi Research Series, Year 10, No. 4, 1979, pp 52
10. Taxation In Mahottari District 1809, Regmi Research Series, Year 3, no. 2, February 1, 1971
11. Taxation In Mahottari District 1809, Regmi Research Series, Year 3, no. 2, February 1, 1971
12. PRNW pp 371
13. Sir Henry Lawrence's journal at Nepal, 23 October and 13 November 1844. Records available in British Library MssEur F85/95. Also see Whelpton, John (1991); Kings, Soldiers and Priests, pp 256
14. Regmi, Mahesh (1985);Eastern Tarai Affairs, A.D. 1846, Regmi Research Series, Year 17, No. 6, June 1985
15. Tandon, Balaram (1953); A Fertile Land the Victim of Neglect, Published in Statesman, Delhi on August 4, 1953
16. Tandon, Balaram (1953); A Fertile Land the Victim of Neglect, Published in Statesman, Delhi on August 4, 1953
17. Nepal (1946-present) - University of Central Arkansas. Downloaded on Dec 21, 2016 from http://uca.edu/politicalscience/dadm-project/asiapacific-region/nepal-1946-present/
18. Karki, Arjun K (2002),Movements from below: land rights movement in Nepal, 2002,pp 10
19. Karki, Arjun K (2002),Movements from below: land rights movement in Nepal, 2002,pp 10
20. Pandey, Binda (2001); Women Participation in Nepali Labour Movement, Studt Report, translated from Nepali, pp 27

21. Pandey, Binda (2001); Women Participation in Nepali Labour Movement, Studt Report, translated from Nepali, pp 27

22. CIA (1952), Origin of Nepal Riots, Central Intelligence Agency, United States of America, declssified document # CIA-RDP82-00457R013300560006-1, dated August 8, 1952

23. Pandey, Binda (2001); Women Participation in Nepali Labour Movement, Studt Report, translated from Nepali, pp 27

24. CIA (1953), Nepal Congress Sponsored Agitation in Biratnagar Area, Central Intelligence Agency, United States of America, declassified document # CIA-RDP80-00810A001800340003-2 , dated July 23, 1953

25. Thapa, Shanker (2001), Peasant insurgence in Nepal, 1951-1960, Nirmala K.C , 2001, pp 77

26. Roy, K.N (1906);The Bengal Tenancy Act: Being Act VIII of 1885, as Amended Up to Date, with Notes, Judicial Rulings, Rules, and Notifications, &c., &c, Majumdar Press, 1906, pp 408

27. Pandey, Binda (2001); Women Participation in Nepali Labour Movement, Studt Report, translated from Nepali, pp 27

28. Pandey, Binda (2001); Women Participation in Nepali Labour Movement, Studt Report, translated from Nepali, pp 25

29. Pandey, Binda (2001); Women Participation in Nepali Labour Movement, Studt Report, translated from Nepali, pp 25

30. Upreti, Bishnu Raj (2008); Land Politics and Conflict in Nepal, Human and Natural Resources Studies Centre (HNRSC), Kathmandu University, 2008, pp 31

31. Gaige, Frederick H (1975); Regionalism and National Unity in Nepal, 1975, pp 115

32. Jha, Navin (2014); Madhes Politics Part 1 - How did Madhes Politics begin in Nepal?, downloaded on Dec 2016 from http://www.dalannepal.net/2014/12/madhes-politics-part-1-how-did-madhes.html

33. Joshi, Bhuwan Lal and Rose Leo E. (1966); Democratic Innovations in Nepal: A Case Study of Political Acculturation, pp 138

34. Rasgotra, Maharajakrishna(2016); A Life in Diplomacy, Penguin UK, Apr 28, 2016

35. Dr. Jogendra Jha was a trained doctor, but set up Nepal's first private construction firm. He also tried to start first Nepali Shipping Company with support from Government. He indirectly dabbled in politics, financing leaders like Tulsi Giri, who was the first Prime Minister under the Panchayat system. Giri and Jha had studied medicine together in Darbhanga, and Giri had encouraged Dr. Jha to migrate to Nepal after they completed their degrees.

36. Dr. Ram Mohan Mahato was an English professor of Patan College, where Prince Gyanendra (who became King in 2001) was studying. Later, Prof. Mahato was offered to tutor Princess Shobha within Royal Palace. Dr. Mahato was pass out of Patna College, and in June 1957 applied for job for Padmakanya Campus after seeing advertisement in Indian paper. Dr. Mahato became head of English department in Patan College. During 1991, he was appointed member of LoksewaAyog (Public Service Commission) selection board.

37. US embassy (1977); New Nepali Ambassador To India, dated 20 May 1977, document # 1977KATHMA02082_c, published on Wikileak. https://wikileaks.org/plusd/cables/1977KATHMA02082_c.html

38. Read Chapter 7 for more details on land reform program.
39. Gaige, Frederick H (1975); Regionalism and National Unity in Nepal, 1975, pp 174
40. Gaige, Frederick H (1975); Regionalism and National Unity in Nepal, 1975, pp 174
41. Gaige, Frederick H (1975); Regionalism and National Unity in Nepal, 1975, pp 175
42. Gaige, Frederick H (1975); Regionalism and National Unity in Nepal, 1975, pp 176
43. Gaige, Frederick H (1975); Regionalism and National Unity in Nepal, 1975, pp 176
44. Gaige, Frederick H (1975); Regionalism and National Unity in Nepal, 1975, pp 177
45. Karki, Arjun K (2002), Movements from below: land rights movement in Nepal, 2002, pp 13
46. Parmanand (1986); The Indian Community in Nepal and the Nepalese Community in India: The Problem of National Integration, Asian Survey, Vol. 26, No. 9 (Sep., 1986), pp 1014
47. US Embassy (1979), GON defends new economic measures, SECRET document # 1975KATHMA01930_b, dated 26 April 1975, published on wikileakshttps://wikileaks.org/plusd/cables/1975KATHMA01930_b.html
48. US Embassy (1979), POLITICAL DEVELOPMENTS IN NEPAL, SECRET document #1979KATHMA05237_e, dated 2 August 1979, published on wikileakshttps://wikileaks.org/plusd/cables/1979KATHMA05237_e.html
49. US Embassy (1979), U.S. ROLE IN NEPAL, SECRET document # 1979KATHMA07210_e, dated 15 November 1979, published on wikileakshttps://wikileaks.org/plusd/cables/1979KATHMA07210_e.html
50. US Embassy (1979), POLITICAL DEVELOPMENTS IN NEPAL, SECRET document #1979KATHMA05237_e, dated 2 August 1979, published on wikileaks. https://wikileaks.org/plusd/cables/1979KATHMA05237_e.html
51. US Embassy (1979), Current Update On Security Situation In Kathmandu And The Terai, SECRET document # 1979KATHMA03117_e, dated 24 May 1979, https://wikileaks.org/plusd/cables/1979KATHMA03117_e.html
52. US Embassy (1979), GON Gives In To All Student Educational Demands, SECRET document #1979KATHMA03054_e, dated 22 May 1979, https://wikileaks.org/plusd/cables/1979KATHMA03054_e.html
53. US Embassy (1979), Political Developments in Nepal, SECRET document #1979KATHMA05237_e, dated 2 August 1979, published on wikileaks. https://wikileaks.org/plusd/cables/1979KATHMA05237_e.html
54. Parmanand (1986); The Indian Community in Nepal and the Nepalese Community in India: The Problem of National Integration, Asian Survey, Vol. 26, No. 9 (Sep., 1986), pp 1014
55. US Embassy (1974), Indian Ambassador's Comments On Indo/Nepalese Relations, SECRET document # 1974KATHMA04836_b, dated 27 November 1974, https://wikileaks.org/plusd/cables/1974KATHMA04836_b.html
56. Dr. Weiner, Myron (1973); The Political Demography of Nepal, Asian Survey, Vol. 13 No. 6, Jun., 1973
57. Joshi, Sushma (2004); Goodwill Hunting, http://sushma.blogspot.com/2004/02/goodwill-hunting-sadbhawana-party.html

58. Nahta, Komal (2001); Did distributors spread anti-Hrithik stories in Nepal?, published Jan 2, 2001 on Rediff. Downloaded from http://m.rediff.com/movies/2001/jan/02hrit.htm

59. Nahta, Komal (2001); Did distributors spread anti-Hrithik stories in Nepal?, published Jan 2, 2001 on Rediff. Downloaded from http://m.rediff.com/movies/2001/jan/02hrit.htm

60. Kakshapati, Nayantara Gurung (2007); In search of reconciliation, Nepali Times, published on Issues # 380, 28 Dec 2007 - 03 Jan 2008

61. Dr. Raut, CK (2013); BairagDekhiBachabSamma (Denial to Defense), Published 2013, pp 3

62. Dhakal, Deependra (2013); Impact Of Quota Phase Out In Garment Industry Of Nepal, A Research Report Submitted to Bodo graduate School of Business, UniversitetiNordland, 2013, pp 34

63. Dastider, Mollica(2007), Understanding Nepal: Muslims in a plural society, Har-Anand Publications, Jun 1, 2007, pp 114

64. Pradhan, Shirish B (2004); Nepal reacts violently to killings in Iraq, rediff news , published on September 1st, 2004, http://www.rediff.com/news/2004/sep/01nep.htm

65. Bell, Thomas (2004); Three dead as Nepalis riot over Iraq deaths, The Telegraph, Published on 2 september 2004, http://www.telegraph.co.uk/news/worldnews/middleeast/iraq/1470820/Three-dead-as-Nepalis-riot-over-Iraq-deaths.html

66. Dixit, Kunda (2004); Black Wednesday, Was this spontaneous combustion or planned conflagration?, Nepali Times, #212, 03 Sept 2004 - 09 Sept 2004

67. Acharya, Bijaya(2006); Interim constitution approved in Nepal, Washigton Post, Published on December 16, 2006. http://www.washingtonpost.com/wp-dyn/content/article/2006/12/16/AR2006121600115.html

68. Ghimire, Yubaraj (2006); Communal clashes in west Nepal, one killed, The Indian Express, Dec 27 2006

69. Kafle, Surendra (2008); Two years on...no compensation in sight, The Himalayan Times, published on December 25, 2008 downloaded from https://thehimalayantimes.com/nepal/two-years-on-no-compensation-in-sight/

70. Elisabeth, Anne (2007); Nepalgunj Riots, anneelisabethblogspot,PublishedMonday, January 22, 2007 downloaded on Dec 2016 from http://anneelisabeth.blogspot.com/2007/01/nepalgunj-riots.html

71. Elisabeth, Anne (2007); Nepalgunj Riots, anneelisabethblogspot,PublishedMonday, January 22, 2007 downloaded on Dec 2016 from http://anneelisabeth.blogspot.com/2007/01/nepalgunj-riots.html

72. Himalayan News Service (2007), Maoist body reshuffled to fight feudalism, The Himalayan Times, published February 04, 2007

73. ICG (2007); Nepal's Troubled Tarai Region, Crisis Group Asia Report, 9 July 2007, pp 12

74. ICG (2007); Nepal's Troubled Tarai Region, Crisis Group Asia Report, 9 July 2007, pp 12

75. ICG (2007); Nepal's Troubled Tarai Region, Crisis Group Asia Report, 9 July 2007, pp 12

76. ICG (2007); Nepal's Troubled Tarai Region, Crisis Group Asia Report, 9 July 2007, pp 13
77. ICG (2007); Nepal's Troubled Tarai Region, Crisis Group Asia Report, 9 July 2007, pp 14
78. ICG (2007); Nepal's Troubled Tarai Region, Crisis Group Asia Report, 9 July 2007, pp 14
79. ICG (2007); Nepal's Troubled Tarai Region, Crisis Group Asia Report, 9 July 2007, pp 14
80. OHCHR Report (2007);Findings of OHCHR-Nepal's Investigations into the 21 March Killings in Gaur and Surrounding Villages ; UN Office of the High Commissioner for Human Rights, Nepal, April 2007 downloaded from http://nepal.ohchr.org/en/resources/Documents/English/reports/IR/Year2007/Gaur.pdf
81. The Madheshi People's Rights Forum (MPRF) led by Upendra Yadav, the Sadbhavana Party (SP) led by RajendraMahato and the Terai-Madhes LoktantrikMurcha (TMDP) led by Mahant Thakur.
82. OHCHR (2008); Summary of human rights concerns arising from the Terai protests of 13 – 29 February 2008, OHCHR-Nepal, Published 27 March 2008, http://nepal.ohchr.org/en/resources/Documents/English/reports/HCR/2008_03_27_Terai_Protest_E.pdf
83. OHCHR (2008); Summary of human rights concerns arising from the Terai protests of 13 – 29 February 2008, OHCHR-Nepal, Published 27 March 2008, http://nepal.ohchr.org/en/resources/Documents/English/reports/HCR/2008_03_27_Terai_Protest_E.pdf
84. Crisis Group (2016); Nepal's Divisive New Constitution: An Existential Crisis, International Crisis Group, Asia Report, N°276, 4 April 2016, pp 4
85. Jha, Navin (2012); The missing voice, Nepali Times, February 14th, 2012 downloaded on Dec 2016 from http://www.nepalitimes.com/blogs/thebrief/2012/02/14/the-missing-voice/
86. UN RHCO (2012); Monthly Update, UN Resident & Humanitarian Coordinator's Office, Nepal, January 2012, pp 3
87. Sah, Laxmi (2014); Demonstrator shot dead in police firing, The Kathmandu Post, Print Edition 2014-10-12http://kathmandupost.ekantipur.com/printedition/news/2014-10-11/demonstrator-shot-dead-in-police-firing.html
88. News (2014); Govt to implement agreements reached with Bara protesters, The Himalayan times, 15 Oct 2014 http://www.thehimalayantimes.com/fullNews.php?headline=Govt+to+implement+agreements+reached+with+Bara+protesters&NewsID=430380
89. Based on author's personal discussion with Simraungarh's resident
90. Build road or hang us. 'सडकदेउयाफाँसीदेउ’ भन्दैप्रधानमन्त्रीलाईज्ञापनपत्र, Ratopati, June 4th, 2015 downloaded on September 18 from http://www.ratopati.com/news/46756 and http://www.ratopati.com/news/47613/
91. Zee news (2014); PM Modi's visit to Janakpur cancelled after protests by opposition parties in Nepal , 24 Nov 2014 http://zeenews.india.com/news/india/pm-modis-visit-to-janakpur-cancelled-after-protests-by-opposition-parties-in-nepal_1502159.html

92. Giri, Anil (2014); Modi's Janakpur visit called off, says Nidhi, The Kathmandu Post, 21 November 2014, http://kathmandupost.ekantipur.com/news/2014-11-21/modis-janakpur-visit-called-off-says-nidhi.html

93. Ekantipur Report (2015); Curfew at Gaur; protestor's death flares up tension , The Kathmandu Post, April 4th, 2015, http://kathmandupost.ekantipur.com/news/2015-04-04/curfew-at-gaur-protestors-death-flares-up-tension.html

94. Ansari,Mohna (2015); Spokeperson, NHRC expresses Concern over Gaur Incidents, National Human Rights Commission, April 5, 2015http://www.nhrcnepal.org/nhrc_new/doc/newsletter/PR-Gaur%20Incident-Strike-Eng-05April2015.pdf

95. 2015; Gaur protest called off, Gorkhapost, April 2015, http://www.gorkhapost.com/gaur-protest-called-off/

96. Editorial (2015); No easy answer, Events in Gaur are a manifestation of the undercurrents of Tarai-Pahad dichotomy, The Kathmandu Post, 7th April 2015, http://kathmandupost.ekantipur.com/news/2015-04-07/no-easy-answer.html

97. Acharya, Ratnaprasad (2015); मध्यरातिधरानमामालपोतरनापीकार्यालय (Dharan have Malpot and Napi office in Midnight), Annapurana Post, June 6th, 2015 http://archive.annapurnapost.com/News.aspx/story/12833

98. Editorial (2015); No easy answer, Events in Gaur are a manifestation of the undercurrents of Tarai-Pahad dichotomy, The Kathmandu Post, 7th April 2015, http://kathmandupost.ekantipur.com/news/2015-04-07/no-easy-answer.html

99. Sah, Tulanarayan (2015); कथाकलैयाको, व्यथामधेसको (Story is of Kalaiya, pain is of Madhesh), Kantipur Daily, 17 Feb 2015 http://kantipur.ekantipur.com/news/2015-02-17/403933.html

100. Jha, Abdesh Kumar (2016); Reforms at Sagarmatha hospital: Lone crusader in hunger strike for past 14 days; The Kathmandu Post, 6 Dec 2016, http://kathmandupost.ekantipur.com/news/2016-12-06/reforms-at-sagarmatha-hospital-lone-crusader-in-hunger-strike-for-past-14-days.html

101. Jha, Jitendra Kumar (2016); Tiwari ends 18-day hunger strike; Myrepublica, Dec 10, 2016 http://www.myrepublica.com/news/10866

102. Post Report (2016); NHRC urges govt to address fasting Tiwari's concerns, The Kathmandu Post, Dec 8, 2016 http://kathmandupost.ekantipur.com/news/2016-12-08/nhrc-urges-govt-to-address-fasting-tiwaris-concerns.html

103. HRW (2015); Like We Are Not Nepali, Protest and Police Crackdown in the Terai Region of Nepal, Human Right Watch, 16 October 2015, pp 3

104. HRW (2015); Like We Are Not Nepali, Protest and Police Crackdown in the Terai Region of Nepal, Human Right Watch, 16 October 2015, pp 3

105. In the donor conference for earthquake relief, Nepal got USD 4.4 billion commitment in June 2015, which was close to government's other revenue for one year. See Shrestha, Prithivi Man (2015); $4.4 bn aid pledged during donor conference, The Kathmandu Post, 2015-06-25. Nepal Govt estimated revenue for 2016 was $4.8 billion (CIA, world factbook).

106. Unofficial translation of sixteen point agreement http://www.satp.org/satporgtp/countries/nepal/document/papers/16-point_Agreement.htm

107. Kamat, Ram Kumar (2015); Apex court stays implementation of 16-point pact, The Himalayan Times, 20-6-2015

108. Kamat, Ram Kumar (2015); Apex court stays implementation of 16-point pact, The Himalayan Times, 20-6-2015
109. Kamat, Ram Kumar (2015); Apex court stays implementation of 16-point pact, The Himalayan Times, 20-6-2015
110. Crisis Group (2016); Nepal's Divisive New Constitution: An Existential Crisis, International Crisis Group, Asia Report, N°276, 4 April 2016, pp 8
111. Crisis Group (2016); Nepal's Divisive New Constitution: An Existential Crisis, International Crisis Group, Asia Report, N°276, 4 April 2016, pp 8
112. Rastriya Samachar Samiti (2015); Janakpur shutdown continues, The Himalayan Times, July 21, 2015
113. Crisis Group (2016); Nepal's Divisive New Constitution: An Existential Crisis, International Crisis Group, Asia Report, N°276, 4 April 2016, pp 9
114. Republica (2015); Strike hits normal life in Terai, Myrepublica, 21 Jul 2015
115. Crisis Group (2016); Nepal's Divisive New Constitution: An Existential Crisis, International Crisis Group, Asia Report, N°276, 4 April 2016, pp 9
116. Special Report (2016); NEPAL: Protest & Repression - State Responsibility for 37 Killings During Protests in Terai The Asian Human Rights Commission (AHRC), and Terai Human Rights Defenders Alliance ('the THRD Alliance'), May 23, 2016, pp 46
117. Crisis Group (2016); Nepal's Divisive New Constitution: An Existential Crisis, International Crisis Group, Asia Report, N°276, 4 April 2016, pp 12
118. Bhusal, Thira L &Dahal, Ashok (2015); Big 3 draw new 7-province map, Myrepublica, 22 Aug 2015
119. Special Report (2016); NEPAL: Protest & Repression - State Responsibility for 37 Killings During Protests in Terai The Asian Human Rights Commission (AHRC), and Terai Human Rights Defenders Alliance ('the THRD Alliance'), May 23, 2016, pp 47
120. NHRC Press Note (2015), Remain on High Alert to cease Repercussion of Tikapur Incident, National Human Rights Commission, Central Office, HariharBhawan, Pulchowk, Lalitpur, Nepal, September 10, 2015
121. Crisis Group (2016); Nepal's Divisive New Constitution: An Existential Crisis, International Crisis Group, Asia Report, N°276, 4 April 2016, pp 12
122. Special Report (2016); NEPAL: Protest & Repression - State Responsibility for 37 Killings During Protests in Terai The Asian Human Rights Commission (AHRC), and Terai Human Rights Defenders Alliance ('the THRD Alliance'), May 23, 2016, pp 48-50
123. Special Report (2016); NEPAL: Protest & Repression - State Responsibility for 37 Killings During Protests in Terai The Asian Human Rights Commission (AHRC), and Terai Human Rights Defenders Alliance ('the THRD Alliance'), May 23, 2016, pp 48-50
124. Special Report (2016); NEPAL: Protest & Repression - State Responsibility for 37 Killings During Protests in Terai The Asian Human Rights Commission (AHRC), and Terai Human Rights Defenders Alliance ('the THRD Alliance'), May 23, 2016, pp 52

125. Special Report (2016); NEPAL: Protest & Repression - State Responsibility for 37 Killings During Protests in Terai The Asian Human Rights Commission (AHRC), and Terai Human Rights Defenders Alliance ('the THRD Alliance'), May 23, 2016, pp 51-53
126. Special Report (2016); NEPAL: Protest & Repression - State Responsibility for 37 Killings During Protests in Terai The Asian Human Rights Commission (AHRC), and Terai Human Rights Defenders Alliance ('the THRD Alliance'), May 23, 2016, pp 54-55
127. Yadav, Brij Kumar (2015); Six killed in police firing in Janakpur- Jaleshwar, The Himalayan Times, September 12, 2015
128. HRW (2015); Like We Are Not Nepali, Protest and Police Crackdown in the Terai Region of Nepal, Human Right Watch, 16 October 2015, pp 1
129. HRW (2015); Like We Are Not Nepali, Protest and Police Crackdown in the Terai Region of Nepal, Human Right Watch, 16 October 2015, pp 1
130. Special Report (2016); NEPAL: Protest & Repression - State Responsibility for 37 Killings During Protests in Terai The Asian Human Rights Commission (AHRC), and Terai Human Rights Defenders Alliance ('the THRD Alliance'), May 23, 2016, pp 56-57
131. Himalayan News Service (2015); Child killed in Rupandehi police firing, The Himalayan Times, 16-9-2015
132. Special Report (2016); NEPAL: Protest & Repression - State Responsibility for 37 Killings During Protests in Terai The Asian Human Rights Commission (AHRC), and Terai Human Rights Defenders Alliance ('the THRD Alliance'), May 23, 2016, pp 56-57
133. Crisis Group (2016); Nepal's Divisive New Constitution: An Existential Crisis, International Crisis Group, Asia Report, N°276, 4 April 2016, pp 17
134. Pandey, Leknath (2015); Modi sends Jaishankar as special envoy on the eve of constitution commencement, The Himalayan Times, published September 17, 2015
135. Myrepublica (2015); Indian Foreign Secretary Jaishankar in Kathmandu, Myrepublica, Sep 18, 2015
136. Pradhan, Prateek (2015); Wrong advice, Myrepublica, Sep 16, 2015
137. Press Release (2015), Nepal Constitutional Process, John Kirby, Department Spokesperson, Washington, DC September 14, 2015
138. Crisis Group (2016); Nepal's Divisive New Constitution: An Existential Crisis, International Crisis Group, Asia Report, N°276, 4 April 2016, pp 18
139. Crisis Group (2016); Nepal's Divisive New Constitution: An Existential Crisis, International Crisis Group, Asia Report, N°276, 4 April 2016, pp 18
140. GoI (2015); Statement on the situation in Nepal, Ministry of External Affairs, Government of India, September 20, 2015, http://www.mea.gov.in/press-releases.htm?dtl/25821/Statement+on+the+situation+in+Nepal
141. UN News Center (2015); In wake of adoption of Nepal's constitution, Ban stresses need for dialogue, non-violence, published 21 September 2015, http://www.un.org/apps/news/story.asp?NewsID=51931
142. Post Report (2015); One protester dies, several hurt in Terai demonstrations, The Kathmandu Post, 2015-09-21

143. Interview with Mahant Thakur, Govt should talk to countrymen to resolve the crisis: Thakur, Myreublica, November 9, 2015 http://admin.myrepublica.com/interview/story/30851.html

144. Crisis Group (2016); Nepal's Divisive New Constitution: An Existential Crisis, International Crisis Group, Asia Report, N°276, 4 April 2016, pp 19

145. Jha, Prashant (2015); In Nepal, where a battle for rights merges with geo-politics, Hindustan Times, Oct 01, 2015

146. GoI (2015); Statement on the situation in Nepal, Ministry of External Affairs, Government of India, September 21, 2015http://www.mea.gov.in/press-releases.htm?dtl/25825/Statement_on_the_situation_in_Nepal

147. Crisis Group (2016); Nepal's Divisive New Constitution: An Existential Crisis, International Crisis Group, Asia Report, N°276, 4 April 2016, pp 20

148. Mishra, Pramod (2015); A case for change, Oped, The Kathmandu Post, 2015-09-17

149. Himalayan News Service (2015); Madhesi Front takes out dhoti rally in Janakpur, The Himalayan Times, Sep 3

150. दिनदिनैमान्छेमर्दैछन्, ओली 'आँपझरेको' भन्दैछन्, Mero Sansar, September 10, 2015 http://www.mysansar.com/2015/09/19333/

151. Special Editorial (2015); As Tarai burns, parties could at least put CA process on hold, The Kathmandu Post, 2015-09-11

152. Crisis Group (2016); Nepal's Divisive New Constitution: An Existential Crisis, International Crisis Group, Asia Report, N°276, 4 April 2016, pp 20

153. Myrepublica (2015); Govt registers amendments to new constitution, Myrepublica, Oct 8, 2015

154. Myrepublica (2015); Amendment proposals unacceptable: Yadav, Myrepublica, Oct 8 2015

155. Jha, Prashant (2015); China 'assures' agitating Tarai leaders it is not anti-Madhesi, Hindustan Times, 8-10-2015

156. AFP (2015); China to donate fuel to Nepal: official, Daily Mail, 25 October 2015

157. Post(2015); 27 tankers of fuel enter nepal via rasuwagadhi, The Kathmandu Post, Nov 8, 2015

158. Associated Press (2015); Fuel-starved Nepal signs agreement with China for oil, ending India's monopoly, Fox news World, Oct 29, 2015, http://www.foxnews.com/world/2015/10/29/fuel-starved-nepal-signs-agreement-with-china-for-oil-ending-india-monopoly.html

159. Myrepublica (2015); China's role against Madhesi movement: RajendraMahato, 3-11-2015

160. TNN (2016); Unfazed by 'China card', India backs Madhesis; asks Nepal to resolve dispute, Times of India, Nov 5, 2015, http://timesofindia.indiatimes.com/india/Unfazed-by-China-card-India-backs-Madhesis-asks-Nepal-to-resolve-dispute/articleshow/49666795.cms

161. Nayak, Nihar R (2015); Nepal's oil diplomacy could hurt India, The Hindu Businessline, 11-November-2015

162. Myrepublica (2015); 58 cargo vehicles including 32 carrying fuel enter Nepal Monday Myrepublica, October 5, 2015, http://admin.myrepublica.com/feature-article/story/29281/32-fuel-tankers-enter-nepal-thru-jogbani.html

163. News (2015); Pahadi community organises rally to support Madhes agitation - Post Report, Sarlahi, The Kathmandu Post, Oct 15, 2016 http://kathmandupost.ekantipur.com/news/2015-10-15/pahadi-community-organises-rally-to-support-madhes-agitation.html

164. JitendraKhadka (2015); मधेसीकोपक्षमासप्तरीमानहाडीसमदायद्वाराप्रदर्शन, Kantipur Post, Oct 28, 2015

165. Interview with Mahant Thakur, सरकारलेमधेशआन्दोलनलाईबेवास्तागरिरहेकोछ-महन्थठाकुर, today Khabar, November 11, 2015 http://www.todaykhabar.com/2015/11/08/32273/

166. In Delhi, Kamal Thapa signed four-point ‘commitment’ to end Nepal crisis, Online Kabar, Dec 5, 2015 http://www.onlinekhabar.com/2015/12/358807/

167. Myrepublica (2015); UDMF officially says four leaders visiting to India, myrepublica, Dec 5, 2016

168. IANS (2015); Nepal's Madhesi Leaders Meet Foreign Minister Sushma Swaraj, NDTV, December 06, 2015

169. External Affair Minister Replying to a debate in Rajya Sabha on India-Nepal relations, Rajya Sabha, 7 Dec 2015http://rstv.nic.in/no-big-brotherly-approach-nepal-want-early-solution-india.html

170. Post (2015); Rae seeks Morcha's take on Cabinet move, Indian envoy urges Madhesi leaders to lift ‘blockage’ and seek solution through dialogue, The Kathmandu Post, Dec 22, 2015, http://kathmandupost.ekantipur.com/printedition/news/2015-12-22/rae-seeks-morchas-take-on-cabinet-move.html

171. Special Report (2016); NEPAL: Protest & Repression - State Responsibility for 37 Killings During Protests in Terai The Asian Human Rights Commission (AHRC), and Terai Human Rights Defenders Alliance (‘the THRD Alliance’), May 23, 2016, pp 62

172. Special Report (2016); NEPAL: Protest & Repression - State Responsibility for 37 Killings During Protests in Terai The Asian Human Rights Commission (AHRC), and Terai Human Rights Defenders Alliance (‘the THRD Alliance’), May 23, 2016, pp 47-48

173. Crisis Group (2016); Nepal's Divisive New Constitution: An Existential Crisis, International Crisis Group, Asia Report, N°276, 4 April 2016, pp 20

174. Post Report (2016); Madhes agitation is not only Nepal's problem: Bihar leader Singh, The Kathmandu Post, Feb 1, 2017

175. https://ckraut.wordpress.com/training-materials/facebook-posts-2015oct/

176. Dr. CK Raut facebook, December 29, 2016. https://www.facebook.com/drckraut/posts/1392121637495989:0

177. Crisis Group (2016); Nepal's Divisive New Constitution: An Existential Crisis, International Crisis Group, Asia Report, N°276, 4 April 2016, pp. 13.

178. Crisis Group (2016); Nepal's Divisive New Constitution: An Existential Crisis, International Crisis Group, Asia Report, N°276, 4 April 2016, pp. 13.

9

Future of Madhesh

Decoding the Madhesi Needs

Like any human being in the world, the basic needs of Madhesis are same. It follows the same pattern that you can see in United States of America, or Africa or Europe or China or Gulf country, etc. Taking help of Maslow hierarchy of needs, we can classify Nepal's plain peoples' needs limited to bottom two levels of Maslow Hierarchy of needs; Physical need and safety need. Physical needs consisting of food, cloth, house, health, road for transportation. Security of body, food, property, employment, resource, morality and family.

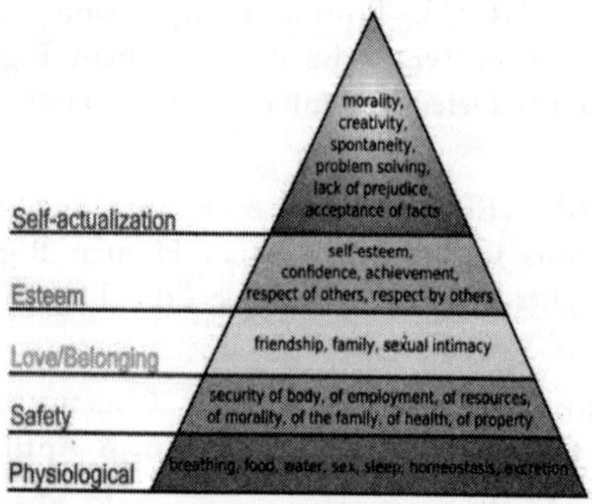

Maslow Hierarchy of Needs

Maslow defines things from an individual, society and group perspective, and ignores the existence of State, government, tax, politics and citizenship card. State, Government, Politics, Citizenship care are human constructs, introduced very recently in the human history, to help in the process of meeting the needs unlisted in Maslow Hierarchy. The human constructs should facilitate rather than create hurdle in meeting the needs.

Citizenship card does certify a sense of emotional belonging to a country, and is of value to the well-off elites. Common people's citizen cards are linked to physical need and security need. Without citizenship card, Madhesi people do not have safety to lands, property, and employment. They cannot inherit the land that they owned before 1964, the year in which the citizenship card was introduced. Today, they neither can get a job nor can open bank account without citizenship card. Recently, there has been discussion of allowing voting only if they have citizenship, and that implies without citizenship their voice will also cease. Citizenship card has instead deteriorated the issue of basic needs for Madhesis, which percolates to level second and level first of the Maslow Hierarchy.

There are justified reasons for plain people to ask for ensuring Maslow Hierarchy 1st and 2nd level needs. First, Kathmandu government claims it represents people of Madhesh and thus collects all the tax and controls resources in Madhesh. In return, Madhesh people are asking for the accountability of the tax, benefit of the tax, and fruits of the resources. What has Hill given to Plain in exchange of foods and Kinds plain has passed to Hill? At the next level of discourse, Madhesis are asking (i) have we outsourced the Madhesh Governance to Hill people? Or (ii) have we collaborated with Hill people to have common government in Kathmandu? These questions are important, because it helps to measure the cost and trust. If outsourced, as Kathmandu likes to behave, then it means Madhesh has to bear the cost of governance that Kathmandu is providing to the people of Madhesh. However the notion of outsourcing itself defies the concept of democracy, equality and participation theme that is the core of governance. Governance means collaboration, rather than outsourcing. Collaboration requires two way flow, two way trust. And probably this is the center of conflict. Hill people want Madhesis to believe that they are ready to provide Governance to the people of Madhesh, however, Hill people are not trusting Madhesis to allow them to share government jobs. Hill people feel they should be allowed to visit and work in Madhesh, however there is no reciprocity where Plain people are allowed to visit and work in Hill. Hill people want Madhesi to accept Hill people as CDO (chief district officer) of their plain district, however Hill people are not ready to accept plain people as CDO of hill districts. As a convenience sampling, one can have a show piece Madhesi on a government role, however population follows census in mass, and the reality of mass sampling shown unequal distribution of trust and acceptability of Madhesi.

While there exists uneven trust between Hills and Plains, people of plains are aspiring to govern on their own needs; physical and security related. In whatever way the future politics takes shape, time will decide, however following SWOT analysis will assist in ensuring basic needs of people.

SWOT Analysis of Plain and it's people

Strength (Internal)

Fertile Land

These lands are most productive in the region. They get plenty of water and nutrient from river flowing from Himalaya and in return gets maximum agri produce, specially the rice grain that consumes plenty of water.

A comparative research was done by A Campbell in 1837 that was submitted to Brian Hodgson[1]. The report illustrates the competitive advantage of plain land in rice production, the main staple of the region, over Tirhut and Nepal Valley.

The produce from transplanted rice in the Terai ranges from 10 to 80 and even to 100 maunds per Bigha. The latter is a very unusual quantity. 20 maunds per Bigha is a fair crop in the best lands under regular cultivation; 30 maunds an excellent one; and 40 maunds may be considered as a high average of the produce in a favorable season. 60 to 80 and 100 maunds per Bigha are only known in single fields and for the most part in newly cultivated lands.

Let us now compare the gross produce of one crop from similar (or very nearly similar) measurements of land in Plain land Terai, Tirhut and Nepal Valley.

The above gives the advantage of Tirhut soils over the Nepal Valley ones, for the production of wheat, as nearly 4 to 1. Terai soils produce double amount of broadcast rice compared to Tirhut. For transplanted rice, Terai produce 25% more than Nepal Valley and 100% more than Tirhut soil. Tirhut land has a productive power by this return, in the pulse crops of nearly 3 to 1 above Nepal Valley. In the production of the sugar cane, the Terai and Tirhut have a decided superiority over Nepal Valley.

Agriculture Grains	Produce of land in the Terai per Bigha in maunds	Produce of land in Tirhut Per Bigha in maunds	Produce of land in Nepal Valley per Bigha in maunds[2]
Wheat	not grown*	30.20.5	8.5.3
Broadcast Sown Rice	80.60.40.20.10	40.30.12.7	none grown
Transplanted Rice	100.80.40.30.15	50.45.15	80.40.30.25.20.8
Masoori (Split Red Lentil)	not known	12.10	4½.4.3
Kerow	20 to 10	12.15	5.4.3.
Moong (Split Green gram)	not known	12.15	4.3.2½
Chana (chickpea)	do do	20.15.10	Scarcely Grown
Oorid (Split Black gram)	not grown	little grown	4½.4.3

*Table: Comparative gross production of crops in Terai, Tirhut and Nepal Valley. Abstracted from A Campbell report of 1837. * Wheat production has started in Terai around 1950s or so. It was not grown before as water content in soil was high before.*

In addition to crop, the plain land has strength in timber production. One of the world's best timber "Sal" is produced in the jungle of Madhesh. British recognized its value early in seventeenth century who used it for making ships in Calcutta. In eighteenth century, Kathmandu valley imported timber from Terai. Every timber long enough for the beam of a house was brought from the Terai[3]. British imported Timber for the railway construction in India and Sal timber was exported to as far as London.

> Letter from Mahommed Reza Khawn, the acting Nawab at Murshedabad, to Souchit Roy Fowzdar at Purnea
>
> Transmitted by Mr Richard Barwell in his Address to the Select Committee as recorded in their Proceedings of the 14th January 1766
>
> HERE are several persons gone into the Morung and are now purchasing and carrying away from thence timbers. As there is a demand for timbers for the Sircar, I write to you, that you should prohibit any persons from purchasing and carrying timbers from thence. In a short time some person will be sent from hence to buy up all the timber of Morung. Look upon these orders as peremptory.

Historical Letter showing British and Murshidabad Nawab's Interest in Terai Timber in 1766 AD. Source Guillaume Bolts[4]

Water Resource

Plain land is at the bottom of Himalayan range, so ideally before reaching water into Ganga, water passes through the plain land networked with multiple rivers and rivulet. During rainy seasons water commonly over flows the river bed and replenish the water reservoirs, ponds and lakes. The fresh water makes ways to the land, and thus the water bed in these area is favorable. After digging 10 feets, we get water table and good drinking water is found at around 100 feets below ground level. In most places, drinking water is plentiful and can be fetched with dug well or tube well. Few places are contaminated with minerals like Arsenic and irons, making it less suitable for drinking water. In few places, water pressure in ground is so high due to Terai being seismic zone between Indian plate and Eurasia plate that on finding a small outlet from ground water keeps coming out without motor engine or mechanical force. The belt between Kurtha and Mujeliya near Janakpur is one where multiple tube wells can be seen throwing water 24 hours, since years, without any external force applied.

Economic activities are productive with the water resources. We have seen above how water helps in maintaining competitive advantage in rice production to Terai land. Rice fields can also be seen having small fish, crabs and snails during August, which helps poor people in getting protein diets. Water reserves, mostly ponds are helping in commercial fish production. Fish species like Silver carp, Grass carp, Bighead carp, Rohu and Naini are commercial preferences. There are few wild fish variety too like; Bowari, Gaincha, Kotri (like Tilapia), Mogra, and Garai. Mogra is carnivores and have been lately introduced with commercial variety too. There are smaller wild fish too like Chenggra, Pothia, and Jhinga being choice of the people.

Dayanagar VDC in Rupendehi district has become one of the model villages for fish farming. Fisheries in Dayanagar started 32 years ago, but commercial farming gained momentum only after the launch of a "fisheries campaign" seven years ago. Around 550 farmers are involved in commercial fish farming in the village, each household having at least a pond, producing nearly 1,000 tonnes of fish annually. Fish species like Silver carp, Grass carp, Bighead carp, Rohu and Naini are raised in 1,200 ponds spread on 167 hectares. Productivity stands at six tonnes per hectare[5].

Dhanusha district, whose capital is Janakpur, produced 305 metric tonnes of fish in 2014-2015, worth NRs. 120 million[6]. There is growing market demand and places like Janakpur too see around 50% of fish imported from Hyderabad, India. Around 20 years back, there was surplus of fish production, and local fish used to make way to Muzaffarpur in India and Kathmandu in Nepal.

There is Fisheries development center in Janakpur, however center has failed to develop the physical infrastructure for increasing and promoting fishery to meet the demand for lack of budget.

Hardworking People

Plain people have garnered multiple appreciations for being hardworking. Hamilton has noted plain people as "hard-favored people"[7]. A Campbell, assistant resident in Kathmandu in 1837, appreciated the plain people saying they are productive class[8].

The whole of plain land was made productive due to hard work of plain people. The produce of Plain land made way to hills in the form of extracts that enabled them to build road and lavish buildings like Singha Durbar. Both Shah and Rana rulers should own debt to plain people for their lavish life style.

Primarily most of the plain people are skilled in agriculture. Gradually, people are getting into other professions too on their own, because of the least opportunities available to them in state employment. Within the government jobs, they are most likely to be found in school teaching jobs.

Today, plain people are in majority in the exported labor groups, working in tough conditions. All these data indicates the hard working nature of plain people and they are not shy of working hard.

Large Group of Expatriate

Based on seven years of trend between 2008 and 2015, 56% of foreign labor immigrants are from plain districts. Top 10 among the labor exporting districts are plain districts[9]. Dhanusha and Mahottari being the first and second most exporting districts. These labor go there to work in hard manual jobs in extreme hot climate of gulf fields. Majority of them are distributed evenly in three destinations; Qatar, Saudi Arabia and Malaysia.

Plain peoples have also migrated to developed countries either in high skill jobs or through higher study opportunities. They are present in Europe,

District	2008-09	2009-10	2010-11	2011-12	2012-13	2013-14	2014-15	Total	%	Rank
Dhanusha	10,950	11,942	11,923	11,643	18,894	21,357	22,259	108,968	5.01%	1
Mahottari	6,136	25,223	13,687	9,476	12,606	15,640	16,740	99,508	4.57%	2
Jhapa	9,535	10,618	11,004	11,778	17,974	18,655	18,182	97,746	4.49%	3
Morang	6,983	9,566	10,399	10,794	16,791	17,829	17,641	90,003	4.14%	4
Siraha	7,508	9,543	10,290	9,223	13,944	17,191	17,072	84,771	3.90%	5
Nawalparasi	5,161	6,461	8,067	8,505	12,310	12,992	12,774	66,270	3.05%	6
Saptari	4,072	7,286	7,480	7,332	11,273	13,418	14,040	64,901	2.98%	7
Sunsari	4,410	5,923	6,620	7,623	11,595	12,774	13,145	62,090	2.85%	8
Sarlahi	3,478	5,200	5,719	5,723	10,335	13,330	14,618	58,403	2.68%	9
Rupandehi	3,419	4,163	5,428	5,986	10,850	11,700	12,325	53,871	2.48%	10
Dang	3,707	5,000	5,169	5,080	8,197	9,994	10,195	47,342	2.18%	11
Chitwan	4,320	4,266	4,841	5,834	9,406	9,547	8,687	46,901	2.16%	12
Makwanpur	2,865	3,447	3,635	4,832	8,527	9,559	9,169	42,034	1.93%	14
Bara	1,774	2,527	3,639	4,158	7,200	8,928	9,014	37,240	1.71%	17
Udaypur	2,989	3,981	3,772	4271	6,360	7,632	7,667	36,672	1.69%	20
Sindhuli	2,416	3,332	3,828	5,091	6,698	7481	7,712	36,558	1.68%	21
Rautahat	1,552	2,134	2,873	3,298	6,606	8,858	9,719	35,040	1.61%	23
Kailali	584	7,385	9,372	7,302	2,572	3,375	3,678	34,268	1.57%	25
Kapilbastu	1,224	2,192	2,994	3,152	6,437	7,118	8,059	31,176	1.43%	33
Banke	993	1,859	2,416	2,538	4,815	5,581	5,977	24,179	1.11%	39
Parsa	885	1,194	1,743	2,244	3,804	6,470	6,167	22,507	1.03%	42
Bardiya	737	1,356	1,995	1,961	3,854	4,385	4,948	19,236	0.88%	46
Kanchanpur	670	1,179	1,705	1,482	2,956	3,438	3,622	15,052	0.69%	54
Surkhet	586	1,079	1,586	1,356	2,898	3,585	3,959	15,049	0.69%	55
Total	86,954	136,856	140,185	140,682	216,902	250,837	257,369	1,229,785	56.52%	

Table: Number of workers issued a labor permit (excluding individual applicants) by Government of Nepal between 2008/09–2014/15. Data Analysis focused on plains districts[10].

primarily Belgium, United States of America, Britain, Australia and few other countries, however their number is estimated not more than 10 thousands together. Among the most successful expatriate person of plain origin are Dr. Upendra Mahato (Businessman), Aditya Jha (Entrepreneur) , Udit Narayan Jha (Singer), and Dr. Sukhdev Shah (ex IMF employee).

Culture (Respect Education, Language, Secular, Open)

Culture is vast area, what to cover and not cover. The focus here is to discuss few aspects of culture. Those are strength, appreciation for education, richness of language, secular social structure and open society. We have seen in Chapter 7, there is lowest amount of government support for educational infrastructure and teacher deployment in Terai. Despite these challenges, people have managed to get educated. Traditionally, education was concentrated among the Brahmins caste, and they commanded respect, and today the lowest among the society have understood the value of education. There has been awareness even in the poorest among the caste to invest in their kids' education. Private English medium schools have come up in towns and villages to cater to the demand for education. For higher education, plain people are recently moving to India and few people who can afford are entering western universities. Before 1990, these students were to be found in border side Indian colleges. After 1990, they completed Inter and graduation in collages located in plains like Janakpur, Biratnagar, Birgunj, Nepalgunj and Kapilbastu. For Master's degree they preferred Kathmandu, where most of the government vacancies are recruited. In the recent time, while getting jobs in government post are becoming tough, the plains students are entering Indian metro cities like Delhi, Banglore and Pune for study and Jobs in private sectors.

Language is another strong area of plain people. Maithili is second largest language group in Nepal and is spoken and understood in region East of Gandaki, center being Rajbiraj. Bhojpuri and Bajika are primarily spoken in the region between Bagmati and Gandaki. In Immediate west of Gandaki, Awadhi is popular, and Tharu is largest group in west of Gandaki.

Each group has its uniqueness and strength. Madhesh has been center of Maithili during Karnat dynasty in 13th-14th centuries. Among the earliest books written in north India are in Maithili; Varna-Ratnakar written by Jyotirisvara (in 14th century) and Vidyapati poems (14th and 15th century).

Maithili is closer to the Bengali language than any other language, and thus Vidyapati used to be regarded as one of the earliest poets of Bengali, primary language of Bangladesh and West Bengal. During 15th century, the script of Maithili was like Bengali Script, however little is known about the history, how it got transferred to Devanagari script during Muslim and British rule. In fact, now Maithili is also considered to be a dialect of Hindi as Awadhi, Brij and Bhojpuri. Newari Kings in Kathmandu have written many poems and literature in Maithili language. Awadhi is language in which Tulsi Das wrote his Ramayana entitled Ramcharitmanas. Awadhi is close to Hindi for all purpose. Bhojpuri is relatively new language, however the language has received lot of significance due to its acceptance in Bollywood movies. Lately, pure Bhojpuri movies are also making market among the regional markets, including at the regions where Maithili is spoken. Tharu is unique in style, however it has borrowed words from the nearest languages across region, from East to West. Though there are variances in these languages and they are different from each other, most of the people can still understand each of these languages. However to have free flow of communication, people jump to Hindi as preference or to Nepali, if they are trained in school.

Secular social structure is the strongest fabric of the plains people. There are many common festivals among Tharu and remaining areas, like; Faguwa, Jitiya, Jursital, Sama chakewa, Makar Sankranti, and etc. Muslim and Hindu celebrate Daha (Tazia) together. Also, Hindu people worship Muslim saints; Mira Sahib and Panchpirs. Muslim saint is also believed to have friendship with Karikh Maharaj, another saint worshipped in the houses of plain's people. There is also a temple of Karikh Maharaj at Paraul village, around 8 km north of Jaleshwar, where devotees go and worship. King Salhesh is another cult followed by almost every caste in plain including Brahmins, though King Salhesh is primarily worshiped by Dusad and Dom.

Society is open and this can be deduced from the fact that plain districts voted and elected hill people, the recent migrants in plains, in 1981 and 1986 elections contradicting the earlier assumptions that only Madhesi could represent them[11].

Marriage Across Border

Indian side leads in the introduction of changes in different area; education, women empowerment, technology adoption, farming methodology, politics and business opportunities. These changes are pushed in frontier villages and cities from bigger cities like Patna, Delhi and Kolkata. Family relationship established through marriage facilitates the movement of these changes into plain land Madhesh. The Brides come as change agent from India to Madhesh.

Few women born in India, married in Madhesh and also made big in public life[12].

Name	Birth Place	Contribution
Mrs. Sita Devi Yadav	Madhubani, Bihar, India	Nepali Congress treasurer 2016, Cabinet minister for Peace and Reconstruction in 2016 during Prachanda Government
Mrs. Babita Labh Kayastha	Delhi, India	Principal of Nepal Armed Police Force School, Kirtipur, Kathmandu
Mrs. Sarita Giri	India	Constituent Assembly (I) member 2008-12 from Sadbhavana Party. Sadbhavana Party president of one of the factions. Minister for Transport and Labor in 2012 during Baburam Bhattarai's government.
Mrs. Mohammadi Siddiqui	Gorakhpur, UP	Ashoka fellowship Award Winner and Constituent Assembly (I) member 2008-12 from Nepali Congress
Mrs. Basanti Devi Jha	Dharkha, India	Constituent Assembly (I) members 2008-12 from Terai Madhesh LP party
Mrs. Chandan Sah	Sitamarhi, Bihar	Constituent Assembly (I) member 2008-12 from Terai Madhesh LP party
Mrs. Karima Begum	India	Constituent Assembly (I) member 2008-12 from Madhesh PRF party
Mrs. Krishna Thakur	India	Constituent Assembly (I) member 2008-12 from Nepali Congress
Mrs. Lila Devi Mehta	Arariya, Bihar	Constituent Assembly (I) member 2008-12 from Maoist party
Ms. Renu Yadav	India	Constituent Assembly (I) member 2008-12 from Madhesh PRF party
Mrs. Munni Kumari Gupta	Supaul, Bihar	Constituent Assembly (I) member 2008-12 from Nepali Congress
Mrs. Nilam Barma	Brahmapuri, Bihar	Constituent Assembly (I) member 2008-12 from Madhesh PRF party
Mrs. Ramani Ram	Madhubani, Bihar, India	Constituent Assembly (I) member 2008-12 from Terai Madhesh LP party
Mrs. Rambha Devi	Eastern Champaran, Bihar	Constituent Assembly (I) member 2008 12 from Madhesh PRF party
Mrs. Shanti Devi Chamar	India	Constituent Assembly (I) member 2008-12 from UML party
Mrs. Surita Sah	Madhubai, India	Constituent Assembly (I) member 2008-12 from Madhesh PRF party

Open Border with India

Open border with India has benefitted Hilly people economically more than plain people. Poor Hill people use the open border facility to look for employment opportunities in India, who have high demand for security jobs and do not require any work permit to work in India. Poor labor of plain had used open border to seek seasonal agricultural jobs or manual jobs in Assam and Punjab before 1990s. In recent time, most of the poor labor find themselves in Gulf countries.

Open border facilitates hawker traders to move across border to sell their goods in weekly haat bazar or villages by roaming. These hawkers earn their livelihood by selling vegetable, fruits, books, cloths, bangles, and fashionable accessories. They transport their goods on cycles and in old days they used either horse or their own head.

Open border gives most benefit to poor people living at the bottom of pyramid across border, who derive their living from informal sectors. Middle class is next to derive the benefit through ease of transportation and communication. Upper class are less likely to promote open border, rather they might prefer closed controlled border, because it will give discretionary power to them to extract tax from poor people.

Border is contiguous to plain and expand around 800 KM, thus it's natural for plain people to get benefitted with freedom in movement; goods and people. Open border also helps sometime in border transportation due to better road and communication features on Indian side. India is expanding road network at frontier. A person in Birgunj is likely to use Indian rail network to reach point close to Siraha. When there is political agitation, a plain person can travel from Biratnagar to Birgunj or Nepalgunj through Indian road, and that was the case during 1950s before construction of East-West highway.

Center of Buddha, Sita, and Janak and Archeological sites

Buddha, Sita and Janak are all world renowned icons and they give enormous branding to plain land. Similarly there are many archeological sites, waiting for excavations, and some had been explored too. These sites are linked to early Gupta period, Licchavi Period, Karnat Dynasty and Sen Kingdoms. The prominent among them are Simraungadh, Lumbini, Janakpur and Salhesh Phulwari. Details have been discussed in chapter 3.

Weakness (Internal)

Caste System

Caste system may be seen traditionally as performing the following functions:

(i) It minimizes economic competition by pre-determining the occupation of various caste groups.

(ii) By restricting and limiting the range of choosing spouse, it helps its members in their endeavor of choosing a life partner. The rules of endogamy are, traditionally, very strict and violations are taken seriously with punishments.

(iii) The economic basis of the caste system is Jajmani system. It is an elaborate division of labor governed by a well-defined system of exchange of goods and services. The higher landed castes, and the lower occupationally specialized castes or 'service castes' are traditionally bound by certain Jajmani obligations. The patrons (jajman) or higher castes who control land ownership exchange the land produce against the services provided by other castes.

Caste may also be seen as a social and psychological resource for its members. Because of a sense of solidarity and common consciousness the members of a caste come to the rescue of fellow casteman.

On the other hand, the traditional caste system is not able to accept a common leader for the whole society consolidating all castes together, rather leaders are accepted from his/her own caste to someone socially close to their caste. Thus, the whole society is segregated in multiple leaders, and in absence of common acceptable leader, the common welfare agenda are not getting attention from government. The divided Madhesi society along castes expose it weak against external pressure. The gap between castes allows external groups to penetrate psychologically, physically, economically and geographically.

Law and Order

Law and order has been intentionally made worse in frontier districts by rulers to derive benefits; political and economical. The unstable frontiers do not allow plain people society to get stronger, thus facilitating hilly ruler in Kathmandu to have grip over plain people.

Before 1814, Musan Raut, a dreaded robber, was protected and promoted by state actors. Musan Raut weakened the local society by unethical practice. He would send his men during off agriculture season to other side of border to Rob, and bring the loot. The loot would be shared among Musan's men and Gurkha officer. These gangs conducted covert operations, carried in dark through masked person, thus British were handicapped. The local people were also impacted directly, when the gangs would target them a few times. And indirectly it damaged the local people's reputation. After pushing for reforms for long time, British were able to get official treaty in 1837 from Bhimsen to control the cross border crime and surrender of Thugs.

The crime was not wiped out completely and continued. Two villages Jhijha and Akaura had been famous in late twentieth century. They were expert in tunnel (surang) making and effecting small thefts. Traditionally, Dusad caste was more prone to this occupation, however other castes were also involved in the act. A Haluwai caste's Sardar in Jaleshwar, in corroboration with government officer, used to go on plundering across border in mid-twenty centuries. The Bihar government gave lands to the families of Jhijha and Akaura to motivate them to give up thieving and many opted for it, too. Nepal government, seeing the decline in covert objective, also offered similar offer to them and a few additional people opted to settle for other profession.

Till 1990s, there were unofficial declaration to use criminals in suppressing the political opponents, especially those political figures who were staying in India. These criminals were getting state protection in return. Many believe the same strategy was replicated during the armed groups uprising during 2008-2010 in Madhesh. The political criminal actors, whose face were masked, were injected to terrorize the common people. The flood of armed groups in masked faces brought discredit to the armed groups like Goit and Jwala Singh, who had initiated the armed movement taking motivation from armed revolution of Maoists.

Infrastructure

The status of Infrastructure is sad, and going to be a major bottleneck for anyone who wants to see a prosperous plain land. The inadequate infrastructure is impacting health sector, and people are forced to go either to Kathmandu or Indian hospitals for health diagnosis and treatment. The inadequate education infrastructure is impacting the literacy rate and this has been discussed in detail in chapter 7. Road transportation is not in good condition and delay in building Postal (Hulaki) road network is hindering progress of the region. The urban centers have additional challenge of managing sewer and solid waste. First, there is inadequate sewer network and most of them end in neighboring vacant lands or ponds. The clogged sewer water becomes the breeding ground for the mosquito, and this has become one of the top issues in plain cities including Janakpur, Jaleshwar, Birgunj, Biratnagar, and etc. Additionally, the flat terrain makes the flow of sewer water difficult as water tends to flow from high land to low land. The state of infrastructure development is static in four ways; exclusive state structure, unique geography, recurring flood and lack of innovation. Government has given open check for the development of new highway from east to west in the middle hill range, which is estimated[13] to cost Rs 43 billion (as of 2014). However when it comes to plain, government of Nepal believes, it is not their responsibility even to maintain the already existing road, which were built by donors like Russia, India and China in 1970s. The road between Janakpur and Bhittamod is one such example, which Nepal government has outsourced to Indian government[14]. The postal road development is totally brushed as if it is Indian government's responsibility, where Indian government is to bear all the project cost of NRs 9 billion as of 2016 arrangement[15] for constructing 600 KM of road in first phase. The worst part of politics is, Nepal government does not want the road projects in plain to be conceptualized, which is illustrated from 4 decades of no movement on postal road[16]. The postal road would connect all the major towns of plains with shortest route and it would improve connectivity that is considered detrimental to Hilly monopoly politics.

The infrastructure design and development in Terai needs paradigm shift, because these regions are prone to high speed water coming from northern hills. They bring silts with them and water flows are concentrated during rainy season only. All these taken together, the highway and roads have to be built in a way, it facilitates uninterrupted human connectivity, at the same time, and the road should give uninterrupted flows to water. The hindrance to water path would create water logs during cultivation season and further allow water to deposit silts. Silts create problem to the agriculture field by making them unproductive as well as, silt deposit makes the river bed to rise. Thus problem spirals into silt-water flow-silt. Today, due to flood problem, a large part of the plain land could be classified as wetland

and the percentage is increasing. The silt is also making the whole plain region rise few inches each decades, thus posing another problem to the permanent structure. After a span of 3-4 decades, a building can be seen pushed inside the ground level with the dual defect of silt and wetland; the effect is more in area close to river.

Another challenge in the plain region is earthquake, which has been noticed in the range of 7.5+ rector, once in a century. The region is on the border of Indian plate that is going below the Eurasian plate.

The building design needs to take care of the problems of flood, silt, wetland, and earthquake for usability and durability. There could be many innovative design available in world that could be adopted in these regions. One of the design could be that adopted in costal New York, where high rise buildings are built over water fully dependent on pillars as base. These buildings are able to sustain costal water waves as well as make use of the unproductive lands too. Another option could be that followed building artificial island in Dubai where sands are deposited to make certain area very high compared to surrounding water.

Industry

Industry is not in such a good shape. There are few private production houses in Biratnagar, however, over all, the condition is becoming unfavorable. Many companies are closing. Those opened are primarily focused on packaging of processed good imported from India or minimal value adds. These industries are focused in catering consumer in Hills rather than the plain people. Also, industry should help in creating employments to the plain peoples, rather than having the same issue of exclusion witnessed in the government structure.

Chure Management

Chure, the smaller hills immediately north of plain, is the first line of defense of flood and silt issue seen in plains. The jungles once dreaded are now limited to very few area. The large portion of these jungles was cut down during Rana rule, specifically during early 20th century when British established Railway from Indian border to deep inside jungle for the sole purpose of transporting timbers. Next planned damage was witnessed during ambitious King Mahindra East-West Highway of 500 miles, and immediately after hill people were promoted to migrate in plain along the East-West

Highway around 1965 through resettlement companies. Most of the migrated people cut down or burnt jungles to make them habitable.

The damage to Chure and immediate forest has made the earth naked that was once covered with green vegetation. The rain water, flood water washes the muds from these places rather than holding the silts which was the case few decades back.

Proper management of remaining forest in Chure and replantation of trees would be first step in managing silt and flood problem seen in plain.

Health

The health system in lowland is in unimpressive condition. Following are the challenges of the health system in lowland:

1. Traditionally there is preference for vegetarian food due to religious reason and other protein sources like milk/lentil are expensive, thus protein intake for the people are way below average.
2. The extractive state structure force the food transportation to the Hill thus creating artificial shortage in the southern plain.
3. People are poor and cannot afford healthy and complete diet.
4. The weather and climate is temperate which decrease the digestion power compared to the cold climate.
5. People's habit for fasting is less constructive to the healthy body.
6. There is tendency of avoiding doctor visit till health degrades to the critical condition.

Below table shows the comparative status of Terai plain health compared to other geographies.

Indicator	Terai	Hill	Mountain
Gini Co-efficient	0.21	0.28	0.18
Children under five years classified as malnourished (Weight-for-height)			
Percentage below -3 SD (Standard Deviation)	3.2%	1.7%	3.2%
Percentage below -2 SD (Standard Deviation)	11.2%	10.6%	10.9%
Prevalence of anemia in children (<11.0 g/dl). Hemoglobin grams per deciliter.	50.2%	41.0%	47.7%
Prevalence of anemia in women (<11.0 g/dl). Hemoglobin grams per deciliter.	42.0%	26.9%	26.9%

Gini co-efficient and Health Indicator. Source: Nepal Demographic and Health Survey 2011, Population Division, Ministry of Health and Population, Kathmandu, Nepal, Published March 2012

Education System

We have discussed in detail the situation of education system in plain land. The literacy rate is at the lowest level. The allocation of teachers is lowest compared to other regions. There is around 2.5 times more population density per teacher compared to Nepal average. Please read chapter 7.

Political Leadership

Political leader is the weakest dimension of the plain people. There has been a number of sub-divisions of the oldest Sadbhavana party, initially started by Gajendra Narayan Singh. All other Madhesh oriented political parties, started after 2007 uprising, have gone through the multiple divisions and still there does not seem a stabilized scenario having been emerged.

Many times people have found themselves on the road doing protest, however leader of the Madhesi oriented party have been found laggard in catching up with the protest. There has been more than 35 negotiations between UDMF and Government in 2015-2016, still issue looks to be stranded at same place as it was before[17], despite having enormous public push. Disconnect between leader and people can also be seen from the fact that most of the leaders have permanently migrated to Kathmandu and have invested in residential house there, rather than sharing the social space with lowland plain mass, which they claim to represent. They visit lowland on their own convenience.

Opportunity (Internal and External)

Tourism Industry

Internal tourism is present however occasional and mostly related to religious purpose. People visit sites like Janakpur, Salhesh Phulwari, Gadhi Mai and Kapilbastu to worship god. Baidyanath Dham (also called Baba Dham or Deoghar) and Pashupati have shiv temples are popular destinations in addition to Ganga Sagar near Kolkata.

Internal tourism spots have scope of growth to attract internal as well as external tourists. Improved management, connectivity, branding and marketing are required in these places to increase the scope of tourists. Janakpur and Kapilbastu have attracted external tourist imagination and they have donated to build Dharamshala (stay house). Janakpur and Kapilbastu are today in neglected condition and it has risk of damage to the heritage sites; like Ashoka Pilar of Kapilbastu.

There are scopes for other avenues to be developed as tourist spot. The opportunities are:

(1) Heritage sites like Simraungadh, Murtiya, and Devadaha for western tourist and Banauli's Vidyapati spot can be destination for Bangla speakers of India and Bangladesh. Historical sites like Makwanpur Gadhi and Haripur Gadhi are yet another destinations unexplored. There are many other places in need of exploration, preservation, and development as tourist spot. These places have been discussed in chapter 3. Many of these places also need archeological research.

(2) There is organic farming based tourism, which is lately capturing imagination in developed countries. Already Dayanagar village is also gaining popularity as a tourist hotspot, with nearly 200 farmers and tourists visiting the village daily. To cater to the visitors, a number of lodgings and restaurants have been set up. Lodging operators take the tourists to the ponds, provide them with the opportunity to fish and serve them with local fish dishes. The farmers plan to develop the area as "fishing tourism center"[18].

(3) Wildlife and Jungle safari based tourist destination has potential for attracting external as well as internal tourists. Chitwan is already one of the identified spot. Other places have scope of growth, given we see Terai has been covered in jungle and still has remaining areas in jungle. Western Plain land has better potential since population density is less compared to jungle density.

Agriculture Produce Industry

There are multiple scopes for leveraging the external market and providing employment to the plain people

1. Lentil is number one in export. The plains district production make them sixth largest producer of lentil in the world. The maximum export is to Bangladesh.

2. Traditionally rice production was in excess and was exported to India and to northern hill districts. Wheat production is also increasing slowly and steadily.
3. Vegetable and Fruits are in deficit for internal market. If surplus produce is there then the Demand from external market can also be met. Potato, Parwal, Cauliflower, Bins, Flat valor (sim), Gourd (Lauki or Sajhman), Chinese okra (Ghiura), Ladies finger, Eggplant, Green Chili, Amorphophallus (Suran or Oal), and Drumstick are potential vegetable produces. Fruits like Mango, Banana, Water Mellon, Custard apple, Guava, Pomegranate, Lemon, Papaya, Lichhi, Jackfruit, etc can be selected for mass production that can meet both internal as well as external demand.
4. Industry based on agriproducts like (a) Sugar factories (b) Paper factories
5. Agriculture bio by-product can make into energy production through technology as (1) Biomass or (2) Gasification. Barren lands or house roofs can be used for tapping solar energy.
6. Daily industry based on cow milk or Buffalo milk is undisputedly the best on returns for both small and big farmers. Similarly, poultry for hen and duck is favorable trade. Related fields are goat farming and Pig farming. The animal produces from these would help in multiple ways including protein diets, animal skins and hides for industrial uses.
7. Fish Production is favorable option in Terai as there is plenty of water.
8. Jungle or unused land could be planted with high prized timbers like Sissoo and Sal, and let them grow till maturity.
9. Herbal produces like Amla and Tulsi are favorable at most of the places. Vegetable spices like Bay leaf and dried Chili or dried ginger are another area of good revenue.
10. Cotton production of different variety like Simmal, Akaun and cotton plant has favorable condition. Sericulture is yet another tried and tested options for silk production based on mulberry plant. Honey production is similarly desirable field.

11. Flowers like Rose, Marigold, and other decorative plants are equally attractive.

Each of the above needs a chapter to discuss in depth, however this is outside the scope of this book. Below given is detail about Lentil, which has established itself in the world market.

Lentil is Nepal's number one export product[19]. Nepal ranks sixth among the world's largest producers of lentils. Over 90% of the total production of about 200,000 tons of lentil in Nepal is produced in twenty Terai districts by about 600,000 smallholder farmers using a cultivated area of about one third of a hectare.

	Area (Ha)	Production (MT)	Yield (MT/ha)
Dang	27,580	27,663	1.003
Kailali	21,500	21,450	0.998
Sarlahi	17,455	18,912	1.083
Rautahat	19,342	15,287	0.790
Bardiya	15,223	14,998	0.985
Bara	12,779	13,566	1.062
Sunsari	7,600	11,400	1.500
Banke	11,323	11,323	1.000
Saptari	7,125	8,776	1.232
Siraha	9,758	8,007	0.821
Parsa	6,985	7,954	1.139
Nawalparasi	8,870	6,968	0.786
Morang	5,700	6,500	1.140
Rupandehi	4,861	5,004	1.029
Chitwan	5,024	4,562	0.908
Kapilbastu	4,545	4,265	0.938
Kanchanpur	3,395	3,667	1.080
Mahottari	4,125	3,659	0.887
Jhapa	2,001	2,198	1.098
Dhanusha	2,565	1,961	0.765
Other districts	9,835	8,749	0.890
Nepal	207,591	206,869	0.997

Table: Area, Production and Yield of Lentil in Nepal, 2010/11. Source USAID[20]

The country grows nearly five percent of the world's lentil. Nepal produced 206,869 tonnes of lentils in 2011, up 36.31 percent to take the sixth place behind Canada, India, Turkey, Australia and the U.S. Bangladesh is the largest buyer of Nepali lentil followed by India, Singapore, the UAE and Bahrain. In 2011-12, Nepal exported 33,151 tonnes of lentil worth Rs. 2.67 billion. Bangladesh alone procured lentil worth Rs. 2.45 billion. In 2008-09, lentil worth Rs. 5.66 billion was exported, making it the country's largest export[21].

Ensure Human Rights

Human Rights is sought after commodity in plains. It is required by all, especially by poor, lower caste and women. There are hardly 5 percent of total population, mostly upper caste (Brahmin, Rajput, Kayastha, and Bhumihar), in lowland plain who can claim to have social equity. However, remaining population needs to feel the sense of social equity and this also means, better law and order implementation at ground that would create environment for ensuring human rights for majority of the population.

Human Resource Export

Human resource is strength of low land. These people migrate to developed destination on temporary basis that helps in gaining money, skills and exposure. There is further scope for improving the Human resources that are going to foreign land for employment. The revenue can be increased in the following three ways: (1) The upward movement in value chain (2) broadening the horizon of area served and (3) adding more people in the employment pool. What that means is, investing in the improvement in the people's skills, so that they can grow upward to the higher position that pays more compensation. The people going abroad are mostly manual labor workers if they happen to possess some technical skill they will get better paid jobs. The skills that can be easily imparted and scaled up are: plumbing, driving, electricity work, carpentry, hair cutting, house painting, tailoring, and etc. Some higher education based certificates like nursing, engineering, accounting can be imparted broadly. Secondly, the employment destination for 95% people are Qatar, Saudi Arabia and Malaysia. The opportunities should be expanded in other countries too. And thirdly, there are still unemployed resource who can be pushed to employment market through first two options.

Technology Adoption

Technology is virgin sector in lowland plains. Every sector we can see needs technology adoption. House construction is old fashioned and should adopt technology for flood, earthquake and silt problems. It should also be weather proof, as both summer and winter is becoming challenge in plains. Similarly, technology is far behind in health sector, education sector, and almost null presence in agriculture field. The latest communication and energy sector technology is evolving rapidly in western countries and that is another bigger challenge to keep pace with ever updating latest art of state technology, which is negligible currently. Internet and solar penetration in lowland plains might be less than one percent[22].

A large Iron ore reserve is found in Nawalparasi is spread over 100 hectares in Pokhari village of Dhaubadhi. The exploration of iron ore reserve would require the latest use of technology for the optimal use of iron. The reserve has been detected over 8-10 km radius and is underground 250 meters[23].

Connect with World

We discussed in strength section of this chapter that there is large group of expatriate people who have migrated to the Gulf, India and Western countries in search of employment and education. Since there is minimal state promotion of plain linked people and values, there lies the scope of them to act like brand ambassador for each of them personally or as group or through culture programs. They can connect with the different lives of the people and register with different organizations interested in South Asia. The established connection would serve in long run benefitting in commerce, tourism, and diplomacy. The importance of China and India connection is discussed in detail in chapter 10.

Threat (External)

Natural Calamity (Flood, Drought/Famine, Earthquake)

Flood

Flood is perennial and seasonal issue of plain, which is lying just below hilly range. The flood water is hardly local, and mostly external which comes down at high speed from hills lying on the north of plain. Small amount of flood is taken as rejoice because it overflows river and surplus water fills the adjoining rice fields that increase agriculture productivity. Along the water, flood water brings nutrients and new layer of mud that further helps increase rice field productivity. Having rice produce is business as usual. In the past, the occurrence of vigorous flood had been less, say once in a decade. Vigorous flood brings sands (or silt) rather than mud with its high speed water. The speeding water (1) uproots the plantation (2) enters the human habitats, damages the infrastructure and blocks the transportation (3) fills the rice field with silt/sand sediments, that decrease the productivity of agriculture field, unlike mud. The vigorous rains in the hill cause landslides there and brings sand with it, which is deposited in the plains, where water speed recedes. Flood is linked to the management of Chure, small range high lands in plain. Rautahat, Sarlahi, Mahottari, and Dhanusha, are seriously affected by flood disasters[24]. The major rivers system linked with flood are Gandaki, Bagmati, Rato, Kamla, and Kosi.

Plains districts are highly prone to flood. In general the Terai Ecological Zone of Western, Central and Eastern Development region are more Flood Prone compared to the other districts and ecological zones[25]. See table below

Flood Risk Exposure	Districts
Very High (0.766-1.000)	Mahottari
High (0.545-0.0.765)	Chitwan, Saptari, Rautahat, Sunsari, Siraha
Moderate (0.352-0.544)	Jhapa, Dhanusha, Parsa, Bara, Morang, Nawalparasi
Low (0.024-0.351)	Kailali, Sarlahi
Very Low (0.000 – 0.023)	Other districts of Nepal

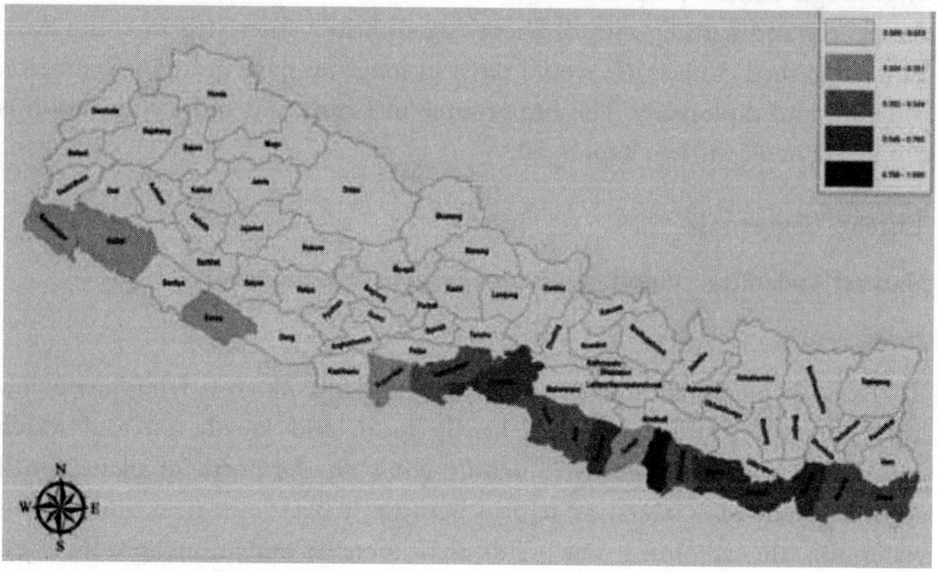

Image showing Flood Risk in Nepal

Drought

Drought and Flood are ideally independent, however in Madhesh they are interlinked too. If region gets lower rain fall, then it is drought in dictionary meaning, and that is true for Madhesh too. Lower rainfalls impact the field plantation. However, in these lowlands, silts are brought through floods, and the new layer of silt on top of soil erode the productivity of fields and also decrease the soil capacity to hold the water, thus decreasing the soil moisture level. Global climate change is impacting the Himalayan range and rain pattern that, in turn, is negatively impacting productivity of plain lands which increase the risk of food security.

Table below showing the drought risk of the districts, in which central Madhesh districts have more risk[26].

Drought Risk/Exposure	Districts
Very High (0.563-1.000)	Saptari, Jajarkot, Siraha, Kalikot, Dailekh, Dadeldhura, Humla, Dhanusha, Jumla, Ramechhap, Achham, Mugu
High (0.348-0.562)	Bajhang, Bajura, Dolakha, Dhading, Doti, Kanchanpur, Sarlahi, Udaypur, Salyan, Darchula, Banke, Baitadi
Moderate (0.24-0.347)	Kathmandu, Kapilbastu, Bardiya, Rolpa, Dolpa, Manang, Rukum, Gorkha, Mustang, Pyuthan, Bhojpur, Lalitpur, Bhaktapur, Arghakhanchi, Rupandehi, Kailali, Dang, Rasuwa, Makwanpur, Mahottari
Low (0.106-0.223)	Rautahat, Panchthar, Sindhuli, Gulmi, Kavrepalanchok, Sunsari, Kaski, Chitwan, Palpa, llama, Nawalparasi, Nuwakot, Okhaldhunga, Baglung, Surkhet, Tanahu, Morang, Taplejung, Tehrathum, Solukhumbu, Myagdi
Very Low (0.000-0.105)	Sankhuwasabha, Sindhupalchok, Parbat, Parsa, Khotang, Bara, Lamjung, Dhankuta, Jhapa, Syangja

that were hitting the plains[27]. Since plains are integrated with Indian plains in geography, climate and economy, we would look into the greatest Famines of times.

Famine of 1770 hit the Bengal presidency including Purnia and Tirhut districts. About one third of people were estimated to have died. In 1896-97 when the famine distress was at its greatest, more than three fifths of the persons were receiving relief in the Division belonging to the districts of Muzaffarpur and Darbhanga. There was another famine in 1873-74. Nowhere did the famine of 1873-74 cause greater suffering than in the district of Tirhut which comprised both Muzaffarpur and Darbhanga. In the Famine of 1866-67, one third of the population was at one period in receipt of relief from Government.

Earthquake

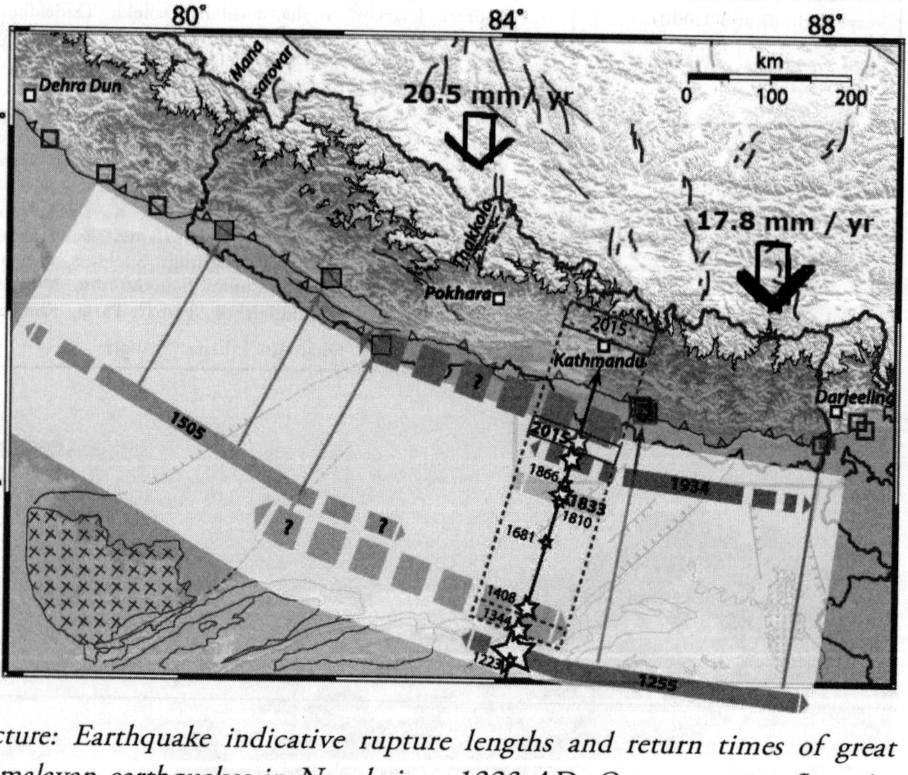

Picture: Earthquake indicative rupture lengths and return times of great Himalayan earthquakes in Nepal since 1223 AD. Open arrows reflect slip up rates across the Himalayan range. Source: Bollinger. L (2016)[28]

Earthquake in this region is linked to the plate movements. The Indian plates are sliding below the Eurasian plate. The researchers have found out that Indian plates move about one-fifth of a centimeter each year inside Chinese plate. This movement causes a great strain inside earth, thus causing an earthquake to release the geographical tension. Chure is the border line of Indian plate compared to Eurasian plate. Major earthquakes are noted in year 1255, 1344, 1408, 1505, 1681, 1810, 1833, 1866, 1934 and 2015. The earthquake of 2015 had negligible damage in plains. The violent damage had been noted in the earthquake of 1934 and 1833.

- **1934 Earthquake**

In the living memory, 1934's earthquake was devastating to plain region, compared to 2015's earthquake that caused bigger damage in hills. 1934's earthquake collapsed every fortress in Mahottari district and Dhanusha district. The fortress of Matihani, Basahiya, Kuwa, and Kapileshwar lay in ruin as did the Laxman, Hanuman Nagar, Ratna Sagar, Rasik Nivas, Dasrath Mandir, Agni Kund, Ram Chandra temple, and Sita Kund Monastery. Only Janaki temple remained standing which was designed by Indian Engineer using steels[29].

In the main epicentral tract, the Sitamarhi and Madhubani subdivisions were the worst affected. In Sitamarhi only one house of any size escaped destruction, and in Madhubani 70 to 80 per cent of the masonry buildings collapsed or were badly damaged[30]. The railway line were seen bent like snake in places.

In Jaleshwar and Hanumannagar [Rajbiraj] all solid houses, of baked brick construction, were destroyed. In Jaleshwar, near Janakpur, the condition was probably worse, and more like that at Sitamarhi and Madhubani[31]. Houses had slumped extensively into the ground. A banyan tree got buried into the fissure. When Mahatma Gandhi visited the Bihar region for earthquake relief works, he also visited Jaleshwar[32].

Large tracts in the district of East Champaran, Sitamarhi, Madhubani, Saharsa and Purnia in a length of about 300 km and average width of about 50 km, slumped into liquefaction of sands and at many places sand-water fountains and sand-boils had occurred on a large scale[33]. Long, wide, and deep fissures were abundant in the entire slump belt. Most large fissures were confined near the epicenter, between rivers Ganga, Gandaki and Kosi.

In Riga, Madhubani, Munger, Motihari, Muzaffarpur, Supaul, Purnia, Raxaul, and Samastipur. A typical fissure at Champaran was 15-feet deep, 30-feet wide, and 300-yards long (approximately 4.57 x 9 x 275 m). At Sitamarhi, a fissure was about 80 yards long and 8 feet wide (70 m x 2 m) and was filled with sand within 1 m of the top. Such fissures were common in the entire affected area[34]. At many places sand and water fountains suddenly erupted. Fountains of water which gushed out from fissures spread all over the cultivated land to a depth varying from a few inches to about three feet[35].

The earthquake of Magh 2, 1990 (January 15, 1934 AD) was followed by drought and hailstorms in 1991 (1934 A.D.) damaging large areas of rice-fields.

- **1833 Earthquake**

Before 1934's the earthquake the Ram Chandra temple in Janakpur stood two stories high and could be seen at a distance[36]. However, James Baillie Fraser described in 1816, the Ram Chandra temple was a building of four stories, from the corner of each of which were suspended seventy-two bells, which might have got collapsed in August 26th, 1833 earthquake that caused big damage in the north Indian cities too. Kamla River was dammed by a landslide that burst 4 days after the earthquake, flooding the village of Baldeah near the India/Nepal border. In Tirhut of India, water was thrown out of tanks, 4 feet deep; the water of which was 3 feet below the edge. Birds were thrown out of their nests; Men could not keep their feet. In Tirhut the earthquake occurred at 6 p.m on 26th of August, with a severe shock. , The earthquake began with a motion from East to West, and was repeated at 11 and 12 with double severity, continuing at intervals throughout the night until 6 am next morning. The two shocks in the middle of the night were most awful, lasting, each time more than a minute[37].

Political Suppression

It is a threat for future if we notice the trend of the past. In 1950s, Madhesis were doing better, but Mahendra intentionally imposed the policies which intended to suppress the Madhesis' progress. Growth and empowerment of plain people are seen as threat by external groups, thus their acts are to suppress plain people. If the trend continues, it poses a big threat to plain people. The suppression could be enforced through violence, as it had been done in the past, and it is convenient for hill group, because they are certified world class Gurkha fighter in addition to not having inclusive state structure.

Evolving Foreign Politics

Nepal perceived itself as a root between two big stones till 1950. Since opening of international connection with Western countries and communist bloc, Nepal has acted as buffer state between neighboring countries. Today, China is more assertive than before, and each day foreign politics is evolving. India is trying to engage in International politics with the strategic partnership of United States of America. As long as foreign politics is unstable, it brings risk to Madhesis, as international power engagement will be limited to the ruling group in Kathmandu.

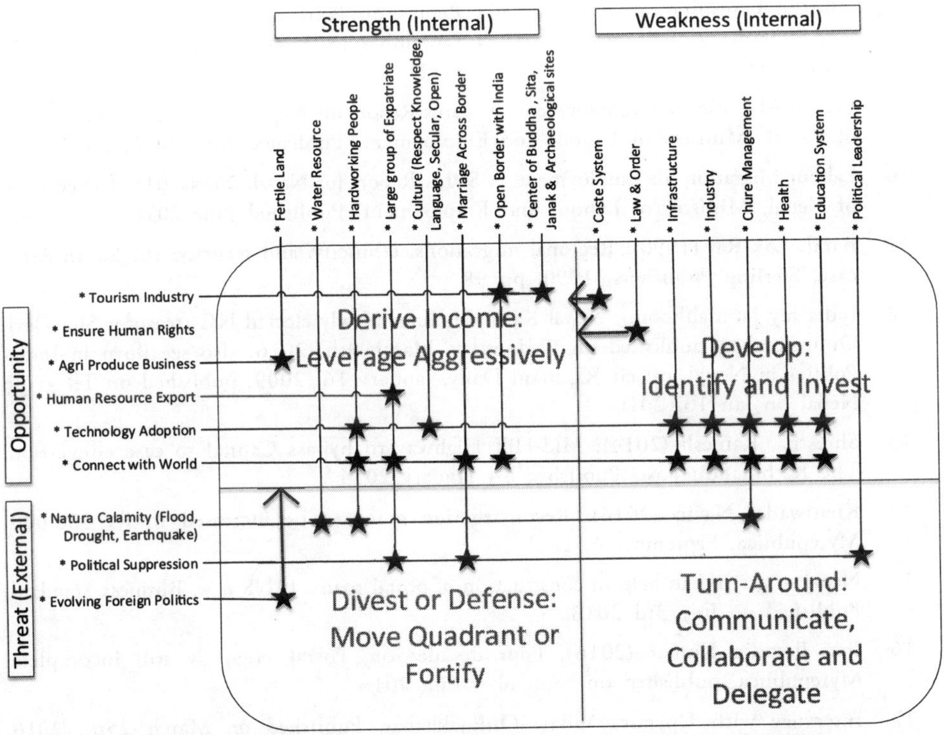

Picture showing SWOT Analysis for Madhesh and its people. The list is of indicative attributes and few possible strategic leverages. The star indicate possible coupling between two factors, such that the favorable factor can be used to nullify effect of adverse factor. The arrow direction shows the scope of moving to different quadrant for the selected factors.

Notes

1. Campbell, A (1837); Notes on the Agriculture and Rural Economy of the Valley of Nepal, Transactions of the Agricultural and Horticultural Society of India, Volume 4, Published By Agricultural & Horticultural Society of India, 1837
2. 25 ropunis is 1 khet, and 6 to 61.5 bigahs equal to 1 khet. 40 Kilo Grams is 1 maunds
3. Lawrence, Honoria (1980); The Journals of Honoria Lawrence, London: Hodder and Stoughton, 1980, pp 179
4. Bolts, Guillaume (1775);Considerations on India Affairs; Particularly Respecting the Present State of Bengal (etc.). 2. Ed, Volume 2, 1772-1775, pp 287
5. Anmol, Amrit (2016); Commercial fish farming gaining popularity, The Kathmandu Post, Published May 5, 2016
6. RSS Nepal, Published on Jan 2nd , 2015
7. Hamilton, Francis, An Account of the Kingdom of Nepal: And of the Territories Annexed to this, pp 169
8. Political Consultation, A Campbell's Report on Political Transactions with Nepal, The Supermacy of Bhimsen Thapa, 1 September 1837, as mentioned in Bikrama Jit Hasrat's History of Nepal (1871) , pp 231
9. Labour Migration for Employment, A Status Report for Nepal: 2014/2015, Government of Nepal, Ministry of Labour and Employment, Published June 2016, pp 73
10. Labour Migration for Employment, A Status Report for Nepal: 2014/2015, Government of Nepal, Ministry of Labour and Employment, Published June 2016
11. Baral, Lok Raj (1990); Regional migrations, ethnicity, and security: the South Asian case, Sterling Publishers, 1990, pp 98
12. India my Janmabhoomi, Nepal Karmabhoomi: Newly-elected NC treasurer Sita Devi, Onlinekhabar, published on Wednesday, March 9th, 2016, also see Born in India-Politics in Nepal, op cit Rajdhani Daily, January 16, 2009, published on Telegraph Nepal on Jan 16, 2016.
13. Shrestha, Ramesh (2014); Mid-Hill Highway to bypass Capital to ease congestion, The Kathmandu Post, Published 14 January 2014
14. Khatiwada, Navin (2016); Reconstruction grant to be increased to Rs 300,000, Myrepublica, September 6, 2016
15. Nepal to get Indian help in construction of postal roads, IANS new, Business Standard, Published on July 3rd 2016.
16. Jha, Jitendra Kumar (2016); Four decades on, Postal Highway still incomplete, Myrepublica, published on September 6th, 2016
17. Interview with Upendra Yadav, Onlinekhabar, Published on March 25th, 2016, Downloaded on Sep 21, 2016 from http://english.onlinekhabar.com/2016/03/25/373325#sthash.lSPR3MT8.dpuf
18. Anmol, Amrit (2016); Commercial fish farming gaining popularity, The Kathmandu Post, Published May 5, 2016 RSS Nepal, Published on Jan 2nd , 2015
19. USAID Nepal, Quarterly Newsletter, April To June, 2013, pp 1

20. Lentil Market Assessment report Nepal, Economic, Agriculture, And Trade Activity, July 2013, pp 82 appendix 5

21. Prasain, Sangam (2013); Bardia lentil farmers buoyed by higher prices, The Kathmandu Post, April 19, 2013 http://kathmandupost.ekantipur.com/printedition/news/2013-04-18/bardia-lentil-farmers-buoyed-by-higher-prices.html

22. Bohannon, John (2016); Who is getting left behind in the internet revolution?, American Association for the Advancement of Science, Published Sep 9, 2016, http://www.sciencemag.org/news/2016/09/who-getting-left-behind-internet-revolution

23. Sharma, Narayan (2016); Nepal's largest iron ore reserves found in Nawalparasi, The Kathmandu Post, Published Mar 16, 2016

24. Khanal, Narendra. R (2007), Preparing for Flood Disaster, Mapping and Assessing Hazard in the Ratu Watershed, International Centre for Integrated Mountain Development (ICIMOD), March 2007 pp 14

25. GoN (2010); Climate Change vulnarability Mapping for Nepal, Ministry of Environment, Government of Nepal, National Adaptation Programme of Action to Climate Change, September 2010, pp 17

26. GoN (2010); Climate Change vulnarabilty Mapping for Nepal, Ministry of Environment, Government of Nepal, National Adaptation Programme of Action to Climate Change, September 2010, pp 18

27. Regmi, Mahesh (1976); Famine in Nepal, Regmi Research Series, Year 8, No. 11, November 1, 1976

28. Bollinger. L (2016); Slip deficit in central Nepal: omen for a repeat of the 1344 AD earthquake?, Springer Link, December 2016

29. Burghart, Richard (1978), History of Janakpurdham, Phd Thesis, 1978, pp 495-496

30. Brett, William Bailie (1935), A Report on the Bihar Earthquake: And on the Measures Taken in Consequence Thereof Up to the 31st December 1934, published 1935

31. Records of the Geological Survey of India, Volume 68 , page 239

32. Based on personal talk with Author uncle Shri Ram Ratan Mehtari Sah, who was 12 years old at that time.

33. Himalayan Geology, Volume 17, Wadia Institute of Himalayan Geology., 1996, pp 34

34. Sinvhal, Amita (2010); Understanding Earthquake Disasters, Tata McGraw-Hill Education, Jan 1, 2010, pp 130

35. Mukerjee, Shyamal (1988); Soil Liquefaction In Nepal-Bihar Earthquake Of August 21, 1988, Proceedings: Fourth International Conference on Case Histories in Geotechnical Engineering, St. Louis, Missouri, March 9-12, 1998.

36. Burghart, Richard (1978), History of Janakpurdham, Phd Thesis, 1978, pp 495-496

37. Bilham, R (1995); Location and magnitude of the 1933 nepal earthquake and its relation to the rupture zones of contiguous great Himalayan earthquakes, Current Science, 69, 101–128 http://www.currentscience.ac.in/Downloads/article_id_069_02_0101_0128_0.pdf

10

Madhesh: Yam between Three Boulders; Delhi, Beijing and Kathmandu

The political chapter of Madhesh will remain incomplete without understanding India-China role in the making of Nepal. Himalaya, mountain range in Asia, divides Indian subcontinent from the Tibetan Plateau. Nepal falls on the south of the Himalaya becoming part of the Indian sub-continent, which makes India to assume its security measure starts at Kodari rather than Raxaul. This assumption became even stronger after annexing of Tibet by China, in 1950's. The Indian concern is the thorny point in Nepalese policy. No two situations are same, however if we have to find a closer analogy, Nepal wants itself to be considered different from India the way Taiwan wants to be looked different from China. China considers the people in Taiwan to be their own, who ran away from mainland China's political regime in 1950's. In the same way, if we go backward 3 centuries, Indian Hindu rulers and their loyalist ran away from mainland India, saving themselves from Muslim/British prosecution, to establish rule in Hilly Range, which is today called Nepal.

Nepal is different from Taiwan, because despite having most of the hate and fear relationship with India, it depends on India the most, for sourcing its daily needs. However, the desire of Nepal to have relationship with China can be understood from the Oli trade treaty, which would cost Nepal NRs 180 per liter to bring Chinese petrol to Kathmandu, compared to costs of NRs 104 per liter imported from India[1]. Nepalese hilly psychology, both hilly indigenous and migrated Indian ruler group, values independence so much that they are ready to pay extra cash to anyone who can make them feel away from India. This psychology is today know to US and western powers, who wants Nepal to remain buffer between India-China. This psychology was known to British India rulers too, who wanted to prevent Nepalese siding with China after 1814-1816 war, thus gifted Madhesh to appease rulers in Kathmandu.

Though British occupied the Terai lowland plains during 1814-1815 war, and despite having upper hand, they sacrificed the land suppressing all the confusions, after Chinese popped into the post-war affair in 1816. Though the war and treaty was over, still the entry of China played the deciding role. The details surrounding Anglo-Nepal War of 1814-1816 have been discussed in chapter 4.

The ultimate looser were plains people after Sugaolee Treaty, and is the looser today, whose resources are being extracted without parity. Everyone is winner, except Madhesh, which sacrificed in past and continues to sacrifice. US knows their role in Nepal and expectation from the relationship. India knows, what they have to expect from Nepal and China knows what they can expect from Nepal. We will discuss the India-China relationship with Nepal in details. Before that, lets understand the US and western expectations.

A US embassy report titled 'U.S. role in Nepal' dating 1979 states[2] "We have no significant interest in Nepal and that instability in the country would not pose a fundamental threat to US interests" and adds "Maintain contact with all major political elements (Congress, Partyless camp, Independents, Moderate communists) in order to encourage their moderation and put the US in a position to deal with them if they later come to have a share of the power. Nurture our good bilateral relations and as appropriate take cognizance of Nepal's moderate and useful role in international and non-aligned fora, by presidential letters and other non-public relationships." US government's favorite investment has been Army, which US strategic report describe as "The army is important to U.S interests in Nepal in the broad perspective of contributing to security and stability in the remote regions of the nation so that other development programs can reach into these areas. Consistent with these objectives, the IMET is professionally oriented, emphasizing training in small unit leadership, counter-insurgency, civil affairs, and maintenance of equipment, and involving exposure to the U.S staff college."[3] The summary of U.S interest in Nepal "derive primarily from its role as a buffer between India and China"[4].

Other western countries have negligible interest in Nepal, except UK which is primarily driven from its desire to maintain Gurkha Army. Thus British wants to have good relationship with Government of Nepal to get assurance of its rights to keep continuing recruitment of low cost fighter from Nepal. Other western countries' interest has to pass through US consent, which states "in the event of clear evidence of foreign intervention in the internal political process, advise the interfering power of our knowledge and disapproval of its interference" [5].

Now we are going to discuss the relations with India and China along with their expectations, since the emergence of Nepal state in mid of 18th century, from Nepal. To start with, let's dive deep into what are the building blocks of Nepal State.

Nepal State Building Blocks

Survival Rather than Growth

King Prithivinarayan strategy of capturing Nepal Valley was, to put Valley through economic sanction, and let the economy suffer till state dies on its own. Prithivinarayan was successful with aggression; however the strategy of isolating the economy from north and south did continue. The ancient trade route of Malla's time between Tibet and India was chopped off, because he perceived "With the merchant comes the musket and with the Bible comes the Bayonet", the popular saying of those days, when British was expanding in India through the trade. The strategy of Rana, to remain isolated, can be summarized from the Jung Bahadur Statement "If a cat is pushed into a corner it will fly at an elephant, but it will always try to keep out of the corner as long as possible."[6] At the same time, he wanted to open the country for trade as much less as possible. Laurence wrote in 1852, "The present policy of the Nepal government is to keep the roads by which their country is approached, in as impassable a state as possible, vainly imagining that in case of a war the badness of the roads would offer an insuperable obstacle to our [British] progress and compel us [British] to relinquish any attempt to penetrate to Katmandu". The strategy of Mahendra was to open the country to foreign countries for a price (read donation), however survive by balancing one country with the other. Mahendra foreign policy is eating up country energy in balancing the conflicting interests of foreign powers, rather than concentrating in growing the country. Read more about Mahendra in Chapter 7 - Encounter with Racist State, Mahendra's Nationalism.

Collectivist Culture Practice (Secrecy, Blood relationship, Exclusion)

State is represented by Hill group, primarily run by Khas with the support of hilly Janajatis. The characteristic of Hill group, as we discussed in chapter six, is collectivist. State is inheriting the collectivist culture of the dominant group in structure. It promotes hilly group, suspicion on people outside hilly group, authoritarianism in decisions, top down approach, and the least open to public opinion on government policies. These all culminate into exclusion of lowland people from the Government and governance.

Dual Definition of Nationalism

- Bollywood movies, Indian TV serials, their actors and music are popular in Hilly public, which is propagating Hindi among people. However in official way they will hate Hindi. Indian Government gives hundreds of scholarships including stipend to study Engineering and other subjects into Indian universities, however when they go to Indian collages, instead of being humble to the Indian students, students rarely miss chance to excite fellow Indian, taking side of Indian rival Pakistan team in Cricket game matches and similar affairs. Nepal depends on India for everything from salt to steel, gets every drop of petrol from India but will show as if they donate instead[7]. Khas Hindu Brahmins will wear Dhoti for all the special religious occasions however they have slang "Dhoti" to irritate Madhesis whose primary traditional wear is "Dhoti". Similarly, elite of Nepal would boost Royal Families ties in India and would curse Madhesis for marrying in India. Additional hilly population would fill their tummy from the grains they extract from Madhes, however they wouldn't digest their food without cursing Madhesi as foreigners. The high of their duplicity is, Indian teachers have educated the whole of Nepal since 1958, when education sector opened up and there were negligible teachers available in Nepal, however these teachers hardly got the acceptance in the public life and many had to return India after retirement due to implicit humiliation, despite having commitment of equal treatment from Indo-Nepal Friendship treaty of 1950.
- Nepalese state, primarily controlled by Khas group, copies everything possible from the surroundings with least acknowledgement. Like,

they copied "Nepal" word for Khas language that originally linked to "Newar" culture. Nepali cap name is derived from Dhaka keyword, the capital of Bangladesh, and cap styles like Kashmiri cap, however Nepali cap has become symbol of "Nepalization". All Army officers, police officers wears western attires Shirt-Pants, however they expect citizens to wear Daura-Suruwal to enter government office. Banknotes released during King Mahendra's and King Birendra's time will show them in western wears, and they will preach others to wear Daura-Suruwal. The building built during and after Rana period will lavishly flash Western architecture, and they claim being protector of Nepal culture. Referring to Singh Durbar, or the home of the Prime Minister, Northey says "there is nothing of Nepalese architecture in this imposing building".

- Gurkha Recruitment: There are Gurkhas (hilly people) in Indian government payroll, British Government payroll, and few more foreign governments' payrolls serving as respective countries' Army officers; still they hold citizenship of Nepal. Nepal government facilitates these recruitments in the form of perks; direct or indirect. This shows dual Royalty in terms of modern state concept.

Nepalese youths gather to "donate petrol" to the Indian Embassy (07 October 2015). Source: BBC

Piggyback on Indian Economy Policy

Myron Weiner, American political scientist, mentioned India as "safety valve" for Nepal because of the employment opportunities gained by Nepalese in India[8]. As per the 1950 treaty, Nepalese are legally allowed to avail equal economic opportunities in India like any other Indian. It is estimated that about 5 to 7 million Nepalese are currently in India and 3 to 5 lakh in Delhi alone,[9] out of total 27million population. Nepalese people find themselves employed in home-office security guard, restaurants, housekeeping, and selected few high end jobs like Information technology and management jobs. A large chunk of Hilly tribes are employed in Indian Army.

As of 1991, there were more than 100,000 Gurkhas serving in over forty Indian infantry battalions and elsewhere in the Indian Army. Many among the Gurkhas serving in 38 battalions in India Army are third or fourth generation soldiers. There are about 1,23,000 ex-servicemen in Nepal who derives pensions from Indian treasury. About NRs 1600 crores (USD $ 160 millions) are added to Nepalese economy by the way of pay and pension annually[10].

Open border facilitates meeting the Nepal's commodities supply, the country produce is sold and exported to Indian market, rich people seek quality education and health service in Indian metros like Delhi, Bangalore, Kolkata and Mumbai.

India supplies[11] around one third of peak electricity demand of Nepal[12], and supplies almost cent percent petroleum energy needs.

This all means, Nepal does not have to worry about planning employment and commodity price in the way other countries have to worry about.

Nepalese currency is pegged to Indian currency at fixed exchange rate of 1 to 1.6. Thus literally, Nepal, which derives 1/3rd of GDP from remittance, is protected from Exchange rate policy.

In future, Nepal has plans to generate surplus electricity, and all those are planned to be exported to India.

Profit over Professionalism and Rent over Responsibilities

The genesis of Kathmandu's state actor interest in commerce started since Jung Bahadur days. He was impressed with East India Company's ability to manage both commercial interests and government. Jung Bahadur's successor tried all the possible trades including Banking, Indigo farming, saltpeter trade, and manufacturing while they were in office. Beyond the border, money from treasury, primarily collected from plain districts, were diverted to Indian financial system, and the investment process was well documented in administrative rule book "*Madhesh Mal ko Swal*". Army was the state machinery from which Rana enforced the authority. Overlapping of authority with commerce gave rise to monopoly. The monopoly covered all lucrative sectors in nineteenth and twentieth centuries. The shadow of monopoly has overlapped in twenty first century too, though conflict of interest between commercial activities and authority has been separated on paper. Behind the scene, there is overlapping interest between commercial activities and authority even today. Nepalese Billionaire Binod Chaudhary, who was nominated Member of first CA (2008-2014) from Nepal Communist Party (UML), has mentioned in his autobiography how in quid pro quo deals he was able to gain in business from his financial support to King and then-king's brother[13]. The space left out from monopoly is covered through the cartels and syndicates between smaller businesses that can be seen in day to day, like hair cutting to public transportation. Government structure have unofficial share without which they would not run.

The unhealthy part of this profit oriented mentality from the public oriented professional service organization can be found in small schools, who would build rentable commercial spots, to big central agencies. Nepal Army is a professional organization with clear responsibility to maintain the securities. However, recently with it's about USD $350 million cash in hand, has pitched to enter profit generating sectors like commercial cloth manufacturing[14], hydropower generation[15]. Nepal army is already owning petrol pump that sells directly to consumer[16], have road construction projects from government and has invested NRs 4.4 billion through its welfare fund in various sectors, including NRs 2.14 billion in a medical college, an oxygen plant and drinking water plants. The biggest of all these profit is coming from mission to United Nations through which it milks the maximum cash that is fueling other ventures. A serving Nepali Army person serving in the UN mission contributes 22 percent of his/her salary earned from the UN Peacekeeping Missions to the Army Fund. An Army official deployed in peacekeeping missions in war-prone countries is paid $1,365 a month[17] and Nepal deploy around 4,000 to 5,000 soldiers each year[18]. There are questions on corruptions[19]; every year, the Welfare Fund is adding Rs 3 billion to its coffers from various sources, including profit, but the increment rate has remained consistent despite accumulating assets over the years, raising serious questions over transparency in the management of the fund[20]. Even before corruption, the question is, should Army hold the income from UN

Mission for their private use rather than depositing income into national treasury, when country is already paying salary for elephant size army of about 91 thousand soldiers? Coming back to the overlapping of interest, should profit[21] take priority over professionalism of Army? Commerce means risk, and the question is asked, who will bail out if those commercial business will make loss? Who will audit business transactions of Army enterprise? Will a private player be interested to invest in a sector in which army enters? Comparing with two neighbors; India[22] has negligible commercial interest and Chinese president Xi has already pushed to end commercial activities of Military in three years[23]. The Chinese Army paper noted "Profits will distract the military from strengthening its combat capabilities" and there is a feeling that paid services can sometimes encourage corruption, and the military should focus on national defense[24].

Today Nepal lives on immigrant labor's remittance contributing about one third of GDP. However start from first day of an individual decision to become foreign land labor, he/she faces extractive state structure. People are poor that's why they are motivated to leave families for foreign employment, however to make passport, which is in Nepal government control, these labors have to spend highest fee in comparison to South Asian neighbors[25]. As of 2013, Nepal charged Rs 5,000 ($57.27) for 60 page passport compared to India's, INRs 1,000 ($20) and INRs 1,500 ($30) for a new passport with 36 pages and 60 pages respectively. The cost of acquiring a passport in Pakistan, Bangladesh, Sri Lanka, Bhutan and the Maldives was $30, $25, $25, $18.4 and $36 respectively. Sri Lanka issues a different passport for workers going to the Middle East and South Asian countries, which cost only $10. In addition to the steep cost, the wait period is two months and to expedite passport delivery, the charge further multiplies by two to become 10,000 ($114.54). In addition to getting the passport from Ministry of Foreign Affairs, labor now have to apply and pay few more fees to Ministry of Labor to receive Labor permit before flying for foreign countries. Workers deposit 1,000 rupees into a Migrant Workers' Welfare Fund, managed by the Foreign Employment Promotion Board, before departing to their destination country. Though there is provision of support to these laborers from Nepal government in need, Government's response had been below expectation. For example, Government is lagging[26] in bringing dead bodies of immigrant workers, and impacts especially poor and those having issues with employers[27]. There is news of misuse[28][29] and corruption in the Migrant Workers Welfare

Fund which was about USD $33 million (Rs 3.3 billion) at the end of Fiscal Year 2014/15. Embassies in 9 foreign countries were accused of misusing migrant workers' welfare fund[30] instead of proving required benefit to the workers[31].

Another instance of profit over professionalism was witnessed during April 2015 earthquake, which was worst hit in last 90 years. Soon after the earthquake, relief help started pouring in from the people outside Nepal. However, in this sensitive time, bureaucratic structure was exploring every opportunity to make profit rather than professionally facilitating the expedition of help delivery to victims. At a time when medical facilities across the country were reeling under an acute scarcity of medicines, essential drugs worth millions of rupees, donated by aid agencies, was decaying at the customs at Tribhuwan International Airport because TIA customs demanded a tariff of 10 percent of the price of the medicines, or over Rs 8.8 million, on the earthquake relief material[32]. Similarly, Rice donated for quake victims by Bangladesh meant for quake victims was sold instead of distributing[33]. Only about 20 percent of the rice was distributed and the rest of it was sold in market[34] around July 2016, after a year of the arrival of such relief material. Likewise, truck carrying tents for the quake victim was stopped[35] at the Birgunj Customs Office[36]. In the similar case, more than 7,000 quintal rice provided by the government of Japan to Nepal Government under food assistance had remained undistributed after six years[37].

In yet another example, Nepal Energy ministry opened a commercial company to serve emerging electricity market. The most puzzling part of "*Vidyut Utpadan Company*" (Electricity Production Company) was the share of ministries that could contribute the least in the production of electricity. The company has 5% share of Law Ministry, 5 % of Finance Ministry, and 20% of Energy Ministry[38].

There is difference in rent and tax. Rent collector considers the property as personal, and feels they have right to collect rent without proving other benefit to the rent payer. This was what happened since King Prithivinarayan Shah till Rana Regime. Tax on the other land is collected on behalf of people with the promise that tax will be invested back into economy to provide benefits to the tax payers. Tax has relationship of responsibilities, whereas rent has negligible responsibilities for the money collector. If we look closely into the nature of operation of a few government agencies, it will indicate the foot print of old days rent regime. Nepal Telecom is opened by Government with people's money. However the nature of operation is to extract as much as possible from the people, and distribute the profit among employees. In today's context, immigrant laborers need connection with families and telecom is one of the first medium to connect with people. The telecom, instead of being enabler of the economy and development of country, is more like rent extractor. There is hardly any evidence to suggest, the service of Nepal telecom is better than the neighbor countries telecom service, however the price of Nepal telecom is way above China, India and Bangladesh. Here, it needs to be understood that price of the telephone is determined by receiving (or terminating) country and dialing (originating) country. If we compare the below mentioned prices of making calls to Nepal and its neighbors, it all points to the high price of making call to Nepal, indicating Nepal overprices the terminating call charges, which finally gets paid by people.

Telecom Service Provider	Calling Country	Receiving Country	Tariff/ min	CCY
Raza	US	India	1.1	US Cent
Raza	US	Nepal	9.0	US Cent
Raza	US	China	0.5	US Cent
Raza	US	Bangladesh	2.1	US Cent
Vodafone Special Rates	Qatar	India	15	Dhs
Vodafone Special Rates	Qatar	Nepal	45	Dhs
Vodafone Special Rates	Qatar	China		Dhs
Vodafone Special Rates	Qatar	Bangladesh	19	Dhs
Hotlink	Malaysia	India	8	SEN
Hotlink	Malaysia	Nepal	40	SEN
Hotlink	Malaysia	China	10	SEN
Hotlink	Malaysia	Bangladesh	10	SEN
call2call	UK	India	2	Pence
call2call	UK	Nepal	3.99	Pence
call2call	UK	China	1	Pence
call2call	UK	Bangladesh	3	Pence
call2call	UK	Pakistan	3.5	Pence

Data as of December 2016. Manually compiled by Author

Violence Justifies All

The history witnesses, whoever took to the violence, could justify his power with proud. Bhimsen Thapa took to violence in 1805 and established himself in the helm of Nepal politics, after killing major opponents of his time, mostly from Pande group. Even after 1814-1816 British-Nepal war defeat, he continued to be Army chief. He ruled Nepal for next three decades. Jung Bahadur killed all the possible opponents of his time to establish himself at the top of affair, he killed even his uncle Mathwar Singh Thapa, and ruled Nepal for next three decades. Kot Massacre, Bhandar Khal Massacre, and Aul Massacre are linked to Jung Bahadur. Maoists used the violence as mean to look for political change, and at the end of decade, around 13000 people were killed in cross-fire between Maoists and Army. Maoists came to power after signing of peace agreement. Around 200 Madhesis were killed by security forces in cold blood, however it is being justified because Madhesis do not have any political backing.

Trust Deficit

Between 1950 and 1990, there were changes in governments 23 times, and in that period 10 people got rotated to become Prime Minister. After restoration of democracy in 1990, governments have changed 25 times in the span of 26 years to give 9 Prime Ministers till 2016. The count of these changes in governments and Prime Ministers depicts the low trust between people and political actors. The trust deficit can also be found in the dealing with the foreign powers, where slowly both neighbors India and China are concluding Nepal is a burden[39]. Nepal has been using one against the other whenever opportunity arises. Also, Nepal has not been able to deliver to International community on the commitments, the recent one being the earthquake relief work for which donors have committed more than USD 4 billion. The trust deficit between State and others prevail even within the internal parties like Tharu, Madhesis and Janajatis, with whom government has made multiple written commitment breaches. Nepal judiciary is not free from trust controversy either; the institute believed to be guardian of country constitution, itself violated principle of inclusion and proportion representation as guaranteed by the 2015's constitution. Of the 80 individuals appointed to be HC judges in January 2017, 83.75 percent, or 62 persons, were from Khas Arya group that accounts for a third of the country's population. Only four persons, or 5 percent, were from the Madhesi community, which forms another one third of population[40]. Even within the transactions of major political parties, it has become a norm to have written commitment broken as the convenient opportunities arises.

Non-Implementation of Sovereign Treaty

Prithivi Narayan Shah was unscrupulous, had little regard for his promise and broke it whenever it suited his purpose[41]. The 1758's treaty between Jay Prakash Malla and Prithivi Narayan Shah was abandoned within a year by Shah King and attacked valley[42]. Similarly, the treaty of 1792 with British was not followed in Nepal, however Nepal continued to derive the benefit of lower custom tax of 2.5 percent on export in India, against its own tax of 10 percent for import in Nepal, till 1834, when Hodgson was trying to improve commercial relationship with Nepal. Similarly, Nepal never reciprocated the 1801's treaty benefit to British India. The 1950's Indo-Nepal Friendship treaty also falls under the similar selective implementation from Nepal side. Despite having commitment of equal treatment of Indian citizens, Nepal government stopped taking Indians in government jobs since 1960s. However, Nepalese continue to get selected in Indian Jobs. The recent news being, 530 Nepalese got government jobs in Himachal-Pradesh[43].

Nepal-China Relationship Characteristic

Priority over the Years

The relationship of Kathmandu with its Northern neighbor has gone through ups and downs in last four centuries. Before Shah Kings, the relation was built and nurtured by Newari Kings.

- 1645-50 Kantipur attack on Tibet: Newar King attacked Tibet in 1645 to enforce Tibet to redirect all the trade between Tibet and Indian plain through the Kathmandu Valley. Newar also got commitment that Tibet would use Kathmandu's currency for circulation in Tibet and Newari merchant will have access to Tibetan market. China was not involved in the deal between Tibet and Nepal Valley. The deal was a big strategic gain for Nepal valley.
- 1788 - 91 War: Newari King had commercial relationship with Tibet, which was inherited by Shah King. The coin which was minted by Newari went to Shah Kings. During the Shah King period, Tibet started complaining the quality of silver coins sent to Tibet, thus the value of Silver coins compared to the exchange of Gold was questioned. The dispute led to the Nepalese attack on Tibet in 1788. After defeat, Tibet asked help of China, and fought together to defeat Nepal in 1791. This was first time, Nepal got interacted with Chinese.

The Chinese perception about Nepalese through that war was that Nepal was the Country of the Thieves[44] because of the plunder Gurkha did in 1788 to Tibetan temples. The treaty between Nepal-Tibet-China also made Nepal pay five yearly tribute to Chinese emperor in Peking. As Tibet invited China for help, so did Gurkha also invite British for help, however British arrived after treaty with China was concluded.

- 1816: While British-Gurkha war was going on, Kathmandu invited Chinese, via Amban in Tibet, to help them repeal British. The Chinese response was very late and too little. When they arrived close to Kathmandu, Sugaolee Treaty was already signed. Chinese rather gave advice to Gurkha to have good terms with British India.
- 1855 Nepal-Tibet War: Mainland China was busy in civil war in 1850, thus was weak to enforce imperial authority on Tibet so far from Beijing. Additionally, Jung Bahadur was looking for opportunity to grab absolute control over the military power. Jang Bahadur Rana, saw an excellent opportunity to press for Nepalese objectives in Tibet without the threat of Chinese interference. Gurkha attacked and defeated the Tibet. Tibet affair was indifferent to Chinese. The strong opposition from Tibet merely gave a face saving financial leverage to Jang Bahadur Rana in the treaty with Tibet. However, Nepal derived terms to establish itself as protector of Tibet if attacked by any other Rajah or in dispute with other countries. Nepal was also allowed to have ambassador in Lhasa. Tibetans were also happy with the face saving Treaty terms because it gave them opportunity to distance from Chinese control. Nepal got right to establish trading establishment at Lhasa.
- 1950 Chinese Army occupation to Tibet: Chinese attitude about Nepal was that it is one among the five figures of the Kingdom that was originally part of China. This caused pain in Kathmandu and brought closer to India, thus concluding 1950's Indo-Nepal Treaty of Peace and Friendship stating "to inform each other of any serious friction or misunderstanding with any neighboring State". After unsuccessful Chinese attempt to capture Nepal with the help of communist in 1952, Nepal took Indian military help to train armies and modernize checkpoints along the Chinese border.

- 1956 Treaty between Nepal and China[45]: The aspiration of King Mahendra was conflicting with the democratic push of India through Nepali Congress. King Mahendra wanted a back door opened which can push back India. So, he stroke a Treaty formally with China on 24th September 1956 that surrendered all the privileges of Nepal on Tibet that were gained through 1855's Nepal-Tibet Treaty. All the Treaties between Nepal-Tibet were abrogated. The Nepalese trader were pushed out of Tibet, and only to be admitted on the future approval of China. In 1962 Nepal withdrew its ambassador from Tibet and appointed a consul general.
- 2005: The falls of Monarchy in Kathmandu changed the China position in Nepal. China had to reach out to multiple political groups to safeguard the Chinese Interest, which they could do before just by negotiating with King.
- 2015: Nepal-China signed Oil trade agreement. China would be second country after India to source Oil product and Nepal became first country for China to supply Oil products[46]. This deal was signed as fall back of Madhesis' blocking of Trade routes that connected India with Kathmandu[47]. In 2016, the first ever transit treaty between Nepal and China was signed[48]. In December 2016, Nepal-China announced the first ever joint military drill[49]. China feels, hit now as iron is hot to mold the Chinese interest in Nepal, when Nepal is itself presenting opportunities in plate. Nepal believes, China has economy and technical power to build railroad from Kathmandu to connect with ocean without paying any overhead cost, thus providing more options to distance from Indian dependence.

China's Future Strategy

China's future interest in Nepal is limited to Tibet and gateway to South Asia commerce.

There is little commercial value of Nepal for China in terms of total export China is making to the world. Even if Nepal becomes gateway for China to export to India, which is least probable given there is shared border between India-China, the total percentage of Chinese export to India is about 2.5 percent.

Nepal is the only country in the world, which was able to rule over Tibet for more than four centuries, and has won wars with Tibet, multiple times. China feels, if there is any military threat to Tibet, it will come from Nepal either alone or with support from someone else. Thus, it becomes important for China to have commitment of Nepal in terms of Tibet policy, for now and for future. This also implies, restricting Tibetan connections with Nepal through strict controls on the border movement.

All the future strategy of China would focus on getting assurance of Nepal to the One-China policy. The aggressive China, after the "US-India Strategic Defense pact", will not necessarily actively participate in internal affairs, as Nepal has been expecting since long time. However China is willing to pay the price that Nepal will be willing to negotiate for One China Policy. Because, the benefits Tibet presents to China is same as Nepal could present to China, however, Tibet is many times bigger than Nepal in terms of land, resources and water. And China will not mind sharing gains from Tibet with Nepal.

China also wants to take the presented opportunity to integrate Nepal with China through the people to people relationship, to fill the gap created by breakage of people to people relationship that existed between Nepal-Tibet prior to 1950. However, this time Chinese ethnic group will be there instead of Tibetan people, and China will be opening commercial houses in Nepal rather than Nepalese competing in Chinese market. Chinese will be generous in opening of Chinese language center, Student Scholarship, cultural centers, etc. Chinese rail up to Kathmandu or closer will just make the process of Chinese integration with Nepal faster.

In this context, Madhesh is far away from Tibet border, and also within the democratic setup, plains people is least likely to have deciding interest in Tibet affair. Thus Madhesh is of little significance to Chinese Interest.

Characteristics of Nepal-India Relationship

Priorities over the Years

Over the last two and a half centuries, Indian priorities have changed over time with respect to Nepal-India relationship. Thus they went for 1791 commerce treaty. In the same treaty there was mention of border management indicating there were crimes along frontier.

- 1791 (Treaty of Commerce): In the initial days of British East India Company, they had assumption that Nepal has gold mines and Nepal is transit to Tibet trades, thus there was temptation to tap the resource and tap Tibet trade opportunities via Nepal transit points. 1791 was first official treaty between British EIC and Gurkha under Maulvi Abdool Kadir Khan Mission to Kathmandu with focus on (1) Increasing trade and (2) to settle and fix the duties payable by the subjects and (3) approach to resolve hurdles in the movement of goods across frontier.
- 1801-1802 (Treaty with the Rajah of Nepaul): the focus of Treaty was to appease King Ran Bahadur by giving him residency in Banaras, and asking for expense from the Nepal government. The treaty also mentions the "fugitives" issue along the frontier needs to be controlled. Mushan Raut was believed to be leader of fugitives, creating plunder across border, under support of Gurkha officers.
- 1816 (Treaty of Peace between the Honorable East India Company and Maharajah): During 1814-1816 war, their priority was to control state violence along frontier, fix the frontier with clean border demarcation, open residency in Kathmandu to understand the affair of Hilly kingdom and annexation of plain lands into British rule.
- 1816 (Addendum): The objective of addendum was reversal of British EIC earlier decision to bring plain Madhesh into British rule. The addendum mentions, Gurkha shouldn't take revenge of loss of war with people of Madhesh because they "favored the cause of the British Government during the war". Because British gave plain land to Gurkha government, thus former annulled the commitment to give sum of two lakhs of Rupees per annum to later.
- 1837 (Regarding the surrender of Thugs): Objective was to control cross border crimes along frontier. This treaty was concession from Bhimsen Thapa to appease British Government to support him, while his power was diminishing in Nepal. British has been asking for the action on crime from Gurkha government long before the treaty.
- 1839 (Stopping secret intrigues and also promote commerce): The period was after fall of Bhimsen Thapa. Suddenly political activities increased in Nepal Valley, in collaboration with Pande group and King Rajendra Bikram, and they sent letters to different Princely

states in Gangetic plain seeking partnership with the intention to weaken British rule. The Gurkha mission was pushed behind the marriage proposals. The British objective was to stop such secret schemes. The British residency was under Brian Hodgson, and his pet mission was to engage Gurkha through commerce that can redirect attention from ballooning army size. Treaty had two more points to ease trade flow (1) uniformity of duties across border as per 1791 treaty and (2) get commitment from Gurkha to regard British subjects on equality as Gurkha subject: "British subjects shall hereafter be regarded as her own subjects in regard to access to the Courts of Law".

- 1841 (Undertaking of 94 Chiefs)[50]: On 21st June 1840, King announced reduction in Army salary, and decision broke revolts in Army. King diplomatically called British Resident Brian Hodgson at the palace next day evening, and held him throughout night talking to him on no serious topics and without disclosing any reason. Next day, the rumor was circulated in Valley that British government has enforced King for reduction in salary. Mutineer gathered in large number at residency to storm the British Residency. The calmness of Brian Hodgson saved the life. This was the period of high political drama on street of Kathmandu in the name of Nationalism, creating anti British-India air in Nepal Valley. The war fever was fanned throughout the country with census counting the fighting population ready for war as four lakh men. Next year in January 1841, Brian Hodgson derived the commitment from all the major chiefs, that anti-British India fever would not be fanned and relationship was going to be normalized.
- 1855 (Mutual surrender of heinous criminals): This agreement is similar to 1837, with additional details on the nature of crime and procedure to surrender of crime perpetrators across border. This treaty also accepted Jung Bahadur as representative of King.
- Treaty of 1860 (Rewarding Gurkha for co-operating with British Army in re-capturing Lucknow and in the final defeat of the 1857 Indian Mutineers): British Government bestowed lowlands between the Rivers Kali and District of Gorakhpur for helping British cause during Indian 1857 mutiny. These gifted lands came to be known

as "Naya Muluk" meaning New Country, and consist of four western Nepal plains districts: Banke, Bardiya, Kanchanpur, and Kailali.

- 1866 (Extending the 1855 Treaty): The extension of 1855 crime list included offences of cattle stealing, embezzlement by public officers and serious thefts.
- 1923 (Rewarding Gurkha for co-operating with British Army in World War I): Around 2 lakh Gurkhas were sent at disposal of British Army by Rana. After the end of war, British rewarded the Rana Prime Minister, when they raised the demand of having more trust on them in terms of International Relationship. Gurkhas were allowed to have direct relationship with other countries and get army supplies, ammunition from countries other than British domination, and British was to provide transit via India.
- 1950 (Stopping the Communist China Growth): India got freedom in August 1947. Two years after, Chinese communist formally announced People's Republic of China taking over government control in October 1, 1949. In January 1950, Chairman Mao announced sending troops to Tibet. The political changes in China frightened Rana, if Chinese might enter Nepal. India was frightened too, if China would break the Himalayan barrier and enter Indian plain. Thus both of them signed agreement to "inform each other of any serious friction or misunderstanding with any neighboring State". India also saw Nepal as buffer state between Indian Gangetic plain and China, accordingly easily agreed to "complete sovereignty, territorial integrity and independence of each other", and even later motivated Nepal to apply for UN membership.

Indian Future Strategy

India has the knowledge of anti-India fever in Nepal because, assumed Indian security measure starts at Himalaya instead of Raxaul. India cannot build strong impenetrable wall on Indo-Nepal border like Himalaya to stop China, which had attacked Indian plains multiple times in History. The first noted Chinese attack was in seventh century towards the end of the reign of King Harshavardhana of Kannauj.

The occupation of Tibet by Chinese in 1950s and subsequent Indo-Chinese war of 1962 have made India believe that, Chinese cannot be easily discounted when it comes to Chinese imperial ambition. This belief further became stronger given the root of communist in China and belief of communist in arms.

The challenge of India is to mitigate the risk of Chinese fear with the help of hostile Nepalese hilly populations.

India has already taken a step to employee and maintain Hilly Tribals (Janajatis) in the Indian army. This might ensure some degree of security.

However the most challenging part still remains to change the attitude of hostile hilly population to be friendly to Indian people.

Thus, Indian strategy will continue to increase people to people integration either through cultural exchanges or marriage or through open border people's movement or through Indian government reaching to the door of people taking different initiatives like (i) School building and bus (ii) small projects impacting community.

But the toughest task for India will be to fill the economic gap between hill and Indian plains. The aspiration of people has been increasing day by day, whereas Nepal government has not been able to produce stable political system since long time that could have taken care of economic aspirations.

Indian response had been and will continue to be to absorb the surplus manpower into India. However, India would be hesitant in providing legal rights; voting rights, Aadhar Card, Bank account. Even if India tries to provide legal rights, it would be very slow and selective. For example, India has recently opened admission to Nepalese in IIT engineering entrance exam competition.

India would also like to fill the gap supposed to be filled by Nepal government in the field of governance and service. For example, India would contribute in Flood management, calamity relief management, opening of colleges, proving scholarships.

India cannot accommodate all the people from Nepal into India, and neither India would like to build aid dependable population. Also, India would be hesitant to see foreign players in its backyard. Thus, India would like to commercially integrate Nepal into India. One of the future commercial integration may be through water resource and electricity.

At last, India would like to ensure its credit goes unnoticed in Nepal, and goodwill keeps building, where there are competing foreign donors.

But, Madhesi misses to fit into the bigger Indian plan for the Nepal. Madhesis are neither hostile to India nor does Madhesh provide the security cover of being habitant of Himalaya. On the other hand, India feels offended, if any foreign donor wants to start a welfare project in Madhesh, which is close to Indian border. The situation of Madhesh is precarious when it comes to Indian interest. India wants infinite control over Madhesh land, however it wants to take zero responsibility. India treats Madhesh like a daughter, who always expects daughter to be nice to fair/unfair husband, and never expects daughter to come to father with any civil grievances. Daughter [Madhesh] suffocates on daily basis for being political sacrifice rather than treated as loved family member.

Madhesis expect India to stand for the welfare of region and people. So, what specifically does Madhesi expect?

The first expectation is treatment of Madhesis at par with Hilly groups. Which means, opportunity in the employment in Indian government jobs, including recruitment in Indian Army[51] like Gurkha Army. The life in the border areas is becoming tougher day by day[52], since the enforcement of citizenship papers on both sides. Thus, to annul the hardship introduced since 1950s, people expect official recognition for the freedom of economic opportunities across border; like ease of opening small business across the border, ease of transportation facilities, protective regime, reservation in educational institutions and friendly rules to allow opening of bank accounts with Nepalese ID card. On day to day basis, small people expect, higher limit for the movement of daily goods for individual uses. Strategically, people expect border management, information sharing and more importantly nurturing of cross border civil society groups recognized by government. Water management across the border is another important issue cutting across border. Additionally, people expect ease of transfer of inputs for agriculture developments, including fertilizer, technology, seeds and improved animal breeds. Last but not the least, official trust in cross border marriage and families.

Madhesh: A Political Sacrifice and Significance in 21st Century

Kathmandu government can save the reign and can stand with the support of the foreigners. However, during the whole process, the meaning of government has changed. The government priority to serve the people has lost somewhere between Delhi and Beijing. The worst victim of this plight is southern Madhesi people.

Whenever Madhesi people have tried to raise the issue of governance, responsibilities, tax accountability and exclusion, the Kathmandu's recorded response is, either you are Indian or India should take care of Madhesis' needs. In case of citizenship and land issue, Kathmandu categorizes native people as Indians, and when southern citizens ask for jobs in Army, the Kathmandu's response is, Delhi should provide the job first to Madhesi, and then Kathmandu will follow. When it comes to building road infrastructure in plain, Kathmandu passes the ball to Delhi.

The frustrated southern people again took to massive street protest for six months starting July 2015. Kathmandu tried guns to suppress the people's plight, which saw more than 50 deaths including one of 4 year boy, grand father-son duo, and women. Once plain people protest was outside the control of Hilly people authority, Kathmandu played the same game like in 1814-1816, and brought India-China together instead of focusing on its own act of aggression in southern plain.

The tactic, which Bhimsen played in 1816, is well stablished in Kathmandu that King Mahendra again played between China-India in 1960's. After World War II, the tactic has provided space for international donors too those willing to pay.

For any issue, Kathmandu tries to propagate Madhesh as India instigated problem. The moment it succeeds in establishing this propaganda, Kathmandu wins 25%. Kathmandu then drags China, even though they might not be interested, showing India fear, and wins another 25%. Once India-China starts clashing with each other to show its presence felt, Kathmandu enjoys the free flow of goods (with no string attached). And remaining 25% is won by bringing EU and US through propaganda that Nepal is getting minced into Indo-China battle. At the end Madhesis voices are crushed to complete 100%.

This is not doing well to Madhesi cause. Madhesis are lacking International approach; their issues are not communicated to international diplomats, focusing on Civil Right violations and exclusionary state structure. Foreign players, with contribution of 25% of government budget, are making matter worse for Madhesis because they are blindly aiding Nepal, whose money is being discretionarily diverted for political suppression. Donor countries tax payers' money is misused and thus they should feel guilty of not been able to stop human right violations in Madhesh instead that is promoting suppression of civil rights and state non-performance.

Time is changing rapidly in 21st century, so is the people's belief, international politics and technology power. And more importantly, Madhesis' desire to redefine the traditional relationship to become self-esteemed daughter rather than political sacrifice and partnership rather than husband-wife relationship. All this would compel the new scenarios to emerge sooner than later.

Technology is pushing for economy of scale, however Nepal lacks the scale that India or China presents.

The economy of Nepal have shrunk and continues to shrink, so has the political clout. Tibet is out of Newari sphere of influence. Kathmandu is growing in mismanagement as the population is increasing there. There is high probability of Cold war like scenario between China and India, in which China enters from north and India enters from south. Additionally, the concepts of 1814s period is vestigial in today's time, both internally and externally.

The notion of Terai being Agriculture basket and source of foreign currency have evaporated today with the migration of working people into Gulf, which is slowly releasing Terai of the economic burdens. Today, Hill is also becoming economically productive and future looks bright with water resources. Geographical importance of Himalaya being impeachable barrier is also changing with the technology and high-tech warfare, thus neighbor's reliance on Nepal will be lighter, when neighbor could come from sky too.

Educated elites, mostly Khas, are migrating to developed western nations for permanent residency, leaving political spaces to be occupied by emerging social groups. On the other hand, confident, skilled and financially successful immigrant labors in their late 40's have started returning from Qatar, Malaysia and Saudi with world class experience and dream to build their own house.

All these presents opportunity for plains to fill the vacuum created by falling Kathmandu. Which looks further prospective, given the global awareness of Human Rights, and increasing number of English speaking plains' populations who have desire to connect with world. The less rigidity on the norms based on caste is strength for overall plain people too. The recent political movements of plains people is simply accelerating the changes to meet the aspirations.

Plain people have the strong foundation of History, Culture, and Heritage. Future is there to be built.

At the end, whoever rules over the people, and whatever shape the border takes, the aspiration of people will remain for (1) Freedom to choose own culture, language or dress (2) Security of employment to live a decent life (3) The expectation of getting return for tax in the form of service and governance (4) No discrimination on civil rights, no differentiation based on one's color, ethnicity and place of origin.

Notes

1 Dhungana, Sujan (2015); Chinese petrol will cost Rs 180 per liter sans tax waiver, Myrepublica, 06 Dec 2015 http://admin.myrepublica.com/feature-article/story/32341/chinese-petrol-will-cost-rs-180-per-liter-sans-tax-waiver.html

2 US diplomatic report (1979); U.S. Role in Nepal, dated 1979 November 15, document # 1979KATHMA07210_e, wikileaks, https://wikileaks.org/plusd/cables/1979KATHMA07210_e.html

3 US diplomatic report (1978), Annual Integrated Assessment Of Security Assistance, dated 1978 July 21, document # 1978KATHMA03745_d, wikileaks https://wikileaks.org/plusd/cables/1978KATHMA03745_d.html

4 CIA (1983); Nepal: Continuity and Change in a Himalayan Monarchy, An Intelligence Assesement, Declassified Document # CIA-RDP84S00927R000200030003-7, NESA 83-10307, November 1983, pp 10, downloaded from https://www.cia.gov/library/readingroom/docs/CIA-RDP84S00927R000200030003-7.pdf

5 US diplomatic report (1979); U.S. Role in Nepal, dated 1979 November 15, document # 1979KATHMA07210_e, wikileaks, https://wikileaks.org/plusd/cables/1979KATHMA07210_e.html

6 Oliphant, Laurence (1852); A journey to Katmandu ... with the camp of Jung Bahadoor

7 Nepal fuel shortages: Petrol 'donated' to India embassy, BBC, Published on 7 October 2015

8 Weiner, Myron (1973); The Political Demography of Nepal, Asian Survey, Vol. 13, No. 6 (Jun., 1973), pp. 617-630

9 Bhattrai, Raju (2007); Open borders, closed citizenships: Nepali labor migrants in Delhi, International migration, multi-local livelihoods and human security, Institute of Social Studies, The Netherlands, 30 and 31 August 2007

10 Singh, R.N.S (2010); The unmaking of Nepal, Lancer Publishers, 2010, pp 84

11 BHATTARAI, KAMAL DEV (2016); India says ready to supply more electricity to Nepal, The Kathmandu Post, Published on 28-06-2016

12 Nepalitimes Editorial (2016); Wired, Nepalitimes, Issue #797, 26 Feb - 3 Mar 2016

13 Report (2016), Peak tycoon - How to win friends and influence people in Nepal, The Economist, May 14th 2016

14 Post Report (2016), Nepal Army permitted to run garment factory, The Kathmandu Post, published 16-03-2016

15 News(2016); Nepal Army to invest in hydropower project, myrepublica, 15 Dec 2015

16 Khanal, Rajesh (2016); Army, police form panels to probe irregularities, The Kathmandu Post, Published 19-03-2015

17 Post Report (2016); NA plans to invest in hydel sector, The Kathmandu Post, published Aug 17, 2016

18 Bhattarai, Rajan (2013); Peacekeeping Contributor Profile: Nepal, Nepal Institute for Policy Studies, Kathmandu downloaded on Oct 2016 from http://www.providingforpeacekeeping.org/2014/04/03/contributor-profile-nepal/

19 Pariyar, Kamal (2016); Army seeks Rs 8.66b for arms procurement, Myrepublica, Dec 16, 2016

20 Pariyar, Kamal (2016); NA welfare fund profit declines despite growing investment, Myrepublica, Aug 17, 2016

21 Pangeni, Rudra (2016); Nepal Army: All eyes on profits, Myrepublica, published December 19, 2016

22 Bedi, Rahul (2011); Armed, dangerous and building their own empires, NZ Herald, Published Aug 20, 2011

23 Hewitt, Duncan (2016), China's Military To End Commercial Activities In 3 Years As President Xi Pushes For Stronger, More Loyal Armed Forces, IB Times, Published March 28, 2016

24 Hewitt, Duncan (2016), China's Military To End Commercial Activities In 3 Years As President Xi Pushes For Stronger, More Loyal Armed Forces, IB Times, Published March 28, 2016

25 Sedhai, Roshan (2013), Nepal's passport costliest in S Asia, The Kathmandu Post, Published on 2013-03-22, www.ekantipur.com/the-kathmandu-post/2013/03/21/top-story/nepals-passport-costliest-in-s-asia/246661.html

26 Khadka, Upasana (2016); Home they bring the workers dead, Nepalitimes, issue #822, 19-25 August 2016

27 Hulakinews, साउदीमा एक मधेशीको लास अलपत्र (A Madhesi corpse stranded in Saudi), Published on Oct 23, 2016, downloaded from www.hulakinews.com/साउदीमा एक मधेशीको लास अलपत्र

28 News (2016); Probe panel to look into alleged misuse of fund, The Kathmandu Post, Published Aug 11, 2016

29 Sedhai, Roshan (2016); Misuse of migrant workers' welfare fund goes rampant, The Kathmandu Post, Mar 3, 2014

30 Bhattarai, Kiran (2016); Embassies in 9 foreign countries accused of misusing migrant workers' welfare fund, myrepublica, Aug 29, 2016

31 News (2016); Stranded Nepali migrant workers in Saudi implore for help, The Kathmandu Post, Mar 13, 2016

32 Poudel, Arjun (2015); Drugs worth millions rotting at TIA customs, Myrepublica, 17 Nov 2015

33 Board, Jack (2016), Donated rice for Nepal earthquake victims to be sold, not distributed, channelnewsasia, April 21, 2016

34 AFP news (2016), Rice donated for quake victims being sold due to lack of storage facilities, Indian Express, Published July 7, 2016

35 Huët, Stéphane (2015); Bureaucracy as usual, Nepalitimes, June 10th, 2015

36 Sharma, Ritu (2015); Aid deliveries for Nepal quake victims hit delays, ucanews, May 4, 2015

37 Sangraula, Bikash (2013); 460,000 kg of Japan-donated rice fails to find takers in Nepal, Japan Times, Published on June 6th, 2013 Downloaded on Dec 2, 2016 from www.japantimes.co.jp/news/2013/06/06/national/460000-kg-of-japan-donated-rice-fails-to-find-takers-in-nepal Also read news '7,000 quintal rice lies undistributed in NFC go-down' The Kathmandu Post, Published on Dec 2, 2016

38 Kantipur Reporter (2016); विद्युत् उत्पादन कम्पनी खुल्यो Kantipur Daily, 2016-11-21 http://kantipur.ekantipur.com/news/2016-11-21/20161121083155.html

39 Myrepublica Interview with Nischalnath Pandey (2017); The real danger is when both India and China conclude Nepal is a burden, Myrepublica, 12 January 2017

40 Rai, Dewan (2017); Judges for high courts: Govt lawyers object to JC recommendations, The Kathmandu Post, Jan 17, 2017 http://kathmandupost.ekantipur.com/news/2017-01-17/govt-lawyers-object-to-jc-recommendations.html

41 Baral, Leelanatheshwar Sharma (1964), Life and Writings of Prithvinarayan Shah, Unpublished PhD dissertation, University of London, 1964, pp 217

42 Baral, Leelanatheshwar Sharma (1964), Life and Writings of Prithvinarayan Shah, Unpublished PhD dissertation, University of London, 1964, pp 217

43 News (2017), हिमाञ्चल प्रदेशमा 530 नेपालीले पाए सरकारी जागिर (540 got government jobs in Himachal Pradesh), Kantipur Daily, 13 January 2017 http://kantipur.ekantipur.com/news/2017-01-13/20170113221955.html

44 Leo E Rose, Strategy of Survival, pp 73

45 Agreement to Maintain the Friendly Relations between the Kingdom of Nepal and the People Republic of China and on Trade and Intercourse between Nepal and the Tibet Region of China, US Foreign Service Dispatch, Dispatch no 548, October 31, 1956 https://www.cia.gov/library/readingroom/docs/CIA-RDP08C01297R000200050002-5.pdf

46 Prasain, Sangam, and Khanal, Rajesh (2015); Nepal inks historic oil agreement with China, The Kathmandu Post, 29/10/2015

47 THT Online (2016); Nepal, China issue joint communique, agree to seal petrol trade deal, The Himalayan Times, March 23, 2016 https://thehimalayantimes.com/nepal/nepal-china-issue-joint-communique-agree-to-seal-petrol-trade-deal/

48 IANS (2016); Nepal, China sign first ever transit treaty, Business Standard, March 21, 2016

49 China, Nepal To Conduct First Ever Joint Military Drill

50 Translation of an Ikrar namah signed by the Gurus Chauntrias Chiefs etc of Nepal dated Saturday Poos Soodi 9th 1897 or January 2nd 1 841 Aitchison's Treaties Engagements and Sanads Vol II, pp 178-179, 1876

51 Ghimire, Yubaraj (2016); How the Gorkha regiments may be on Nepal PM's agenda in India, A prominent Madhesi leader told Dahal that the Madhesis should get around 50 per cent quota in the Gorkha regiments, Indian Express, September 15, 2016

52 Paudel, Manoj (2016); कष्टकर छसीमा क्षेत्रको जीवन (life becoming tougher on border), Kantipur Daily, 2016-09-16 http://kantipur.ekantipur.com/news/2016-09-16/20160916094436.html

Appendix I: Major Category/Group Sub-Category Caste and Ethnic Groups in the 2011 Census

Major Category/Group	Sub-Category	Caste and Ethnic Groups
1 Hill caste	1.1 Hill Brahmans 1.2 Hill Chhetris	
2 Tarai/Madhesi castes	2.1 Tarai/Madhesi Brahmans/Chhetris 2.2 Tarai/Madhesi other castes	2.1 Tarai Brahman, Nurang, Rajput, Kayastha 2.2 Badhaee, Barai, Bin, Dev, Dhunia, Gaderi/Bhedihar, Hajam/ Thakur, Haluwai, Kahar, Kalwar, Kamar, Kanu, Kathabaniyan, Kewat, Koiri/ Kushwaha, Kori, Kumhar, Kurmi, Lodh, Lohar, Mali, Mallaha, Nuniya, Rajbhar, Rajdhob, Sonar, Sudhi, Teli, Yadav
3 Dalits	3.1 Hill Dalits 3.2 Tarai/Madhesi Dalits	3.1 Badi, Damai/Dholi, Gaine, Kami, Sarki 3.2 Bantar/Sardar, Chamar/ Harijan/Ram, Chidimar, Dhandi, Dhankar/ Dharikar, Dhobi, Dom, Dusadh/Paswan/Pasi, Halkhor, Kalar, Khatwe, Musahar, Natuwa, Sarbaria, Tatma/Tatwa
4 Janajatis	4.1 Mountain Janajatis 4.2 Hill Janajatis 4.3 Bhitri (Inner) Madhesi Janajatis 4.4 Tarai/Madhesi Janajatis	4.1 Bhote, Byasi/Sauka, Dolpo, Lhomi, Lhopa, Sherpa, Thakali, Topkegola, Walung 4.2 Athpariya, Bahing, Bantawa, Brahmu/Baramo, Chamling, Chepang/ Praja, Chhantyal/Chantel, Dura, Ghale, Gharti/Bhujel, Gurung, Hayu, Hyolmo, Jirel, Khaling, Khawa, Kulung, Kusunda, Lepcha, Limbu, Loharung, Magar, Mewahang/Bala, Nachhiring, Newar, Pahari, Rai, Sampang, Sunuwar, Tamang, Thami, Thulung, Yakkha, Yamphu 4.3 Bote, Danuwar, Darai, Kumal, Majhi, Raji, Raute 4.4 Amat, Dhanuk, Dhimal, Gangai, Jhangad/Dhagar, Kisan, Koche, Meche, Munda, Pattharkatta/ Kuswadia, Rajbanshi, Satar/Santhal, Tajpuriya, Tharu
5 Muslim 6 Others	5 Muslim 6 Others	5 Muslim 6 Bengali, Marwari, Punjabi/Sikh, Foreigners

Source: Nepal Human Development Report 2014 with additional input from the Author.

Appendix II: State of Castes/Ethnic Inclusion in the Nepalese Army

(As of August 26, 2016)

S.No.	Caste/Ethnic Groups	Representation in NA	Representation in NA
1	Kshatri	39721	43.176 %
2	Brahman	8093	8.797 %
3	Magar	7253	7.884 %
4	Newar	5577	6.062 %
5	Tamang	4934	5.363 %
6	Thakuri	3213	3.492 %
7	Tharu	3021	3.284 %
8	Kami	2891	3.142 %
9	Gurung	2753	2.992 %
10	Rai	2278	2.476 %
11	Chaudhari	1773	1.927 %
12	Jogi	1718	1.867 %
13	Pariyar	1074	1.167 %
14	Sarki	969	1.053 %
15	Limbu	717	0.779 %
16	Kumal	698	0.759 %
17	Thakur	664	0.722 %
18	Damai	662	0.72 %
19	Bhujel	494	0.537 %
20	Gharti	373	0.405 %
21	Nepali	340	0.37 %
22	Majhi	273	0.297 %
23	Sunuwar	262	0.285 %
24	Yadav	240	0.261 %
25	Pode	144	0.157 %
26	Dura	138	0.15 %
27	Danuwar	126	0.137 %
28	Darai	117	0.127 %
29	Sherpa	115	0.125 %
30	Rajbanshi	114	0.124 %
31	Rana	89	0.097 %
32	Dhimal	82	0.089 %
33	Madhesi	57	0.062 %
34	Khatwe	55	0.06 %
35	Chamar	50	0.054 %
36	Jirel	49	0.053 %
37	Mahato	35	0.038 %
38	Mandal	34	0.037 %
39	Dhanuk	33	0.036 %
40	Bote	33	0.036 %
41	Teli	33	0.036 %
42	Dom	32	0.035 %
43	Pahari	31	0.034 %
44	Muslim	27	0.029 %
45	Kasai	24	0.026 %
46	Meche	23	0.025 %
47	Nau	22	0.024 %
48	Dusadh	22	0.024 %

49	Dhobi	21	0.023 %
50	Tatma	21	0.023 %
51	Mehata	19	0.021 %
52	Sah	19	0.021 %
53	Hayu	15	0.016 %
54	Rajput	15	0.016 %
55	Chepang	15	0.016 %
56	Gaine	14	0.015 %
57	Kurmi	13	0.014 %
58	Thami	13	0.014 %
59	Gupta	13	0.014 %
60	Badi	13	0.014 %
61	Tamata	12	0.013 %
62	Shah	11	0.012 %
63	Jha	11	0.012 %
64	Urawa	10	0.011 %
65	Kuber	10	0.011 %
66	Paswan	9	0.01 %
67	Sada	9	0.01 %
68	Thakali	8	0.009 %
69	Kumal	8	0.009 %
70	Raji	8	0.009 %
71	Musahar	8	0.009 %
72	Kanu	7	0.008 %
73	Das	6	0.007 %
74	Lawad	6	0.007 %
75	Kuswaha	6	0.007 %
76	Tajpuriya	6	0.007 %
77	Sudhi	5	0.005 %
78	Sardar	5	0.005 %
79	Santhal	5	0.005 %
80	Jhagad	5	0.005 %
81	Od	5	0.005 %
82	Kapar	4	0.004 %
83	Tiruwa	4	0.004 %
84	Chunara	4	0.004 %
85	Malaha	4	0.004 %
86	Kalar	3	0.003 %
87	Rajdhob	3	0.003 %
88	Satar	3	0.003 %
89	Sahani	3	0.003 %
90	Pharswan	3	0.003 %
91	Pasi	3	0.003 %
92	Barma	3	0.003 %
93	Srivastava	3	0.003 %
94	Dhal	2	0.002 %
95	Dhega	2	0.002 %
96	Gurdhami	2	0.002 %
97	Kewar	2	0.002 %
98	Chhantyal	2	0.002 %
99	Johari	2	0.002 %
100	Kabirath	2	0.002 %
101	Daudi	2	0.002 %
102	Deo	2	0.002 %
103	Gahate	2	0.002 %
104	Devjan	2	0.002 %

105	Kewat	2	0.002 %
106	Sinha	2	0.002 %
107	Samat	2	0.002 %
108	Kumhar	2	0.002 %
109	Pawe	2	0.002 %
110	Lodh	2	0.002 %
111	Sutihar	2	0.002 %
112	Makra	2	0.002 %
113	Tabdar	1	0.001 %
114	Sutparai	1	0.001 %
115	Chilaune	1	0.001 %
116	Chitaure	1	0.001 %
117	Chundali	1	0.001 %
118	Chuwain	1	0.001 %
119	Dala	1	0.001 %
120	Suli	1	0.001 %
121	Tadi	1	0.001 %
122	Shekh	1	0.001 %
123	Chaihan	1	0.001 %
124	Datta	1	0.001 %
125	Shahu	1	0.001 %
126	Daut	1	0.001 %
127	Dayale	1	0.001 %
128	Serma	1	0.001 %
129	Sauke	1	0.001 %
130	Dhadi	1	0.001 %
131	Sanwat	1	0.001 %
132	Sob	1	0.001 %
133	Belal	1	0.001 %
134	Bachhar	1	0.001 %
135	Wayak	1	0.001 %
136	Bag	1	0.001 %
137	Bahakari	1	0.001 %
138	Baitha	1	0.001 %
139	Baraghare	1	0.001 %
140	Barakoti	1	0.001 %
141	Barghare	1	0.001 %
142	Titara	1	0.001 %
143	Barwati	1	0.001 %
144	Chandraban	1	0.001 %
145	Begnasi	1	0.001 %
146	Saithbar	1	0.001 %
147	Bhiyal	1	0.001 %
148	Bhujawa	1	0.001 %
149	Thyaita	1	0.001 %
150	Bhumihar	1	0.001 %
151	Thamphara	1	0.001 %
152	Tariya	1	0.001 %
153	Chachhara	1	0.001 %
154	Chadaro	1	0.001 %
155	Raut Kurmi	1	0.001 %
156	Takmel	1	0.001 %
157	Bashahi	1	0.001 %
158	Lothyal	1	0.001 %
159	Mudiyari	1	0.001 %

160	Medaniya	1	0.001 %
161	Marwodi	1	0.001 %
162	Marik	1	0.001 %
163	Kahar	1	0.001 %
164	Kalal	1	0.001 %
165	Marau	1	0.001 %
166	Kamat	1	0.001 %
167	Madarniya	1	0.001 %
168	Roshyara	1	0.001 %
170	Nuniya	1	0.001 %
171	Kausha	1	0.001 %
172	Loppa	1	0.001 %
173	Loniya	1	0.001 %
174	Khadluk	1	0.001 %
175	Khang	1	0.001 %
176	Kohar	1	0.001 %
177	Koli	1	0.001 %
178	Lekhi	1	0.001 %
179	Yola	1	0.001 %
180	Ansari	1	0.001 %
181	Mabo	1	0.001 %
182	Garanga	1	0.001 %
183	Kupar	1	0.001 %
184	Diyal	1	0.001 %
185	Kumar	1	0.001 %
186	Dumjan	1	0.001 %
187	Raub	1	0.001 %
188	Dural	1	0.001 %
189	Ram	1	0.001 %
190	Gadariya	1	0.001 %
191	Gaderi	1	0.001 %
192	Rajwar	1	0.001 %
193	Mudvari	1	0.001 %
194	Gamal	1	0.001 %
195	Murau	1	0.001 %
196	Garedi	1	0.001 %
197	Gharala	1	0.001 %
198	Phulara	1	0.001 %
199	Godiya	1	0.001 %
200	Gorathoki	1	0.001 %
201	Goth	1	0.001 %
202	Guiche	1	0.001 %
203	Pela	1	0.001 %
204	Pabe	1	0.001 %
205	Sai	1	0.001 %
206	Podar	1	0.001 %
	Total	91998	100.00%

Source: Ag Dept (Army Records Office), Army Hq.

Appendix III: Table showing Population, Schools and Teachers, and their relationship with district literacy. Literacy ranking 1 represents best. Red color represent bottom of ranking and green represent best in ranking. Tabular representation compiled by Author based on 2011 Nepal census data.

Division	District	Population	Schools	Teachers	Ratio: Popu/ School	Ratio: Popu/ Teacher	Literacy Rank
Hill Far-Western	Achham	257477	502	3393	513	76	61
Hill Far-Western	Doti	211746	381	3041	556	70	58
Hill Far-Western	Baitadi	250898	554	3224	453	78	45
Hill Far-Western	Dadeldhura	142094	263	2151	540	66	41
Hill Mid-Western	Jajarkot	171304	430	1671	398	103	56
Hill Mid-Western	Rolpa	224506	423	2269	531	99	53
Hill Mid-Western	Rukum	208567	391	1614	533	129	51
Hill Mid-Western	Dailekh	261770	508	2412	515	109	48
Hill Mid-Western	Salyan	242444	454	1907	534	127	44
Hill Mid-Western	Pyuthan	228102	373	2434	612	94	35
Hill Western	Gorkha	271061	553	3769	490	72	36
Hill Western	Lamjung	167724	424	3344	396	50	22
Hill Western	Myagdi	113641	273	1617	416	70	20
Hill Western	Baglung	268613	594	4255	452	63	19
Hill Western	Gulmi	280160	615	4610	456	61	18
Hill Western	Arghakhanchi	197632	451	2693	438	73	16
Hill Western	Parbat	146590	369	2911	397	50	14
Hill Western	Tanahu	323288	650	4856	497	67	11
Hill Western	Palpa	261180	496	4723	527	55	8
Hill Western	Syangja	289148	637	5983	454	48	7
Hill Western	Kaski	492098	645	8597	763	57	3
Hill Central	Nuwakot	277471	521	2813	533	99	54
Hill Central	Ramechhap	202646	492	3018	412	67	50
Hill Central	Dhading	336067	634	4647	530	72	46
Hill Central	Kavrepalanchok	381937	696	7580	549	50	27
Hill Central	Bhaktapur	304651	355	5724	858	53	4
Hill Central	Lalitpur	468132	488	7110	959	66	2
Hill Central	Kathmandu	1744240	1370	18827	1273	93	1
Hill Eastern	Okhaldhunga	147984	368	2272	402	65	42
Hill Eastern	Khotang	206312	484	2972	426	69	31
Hill Eastern	Bhojpur	182459	404	2472	452	74	30
Hill Eastern	Panchthar	191817	436	3298	440	58	17

Hill Eastern	Dhankuta	163412	340	2261	481	72	13
Hill Eastern	Tehrathum	101577	253	1764	401	58	12
Hill Eastern	Ilam	290254	494	3695	588	79	5
Mountain Far-Western	Bajhang	195159	457	3230	427	60	62
Mountain Far-Western	Bajura	134912	262	2312	515	58	60
Mountain Far-Western	Darchula	133274	361	2053	369	65	40
Mountain Mid-Western	Humla	50858	135	636	377	80	72
Mountain Mid-Western	Mugu	55286	152	701	364	79	69
Mountain Mid-Western	Dolpa	36700	121	723	303	51	66
Mountain Mid-Western	Jumla	108921	155	1123	703	97	64
Mountain Mid-Western	Kalikot	136948	288	2149	476	64	57
Mountain Western	Mustang	13452	70	506	192	27	38
Mountain Western	Manang	6538	32	223	204	29	10
Mountain Central	Rasuwa	43300	113	702	383	62	67
Mountain Central	Sindhupalchok	287798	556	3707	518	78	55
Mountain Central	Dolakha	186557	431	3166	433	59	47
Mountain Eastern	Solukhumbu	105886	290	1601	365	66	43
Mountain Eastern	Sankhuwasabha	158742	414	2622	383	61	29
Mountain Eastern	Taplejung	127461	339	2439	376	52	21
Terai Far-Western	Kailali	775709	605	5498	1282	141	37
Terai Far-Western	Kanchanpur	451248	430	3506	1049	129	24
Terai Mid-Western	Banke	491313	436	4026	1127	122	49
Terai Mid-Western	Bardiya	426576	350	3369	1219	127	39
Terai (Inner) Mid-Western	Dang	552583	512	4942	1079	112	26
Terai (Inner) Mid-Western	Surkhet	350804	581	3469	604	101	15
Terai Western	Kapilbastu	571936	511	4253	1119	134	63
Terai Western	Rupandehi	880196	597	9081	1474	97	28
Terai Western	Nawalparasi	643508	706	6502	911	99	23
Terai Central	Rautahat	686722	487	2531	1410	271	75
Terai Central	Sarlahi	769729	745	3064	1033	251	74
Terai Central	Mahottari	627580	415	2801	1512	224	73
Terai Central	Dhanusha	754777	397	2850	1901	265	70
Terai Central	Bara	687708	418	3225	1645	213	68
Terai Central	Parsa	601017	392	3282	1533	183	59
Terai (Inner) Central	Sindhuli	296192	581	3838	510	77	52
Terai (Inner) Central	Makwanpur	420477	597	5079	704	83	34
Terai (Inner) Central	Chitwan	579984	543	6745	1068	86	6
Terai Eastern	Siraha	637328	469	2952	1359	216	71
Terai Eastern	Saptari	639284	484	2973	1321	215	65
Terai Eastern	Sunsari	763487	745	5120	1025	149	33
Terai (Inner) Eastern	Udaypur	317532	472	3190	673	100	32

Appendix IV: Table: Showing pattern for the literacy ranking for past 70 years. The district wise literacy data is enriched with the migration data to understand the impact of migrants in influencing the literacy. There were 55 districts reported in 1960 census and numbers were 54 in 1952-54 census. In 1971, the new districts were formed by reorganization of old district. Tabular representation compiled by Author based on Nepal census data. Statistical modelling was used to adjust the 1960 and 1952-54 ranking number for newly created districts.

Division	District	1952 - 54	1961	1971	1981	1991	2001	2011	Population increase 1961-2011
Hill Central	Kathmandu	1	1	1	1	1	1	1	676%
Hill Central	Lalitpur	2	2	2	2	2	4	2	222%
Hill Central	Bhaktapur	3	3	4	9	3	5	4	239%
Hill Central	Kavrepalanchok	33	20	45	23	34	12	27	76%
Hill Central	Dhading	54	55	71	59	48	53	46	66%
Hill Central	Ramechhap	45	51	49	50	52	62	50	64%
Hill Central	Nuwakot	55	47	59	45	49	40	54	210%
Hill Eastern	Ilam	16	4	17	7	8	8	5	377%
Hill Eastern	Tehrathum	37	28	15	5	6	20	12	-76%
Hill Eastern	Dhankuta	29	16	19	12	12	11	13	141%
Hill Eastern	Panchthar	16	4	29	25	21	29	17	201%
Hill Eastern	Bhojpur	34	41	35	27	26	30	30	-12%
Hill Eastern	Khotang	34	41	40	30	30	43	31	19%
Hill Eastern	Okhaldhunga	39	45	46	51	36	46	42	67%
Hill Far-Western	Dadeldhura	12	29	26	34	40	39	41	72%
Hill Far-Western	Baitadi	19	30	27	40	41	38	45	142%
Hill Far-Western	Doti	47	60	61	68	60	54	58	52%
Hill Far-Western	Achham	47	74	68	60	70	71	61	69%
Hill Mid-Western	Pyuthan	38	43	31	54	46	50	35	7%
Hill Mid-Western	Salyan	59	65	54	64	53	48	44	101%
Hill Mid-Western	Dailekh	65	63	55	43	54	49	48	110%
Hill Mid-Western	Rukum	59	65	63	63	57	60	51	154%
Hill Mid-Western	Rolpa	59	65	64	61	62	64	53	62%
Hill Mid-Western	Jajarkot	59	65	73	72	69	61	56	132%
Hill Western	Kaski	4	8	3	4	4	2	3	286%
Hill Western	Syangja	13	15	11	17	10	7	7	-15%
Hill Western	Palpa	5	11	5	16	16	9	8	51%
Hill Western	Tanahu	6	13	12	20	11	15	11	153%
Hill Western	Parbat	55	48	14	10	9	25	14	127%
Hill Western	Arghakhanchi	14	36	22	21	23	27	16	80%
Hill Western	Gulmi	14	36	16	11	18	23	18	46%
Hill Western	Baglung	21	38	28	29	29	16	19	75%
Hill Western	Myagdi	21	38	32	33	33	28	20	121%

Hill Western	Myagdi	21	38	32	33	33	28	20	121%
Hill Western	Lamjung	10	24	13	8	17	26	22	35%
Hill Western	Gorkha	32	44	41	46	22	31	36	79%
Mountain Central	Dolakha	42	59	52	53	43	41	47	41%
Mountain Central	Sindhupalchok	63	57	58	58	55	59	55	54%
Mountain Central	Rasuwa	55	48	65	74	72	69	67	378%
Mountain Eastern	Taplejung	29	16	25	15	19	36	21	139%
Mountain Eastern	Sankhuwasabha	29	16	30	19	15	32	29	121%
Mountain Eastern	Solukhumbu	39	45	34	35	37	51	43	40%
Mountain Far-Western	Darchula	19	30	23	32	27	45	40	141%
Mountain Far-Western	Bajura	47	60	75	71	67	70	60	161%
Mountain Far-Western	Bajhang	47	60	53	67	63	66	62	114%
Mountain Mid-Western	Kalikot	71	69	60	75	75	63	57	1435%
Mountain Mid-Western	Jumla	71	69	66	47	66	73	64	0%
Mountain Mid-Western	Dolpa	71	69	70	70	71	67	66	116%
Mountain Mid-Western	Mugu	71	69	72	73	73	74	69	141%
Mountain Mid-Western	Humla	71	69	67	66	74	75	72	93%
Mountain Western	Manang	10	24	74	39	24	18	10	-1%
Mountain Western	Mustang	21	38	10	28	14	37	38	-44%
Terai (Inner) Central	Chitwan	70	21	6	6	7	3	6	754%
Terai (Inner) Central	Makwanpur	46	50	37	24	38	13	34	165%
Terai (Inner) Central	Sindhuli	58	54	51	41	45	42	52	184%
Terai (Inner) Eastern	Udaypur	52	52	50	42	39	33	32	255%
Terai (Inner) Mid-Western	Surkhet	65	63	48	36	25	14	15	318%
Terai (Inner) Mid-Western	Dang	64	12	47	37	32	21	26	460%
Terai Central	Parsa	51	33	24	38	47	56	59	337%
Terai Central	Bara	24	19	43	49	61	55	68	175%
Terai Central	Dhanusha	26	22	38	44	51	47	70	206%
Terai Central	Mahottari	26	22	44	55	65	68	73	159%
Terai Central	Sarlahi	44	32	56	57	64	65	74	372%
Terai Central	Rautahat	41	34	57	69	68	72	75	214%
Terai Eastern	Saptari	18	9	21	22	42	44	65	113%
Terai Eastern	Siraha	43	35	36	52	58	58	71	203%
Terai Eastern	Sunsari	7	6	9	13	20	17	33	451%
Terai Eastern	Morang	7	6	8	14	13	24	25	416%
Terai Eastern	Jhapa	36	10	7	3	5	6	9	579%
Terai Far-Western	Kanchanpur	67	75	42	26	28	19	24	2290%
Terai Far-Western	Kailali	68	56	62	56	50	35	37	764%
Terai Mid-Western	Bardiya	69	58	69	62	56	52	39	530%
Terai Mid-Western	Banke	25	14	33	48	44	22	49	416%
Terai Western	Nawalparasi	53	53	20	31	35	34	23	304%
Terai Western	Rupandehi	28	27	18	18	31	10	28	298%
Terai Western	Kapilbastu	9	26	39	65	59	57	63	1427%
	Nepal								-179.8%

Index

A

B

C

J

K

L

M

N

Q

R

S

T

U

V

W

■■■

सखी आज कैसी मनोहर घड़ी है

सखी आज कैसी मनोहर घड़ी है!
गलेआनी जयमाला सुन्दर पड़ी है
जरा कोई संभाले बनी का मनटिका
लिये रंगभूमि में सुनरा खड़ी है

सखी आज कैसी मनोहर घड़ी है !
गलेआनी जयमाला सुन्दर पड़ी है
जरा कोई संभाले ये बना का लहंगा
लिये रंगभूमि मे बज्जबा खड़ी है

सखी आज कैसी मनोहर घड़ी है !
गलेआनी जयमाला सुन्दर पड़ी है
जरा कोई संभाले फूलो का माला
लिए आँगन में माली खड़ी है

सखी आज कैसी मनोहर घड़ी है !
गलेआनी जयमाला सुन्दर पड़ी है
जरा कोई संभाले दूल्हा का जूता
लिए आँगन में मोची खड़ी है

सखी आज कैसी मनोहर घड़ी है !
गलेआनी जयमाला सुन्दर पड़ी है
जरा कोई संभाले ये बना के बनी
लिये रंगभूमि मे बाबूजी खड़ी है

सखी आज कैसी मनोहर घड़ी है !
गलेआनी जयमाला सुन्दर पड़ी है

- सुनीता पुर्बे

Friend I wonder, how beautiful is this time !
(Ethnic Marriage Song translated in English)

Friend I wonder, how beautiful is this time !
Greeting Garland is beautiful prime
Someone hold please Bridal forehead Jeweler
Goldsmith is standing taking in hand

Friend I wonder, how beautiful is this time !
Greeting Garland is beautiful prime
Someone hold please Bridal wedding dress
Tailor is standing taking in hand

Friend I wonder, how beautiful is this time !
Greeting Garland is beautiful prime
Someone hold please flower's garland
Gardner is standing taking in hand

Friend I wonder, how beautiful is this time !
Greeting Garland is beautiful prime
Someone hold please groom's shoe
Cobbler is standing taking in hand

Friend I wonder, how beautiful is this time !
Greeting Garland is beautiful prime
Someone hold please Groom's Bride
Daddy is standing together withher

Friend I wonder, how beautiful is this time !
Greeting Garland is beautiful prime

\- Sunita Purbe

CULTURE PHOTO

Dashain procession in 1967-69 in a village near Jaleswar carries the idol of Durga to a local river for submersion, marking the end of a 10-day festival in Durga's honor.
Photo Credit Hank Lacy

A village boy playing on makeshift swing in agriculture field.
Photo Credit Author

Community feast for villager on marriage.
Photo Credit Author

Farmer couple in Mango Grove with temporary setup.
Photo Credit Author

Morning shaves amidst the harvest rice hay in a terai village during 1967-69.
Photo Credit Hank Lacy

Salhes Sthan under Pipal tree.
Photo Credit Author

Salhesh Statue in Jaleshwar.
Photo Credit Rakesh Prasad chaudhary

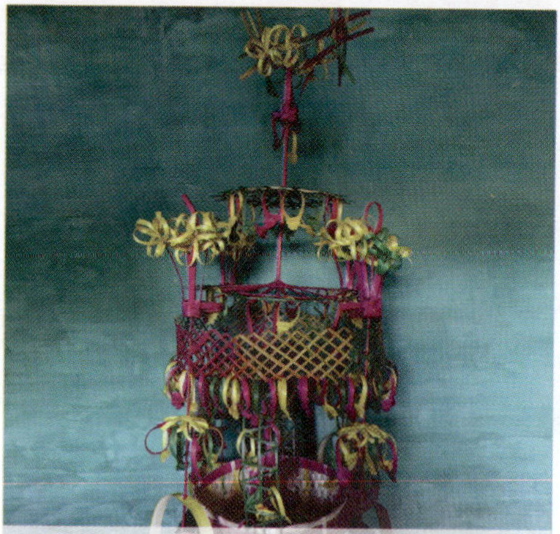

Traditional decorative artistic Basket called Dala-Hara sent from Groom to Bride House during Marriage. Photo Credit Author

Traditional Mithila Art on wall forming part of marriage ritual. Photo Credit Author

Traditional musician from Chamar caste playing in marraige. Photo Credit Author

Vendor selling spices in weekly Haat-Bazar. Photo Credit Author

Villager engaged in Bhajan-Kirtan. Photo Credit Author

Women cutting vegetable for community feast. Photo Credit Author

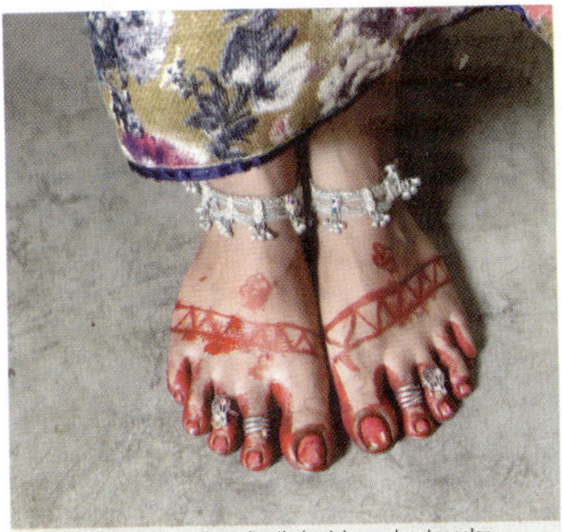

Women foot makeup in ethnic style - red water color with foot jewelleries. Photo Credit Author

Women Selling Goat in weekly Haat-Bazar. Photo Credit Author

Women Selling Traditional Fan made of Bamboo locally called Bena. Photo Credit Author

Artesian water is common in the eastern terai. It is usually clean and runs 24 by 7. Photo Credit Hank Lacy

Jaleswar's weekly haat bazaar with sellers and buyers of a wide variety of produce, goods, and services. Photo Credit Hank Lacy

Jhijhiya pot on Women Head during the Durgapuja Celebration in 1967-69. Photo Credit Hank Lacy

The Traverse of Madhesh Protest Activity 2007 - 2008

Media Professional Protest Rally in Birgunj.

Photo Credit Madhesi

Protest with Demand list in Janakpur.

Photo Credit Madhesi

A protesting women being taken into police custody.

Photo Credit Madhesi

Civil society of Jaleshwor, Dhanusa and young people organized a peaceful demonstration. Participants of the rally wore dhoti-kurta.

Photo Credit Author

Janakpur Protest Infront of Bhanu Chowk.

Photo Credit Madhesi

Local young folks of Ghadiarwa, Birgunj took out a torchlight rally.

Photo Credit Author

Medical Professional's Protest Rally in Birgunj.

Photo Credit Madhesi

Members of Mahottari district Movement Committee took out a rally in Jaleshwor putting forward five demands.

Photo Credit Author

People listening to local FM radio for getting the news during movements in Birjung.

Photo Credit Author

People of hill origin living in Madhesh took out a peace rally in Lahan, Siraha on Saturday 3 Feb . Photo Credit Author

Protest with Demand list in Janakpur.

Photo Credit Author

Student Protest Rally in Birgunj.

Photo Credit Author

Women confronting with riot police in Birgunj.

Photo Credit Author

The Traverse of Madhesh Protest Activity - 2015

Dead body procession in Dhanusha, Janakpur September 2015.
Photo Credit THRD Alliance

Dr Raghubansh P Singh with Madhesi at Jantarmantar, Delhi Feb 23.
Photo Credit United Madhesis of Nepal

Human Chain formed over Kamala River.
Photo Credit Madhesiyouth

Lathi Protest in Sarlahi January 2016.
Photo Credit Author

100th Days Protest Nepal Observed, Forming Human Structure of 100.
Photo Credit Madhesi Youth

Madhesis in Delhi showing Black flag to PM KP Oli March 2016.
Photo Credit United Madhesis of Nepal

Madhesis - Protesting in Front of White House in Washington DC USA. Photo Credit Madhesi Youth

A scene from Madhesi indefinite bandh, 2016 Jan.
Photo Credit Hulakinews

Nepal Army deployed in Janakpur.
Photo Credit Author

People having placard hailing Madhesh-Tharuhat 2016 Feb.
Photo Credit THRD Alliance

Protest March in a Saptari Village.
Photo Credit THRD Alliance

Police Beating a Protester Encircling him.
Photo Credit THRD Alliance

Protest March in Biratnagar on 2016 Feb 19 .
Photo Credit Hulakinews

UDMF and PoliceFacing each other on Indo-Nepal Border in Birjung Maitri Bridge 40th Day.
Photo Credit Madhesi Youth